Annual Editions: Sociology, 43/e

Kurt Finsterbusch

http://create.mheducation.com

ISBN-10: 1260180301   ISBN-13: 9781260180305

Contents

Unit 6   145

Detailed Table of Contents

Unit 1: Culture

How to Buy Happiness: What the Social Science Says, Isabella Kwai, *The Atlantic*, 2017
The point of this article is that money buys happiness if it is used in the right way. It increases our happiness more if it is spent on experiences rather than on things and if the purchase is shared rather than if used by the purchaser alone.

Pluribus et Unum: The History of American Politics as a Tug-of-War between Our Individualist and Collectivist Identities, Jennifer Miller, *Washington Monthly*, 2016
The title means that out of many, we are one. Thus, though we have many individualist identities nevertheless, we are one united country. Both gay rights' advocates and gun enthusiasts argue for the individual's right to self-determine. On the flip side, proponents of both "traditional" marriage and gun control believe their positions strengthen the collective.

The Myth of the "Culture of Poverty", Paul Gorski, *Educational Leadership*, 2008
The culture of poverty myth accuses the poor of having beliefs, values, and behaviors that prevent them from achieving. Thus their failure is their fault. This myth must be challenged. Most poor people do have the work ethic, value education, and possess other characteristics that contradict the culture of poverty myth. Opportunity structures play a big role in poverty.

American Muslims in the United States, Interfaith Alliance & Religious Freedom Education Project/First Amendment Center, www.interfaithalliance.org, 2017
This article provides a description of Muslims in America, which contradicts many of the negative stereotypes commonly believed. American Muslims take part in all aspects of American civic life. Many American Muslim leaders and organizations have repeatedly denounced extremist violence in the strongest possible terms. Most American Muslims, like most other Americans, are deeply concerned about the problem of extremist violence committed in the name of Islam.

The Common Good, Manuel Velasquez et al., *Markkula Center for Applied Ethics*, 2014
The common good is a good to which all members of society have access and from whose enjoyment no one can be easily excluded. All persons, for example, enjoy the benefits of clean air or an unpolluted environment. This article advocated efforts to advance the common good against the groups that promote special interests and oppose benefits for disadvantaged groups.

What Do We Deserve? Namit Arora, *The Humanist*, 2011
A major key to political, economic, and cultural issues is the question "What is just or right?" Namit Arora uses Michael Sandel's book, Justice, to explore this question. People should be rewarded for their skill and effort, but since chance and innate advantages play such a large role in outcomes, some adjustments are required for outcomes to be considered fair. How these adjustments are made shapes political philosophies and differentiates societies.

Unit 2: Socialization and Social Control

Sex Slavery/Trafficking, Soroptimist, 2012
Soroptimist is an organization that fights human trafficking for slavery and sex trafficking. This article is a full description of these practices. Human trafficking is a $32 billion annual industry. Sex trafficking or slavery is the exploitation of women and children, within national or across international borders, for the purposes of forced sex work. Unaware of the extent of force and exploitation, many countries largely tolerate the practice.

explain why the growth has been slow and blames it on depopulation, deleveraging, and deglobalization. Between the end of World War II and the financial crisis of 2008, the global economy was supercharged by explosive population growth, a debt boom that fueled investment and boosted productivity, and an astonishing increase in cross-border flows of goods, money, and people. Today, all three trends have begun to sharply decelerate.

The Return of Monopoly, Matt Stoller, *New Republic*, 2017
Over the past three decades, the U.S. government has permitted corporate giants to take over an ever-increasing share of the economy. Monopoly—the ultimate enemy of free-market competition—now pervades every corner of American life: every transaction we make, every product we consume, every news story we read, and every piece of data we download. As a result, they have been able to fix the price of almost everything in the economy.

Hard at Work in the Jobless Future, James H. Lee, *The Futurist*, 2012
James H. Lee is also pessimistic about America's economic future. Automation and new technologies will make many workers redundant including white-collar and professional workers. The jobless future in his title is exaggerated, but a severe shortage of jobs is to be expected. The ramifications are worrisome.

The Case for Less, Tim Wu, *The New Republic*, 2013
Tim Wu presents the case for less against the dominant ideology that ever-increasing abundance is the main national and personal objective. Obviously, poverty, hunger, and miserable conditions should be overcome by economic advancement and widespread abundance, but Wu argues against excessive abundance, which has contributed to widespread obesity, information overload, high indebtedness, growing inequality, and lessening of self-control.

Why For-Profit Education Fails: Moguls' Good Intentions Too Often Betray Them, Jonathan A. Knee, *The Atlantic*, 2016
Many corporations have tried to have a successful for-profit educational system that would be superior to public education and therefore have thousands of contracts to replace public school systems. Many of those companies have gone out of business since their results were not that good. This article presents the pros and cons of for-profit educational systems citing more cons than pros.

Noam Chomsky on How the United States Developed Such a Scandalous Health System, C. J. Polychroniou, *Truthout*, 2017
America is exceptional among developed countries in not believing that health care is a right. Each person is responsible to provide his own health care. As a result, 30 million have no health-care insurance. Other factors are the brutal fight of corporations against workers and the lack of public demand for adequate coverage. Drugs are also about twice as high in America than in Europe.

A Thousand Years Young, Aubrey de Grey, *The Futurist*, 2012
How would you like to live a 1,000 years? Aubrey de Gray says that advances in medical and biochemical treatments can overcome the aging process and keep us young for many centuries.

American Religion Has Never Looked Quite Like It Does Today, Antonia Blumberg, *Huffington Post*, 2016
Bloomberg presents the major changes in religion in America over the past century. They include a drop of 12 percent in belief in God, an 8 percent decline in those who identify as Christian, More and more Americans identify as spiritual but not religious, less church attendance, more women entering the ministry, increase in non-Christian faiths, the spirituality marketplace exploded, and so on.

Unit 6: Social Change and the Future

Full Planet, Empty Plates, Lester R. Brown, *Population Press*, 2012
According to Lester R. Brown, the world is in a long-term worsening food crisis that will have troubling economic, social, and political impacts. Population growth, billions moving up the food chain, and the use of grains for fuel increase the demand for food while supply problems are increasing due to soil loss, increasing water scarcity, expansion of deserts, adverse weather changes, and the leveling off of acreage productivity in developed countries. Brown suggests what needs to be done.

The Greatest Story Too Rarely Told: America Is an Oligarchy, John Atcheson, *Common Dreams*, 2017

We live in a nation controlled by corporate power and the individually wealthy. And the major press, of course, is in on the con. The Republican Party has complete disdain for facts, reality, or the scientific method. To deny the existence of climate change in the face of the data is irrational. The same is true of their position on health care, national budgets, state budgets, and tax policy. In all cases, their policies are counterfactual and counterproductive. Consider the collapse of the economy in Kansas after they adopted supply-side and trickle-down-economics. Or the fact that the three biggest economic collapses in US history followed periods when the Republicans were in control and they'd implemented their destructive laissez-faire economic policies. Or watch as they fumble with health care, literally threatening death to hundreds of thousands in the process, and leaving 22 million more Americans uninsured. But the press still covers all this in a way that is "balanced," rather than accurate. This is clearly one sided but worthy of discussion.

Understanding Populist Challenges to the Liberal Order, Pranab Bardhan, *Boston Review*, 2017

Bardhan identifies the growth of populism throughout the world. Trump in the United States, Modi in India, Britain's Brexit, France's Marine Le Pen, Russia's Vladimir Putin, Hungary's Viktor Orbán, Poland's Jarosław Kaczyński, Turkey's Recep Tayyip Erdoğan, and the Philippines's Rodrigo Duterte are current examples. This is not explained by increasing inequality because these developments are allied to crony capitalism. Rather it is allied to anti globalism, loss of jobs, antigovernment, and cultural values.

Preface

These past few years have changed so many things and confront us with many new and difficult issues, while many of the old issues remain unresolved. There is much uncertainty. Almost all institutions are under stress. The political system is held in low regard because it seems to accomplish so little, cost so much, and focus on special interests more than on the public good. The economy is still in crisis. In the long term, it suffers from massive debt, foreign competition, trade deficits, increasing inequality, economic uncertainties, and a worrisome concentration of economic power in the hands of relatively few multinational corporations. Complaints about the education system continue, because grades K–12 do not teach basic skills well and college costs are too high. Healthcare is too expensive and medical mistakes are too numerous. Many Americans still lack healthcare coverage, and some diseases are becoming resistant to our medicines. The entertainment industry is booming, but many people worry about its impact on values and behavior.

News media standards seem to be set by the Internet. Furthermore, the dynamics of technology, globalization, and identity groups are creating crises, changes, and challenges. Street crime rates have declined significantly, but white collar crime is now recognized as costing trillions of dollars, harming the economy, and largely going unpunished. Many criminologists question the recent policy of more police, more jails, and tougher sentences. Social policies seem to create almost as many problems as they solve. The use of toxic chemicals has been blamed for increases in cancer, sterility, and other health problems. Marriage and the family have been transformed, in part by the women's movement and in part by the stress that current conditions create for women who try to combine family and careers. Schools, television, and corporations are commonly vilified. Many claim that morality has declined to shameful levels although this claim can be challenged. Add to all this the worldwide problems of ozone depletion, global warming, deforestation, soil loss, desertification, and species loss, and it is easy to be pessimistic. Nevertheless, crises and problems also create opportunities.

The present generation may determine the course of history for the next 200 years. Great changes are taking place and new solutions are being sought where old answers no longer work. The issues that the current generation is facing are complex and must be interpreted within a sophisticated framework. The sociological perspective provides such a framework. It expects people to act in terms of their positions in the social structure, within the political, economic, and social forces operating on them, and guided by the norms that govern the situation.

Annual Editions: Sociology should help you to develop the sociological perspective that will enable you to determine how the issues of the day relate to the way that society is structured. The articles provide not only information, but also models of interpretation and analysis that will guide you as you form your own views.

This edition of *Annual Editions: Sociology* emphasizes social change, institutional crises, and prospects for the future. It provides intellectual preparation for taking action for the betterment of humanity in times of critical change. The sociological perspective is needed more than ever as humankind tries to find a way to peace, prosperity, health, and well-being that can be maintained for generations in an improving environment. The numerous obstacles that lie in the path of these important goals require sophisticated responses. The goals of this edition are to communicate to students the excitement and importance of the study of the social world and to provoke interest in, and enthusiasm for, the study of sociology.

A number of features are designed to make this volume useful for students, researchers, and professionals in the field of sociology. Each unit is preceded by an overview, which provides a background for informed reading of the articles and emphasizes critical issues. *Learning Outcomes* accompany each article and outline the key concepts that students should focus on as they are reading the material. *Critical Thinking* questions found at the end of each article allow students to test their understanding of the key points of the article. The *Internet References* section can be used to further explore the topics online.

Annual Editions: Sociology depends upon reader response in order to develop and change. We welcome your recommendations of articles that you think have sociological merit for subsequent editions, as well as your advice on how the anthology can be made more useful as a teaching and learning tool.

Editor

Kurt Finsterbusch is a professor of sociology at the University of Maryland at College Park. He received a BA in history from Princeton University in 1957, a BD from Grace Theological Seminary in 1960, and a PhD in sociology from Columbia University in 1969. He is the author of *Understanding Social Impacts* (Sage Publications, 1980), and he is the co-author, with Annabelle Bender Motz, of *Social Research for Policy Decisions* (Wadsworth, 1980) and, with Jerald Hage, of *Organizational Change as a Development Strategy* (Lynne Rienner, 1987). He is the editor of *Annual Editions: Sociology* (McGraw-Hill/Contemporary Learning Series); *Annual Editions: Social Problems* (McGraw-Hill/Contemporary Learning Series); and *Sources: Notable Selections in Sociology,* 3rd ed. (McGraw-Hill/Dushkin, 1999).

Academic Advisory Board

Members of the Academic Advisory Board are instrumental in the final selection of articles for the *Annual Editions* series. Their review of the articles for content, level, and appropriateness provides critical direction to the editor(s) and staff. We think that you will find their careful consideration reflected in this book.

Unit 1

UNIT

Prepared by: Kurt Finsterbusch, *University of Maryland, College Park*

Culture

The ordinary, everyday objects of living and the daily routines of life provide a structure to social life that is regularly punctuated by festivals, celebrations, and other special events (both happy and sad). These routine and special times are the stuff of culture, for culture is the sum total of all the elements of one's social inheritance. Culture includes language, tools, values, habits, science, religion, literature, and art.

It is easy to take one's own culture for granted, so it is useful to pause and reflect on the shared beliefs and practices that form the foundations for our social life. Students share beliefs and practices, and thus have a student culture. Obviously, the faculty has one also. Students, faculty, and administrators share a university culture. At the national level, Americans share an American culture. These cultures change through the decades and especially between generations. As a result, there is much variety among cultures across time and across nations, tribes, and groups. It is fascinating to study these differences and to compare the dominant values and signature patterns of different groups.

Article   Prepared by: Kurt Finsterbusch, *University of Maryland, College Park*

How to Buy Happiness: What the Social Science Says

Isabella Kwai

Learning Outcomes

After reading this article, you will be able to:

- Understand how money can buy happiness.
- Understand why money often does not buy happiness.
- Understand the value of sharing experiences.

"There's nothing in the world so demoralizing as money," a character proclaims gloomily in Antigone, but maybe he didn't know how to use his cash. If we spend it right, research suggests, money can, in fact, buy happiness.

According to one oft-repeated rule of thumb, spending on experiences rather than objects makes us happiest. When asked to reflect on a purchase, people who described experiential ones—travel, say, or concerts—were much happier than those who described material ones [1]. Psychologists believe the "hedonic treadmill"—our tendency to eventually revert to our original level of happiness following a change—operates more swiftly after material purchases than after experiential ones: A new table is easier to get used to than a trip to Chile. They also say we are better at making peace with bad experiences ("It brought us closer together") than with regrettable objects [2].

Not all experiences are equally worthwhile, however. In one study, when experiential purchases were categorized as either solitary or social in nature, social expenses brought more happiness. People who spent on solitary experiences valued them no more in hindsight than they valued possessions [3]. It's not so much that doing things makes us happier than having things—it's that we like doing things with people. This is particularly true for extroverts: In one study, they got significantly happier after shopping with others, no matter what they bought [4].

University of Cambridge researchers joined with a bank to analyze the relationship between customers' spending habits, personality, and happiness. They found that the "Big Five" personality traits—extroversion, openness to experience, conscientiousness, agreeableness, and neuroticism—predicted spending. Outgoing people splurged on restaurants and entertainment, while self-controlled, conscientious types shelled out for fitness and insurance. And those whose spending fit their personality were happier than those who spent against type. In one case, extroverts and introverts received vouchers for either a bar or a bookstore. Extroverts were happier when forced to spend money at the bar, while introverts were happier spending at the bookstore [5].

But before you go on a spending spree, a caution: More than income, investments, or debt, the amount of cash in one's checking account correlates with life satisfaction [6]. That doesn't mean you should be stingy, though: When people were assigned to buy goodies for either a hospitalized child or themselves, those who bought treats for a sick child reported more positive feelings. The effect was the same in a rich country (Canada) as in a poor one (South Africa) [7]. Spending on friends and family likewise gives us a boost because—unsurprisingly—it brings us closer to them [8].

So how do you turn cash into fun? First, figure out whether you're an extrovert or an introvert. Then, head to a bar, bookstore, or hospital, with a Canadian in tow. There must be a joke in there somewhere.

References

[1]   Gilovich and Van Boren, "To Do or to Have? That Is the Question" (Journal of Personality and Social Psychology. December 2003).

[2] Gilovich et al., "A Wonderful Life" (Journal of Consumer Psychology. January 2015).

[3] Caprarlello and Reis, "To Do. to Have, or to Share?" (Journal of Personality and Social Psychology, February 2013).

[4] Goldsmith, "The Big Five, Happiness and Shopping" (Journal of Retailing and Consumer Services, July 2016).

[5] Matz et al., "Money Buys Happiness When Spending Fits Our Personality" (Psychological Science, May 2016).

[6] Ruberton, "How Your Bank Balance Buys Happiness" (Emotion, August 2016).

[7] Aknin, "Prosocial Spending and Well-Being" (Journal of Personality and Social Psychology. April 2013).

[8] Yamaguchl et al., "Experiential Purchases and Prosocial Spending Promote Happiness by Enhancing Social Relationships" (The Journal of Positive Psychology, September 2016).

Critical Thinking

1. How do extroverts differ from introverts in spending patterns?
2. How do private experiences differ from shared experiences in happiness results?
3. To what extent can happiness be bought?

Internet References

Psychology Today
https://www.psychologytoday.com/basics/happiness

Sociology—Study Sociology Online
http://edu.learnsoc.org/

Sociology Web Resources
http://www.mhhe.com/socscience/sociology/resources/index.htm

Sociosite
http://www.topsite.com/goto/sociosite.net

Socioweb
http://www.topsite.com/goto/socioweb.com

Article   Prepared by: Kurt Finsterbusch, *University of Maryland, College Park*

Pluribus et Unum: The History of American Politics as a Tug-of-War between Our Individualist and Collectivist Identities

JENNIFER MILLER

Learning Outcomes

After reading this article, you will be able to:

- See how the struggle between individualism and collectivism plagued American history.

- Understand how Trump and Clinton stood for opposing American values.

- Understand how gay rights and gun ownership fit into the individualist/collectivist traditions.

This past July, presidential candidates Hillary Clinton and Donald Trump took the stage to accept their parties' nominations for president and articulate their visions for America. By all accounts, neither speech towed the traditional party line. Instead of espousing small government, the beating heart of American conservatism, Trump championed the power of the presidency, with himself as savior in chief. "I alone can fix it," he declared. "I will restore law and order . . . I have made billions of dollars in business making deals—now I am going to make our country rich again . . . I am your voice."

In contrast, the Democratic convention sounded downright Republican. "Over four flag-waving days in Philadelphia, Democrats stole the Republicans' mojo," wrote CNN's Nicole Gaouette. Clinton's theme was American unity: our exceptional patriotism, greatness, and strength. "Powerful forces are threatening to pull us apart," she warned. "We have to decide whether we all will work together so we all can rise together. Our country's motto is e pluribus unum: out of many, we are one."

But pan out a couple of centuries—or even just a few decades—and you quickly realize that Trump's expression of oligarchic individualism and Clinton's mighty collective are precisely the competing facets of American identity that have always divided us. This argument is at the center of a new book, American Character: A History of the Epic Struggle Between Individual Liberty and the Common Good, by the journalist and historian Colin Woodard. Early on, he asks, "When individual liberty and the common good come into conflict, with which principle will you side?"

Don't be too quick to answer. Woodard reminds us that the two philosophies have been trumpeted and twisted for both good and evil, and neither is the battle cry of any single faction. Both gay rights' advocates and gun enthusiasts argue for the individual's right to self-determine. On the flip side, proponents of "traditional" marriage and gun control both believe their positions strengthen the collective. So how do we reconcile these competing facets of American identity? How do we possibly come together? This is the question Woodard seeks to answer.

American Character isn't a long book, but it is sweeping in its scope. Woodard's exploration of individualism and collectivism begins with the very origins of human civilization over a million years ago. He touches on John Locke's antimonarchical influence over the British aristocracy in the seventeenth century, before exploring the divisions between Thomas Jefferson's libertarianism and Alexander Hamilton's

Federalism. In a chapter that synopsizes his excellent 2011 book American Nations, he explains how these competing philosophies were adopted and rejected on a regional basis. He then presents the rise of unchecked laissez-faire individualism and the backlash of Teddy Roosevelt's Progressive Movement. He moves us through the vast expansion of government under Franklin D. Roosevelt, the refreshingly sane national liberal policies of Dwight Eisenhower and John F. Kennedy, and the eventual hijacking of these policies by Ronald Reagan, Newt Gingrich, and the Tea Party.

Many of Woodard's chapters read like chronological surveys: the administrations, national conflicts, and policy debates fly by at ferocious speeds. It's a rough ride, especially with such frequent toggling back and forth between examples of individualism, collectivism, and their economic and social consequences. At times, we are desperate for Woodard to slow the bus down, get on the intercom, and take up an active role as tour guide. Unfortunately, we don't hear much from him until the end of the trip. This lack of authorial intervention means that readers will likely impose their own framework and analysis on the history presented here.

That's not inherently a problem. Readers should be encouraged to think for themselves now and then. But because we're in the middle of a madcap presidential election, many of the details in American Character feel supercharged with political subtext. When Woodard praises New York's seventeenth-century forebears for establishing an environment with a "profound tolerance for diversity," and calls it a "refuge for those persecuted by other regional cultures," it's impossible for liberal-minded readers not to seethe with frustration over today's immigration debates and Trump's anti-Muslim rhetoric. Just as easily, anyone who championed Ted Cruz's "New York values" statement last April is likely to feel smugly self-righteous over Woodard's comment that the region has never been "particularly democratic or concerned with great moral questions."

Similarly, it is near impossible to read about Andrew Jackson's attack on government bureaucracy and his mass firing of civil servants without immediately thinking of Trump's populist anti-intellectualism. (Depending on where you live and your own economic situation, this is something to either celebrate or decry.) And, of course, when Woodard points out that "in 1890, the richest 1 percent of Americans had the same combined income as the bottom 50 percent and owned more property than the other 99 percent," it's impossible not to think about the Bernie Bros and the terrible income inequality that is wrenching our country apart.

Even Woodard's discussion of evolutionary biology feels political. "Far from being naturally solitary, humans have always existed in a social state," he writes in the first chapter, titled "Maintaining Freedom." He continues, "Our evolutionary ancestors, Homo erectus, were using fire a million years ago, a game-changing innovation that led them to live in group camp-sites [and] share tasks, responsibilities, and resources." Like any responsible historian, Woodard is simply trying to contextualize his argument. And yet given the virulence of today's small-government evangelists and Ayn Rand individualists, it's difficult not to wonder: Is this how far back we need to go to make a case for the collective? To fire?

Well, yes. The best chapter in American Character is called "Two Paths to Tyranny." It's here, through a discussion of the oligarchic slaveholding South and communist Europe, that Woodard explores how individualism and collectivism have been taken to dangerous extremes. The chapter is unusual for a work of American history: half of it takes place abroad, detailing life behind the Iron Curtain, with its armed police, banned typewriters, and bugged classrooms. But these examples help underscore America's historic fear of the collective and the "radical counter-reaction" of ardent individualists, which eventually led to the creation of the John Birch Society, the Heritage Foundation, and the Tea Party.

Although not explicitly discussed in these pages, Woodard's chapter on extremes also helps explain the rise of Donald Trump. So much of the anger on display at Trump rallies stems from a combined fear and resentment of immigrants and minorities. To many working-class Americans, these are massive, faceless groups of people—collectives, if you will—who pose a direct threat to the individual's freedom and happiness. It's a bigoted, misguided point of view, but it too stems from the collective-individualist divide. The Donald's detractors see him as a symbol of extreme selfishness in the vein of the pre-Progressive oligarchs. His working-class supporters (most of whom have directly benefited from the protections afforded by Progressive reformers) see him as a symbol of self-determination. To them, he's a powerful individual who does not bow to group will—including that of the party that nominated him.

So what's the solution? Woodard ends his book with an appeal to fairness. "In the early twenty-first century, fairness must be reasserted as the central issue of our political discourse and made the central value of a new political coalition," he writes in the final chapter, "A Lasting Union." This compromise, he says, would champion "individual achievement and investments in our shared institutions and resources." It would "protect the competitiveness and security of the market and the health of consumers, workers, and the environment." And it would also reform the tax code so that "the rich and ultrarich pay a larger share of the burden of maintaining a civilization that has served them so well."

In theory, this sounds like the perfect solution. The problem is that it requires not simply a tremendous degree of compromise to achieve but also a unified definition of what is fair. All along, Woodard has argued that in this country, there are no common definitions. To one group, individualism means economic deregulation; to another it means upholding civil rights. To one group, supporting the collective means strengthening social services; to another it means strengthening the military. And so as much as our history has been a debate between individual liberty and the common good, it has also been a struggle between factions who champion both philosophies as uniquely American—and uniquely their own.

Critical Thinking

1. What was the publics' response to the two candidates?

2. What are some of the problems that extreme forms of individualism or collectivism can lead to?

3. Understand how both individualism and collectivism can be supportive of very different political positions.

Internet References

Refugee Center
www.therefugeecenter.org/AmericanValues

Sociology—Study Sociology Online
http://edu.learnsoc.org/

Sociology Web Resources
http://www.mhhe.com/socscience/sociology/resources/index.htm

Sociosite
http://www.topsite.com/goto/sociosite.net

Socioweb
http://www.topsite.com/goto/socioweb.com

JENNIFER MILLER is the author of two novels, The Year of the Gadfly and The Heart You Carry Home. Her journalism can be found in the New York Times, the Washington Post, and Slate.

Article Prepared by: Kurt Finsterbusch, *University of Maryland, College Park*

The Myth of the "Culture of Poverty"

Instead of accepting myths that harm low-income students, we need to eradicate the systemwide inequities that stand in their way.

PAUL GORSKI

Learning Outcomes

After reading this article, you will be able to:

- Assess the role of culture in the condition of the poor.
- Discuss the role of opportunity structures in contributing to the conditions of the poor.
- Evaluate how different the poor are from the middle class.

As the students file out of Janet's classroom, I sit in the back corner, scribbling a few final notes. Defeat in her eyes, Janet drops into a seat next to me with a sigh.

"I love these kids," she declares, as if trying to convince me. "I adore them. But my hope is fading."

"Why's that?" I ask, stuffing my notes into a folder.

"They're smart. I know they're smart, but . . . "

And then the deficit floodgates open: "They don't care about school. They're unmotivated. And their parents—I'm lucky if two or three of them show up for conferences. No wonder the kids are unprepared to learn."

At Janet's invitation, I spent dozens of hours in her classroom, meeting her students, observing her teaching, helping her navigate the complexities of an urban midwestern elementary classroom with a growing percentage of students in poverty. I observed powerful moments of teaching and learning, caring and support. And I witnessed moments of internal conflict in Janet, when what she wanted to believe about her students collided with her prejudices.

Like most educators, Janet is determined to create an environment in which each student reaches his or her full potential. And like many of us, despite overflowing with good intentions, Janet has bought into the most common and dangerous myths about poverty.

Chief among these is the "culture of poverty" myth—the idea that poor people share more or less monolithic and predictable beliefs, values, and behaviors. For educators like Janet to be the best teachers they can be for all students, they need to challenge this myth and reach a deeper understanding of class and poverty.

Roots of the Culture of Poverty Concept

Oscar Lewis coined the term *culture of poverty* in his 1961 book *The Children of Sanchez*. Lewis based his thesis on his ethnographic studies of small Mexican communities. His studies uncovered approximately 50 attributes shared within these communities: frequent violence, a lack of a sense of history, a neglect of planning for the future, and so on. Despite studying very small communities, Lewis extrapolated his findings to suggest a universal culture of poverty. More than 45 years later, the premise of the culture of poverty paradigm remains the same: that people in poverty share a consistent and observable "culture."

Lewis ignited a debate about the nature of poverty that continues today. But just as important—especially in the age of data-driven decision making—he inspired a flood of research. Researchers around the world tested the culture of poverty concept empirically (see Billings, 1974; Carmon, 1985; Jones & Luo, 1999). Others analyzed the overall body of evidence regarding the culture of poverty paradigm (see Abell & Lyon, 1979; Ortiz & Briggs, 2003; Rodman, 1977).

These studies raise a variety of questions and come to a variety of conclusions about poverty. But on this they all agree: *There is no such thing as a culture of poverty.* Differences in values and behaviors among poor people are just as great as those between poor and wealthy people.

In actuality, the culture of poverty concept is constructed from a collection of smaller stereotypes which, however false, seem to have crept into mainstream thinking as unquestioned fact. Let's look at some examples.

Myth: Poor people are unmotivated and have weak work ethics.

The Reality: Poor people do not have weaker work ethics or lower levels of motivation than wealthier people (Iversen & Farber, 1996; Wilson, 1997). Although poor people are often stereotyped as lazy, 83 percent of children from low-income families have at least one employed parent; close to 60 percent have at least one parent who works full-time and year-round (National Center for Children in Poverty, 2004). In fact, the severe shortage of living-wage jobs means that many poor adults must work two, three, or four jobs. According to the Economic Policy Institute (2002), poor working adults spend more hours working each week than their wealthier counterparts.

Myth: Poor parents are uninvolved in their children's learning, largely because they do not value education.

The Reality: Low-income parents hold the same attitudes about education that wealthy parents do (Compton-Lilly, 2003; Lareau & Horvat, 1999; Leichter, 1978). Low-income parents are less likely to attend school functions or volunteer in their children's classrooms (National Center for Education Statistics, 2005)—not because they care less about education, but because they have less access to school involvement than their wealthier peers. They are more likely to work multiple jobs, to work evenings, to have jobs without paid leave, and to be unable to afford child care and public transportation. It might be said more accurately that schools that fail to take these considerations into account do not value the involvement of poor families as much as they value the involvement of other families.

Myth: Poor people are linguistically deficient.

The Reality: All people, regardless of the languages and language varieties they speak, use a full continuum of language registers (Bomer, Dworin, May, & Semingson, 2008). What's more, linguists have known for decades that all language varieties are highly structured with complex grammatical rules (Gee, 2004; Hess, 1974; Miller, Cho, & Bracey, 2005). What often are assumed to be *deficient* varieties of English—Appalachian varieties, perhaps, or what some refer to as Black English Vernacular—are no less sophisticated than so-called "standard English."

Myth: Poor people tend to abuse drugs and alcohol.

The Reality: Poor people are no more likely than their wealthier counterparts to abuse alcohol or drugs. Although drug sales are more visible in poor neighborhoods, drug use is equally distributed across poor, middle class, and wealthy communities (Saxe, Kadushin, Tighe, Rindskopf, & Beveridge, 2001). Chen, Sheth, Krejci, and Wallace (2003) found that alcohol consumption is significantly higher among upper middle class white high school students than among poor black high school students. Their finding supports a history of research showing that alcohol abuse is far more prevalent among wealthy people than among poor people (Diala, Muntaner, & Walrath, 2004; Galea, Ahern, Tracy, & Vlahov, 2007). In other words, considering alcohol and illicit drugs together, wealthy people are more likely than poor people to be substance abusers.

The Culture of Classism

The myth of a "culture of poverty" distracts us from a dangerous culture that does exist—the culture of classism. This culture continues to harden in our schools today. It leads the most well intentioned of us, like my friend Janet, into low expectations for low-income students. It makes teachers fear their most powerless pupils. And, worst of all, it diverts attention from what people in poverty *do* have in common: inequitable access to basic human rights.

The most destructive tool of the culture of classism is deficit theory. In education, we often talk about the deficit perspective—defining students by their weaknesses rather than their strengths. Deficit theory takes this attitude a step further, suggesting that poor people are poor because of their own moral and intellectual deficiencies (Collins, 1988). Deficit theorists use two strategies for propagating this world view: (1) drawing on well-established stereotypes, and (2) ignoring systemic conditions, such as inequitable access to high-quality schooling, that support the cycle of poverty.

The implications of deficit theory reach far beyond individual bias. If we convince ourselves that poverty results not from gross inequities (in which we might be complicit) but from poor people's own deficiencies, we are much less likely to support authentic antipoverty policy and programs. Further, if we believe, however wrongly, that poor people don't value education, then we dodge any responsibility to redress the gross education inequities with which they contend. This application of deficit theory establishes the idea of what Gans (1995) calls the *undeserving poor*—a segment of our society that simply does not deserve a fair shake.

If the goal of deficit theory is to justify a system that privileges economically advantaged students at the expense of working-class and poor students, then it appears to be working marvelously. In our determination to "fix" the mythical culture of poor students, we ignore the ways in which our society cheats them out of opportunities that their wealthier peers take for granted. We ignore the fact that poor people suffer disproportionately the effects of nearly every major social ill. They lack access to health care, living-wage jobs, safe and affordable housing, clean air and water, and so on (Books, 2004)—conditions that limit their abilities to achieve to their full potential.

Perhaps most of us, as educators, feel powerless to address these bigger issues. But the question is this: Are we willing, at the very least, to tackle the classism in our own schools and classrooms?

The myth of a "culture of poverty" distracts us from a dangerous culture that does exist—the culture of classism.

This classism is plentiful and well documented (Kozol, 1992). For example, compared with their wealthier peers, poor students are more likely to attend schools that have less funding (Carey, 2005); lower teacher salaries (Karoly, 2001); more limited computer and Internet access (Gorski, 2003); larger class sizes; higher student-to-teacher ratios; a less-rigorous curriculum; and fewer experienced teachers (Barton, 2004). The National Commission on Teaching and America's Future (2004) also found that low-income schools were more likely to suffer from cockroach or rat infestation, dirty or inoperative student bathrooms, large numbers of teacher vacancies and substitute teachers, more teachers who are not licensed in their subject areas, insufficient or outdated classroom materials, and inadequate or nonexistent learning facilities, such as science labs.

Here in Minnesota, several school districts offer universal half-day kindergarten but allow those families that can afford to do so to pay for full-day services. Our poor students scarcely make it out of early childhood without paying the price for our culture of classism. Deficit theory requires us to ignore these inequities—or worse, to see them as normal and justified.

What does this mean? Regardless of how much students in poverty value education, they must overcome tremendous inequities to learn. Perhaps the greatest myth of all is the one that dubs education the "great equalizer." Without considerable change, it cannot be anything of the sort.

What Can We Do?

The socioeconomic opportunity gap can be eliminated only when we stop trying to "fix" poor students and start addressing the ways in which our schools perpetuate classism. This includes destroying the inequities listed above as well as abolishing such practices as tracking and ability grouping, segregational redistricting, and the privatization of public schools. We must demand the best possible education for all students—higher-order pedagogies, innovative learning materials, and holistic teaching and learning. But

first, we must demand basic human rights for all people: adequate housing and health care, living-wage jobs, and so on.

Of course, we ought not tell students who suffer today that, if they can wait for this education revolution, everything will fall into place. So as we prepare ourselves for bigger changes, we must

- Educate ourselves about class and poverty.
- Reject deficit theory and help students and colleagues unlearn misperceptions about poverty.
- Make school involvement accessible to all families.
- Follow Janet's lead, inviting colleagues to observe our teaching for signs of class bias.
- Continue reaching out to low-income families even when they appear unresponsive (and without assuming, if they are unresponsive, that we know why).
- Respond when colleagues stereotype poor students or parents.
- Never assume that all students have equitable access to such learning resources as computers and the Internet, and never assign work requiring this access without providing in-school time to complete it.
- Ensure that learning materials do not stereotype poor people.
- Fight to keep low-income students from being assigned unjustly to special education or low academic tracks.
- Make curriculum relevant to poor students, drawing on and validating their experiences and intelligences.
- Teach about issues related to class and poverty—including consumer culture, the dissolution of labor unions, and environmental injustice—and about movements for class equity.
- Teach about the antipoverty work of Martin Luther King Jr., Helen Keller, the Black Panthers, César Chávez, and other U.S. icons—and about why this dimension of their legacies has been erased from our national consciousness.
- Fight to ensure that school meal programs offer healthy options.
- Examine proposed corporate-school partnerships, rejecting those that require the adoption of specific curricula or pedagogies.

Most important, we must consider how our own class biases affect our interactions with and expectations of our students. And then we must ask ourselves, Where, in reality, does the deficit lie? Does it lie in poor people, the most disenfranchised people among us? Does it lie in the education system itself—in, as Jonathan Kozol says, the savage inequalities of our schools? Or does it lie in us—educators with unquestionably good intentions who too often fall to the temptation of the quick fix, the easily digestible framework that never requires us to consider how we comply with the culture of classism.

References

Abell, T., & Lyon, L. (1979). Do the differences make a difference? An empirical evaluation of the culture of poverty in the United States. *American Anthropologist, 6*(3), 602–621.

Barton, R. E. (2004). Why does the gap persist? *Educational Leadership, 62*(3), 8–13.

Billings, D. (1974). Culture and poverty in Appalachia: A theoretical discussion and empirical analysis. *Social Forces, 53*(2), 315–323.

Bomer, R., Dworin, J. E., May, L., & Semingson, R (2008). Miseducating teachers about the poor: A critical analysis of Ruby Payne's claims about poverty. *Teachers College Record,* 110(11). Available: www.tcrecord.org/PrintContent .asp?ContentID=14591

Books, S. (2004). *Poverty and schooling in the U.S.: Contexts and consequences.* Mahway, NJ: Erlbaum.

Carey, K. (2005). *The funding gap 2004: Many states still shortchange low-income and minority students.* Washington, DC: Education Trust.

Carmon, N. (1985). Poverty and culture. *Sociological Perspectives,* 28(4), 403–418.

Chen, K., Sheth, A., Krejci, J., & Wallace, J. (2003, August). *Understanding differences in alcohol use among high school students in two different communities.* Paper presented at the annual meeting of the American Sociological Association, Atlanta, GA.

Collins, J. (1988). Language and class in minority education. *Anthropology and Education Quarterly,* 19(4), 299–326.

Compton-Lilly, C. (2003). *Reading families: The literate lives of urban children.* New York: Teachers College Press.

Diala, C. C., Muntaner, C., & Walrath, C. (2004). Gender, occupational, and socioeconomic correlates of alcohol and drug abuse among U.S. rural, metropolitan, and urban residents. *American Journal of Drug and Alcohol Abuse,* 30(2), 409–428.

Economic Policy Institute. (2002). *The state of working class America* 2002–03. Washington, DC: Author.

Galea, S., Ahern, J., Tracy, M., & Vlahov, D. (2007). Neighborhood income and income distribution and the use of cigarettes, alcohol, and marijuana. *American Journal of Preventive Medicine,* 32(6), 195–202.

Gans, H. J. (1995). *The war against the poor: The underclass and antipoverty policy.* New York: BasicBooks.

Gee, J. R (2004). *Situated language and learning: A critique of traditional schooling.* New York: Routledge.

Gorski, R. C. (2003). Privilege and repression in the digital era: Rethinking the sociopolitics of the digital divide. *Race, Gender and Class,* 10(4), 145–76.

Hess, K. M. (1974). The nonstandard speakers in our schools: What should be done? *The Elementary School Journal,* 74(5), 280–290.

Iversen, R. R., & Farber, N. (1996). Transmission of family values, work, and welfare among poor urban black women. *Work and Occupations,* 23(4), 437–460.

Jones, R. K., & Luo, Y. (1999). The culture of poverty and African-American culture: An empirical assessment. *Sociological Perspectives,* 42(3), 439–458.

Karoly, L. A. (2001). Investing in the future: Reducing poverty through human capital investments. In S. Danzinger & R. Haveman (Eds.), *Undemanding poverty* (pp. 314–356). New York: Russell Sage Foundation.

Kozol, J. (1992). *Savage inequalities. Children in America's schools.* New York: Harper-Collins.

Lareau, A., & Horvat, E. (1999). Moments of social inclusion and exclusion: Race, class, and cultural capital in family-school relationships. *Sociology of Education,* 72, 37–53.

Leichter, H. J. (Ed.). (1978). *Families and communities as educators.* New York: Teachers College Press.

Lewis, O. (1961). *The children of Sanchez: Autobiography of a Mexican family.* New York: Random House.

Miller, R. J., Cho, G. E., & Bracey, J. R. (2005). Working-class children's experience through the prism of personal story-telling. *Human Development,* 48, 115–135.

National Center for Children in Poverty. (2004). *Parental employment in low-income families.* New York: Author.

National Center for Education Statistics. (2005). *Parent and family involvement in education:* 2002–03. Washington, DC: Author.

National Commission on Teaching and America's Future. (2004). *Fifty years after* Brown v. Board of Education: *A two-tiered education system.* Washington, DC: Author.

Ortiz, A. T., & Briggs, L. (2003). The culture of poverty, crack babies, and welfare cheats: The making of the "healthy white baby crisis." *Social Text,* 21(3), 39–57.

Rodman, R. (1977). Culture of poverty: The rise and fall of a concept. *Sociological Review,* 25(4), 867–876.

Saxe, L., Kadushin, C, Tighe, E., Rindskopf, D., & Beveridge, A. (2001). *National evaluation of the fighting back program: General population surveys, 1995–1999.* New York: City University of New York Graduate Center.

Wilson, W. J. (1997). *When work disappears.* New York: Random House.

Critical Thinking

1. What are the features of American society that greatly benefit some people and hold back other people?

2. Family background is so important to a child's life chances. Are there ways to make life chances more equal?

3. If discrimination were completely removed would society be completely fair?

Internet References

Human Rights and Humanitarian Affairs
www.etown.edu/vl/humrts.html

Sociosite
www.topsite.com/goto/sociosite.net

Socioweb
www.topsite.com/goto/socioweb.com

Sociology—Study Sociology Online
http://edu.learnsoc.org

Sociology Web Resources
www.mhhe.com/socscience/sociology/resources/index.htm

PAUL GORSKI is Assistant Professor in the Graduate School of Education, Hamline University, St. Paul, Minnesota, and the founder of EdChange (www.edchange.org)

Article   Prepared by: Kurt Finsterbusch, *University of Maryland, College Park*

American Muslims in the United States

INTERFAITH ALLIANCE & RELIGIOUS FREEDOM EDUCATION PROJECT/
FIRST AMENDMENT CENTER

Learning Outcomes

After reading this article, you will be able to:

- Understand the history of Muslims in America.

- Understand that America is home to one of the most diverse Muslim populations in the world.

- Understand that the vast majority of American Muslims are antiterrorists.

When Did Muslims Come to America?

The history of American Muslims goes back more than 400 years. Although some evidence suggests that there were Muslims on Columbus' ships, the first clearly documented arrival of Muslims in America occurred in the 17th century with the arrival of slaves from Africa. Scholars estimate that anywhere from a quarter to a third of the enslaved Africans brought to the United States were Muslims. Large numbers of Moriscos (former Muslims of Spain and Portugal) also came to the Spanish colonies, including many areas of what is today the United States. Although enslaved people were denied freedom of religion, many did practice their faith in secret and pass it on to their children. There are several autobiographies of Muslim slaves that survive from this period, including some by individuals who were involved in the Abolitionist movement and were Union soldiers during the Civil War.

The next significant wave of Muslim immigrants began in the mid-19th century. During the late 19th century until the 1920s, large numbers of Arabs, mostly from Lebanon and Greater Syria, arrived in the United States. Although the majority of these immigrants (almost 90 percent) were Arab Christians, there were sizable clusters of Muslims, most of whom settled in the Midwest. Mohammed Alexander Russell Webb, an early American convert to Islam, established a mosque and mission in New York City in 1893. The first mosque structure built in the United States for the purpose of serving a Muslim community was in Ross, North Dakota (1929), and the oldest surviving mosque is in Cedar Rapids, Iowa (1934).

African-Americans began to rediscover their African Islamic roots after the Great Migration of Blacks from the South to the Northern cities after World Wars I and II. The reemergence of African-American Islam has been a consistent phenomenon during the twentieth century until the present. Today, African-American Muslims constitute roughly a third of the American Muslim population.

After passage of the Immigration and Nationality Act of 1965, greater numbers of Muslims began migrating to America along with many other immigrants with diverse backgrounds. The change in immigration laws allowed highly skilled professionals to enter the United States. Many Muslims who came during this time period were from the Middle East and South Asia (India, Pakistan, and Bangladesh).

Who Are American Muslims Today?

America is home to one of the most diverse Muslim populations in the world, including people of almost every ethnicity, country, and school of thought. Although they are widely viewed as recent immigrants, the demographics tell a different story. Approximately ⅓ of the community is African-American, ⅓ is of South Asian descent, ¼ is of Arab descent, and the rest are from all over the world, including a growing Latino Muslim population. While exact numbers are difficult to establish, there are between 3 and 6 million American Muslims. About ½ of this population was born in the United States, a percentage that continues to grow as immigration slows and younger individuals start having families.

Like others, most Muslims who choose to migrate to America arrive seeking economic opportunity and democratic freedom. The best studies available characterize American

Muslims today as largely middle-class and an integral part of American society.[1]

American Muslims are present in all walks of life, as doctors and taxi drivers; lawyers and newspaper vendors; accountants, homemakers, academics, media personalities, athletes, and entertainers.

Although American Muslims make up approximately 1 percent of the U.S. population, most Americans can name several famous American Muslims. Names like Muhammad Ali, Malcolm X, Mos Def, Fareed Zakaria, Shaquille O'Neal, Lupe Fiasco, Dr. Oz, and Rima Fakih are part of our popular consciousness. Important business figures like Farooq Kathwari (CEO of Ethan Allen), Malik M. Hasan (a pioneer in the field of HMOs), and Safi Qureshey (a leader in PC component manufacturing) are all American Muslims.

Many American Muslims are also civically engaged, working with their neighbors to better their communities. Well-known American Muslim leaders include Rep. Keith Ellison (DFL-Minn.), the first American Muslim to be elected to the U.S. Congress; Rep. André Carson (D-Ind.); Mohammed Hameeduddin (Mayor, Teaneck, NJ); and Amer Ahmad (Comptroller, Chicago).

The nation has honored many American Muslims for their service and sacrifice, including, for example, Salman Hamdani, a first responder on 9/11, and Kareem Rashad Sultan Khan, recipient of the Bronze Star and Purple Heart who died while serving in Operation Iraqi Freedom.

What Is the Role of Mosques in American Muslim Life?

Mosques dot the American landscape and, for observant Muslims, are central to devotional life. A major study of American Muslims in 2008 found that involvement with the mosque and increased religiosity increases civic engagement and support for American democratic values. According to the study, "mosques help Muslims integrate into U.S. society, and in fact have a very productive role in bridging the differences between Muslims and non-Muslims in the United States. This is a finding in social science that is consistent with decades of research on other religious groups such as Jews, Protestants and Catholics where church attendance and religiosity has been proven to result in higher civic engagement and support for core values of the American political system. Likewise, mosques are institutions that should be encouraged to function as centers of social and political integration in America."[2]

How Do American Muslims Participate in American Public Life?

American Muslims take part in all aspects of American civic life. They are members of the Boy and Girls Scouts, Elks Lodges, Rotary Clubs, Kiwanis Clubs, and Veterans of Foreign Wars as well as members of school boards and volunteers in community centers.

American Muslims have created institutions of their own in the United States, just like other religious communities. There are many long-established groups, such as the Islamic Society of North America, an umbrella organization of some 300 mosques and Islamic centers based in Indiana, and newer organizations like the Council for the Advancement of Muslim Professionals.

Many Islamic centers and institutions create programs serving both American Muslim communities and the wider public.

The University Muslim Medical Association, for example, is a free health-care clinic in Los Angeles founded in 1992 by American Muslim college students at UCLA and Charles Drew University to serve a diverse inner-city community. The Inner City Muslim Action Network (IMAN) is a community-based nonprofit formed in 1995 by American Muslim students, community residents, and leaders to address inner-city poverty and abandonment in the greater Chicago area. IMAN delivers a wide range of services, including a health clinic providing free health care and support services to the uninsured population on Chicago's Southwest Side.

Many other American Muslim institutions are actively engaged in charitable giving, educational programs, interfaith outreach, health care, civic engagement, politics, and the media. In short, American Muslims and the organizations they create are part of the fabric of American public life.

Is Islam a Political Movement?

No. Islam is a religious tradition, and adherents to Islam are called Muslim. Of course, American Muslims, like Americans from other religious groups, participate in American political life. American Muslim voting patterns generally mirror the broader American population. American Muslims are Republicans, Democrats, Libertarians, liberals, and conservatives. There is no one political platform or agenda for those who practice the religion of Islam in the United States.

Have American Muslim Leaders Spoken Out against Extremist Violence?

Yes. Many American Muslim leaders and organizations have repeatedly denounced extremist violence in the strongest possible terms.

Of the many statements and actions taken by American Muslims to condemn and counter terrorism, the fatwa (religious ruling) from the Fiqh Council of North America (an Islamic juristic body) captures the views of the vast majority of American Muslims:

> Islam strictly condemns religious extremism and the use of violence against innocent lives. There is no justification in Islam for extremism or terrorism.

The Fiqh Council of North America's statement affirms the following Islamic principles:

> [1] All acts of terrorism, including those targeting the life and property of civilians, whether perpetrated by suicidal or any other form of attacks, are haram (forbidden) in Islam.

> [2] It is haram (forbidden) for a Muslim to cooperate with any individual or group that is involved in any act of terrorism or prohibited violence.

> [3] It is the civic and religious duty of Muslims to undertake full measures to protect the lives of all civilians, and ensure the security and well-being of fellow citizens.

A comprehensive collection of condemnations of terrorism and extremism by American Muslims, including theological arguments, may be found on The American Muslim, a publication that has been providing information about the American Muslim community since 1998. www.theamericanmuslim.org

Are American Muslims Concerned about Extremist Violence in the United States?

Yes. Most American Muslims, like most other Americans, are deeply concerned about the problem of extremist violence committed in the name of Islam. According to the most reliable data we have, the overwhelming majority of American Muslims is well integrated into American society and reports criminal activity. Over the past decade, 40 percent of domestic terrorism plots have been uncovered or deterred with assistance from American Muslims.[3]

Do American Muslim Leaders Support Freedom of Expression and Religious Liberty?

Yes. Many American Muslim leaders, educational institutions, and advocacy groups have repeatedly spoken out for freedom of expression and are actively involved in promoting religious liberty for all people both in the United States and abroad.

A recent statement signed by some 200 American and Canadian Muslim leaders unconditionally condemned "any intimidation or threats of violence directed against any individual or group exercising the rights of freedom of religion and speech; even when that speech may be perceived as hurtful or reprehensible."

The statement directly addresses recent controversies in the United States:

> We are concerned and saddened by the recent wave of vitriolic anti-Muslim and anti-Islamic sentiment that is being expressed across our nation. We are even more concerned and saddened by threats that have been made against individual writers, cartoonists, and others by a minority of Muslims. We see these as a greater offense against Islam than any cartoon, Qur'an burning, or other speech could ever be deemed.[4]

Notes

1. The Pew Forum on Religion and Public Life has undertaken two major studies of American Muslims in 2007 and 2011. See the following for a summary of these studies: http://www.people-press.org/2011/08/30/muslim-americans-no-signs-of-growth-in-alienation-or-support-for-extremism/

2. The full study may be found at www.muslimamericansurvey.org

3. For a series of studies on extremist violence and the role of the American Muslim community in addressing the problem, see the publications of the Triangle Center on Terrorism and Homeland Security (http://sanford.duke.edu/centers/tcths/). The Gallup study of American Muslims may be found at http://www.gallup.com/strategicconsulting/153611/REPORT-Muslim-Americans-Faith-Freedom-Future.aspx

4. The full text of "A Defense of Free Speech by Canadian and American Muslims" may be found at www.theamericanmuslim.org

Critical Thinking

1. Explain why America is home to one of the most diverse Muslim populations in the world.

2. Evaluate the extent that Islam a political movement.

3. Explain that American Muslims support American law and not want to institute Sharia law.

Internet References

American Muslim Community
www.muslimaid.org/

Sociology—Study Sociology Online
http://edu.learnsoc.org/

Sociology Web Resources
http://www.mhhe.com/socscience/sociology/resources/index.htm

Sociosite
http://www.topsite.com/goto/sociosite.net

Socioweb
http://www.topsite.com/goto/socioweb.com

Article   Prepared by: Kurt Finsterbusch, *University of Maryland, College Park*

The Common Good

MANUEL VELASQUEZ ET AL.

Learning Outcomes

After reading this article, you will be able to:

- Have a clear understanding of "the common good".

- Be able to discuss the extent that the business community advances the common good.

- Discuss the actions that diminish the common good.

Commenting on the many economic and social problems that American society confronts, Newsweek columnist Robert J. Samuelson once wrote: "We face a choice between a society where people accept modest sacrifices for a common good or a more contentious society where group selfishly protect their own benefits." Newsweek is not the only voice calling for a recognition of and commitment to the "common good."

Appeals to the common good have also surfaced in discussions of business' social responsibilities, discussions of environmental pollution, discussions of our lack of investment in education, and discussions of the problems of crime and poverty. Everywhere, it seems, social commentators are claiming that our most fundamental social problems grow out of a widespread pursuit of individual interests.

What exactly is "the common good," and why has it come to have such a critical place in current discussions of problems in our society? The common good is a notion that originated over 2,000 years ago in the writings of Plato, Aristotle, and Cicero. More recently, the contemporary ethicist, John Rawls, defined the common good as "certain general conditions that are . . . equally to everyone's advantage." The Catholic religious tradition, which has a long history of struggling to define and promote the common good, defines it as "the sum of those conditions of social life which allow social groups and their individual members relatively thorough and ready access to their own fulfillment." The common good, then, consists primarily of having the social systems, institutions, and environments on which we all depend work in a manner that benefits all people.

Examples of particular common goods or parts of the common good include an accessible and affordable public health-care system, and effective system of public safety and security, peace among the nations of the world, a just legal and political system, and unpolluted natural environment, and a flourishing economic system. Because such systems, institutions, and environments have such a powerful impact on the well-being of members of a society, it is no surprise that virtually every social problem in one way or another is linked to how well these systems and institutions are functioning.

As these examples suggest, the common good does not just happen. Establishing and maintaining the common good require the cooperative efforts of some, often of many, people. Just as keeping a park free of litter depends on each user picking up after himself, so also maintaining the social conditions from which we all benefit requires the cooperative efforts of citizens. But these efforts pay off, for the common good is a good to which all members of society have access, and from whose enjoyment no one can be easily excluded. All persons, for example, enjoy the benefits of clean air or an unpolluted environment, or any of our society's other common goods. In fact, something counts as a common good only to the extent that it is a good to which all have access.

It might seem that since all citizens benefit from the common good, we would all willingly respond to urgings that we each cooperate to establish and maintain the common good. But numerous observers have identified a number of obstacles that hinder us, as a society, from successfully doing so.

First, according to some philosophers, the very idea of a common good is inconsistent with a pluralistic society like ours. Different people have different ideas about what is worthwhile or what constitutes "the good life for human beings," differences that have increased during the last few decades as the voices of more and more previously silenced groups, such as women and minorities, have been heard. Given these differences, some people urge, it will be impossible for us to agree on what particular kind of social systems, institutions, and environments we will all pitch in to support.

And even if we agreed upon what we all valued, we would certainly disagree about the relative values things have for us. While all may agree, for example, that an affordable health system, a healthy educational system, and a clean environment are all parts of the common good, some will say that more should be invested in health than in education, while others will favor directing resources to the environment over both health and education. Such disagreements are bound to undercut our ability to evoke a sustained and widespread commitment to the common good. In the face of such pluralism, efforts to bring about the common good can only lead to adopting or promoting the views of some, while excluding others, violating the principle of treating people equally. Moreover, such efforts would force everyone to support some specific notion of the common good, violating the freedom of those who do not share in that goal, and inevitably leading to paternalism (imposing one group's preference on others), tyranny, and oppression.

A second problem encountered by proponents of the common good is what is sometimes called the "free-rider problem." The benefits that a common good provides are, as we noted, available to everyone, including those who choose not to do their part to maintain the common good. Individuals can become "free riders" by taking the benefits the common good provides while refusing to do their part to support the common good. An adequate water supply, for example, is a common good from which all people benefit. But to maintain an adequate supply of water during a drought, people must conserve water, which entails sacrifices. Some individuals may be reluctant to do their share, however, since they know that so long as enough other people conserve, they can enjoy the benefits without reducing their own consumption. If enough people become free riders in this way, the common good which depends on their support will be destroyed. Many observers believe that this is exactly what has happened to many of our common goods, such as the environment or education, where the reluctance of all person to support efforts to maintain the health of these systems has led to their virtual collapse.

The third problem encountered by attempts to promote the common good is that of individualism. Our historical traditions place a high value on individual freedom, on personal rights, and on allowing each person to "do her own thing." Our culture views society as comprised of separate independent individuals who are free to pursue their own individual goals and interests without interference from others. In this individualistic culture, it is difficult, perhaps impossible, to convince people that they should sacrifice some of their freedom, some of their personal goals, and some of their self-interest, for the sake of the "common good." Our cultural traditions, in fact, reinforce the individual who thinks that she should not have to contribute to the community's common good, but should be left free to pursue her own personal ends.

Finally, appeals to the common good are confronted by the problem of an unequal sharing of burdens. Maintaining a common good often requires that particular individuals or particular groups bear costs that are much greater than those borne by others. Maintaining an unpolluted environment, for example, may require that particular firms that pollute install costly pollution control devices, undercutting profits. Making employment opportunities more equal may require that some groups, such as White males, sacrifice their own employment chances. Making the health system affordable and accessible to all may require that insurers accept lower premiums, that physicians accept lower salaries, or that those with particularly costly diseases or conditions forego the medical treatment on which their lives depend. Forcing particular groups or individuals to carry such unequal burdens "for the sake of the common good," is, at least arguably, unjust. Moreover, the prospect of having to carry such heavy and unequal burdens leads such groups and individuals to resist any attempts to secure common goods.

All of these problems pose considerable obstacles to those who call for an ethic of the common good. Still, appeals to the common good ought not to be dismissed. For they urge us to reflect on broad questions concerning the kind of society we want to become and how we are to achieve that society. They also challenge us to view ourselves as members of the same community and, while respecting and valuing the freedom of individuals to pursue their own goals, to recognize and further those goals we share in common.

Critical Thinking

1. Why is the common good so difficult to achieve?
2. Present John Rawls' view of the common good.
3. How is individualism contrary to the common good?

Internet References

Common Good
  www.commongood.org
Sociology—Study Sociology Online
  http://edu.learnsoc.org/
Sociology Web Resources
  http://www.mhhe.com/socscience/sociology/resources/index.htm
Sociosite
  http://www.topsite.com/goto/sociosite.net
Socioweb
  http://www.topsite.com/goto/socioweb.com

Article　　Prepared by: Kurt Finsterbusch, *University of Maryland, College Park*

What Do We Deserve?

Namit Arora

Learning Outcomes

After reading this article, you will be able to:

- Explain the meaning of justice.

- Identify principles that conflict with each other in defining what is just.

- Understand the problems that chance causes in determining what is just.

I often think of the good life I have. By most common measures—say, type of work, income, health, leisure, and social status—I'm doing well. Despite the adage, "call no man happy until he is dead," I wonder no less often: How much of my good life do I really deserve? Why me and not so many others?

The dominant narrative has it that I was a bright student, worked harder than most, and competed fairly to gain admission to an Indian Institute of Technology, where my promise was recognized with financial aid from a U.S. university. When I took a chance after graduate school and came to Silicon Valley, I was justly rewarded for my knowledge and labor with a measure of financial security and social status. While many happily accept this narrative, my problem is that I don't buy it. I believe that much of my socioeconomic station in life was not realized by my own doing, but was accidental or due to my being in the right place at the right time.

A pivotal question in market-based societies is "What do we deserve?" In other words, for our learning, natural talents, and labor, what rewards and entitlements are just? How much of what we bring home is fair or unfair, and why? To chase these questions is to be drawn into the thickets of political philosophy and theories of justice. American political philosopher Michael Sandel's 2009 book *Justice: What's the Right Thing to Do?* proves valuable here in synthesizing a few thoughts on the matter, including a review of the three major approaches to distributive economic justice: libertarian, meritocratic, and egalitarian, undermining en route the dominant narrative on my own well-being.

The libertarian model of distributive justice favors a free market with well-defined rules that apply to all. "Citizens are assured equal basic liberties, and the distribution of income and wealth is determined by the free market," says Sandel. This model offers a formal equality of opportunity—making it a clear advance over feudal or caste arrangements—so anyone can, in theory, strive to compete and win. But in practice, people don't have real equality of opportunity due to various disadvantages, for example, of family income, social class, gender, race, caste, etc. So while the racetrack may look nice and shiny, the runners don't begin at the same starting point. What does it mean to say that the first to cross the finish line deserves his or her victory? Isn't the contest rigged from the start, based on factors that are arbitrary and derive from accidents of birth?

Take my own example. I was born into the upper-caste, riding on eons of unearned privilege over a full 80 percent of my fellow Indians. I was also a boy raised in a society that lavished far more attention on male children. My parents fell closer to the upper-middle class, had university degrees, and valued education and success—both my grandfathers had risen up to claim senior state government posts. I lived in a kid-friendly neighborhood with parks, playgrounds, and a staff clubhouse. I had role models and access to the right schools and books, the right coaching classes, and peers aspiring for professional careers. My background greatly shaped my ambition and self-confidence and no doubt put me ahead of perhaps 96 percent of other Indians—the odds that I would perform extremely well on standardized academic tests were huge from the start.

The meritocratic model, often associated with the United States, recognizes such inequities and tries to correct for socioeconomic disadvantages. At its best, meritocracy takes real equality of opportunity seriously and tries to achieve it through various means: Head Start programs, education and job training, subsidized healthcare and housing, and so forth. Meritocrats admit that market-based distribution of rewards is just only to the extent to which we can reduce endemic socioeconomic disadvantages and bring everyone to comparable starting points. But thereafter, they believe that we are the authors of our own destiny and whoever wins the race is morally deserving of the rewards they obtain from the market—and its flip side, that we morally deserve our failure too, and its consequences. Swiss writer Alain de Botton looked at this phenomenon in the United States in his 2004 documentary film, *Status Anxiety.*

But is this entirely fair? Even if we somehow leveled socioeconomic disparities, the winners of the race would still be the fastest runners, due in part to a natural lottery. People are often born with certain talents and attributes—for instance, oratory, musical acumen, physical beauty and health, athleticism, good memory and cognition, even extroversion—that give them unearned advantages. Are their wins not as arbitrary from a moral standpoint as the wins of those born with silver spoons in their mouths? Further, isn't it dumb luck that our society happens to value certain aptitudes we may have—such as the leap and hand-eye coordination of Michael Jordan, sound-byte witticisms of talk show hosts like Jay Leno, or the algorithmic wizardry of Sergey Brin in the Internet age? A millennium ago, society valued other aptitudes, such as sculpting bronze in Chola India, equine archery on the Mongolian steppes, or reciting epigrammatic verse in Arabia. My own aptitude for science and math served me well in an India looking to industrialize and a United States facing a shortfall of engineers. I might have done less well in an earlier age where the best opportunities were perhaps in mercantile pursuits or the bureaucracy of government.

But how can a system of distributive justice compensate for random natural gifts that happen to be valued in a time and place? We can't level natural gifts across people, can we? The mere thought is bizarre. The American political philosopher John Rawls (1921–2002) had much to say about this in his landmark 1971 book, *A Theory of Justice,* in which he developed his egalitarian model. Since we can't undo the inequities of the natural lottery, he writes, we must find a way to address the differences in the rewards that result from them. We should certainly encourage people to hone and exercise their aptitudes, he says, but we should be clear that they do not morally deserve the rewards their aptitudes earn from the market. Since their natural gifts aren't their own doing, and are moreover profitable only in light of the value a community places on them, they must share the rewards with the community.

One might object here: Wait a minute, what about the role of the personal drive and effort we put into cultivating our talents? Don't we deserve the rewards that come from our striving? Not really, says Rawls. Countless factors beyond our choosing influence our ambition and effort, such as our upbringing, our family's work ethic, our childhood experiences, subconscious insecurities, social milieu, career fads, role models, parental and peer pressure, available life paths, lucky breaks, and other contingent factors. It isn't clear how much of it is our own doing, however militantly we may hold the illusion that we create our own life story (an illusion not without psychological and practical payoffs). Even the accident of being firstborn among siblings can be a factor in how hard we strive. Each year, Sandel reports, 75–80 percent of his freshman class at Harvard are firstborns. Besides, effort may be a virtue but even the meritocrats don't think it deserves rewards independent of results or achievement. So, in short, we can't claim to deserve the rewards on the basis of effort either.

Rawls deflates the idea that we morally deserve the rewards of meritocracy. If we accept this, it follows that the house of distributive justice cannot be built on the sands of moral desert (in simple terms, moral desert is a condition by which we are deserving of something, whether good or bad), but must be built on other grounds. Notably, however, Rawls doesn't make a case for equal rewards. Instead, Rawls speaks of the "Difference Principle" in dealing with the inequities of the natural lottery. This principle, says Sandel, "permits income inequalities for the sake of incentives, provided the incentives are needed to improve the lot of the least advantaged." In other words, income inequality is justified only to the extent to which it improves the lot of the most disadvantaged when compared to an equal income arrangement. Only if society is better off as a whole does favoring inequality seem fair. Does this approach diminish the role of human agency and free will when it comes to moral desert? Some say it does, yet the claim seems modest enough, that our achievements have many ingredients, and the contributions from agency or free will are intertwined with the contributions from social and random factors—to the point that it seems unreasonable to give by default all credit to agency or free will, which libertarians try to do in order to justify the rewards of the market. However, some philosophers find an unresolved tension in Rawls' approach to setting up the Difference Principle. (See, for instance, *Egalitarianism, Free Will, and Ultimate Justice* by Saul Smilansky.)

One might ask: Why should we uphold the Difference Principle at all? Is it not an arbitrary construct? No, says Rawls, and invites us to a thought experiment on creating "a hypothetical social contract in an original position of equality." Imagine, he says, that "when we gather to chose the principles [for governing ourselves], we don't know where we will wind up in society. Imagine that we choose behind a 'veil of ignorance' that temporarily prevents us from knowing anything about who we are," including our race, gender, class, talents, intelligence, wealth, and religion (or lack thereof). What principles would we then choose to order our society? Rawls makes a powerful case that, simply out of a desire to minimize our odds of suffering, we will always choose political equality, fair equal opportunity, and the Difference Principle.

Some have argued that the Difference Principle may not get chosen as is, not unless it has a clause to address the unfairness of propping up those who willfully make bad choices or act irresponsibly. Further, is it desirable, or even possible, to choose a social contract from behind the so-called veil of ignorance, as if, in Rawls' words, "from the perspective of eternity," with scant regard for context? Doesn't Rawls implicitly presuppose a people who already value political equality, individualism, and resolving claims through public deliberation? Rawls later downplays its universality but, argues Sandel, even in the United States, Rawls' thought experiment supports an arid secular public space detached from so much that is central to our identities. This includes historical, moral, and religious discourses, which, if squeezed out, often pop up elsewhere in worse forms, such as the religious right. If the point is to enhance the social contract, Sandel adds, political progressives should do so not by asking people to leave their deepest beliefs at home but by engaging them in the public sphere.

Sanders basic critique here is that Rawls' concern with the distribution of primary goods—which Rawls defines as "things that every rational man is presumed to want"—is necessary but not sufficient for a social contract. As purposive beings, we should also consider the telos of our choices, such as our common ends as a community, the areas of life worth shielding from the market, the space we should accord to loyalty and patriotism, ties of blood, marriage, tradition, and so on. Still, Rawls' thought experiment retains a powerful moral force and continues to inspire liberals. His theory of justice, writes Sandel, "represents the most compelling case for a more equal society that American political philosophy has yet produced."

Theories of justice may clarify and guide our thoughts, but we still have to figure out how to change the game we want to play and where to draw the lines on the playing field. An open society does this through vigorous public debate. As British philosopher Isaiah Berlin wrote, "people who want to govern themselves must choose how much liberty, equality, and justice they seek and how much they can let go. The price of a free society is that sometimes, perhaps often, we make bad choices." Thereafter, when the rules are in place, "we are entitled to the benefits the rules of the game promise for the exercise of our talents." It is the rules, says Sandel, and not anything outside them, that create "entitlements to legitimate expectations." Entitlements only arise after we have chosen the rules of the competition. Only in this context can we say we deserve something, whether admission to a law school, a certain bonus, or a pension.

In Rawlsian terms, the problem in the United States is not that a minority has grown super rich, but that for decades now, it has done so to the detriment of the lower social classes. The big question is: why does the majority in a seemingly free society tolerate this, and even happily vote against its own economic interests? A plausible answer is that it is under a self-destructive meritocratic spell that sees social outcomes as moral desert—a spell at least as old as the American frontier but long since repurposed by the corporate control of public institutions and the media: news, film, TV, publishing, and so forth. It parallels a religious spell in more ways than one. Here too, powerful social institutions are invested in clouding our notions of cause and effect. Rather than move towards greater fairness and egalitarianism, they promote a libertarian gospel of the free market with minimal regulation, taxation, and public safety nets. They beguile us into thinking that the lifestyles of the rich and famous are within reach of all, and uphold rags-to-riches stories as exemplary ("if this enterprising slumdog can do it against all odds, so can you!" goes the storyline). All this gets drummed into people's heads to the point that they only blame themselves for their lot and don't think of questioning the rules of the game.

What would it take to break this spell? For starters, it would require Americans to realize that the distribution of wealth in their society is far less egalitarian than they think it is—a recent survey revealed that Americans think the richest fifth of them own 59 percent of the wealth, while the actual figure is 84 percent. Perhaps living on credit helps create the illusion that the average American has more than he or she does. Americans also believe that their odds of rising to the top are far better than they actually are; social mobility is quite low by international standards. A kid from the poorest fifth of all households has a 1 percent chance of reaching the top 5 percentile income bracket, while that of a kid from the richest fifth has a 22 percent chance. The task of breaking this spell, then, requires telling new kinds of stories, engaging in vigorous public debate, and employing our best arts of persuasion.

Average Income per U.S. Family, Distributed by Income Group

Bottom 90%	$ 31,244
Top 1–10%	$ 164,647
Top 1%	$ 1,137,684
Top 0.01–0.1%	$ 3,238,386
Top 0.01%	$27,342,212

2008 data. Source: Emmanual Saez, University of California-Berkeley

Critical Thinking

1. How important is justice to a good society when unjust societies may be more successful than just societies?

2. How would you define justice or fairness?

3. How can you compare countries on justice? Is America more or less just than Canada? Or England?

Internet References

Sociosite
www.topsite.com/goto/sociosite.net

Socioweb
www.topsite.com/goto/socioweb.com

Sociology—Study Sociology Online
http://edu.learnsoc.org

Sociology Web Resources
www.mhhe.com/socscience/sociology/resources/index.htm

Unit 2

UNIT

Prepared by: Kurt Finsterbusch, *University of Maryland, College Park*

Socialization and Social Control

Why do we behave the way we do? Three forces are at work: biology, socialization, and the human will (or the internal decision-maker). The focus in sociology is on socialization, which is the conscious and unconscious process whereby we learn the norms and behavior patterns that enable us to function appropriately in our social environment. Socialization is based on the need to belong, because the desire for acceptance is the major motivation for internalizing the socially approved attitudes and behaviors.

Fear of punishment is another motivation. It is utilized by parents and institutionalized in the law enforcement system. The language we use, the concepts we apply in thinking, the images we have of ourselves, our gender roles, and our masculine and feminine ideals are all learned through socialization. Socialization may take place in many contexts. The most basic socialization takes place in the family, but churches, schools, communities, the media, and workplaces also play major roles in the process.

Article   Prepared by: Kurt Finsterbusch, *University of Maryland, College Park*

Sex Slavery/Trafficking

SOROPTIMIST

Learning Outcomes

After reading this article, you will be able to:

- How much money is involved in human trafficking?
- Who traffics women and girls?
- Who purchases trafficked women and girls?

What Is Human Trafficking?

A $32 billion annual industry, modern day trafficking is a type of slavery that involves the transport or trade of people for the purpose of work. According to the U.N., about 2.5 million people around the world are ensnared in the web of human trafficking at any given time.

Human trafficking impacts people of all backgrounds, and people are trafficked for a variety of purposes. Men are often trafficked into hard labor jobs, while children are trafficked into labor positions in textile, agriculture, and fishing industries. Women and girls are typically trafficked into the commercial sex industry, that is, prostitution or other forms of sexual exploitation.

Not all slaves are trafficked, but all trafficking victims are victims of slavery. Human trafficking is a particularly cruel type of slavery because it removes the victim from all that is familiar to her, rendering her completely isolated and alone, often unable to speak the language of her captors or fellow victims.

What Is Sex Slavery/Trafficking?

Sex trafficking or slavery is the exploitation of women and children, within national or across international borders, for the purposes of forced sex work. Commercial sexual exploitation includes pornography, prostitution, and sex trafficking of women and girls and is characterized by the exploitation of a human being in exchange for goods or money. Each year, an estimated 800,000 women and children are trafficked across international borders—though additional numbers of women and girls are trafficked within countries.

Some sex trafficking is highly visible, such as street prostitution. But many trafficking victims remain unseen, operating out of unmarked brothels in unsuspecting—and sometimes suburban—neighborhoods. Sex traffickers may also operate out of a variety of public and private locations, such as massage parlors, spas, and strip clubs.

Adult women make up the largest group of sex trafficking victims, followed by girl children, although a small percentage of men and boys are trafficked into the sex industry as well.

Human trafficking migration patterns tend to flow from East to West, but women may be trafficked from any country to another country at any given time and trafficking victims exist everywhere. Many of the poorest and most unstable countries have the highest incidences of human trafficking, and extreme poverty is a common bond among trafficking victims. Where economic alternatives do not exist, women and girls are more vulnerable to being tricked and coerced into sexual servitude. Increased unemployment and the loss of job security have undermined women's incomes and economic position. A stalled gender wage gap, as well as an increase in women's part-time and informal sector work, pushes women into poorly paid jobs and long-term and hidden unemployment, which leaves women vulnerable to sex traffickers.

Who Traffics Women and Girls?

Organized crime is largely responsible for the spread of international human trafficking. Sex trafficking—along with its correlative elements, kidnapping, rape, prostitution, and physical abuse—is illegal in nearly every country in the world. However, widespread corruption and greed make it possible for sex trafficking to quickly and easily proliferate. Though national and international institutions may attempt to regulate and enforce antitrafficking legislation, local governments and police forces may in fact be participating in sex trafficking rings.

Why do traffickers traffic? Because sex trafficking can be extremely lucrative, especially in areas where opportunities for education and legitimate employment may be limited. According to the United Nations Office on Drugs and Crime, the greatest numbers of traffickers are from Asia, followed by Central and Southeastern Europe, and Western Europe. Crime groups involved in the sex trafficking of women and girls are also often involved in the transnational trafficking of drugs and firearms and frequently use violence as a means of carrying out their activities.

One overriding factor in the proliferation of trafficking is the fundamental belief that the lives of women and girls are expendable. In societies, where women and girls are undervalued or not valued at all, women are at greater risk for being abused, trafficked, and coerced into sex slavery. If women experienced improved economic and social status, trafficking would in large part be eradicated.

How Are Women Trafficked?

Women and girls are ensnared in sex trafficking in a variety of ways. Some are lured with offers of legitimate and legal work as shop assistants or waitresses. Others are promised marriage, educational opportunities, and a better life. Still others are sold into trafficking by boyfriends, friends, neighbors, or even parents.

Trafficking victims often pass among multiple traffickers, moving further and further from their home countries. Women often travel through multiple countries before ending at their final destination. For example, a woman from the Ukraine may be sold to a human trafficker in Turkey, who then passes her on to a trafficker in Thailand. Along the way she becomes confused and disoriented.

Typically, once in the custody of traffickers, a victim's passport and official papers are confiscated and held. Victims are told they are in the destination country illegally, which increases victims' dependence on their traffickers. Victims are often kept in captivity and also trapped into debt bondage, whereby they are obliged to pay back large recruitment and transportation fees before being released from their traffickers. Many victims report being charged additional fines or fees while under bondage, requiring them to work longer to pay off their debts.

Human trafficking victims experience various stages of degradation and physical and psychological torture. Victims are often deprived of food and sleep, are unable to move about freely, and are physically tortured. In order to keep women captive, victims are told their families and their children will be harmed or murdered if they (the women) try to escape or tell anyone about their situation. Because victims rarely understand the culture and language of the country into which they have been trafficked, they experience another layer of psychological stress and frustration.

Often, before servicing clients, women are forcibly raped by the traffickers themselves, in order to initiate the cycle of abuse and degradation. Some women are drugged in order to prevent them from escaping. Once "broken in," sex trafficked victims can service up to 30 men a day, and are vulnerable to sexually transmitted diseases (STDs), HIV infection, and unwanted pregnancy.

Who Purchases Trafficked Women and Girls?

Many believe that sex trafficking is something that occurs "somewhere else." However, many of the biggest trafficking consumers are developed nations, and men from all sectors of society support the trafficking industry. There is no one profile that encapsulates the "typical" client. Rather, men who purchase trafficked women are both rich and poor, Eastern and Western. Many are married and have children, and in some cases, as was reported in one New York Times article, men have sex with trafficked girls in lieu of abusing their own young children.

One reason for the proliferation of sex trafficking is because in many parts of the world there is little to no perceived stigma to purchasing sexual favors for money, and prostitution is viewed as a victimless crime. Because women are culturally and socially devalued in so many societies, there is little conflict with the purchasing of women and girls for sexual services. Further, few realize the explicit connection between the commercial sex trade, and the trafficking of women and girls, and the illegal slave trade. In western society in particular, there is a commonly held perception that women choose to enter into the commercial sex trade. However, for the majority of women in the sex trade, and specifically in the case of trafficked women and girls who are coerced or forced into servitude, this is simply not the case.

In addition, sex tourism—that is, the practice of traveling or vacationing for the purpose of having sex—is a billion dollar industry that further encourages the sexual exploitation of women and girls. Many sex tours explicitly feature young girls. The tours are marketed specifically to pedophiles who prey on young children, and men who believe that having sex with virgins or young girls will cure STDs. Often, these men spread HIV and other STDs to their young victims, creating localized disease epidemics.

What Is the Impact of Sex Trafficking?

Trafficking has a harrowing effect on the mental, emotional, and physical well-being of the women and girls ensnared in its web. Beyond the physical abuse, trafficked women suffer extreme emotional stress, including shame, grief, fear, distrust, and suicidal thoughts. Victims often experience post-traumatic stress disorder, and with that, acute anxiety, depression, and insomnia. Many victims turn to drugs and alcohol to numb the pain.

Sex trafficking promotes societal breakdown by removing women and girls from their families and communities. Trafficking fuels organized crime groups that usually participate in many other illegal activities, including drug and weapons trafficking and money laundering. It negatively impacts local and national labor markets, due to the loss of human resources. Sex trafficking burdens public health systems. And trafficking erodes government authority, encourages widespread corruption, and threatens the security of vulnerable populations.

What Is Soroptimist Doing to Stop Human Trafficking?

As an organization of business and professional women working to improve the lives of women and girls and local communities throughout the world, Soroptimist undertakes a number of projects that directly and indirectly help potential trafficking victims. In late 2007, the organization launched a major campaign aimed at raising awareness about the devastating practice of sex trafficking. Soroptimist club members place the cards about sex trafficking in highly visible locations including police stations, women's centers, hospitals, legal aid societies, and so on. In addition, the organization is calling on the public to do its part to end this heinous practice.

Soroptimist undertakes a number of other projects that directly and indirectly help victims and potential victims. These projects provide direct aid to women and girls—giving women economic tools and skills to achieve financial empowerment and independence:

The Live Your Dream Awards program—Soroptimist's major project—provides women who are heads of households with the resources they need to improve their education, skills, and employment prospects. By helping women to receive skill

and resource training, Soroptimist provides trafficking and potential trafficking victims with economic options.

The Soroptimist Club Grants for Women and Girls program provides Soroptimist clubs with cash grants for innovative projects benefiting women and girls. Many clubs undertake projects that directly and indirectly benefit trafficking victims: a Soroptimist club in the Philippines supports a shelter for abused women and girls escaping from sex trafficking; a club in California held a conference in support of the Western Regional Task Force to Stop Human Trafficking and a club in Chicago has held several educational events related to trafficking.

Soroptimist presents Human Trafficking Facts that Making a Difference for Women Award program honors women who work to improve the lives of women and girls. Kathryn Xian is a recent recipient. In 2004, she led a grassroots campaign against a local tour company offering Asian sex tours. She also testified at a Hawaii State House of Representatives hearing on trafficking. The hearings resulted in the passage of Act 82, which makes "promoting travel for prostitution" a Class C felony violation. Act 82 now serves as model legislation for other states. Soroptimist [strives to present] Human Trafficking Facts that make a difference in women's lives worldwide.

Soroptimist's Disaster Relief Fund provides financial assistance to regions affected by natural disasters or acts of war, with special attention paid to services benefiting women and girls. Women and girls affected by disasters are often vulnerable to traffickers.

Critical Thinking

1. Understand the role of deception in many human trafficking cases.
2. How the human trafficking system normally operates.
3. Understand how sex trafficking affects individuals and society.

Internet References

Sociology—Study Sociology Online
  http://edu.learnsoc.org/
Sociology Web Resources
  http://www.mhhe.com/socscience/sociology/resources/index.htm
Sociosite
  http://www.topsite.com/goto/sociosite.net
Socioweb
  http://www.topsite.com/goto/socioweb.com

Article   Prepared by: Kurt Finsterbusch, *University of Maryland, College Park*

Getting Tough on Devastating Corporate Crime

RALPH NADER

Learning Outcomes

After reading this article, you will be able to:

- Understand how white-collar criminals are seldom punished for their crimes.
- Know that America is tough on crime but not white-collar crime.
- Corporate power affects laws and law enforcement and protects white-collar criminals.

Politicians looking to bolster their appeal to voters like to talk about being "tough on crime." They think this creates a winning public image. And why wouldn't it? Anyone who has ever seen an old western knows that the bandits in the black hats are bad and the lawmen in the white hats are good. Consequently, many elected officials, desperate to be perceived as White-hatters, carry the "tough on crime" banner. A result is the United States now has more incarcerated people than any other country in the world, including China and Russia. Imagine—over 2 million Americans are currently serving time in prison.

Yet despite all the tough talk from elected officials, a corporate crime wave has long swept our nation, draining people's hard-earned savings and severely harming the health and safety of millions more. The pinstripe-suit wearing perpetrators of this spree are, far more often then not, getting away scot-free. Ironically, it's many of the same politicians who say they are "tough on crime" that are collecting millions of dollars in campaign money from the biggest crooks in America. A smart politician looking to win a campaign would never knowingly accept cash from street thugs, muggers, and thieves. But corporate thugs, corporate muggers, and corporate thieves? No problem! When it comes to corporate crime, where are the heroes in the white hats?

The corporate crime wave is a result of decades of concentrated effort by big business and its lobbyists to weaken and dismantle the policing agencies responsible for keeping watch over them—a tactic that has been cleverly dubbed "deregulation," a term that effectively sidesteps any connotation of blatant wrongdoing. (See the new book *Freedom to Harm* by Thomas O. McGarity.)

It was the effects of wild "deregulation" that led to the global financial collapse in 2008 and its catastrophic effect on the world economy. In 2011, Charles Ferguson, director of the documentary film *Inside Job*, took the stage to accept his Academy Award and said: "Three years after a horrific financial crisis caused by massive fraud, not a single financial executive has gone to jail, and that's wrong." It's now two years later, and relatively nothing has changed. By comparison, in the savings and loan crisis 33 years ago, hundreds of S&L officials were convicted and sent to jail.

Grant, JPMorgan Chase and its CEO Jamie Dimon are currently in the media spotlight for their questionable dealings, resulting in billions of dollars in easily absorbed losses for the bank, yet none of its executives have been punished or charged with a crime and Dimon remains in his lofty, lucrative position. It's just another chapter in the sordid tale of big banks receiving a slap on the wrist for their excesses. The attorney General of the United States, Eric Holder, has publicly admitted that the enormous size of financial institutions has made them too difficult to prosecute. Even conservative columnist George Will wants the big banks broken up.

Once again, where are the heroes in the white hats? One of the primary issues in presenting the seriousness of the corporate crime wave is the perceived lack of physical danger from the public—after all; corporate criminals do not rob you at knifepoint in a dark alley. But corporate crime does take a physical toll. Roughly 60,000 Americans die every year from workplace-related diseases and injuries, hundreds of thousands more from medical malpractice or hospital-induced infections, tens of thousands more from air pollution and from dangerous pharmaceuticals—much of which is a direct result of corporate wrongdoing and could be prevented.

About 400,000 Americans die each year as a result of smoking-related illness, thanks to the tobacco industry, which for years covered up the harmful effects of its product and hooked youngsters with deliberate marketing. In comparison to the nearly 15,000 yearly homicide deaths in the United States, the corporate death toll is sky high.

One of the most important tools in battling corporate crime and informing the public about its long ranging and harmful effects would be the creation of comprehensive corporate crime database. Such a database, run by the Justice Department, would compile detailed statistics and data on corporate crime, searchable by name of corporation and crime committed, and produce an annual report. Such a database would make information on corporate crime easily available to both law enforcement and the media and would place the issue of patterns and costs of corporate crime on the table for national discourse.

So far, all attempts to create such a public record of corporate crime have been met with little enthusiasm or action from the major political parties and successive Attorneys General, including the current AG Eric Holder. In late 2010, as Chair of the House Judiciary Committee, and again in 2011, Rep. John Conyers (D-Mich.) introduced The Corporate Crime Database Act that aimed to establish such a database. (Alongside it, Conyers also introduced the Dangerous Products Warning Act, which would make it a crime for a corporate official to knowingly place a dangerous product into the stream of commerce.) Neither bill gained any traction at all in Congress.

Further steps need to be taken as well. There should be more funding for the Justice Department's tiny corporate crime division, so that they have the prosecutorial tools and resources to adequately go after violators. Congress needs to take steps so that companies that commit corporate crime are not on the federal dole—taxpayer money should never be used to buy goods and services from corporate criminals. It's time to crack down on corporate tax avoidance—a worker on the minimum wage should not be paying more in sheer federal tax dollars than a large, very profitable corporation like General Electric. Going further, shareholders should have the final say in corporate governance, with the right to approve major business decisions and executive compensation—similar to the referendum recently passed in Switzerland. After all, it's the shareholders—not the executives—who ultimately pay the fines when wrongdoing is discovered.

Most importantly, the obsolete and weak federal corporate crime laws need to be upgraded for the times, toughened and clearly defined. Congress and President Obama have to seek law and order for crime in the suites. For rampant, corporate crime is going to continue unless we start punishing and deterring these violations that devastate so many innocent people.

Critical Thinking

1. Would you say that producing and promoting cigarettes is a crime?
2. What kind of criminals give campaign contributions?
3. Are the evils in the criminal justice system likely to be fixed?

Internet References

Sociology—Study Sociology Online
  http://edu.learnsoc.org/
Sociology Web Resources
  http://www.mhhe.com/socscience/sociology/resources/index.htm
Sociosite
  http://www.topsite.com/goto/sociosite.net
Socioweb
  http://www.topsite.com/goto/socioweb.com
White-collar Crime
  https://www.nytimes.com/column/white-collar-watch

Article　　　　　Prepared by: Kurt Finsterbusch, *University of Maryland, College Park*

Wrongful Convictions

RADLEY BALKO

Learning Outcomes

After reading this article, you will be able to:

- Describe specific cases of wrongful convictions and understand some of the inexcusable actions by authorities that lead to these wrongful convictions.

- Understand the very large gap between proven wrongful convictions and the actual number of wrongful convictions.

- Understand the main reasons for wrongful convictions.

How many innocent Americans are behind bars? When Paul House was finally released from prison in 2008, he was a specter of the man who had been sentenced to death more than 22 years earlier. When I visit his home in Crossville, Tennessee, in March, House's mother Joyce, who has cared for him since his release, points to a photo of House taken the day he was finally allowed to come home. In that photo and others from his last days in prison, House is all of 150 pounds, ashen and drawn, his fragile frame nearly consumed by his wheelchair. In most of the images he looks days away from death, although in one he wears the broad smile of a man finally escaping a long confinement.

When House's aunt called to congratulate him on his first day back, his mother handed him her cell phone so he could chat. He inspected the phone, gave her a frustrated look, and asked her to find him one that worked. That kind of Rip Van Winkle moment is common among people freed after a long stint in prison. Dennis Fritz, one of the two wrongly convicted men profiled in John Grisham's 2006 book *The Innocent Man,* talks about nearly calling the police upon seeing someone use an electronic key card the first time he found himself in a hotel after his release. He thought he'd witnessed a burglar use a credit card to jimmy open a door.

"Paul's first meal when he got home was chili verde," Joyce House says. "It's his favorite. And I had been waiting a long time to make it for him." And apparently quite a few meals after that. House, now 49, has put on 75 pounds since his release. More important, he has been getting proper treatment for his advanced-stage multiple sclerosis, treatment the Tennessee prison system hadn't given him.

The years of inadequate care have taken a toll. House can't walk, and he needs help with such basic tasks as bathing, feeding himself, and maneuvering around in his wheelchair. His once distinctively deep voice (which had allegedly been heard by a witness at the crime scene) is now wispy and high-pitched. He spends his time playing computer games and watching game shows.

In the hour or so that I visit with House, his mental facilities fade in and out. Communicating with him can be like trying to listen to a baseball game broadcast by a distant radio station. He will give a slurred but lucid answer to one question, then answer the next one with silence, or with the answer to a previous question, or just with a random assortment of words. He frequently falls back on the resigned refrain, "Oh, well," delivered with a shrug. The gesture and phrasing are identical every time he uses them. It's what House says to kill the expectation that he will be able to deliver the words others in the room are waiting for. It's his signal to stop waiting for him and move on.

In 1986 House was convicted of murdering Carolyn Muncey in Union County, Tennessee, a rural part of the state that shoulders Appalachia. He was sentenced to death. His case is a textbook study in wrongful conviction. It includes mishandled evidence, prosecutorial misconduct, bad science, cops with tunnel vision, DNA testing, the near-execution of an innocent man, and an appellate court reluctant to reopen old cases even in the face of new evidence that strongly suggests the jury got it wrong.

House also embodies the tribulations and frustrations that the wrongly convicted encounter once they get out. According to the doctors treating him, his current condition is the direct result of the inadequate care he received in prison. If he is ever granted a formal exoneration—a process that can be as much political as it is judicial—he will be eligible for compensation for his years behind bars, but even then the money comes with vexing conditions and limitations.

Since 1989, DNA testing has freed 268 people who were convicted of crimes they did not commit. There are dozens of other cases, like House's, where DNA strongly suggests innocence but does not conclusively prove it. Convicting and imprisoning an innocent person is arguably the worst thing a government can do to one of its citizens, short of mistakenly executing him. (There's increasing evidence that this has happened too.) Just about everyone agrees that these are unfathomable tragedies. What is far less clear, and still hotly debated, is what these cases say about the way we administer justice in America, what we owe the wrongly convicted, and how the officials who send innocent people to prison should be held accountable.

How Many Are Innocent?

According to the Innocence Project, an advocacy group that provides legal aid to the wrongly convicted, the average DNA exoneree served 13 years in prison before he or she was freed. Seventeen had been sentenced to death. Remarkably, 67 percent of the exonerated were convicted after 2000, the year that marked the onset of modern DNA testing. Each new exoneration adds more urgency to the question that has hovered over these cases since the first convict was cleared by DNA in 1989: How many more innocent people are waiting to be freed?

Given the soundness of DNA testing, we can be nearly certain that the 268 cleared so far didn't commit the crimes for which they were convicted. There are hundreds of other cases where no DNA evidence exists to definitively establish guilt or innocence, but a prisoner has been freed due to lack of evidence, recantation of eyewitness testimony, or police or prosecutorial misconduct. Those convictions were overturned because there was insufficient evidence to overcome reasonable doubt; it does not necessarily mean the defendant didn't commit the crime. It's unclear whether and how those cases should be factored into any attempt to estimate the number of innocent people in prison.

In a country where there are 15,000 to 20,000 homicides each year, 268 exonerations over two decades may seem like an acceptable margin of error. But reform advocates point out that DNA testing is conclusive only in a small percentage of criminal cases. Testing is helpful only in solving crimes where exchange of DNA is common and significant, mostly rape and murder. (And most murder exonerations have come about because the murder was preceded by a rape that produced testable DNA.) Even within this subset of cases, DNA evidence is not always preserved, nor is it always dispositive to the identity of the perpetrator.

Death penalty cases add urgency to this debate. In a 2007 study published in the *Journal of Criminal Law and Criminology,* the Seton Hall law professor Michael Risinger looked at cases of exoneration for capital murder-rapes between 1982 and 1989, compared them to the total number of murder-rape cases over that period for which DNA would be a factor, and estimated from that data that 3 percent to 5 percent of the people convicted of capital crimes probably are innocent. If Risinger is right, it's still unclear how to extrapolate figures for the larger prison population. Some criminologists argue that there is more pressure on prosecutors and jurors to convict someone, anyone, in high-profile murder cases. That would suggest a higher wrongful conviction rate in death penalty cases. But defendants also tend to have better representation in capital cases, and media interest can also mean more scrutiny for police and prosecutors. That could lead to fewer wrongful convictions.

In a study published in the *Journal of Criminal Law and Criminology* in 2005, a team led by University of Michigan law professor Samuel Gross looked at 328 exonerations of people who had been convicted of rape, murder, and other felonies between 1989 and 2003. They found that while those who have been condemned to die make up just 1 percent of the prison population, they account for 22 percent of the exonerated. But does that mean capital cases are more likely to bring a wrongful conviction? Or does it mean the attention and scrutiny that death penalty cases get after conviction—particularly as an execution date nears—make it more likely that wrongful convictions in capital cases will be discovered?

Many states have special public defender offices that take over death penalty cases after a defendant has exhausted his appeals. These offices tend to be well-staffed, with enough funding to hire their own investigators and forensic specialists. That sometimes stands in stark contrast to the public defender offices that handled the same cases at trial. Perversely, this means that in some jurisdictions, a defendant wrongly convicted of murder may be better off with a death sentence than with life in prison.

Even if we were to drop below the floor set in the Risinger study and assume that 2 percent of the 2008 prison population was innocent, that would still mean about 46,000 people have been convicted and incarcerated for crimes they didn't commit. But some skeptics say even that figure is way too high.

Joshua Marquis, the district attorney for Clatsop County, Oregon, is an outspoken critic of the Innocence Project and of academics like Risinger and Gross. He is skeptical of the belief that wrongful convictions are common. "If I thought that 3 to 5 percent of people in prison right now were innocent, I'd quit my job," Marquis says. "I'd become a public defender or something. Maybe an activist. Look, nobody but a fool would say that wrongful convictions don't happen. As a prosecutor, my worst nightmare is not losing a case—I've lost cases; I'll lose cases in the future. My worst nightmare is convicting an innocent person, and I tell my staff that. But the question here is whether wrongful convictions are epidemic or episodic. And I just don't think it's possible that the number could be anywhere near 3 to 5 percent."

Marquis and Gross have been butting heads for several years. In a 2006 *New York Times* op-ed piece, Marquis took the 328 exonerations Gross and his colleagues found between 1989 and 2003, rounded it up to 340, then multiplied it by 10—a charitable act, he wrote, to "give the professor the benefit of the doubt." He then divided that number by 15 million, the total number of felony convictions during the same period, and came up with what he said was an error rate of just 0.027 percent. His column was later quoted in a concurring opinion by U.S. Supreme Court Justice Antonin Scalia in the 2006 case *Kansas v. Marsh,* the same opinion where Scalia made the notorious claim that nothing in the U.S. Constitution prevents the government from executing an innocent person.

Gross responded with a 2008 article in the *Annual Review of Law and Social Science,* pointing out that his original number was by no means comprehensive. Those were merely the cases in which a judicial or political process had exonerated someone. The figure suggested only that wrongful convictions happen. "By [Marquis'] logic we could estimate the proportion of baseball players who've used steroids by dividing the number of major league players who've been caught by the total of all baseball players at all levels: major league, minor league, semipro, college and Little League," Gross wrote, "and maybe throw in football and basketball players as well."

Whatever the total number of innocent convicts, there is good reason to believe that the 268 cases in which DNA evidence has proven innocence don't begin to scratch the surface. For one thing, the pace of these exonerations hasn't slowed down: There were 22 in 2009, making it the second busiest name-clearing year to date. Furthermore, exonerations are expensive in both time and resources. Merely discovering a possible case and requesting testing often isn't enough. With some commendable exceptions . . . prosecutors tend to fight requests for post-conviction DNA testing. (The U.S. Supreme Court held in 2009 that there is no constitutional right to such tests.) So for now, the pace of genetic exonerations appears to be limited primarily by the amount of money and staff that legal advocacy groups have to uncover these cases and argue them in court, the amount of evidence available for testing, and the willingness of courts to allow the process to happen, not by a lack of cases in need of further investigation.

It's notable that one of the few places in America where a district attorney has specifically dedicated staff and resources to seeking out bad convictions—Dallas County, Texas—has produced more exonerations than all but a handful of states. That's partly because Dallas County District Attorney Craig Watkins is more interested in reopening old cases than his counterparts elsewhere, and partly because of a historical quirk: Since the early 1980s the county has been sending biological crime scene evidence to a private crime lab for testing, and that lab has kept the evidence well preserved. Few states require such evidence be preserved once a defendant has exhausted his appeals, and in some jurisdictions the evidence is routinely destroyed at that point.

"I don't think there was anything unique about the way Dallas was prosecuting crimes," Watkins told me in 2008. "It's unfortunate that other places didn't preserve evidence too. We're just in a unique position where I can look at a case, test DNA evidence from that period, and say without a doubt that a person is innocent. . . . But that doesn't mean other places don't have the same problems Dallas had."

If the rest of the country has an actual (but undetected) wrongful conviction rate as high as Dallas County's, the number of innocents in prison for felony crimes could be in the tens of thousands.

The Trial and Conviction of Paul House

As with many wrongful convictions, the case against Paul House once seemed watertight. House was an outsider, having only recently moved to Union County when Carolyn Muncey was murdered in 1985, and he was an ex-con, having served five years in a Utah prison for sexual assault. He got into scuffles with locals, although he considered Muncey and her husband, Hubert, friends. When Muncey turned up dead, House was a natural suspect.

House has claimed he was innocent of the Utah charge. His mother, Joyce, says it was a he said/she said case in which her son pleaded guilty on the advice of his attorney. "He could have been paroled earlier if he had shown some remorse," she says. "But he said, 'I pled guilty the one time, because that's what the lawyer told me I should do. I'm not going to say again that I did something I didn't do.' He said he'd rather serve more time than admit to the rape again." Joyce House and Mike Pemberton, Paul House's attorney, are hesitant to go into much detail about the Utah case, and public records aren't available due to the plea bargain. But while what happened in Utah certainly makes House less sympathetic, it has no bearing on whether House is the man who killed Carolyn Muncey.

House also didn't do himself any favors during the Muncey investigation. In initial questioning, he lied to the police about where he was the night of the murder, saying he was with his girlfriend all night. But he later admitted he had gone for a walk at one point and had come back without his shoes and with scratches on his arms. He initially lied to police about the scratches too, saying they were inflicted by his girlfriend's cats. House later said he'd been accosted by some locals while on his walk, scuffled with them, then fled through a field, where he lost his shoes. (House would learn years later that his shoes were found by police before his trial. There was no blood or other biological evidence on them, potentially exculpatory information that was never turned over to House's lawyers.)

"I think it was a situation where you're on parole, you're an outsider, and this woman has just been killed near where you live," says Pemberton, House's attorney. "It wasn't smart of him to lie to the police. But it was understandable."

Carolyn Muncey's husband, who House's attorneys would later suspect was her killer, also lied about where he was when she was killed. He would additionally claim, falsely, that he had never physically abused her. Still, House was clearly the early suspect.

The strongest evidence against House was semen found on Muncey's clothing, which an FBI agent testified at trial "could have" belonged to House. DNA testing didn't exist in 1986, but the agent said House was a secretor, meaning he produced blood type secretions in other body fluids, including semen, and that the type secreted in semen found on Muncey's nightgown was a match to House's type A blood. About 80 percent of people are secretors, and about 36 percent of Americans have type A blood. The agent also said the semen found on Muncey's panties included secretions that didn't match House's blood type, but added, inaccurately, that House's secretion could have "degraded" into a match. Muncey's husband was never tested.

The other strong evidence against House was some blood stains on his jeans that matched Muncey's blood type, but not his own. Those stains on House's jeans did turn out to have been Muncey's blood; the question is how they got there.

House was never charged with rape; there were no physical indications that Muncey had been sexually assaulted. But the semen was used to put him at the crime scene, and the state used the possibility of rape as an aggravating circumstance in arguing that House should receive the death penalty.

House was convicted in February 1986. The morning after his conviction, just hours before the sentencing portion of his trial, House slashed his wrists with a disposable razor. He left behind a suicide note in which he professed his innocence. Jail officials rushed him to a hospital in Knoxville, where doctors saved his life and stitched up his wounds. He was then sent back to the courthouse, where a jury sentenced him to death.

It wasn't until more than a decade later, in 1999, that the case against House began to erode. New witnesses came forward with accusations against Hubert Muncey, Carolyn's husband. Several said he was an alcoholic who frequently beat her. At an ensuing evidentiary hearing, two other women said Hubert had drunkenly confessed to killing his wife several months after the murder. When one went to the police with the information the next day, she said at the hearing, the sheriff brushed her off. Another witness testified that Hubert Muncey had asked her to lie to back up his alibi.

But it was the forensic evidence presented at that 1999 hearing that really unraveled the state's case. When House's attorneys were finally able to get DNA testing for the semen found on Carolyn Muncey's clothes, it showed that the semen was a match to Muncey's husband, not House. The state responded that rape was never part of their case against House (though it is why he was initially a suspect, it was the only conceivable motive, and it was presented as evidence in the sentencing portion of his trial). Besides, prosecutors argued, there was still the blood on House's jeans.

Except there were problems with that too. Cleland Blake, an assistant chief medical examiner for the state of Tennessee, testified that while the blood did belong to Muncey, its chemical composition indicated it was blood that had been taken after she had been autopsied. Worse still, three-quarters of a test tube of the blood taken during Muncey's autopsy went missing between the time of the autopsy and the time House's jeans arrived at the FBI crime lab for testing. The test tubes with Muncey's blood and House's jeans were transported in the same Styrofoam box. The blood on House's jeans, his attorneys argued, must have either been planted or spilled because of sloppy handling of the evidence.

It is extraordinarily difficult to win a new trial in a felony case, even in fight of new evidence, and House's case was no exception. A federal circuit court judge denied his request for post-conviction relief, and the U.S. Court of Appeals for the 6th Circuit affirmed that decision. Somewhat surprisingly, the U.S. Supreme Court agreed to hear House's case, and in 2006 issued a rare, bitterly divided 5-to-3 ruling granting House a new trial.

The Supreme Court has occasionally thrown out death penalty convictions because of procedural errors or constitutional violations, but it's rare for the Court to methodically review the evidence in a capital case. Writing for the majority, Justice Anthony Kennedy did exactly that, finding in the end that "although the issue is close, we conclude that this is the rare case where—had the jury heard all the conflicting testimony— it is more likely than not that no reasonable juror viewing the record as a whole would lack reasonable doubt."

It was a surprising and significant victory for House. But it would be another three years before he would be released from prison.

How Do Wrongful Convictions Happen?

The most significant consequence of the spate of DNA exonerations has been a much-needed reassessment of what we thought we knew about how justice is administered in America. Consider the chief causes of wrongful convictions:

Bad Forensic Evidence

DNA technology was developed by scientists, and it has been thoroughly peer-reviewed by other scientists. Most of the forensic science used in the courtroom, on the other hand, was either invented in police stations and crime labs or has been refined and revised there to fight crime and obtain convictions. Most forensic evidence isn't peer-reviewed, isn't subject to blind testing, and is susceptible to corrupting bias, both intentional and unintentional. The most careful analysts can fall victim to cognitive bias creeping into their work, particularly when their lab falls under the auspices of a law enforcement agency. Even fingerprint analysis isn't as sound as is commonly believed.

A congressionally commissioned 2009 report by the National Academy of Sciences found that many other forensic specialties that are often presented in court with the gloss of science—hair and carpet fiber analysis, blood spatter analysis, shoe print identification, and especially bite mark analysis—lack the standards, peer review, and testing procedures of genuinely scientific research and analysis. Some are not supported by any scientific literature at all. Moreover, the report found, even the forensic specialties with some scientific support are often portrayed in court in ways that play down error rates and cognitive bias.

According to an Innocence Project analysis of the first 225 DNA exonerations, flawed or fraudulent forensic evidence factored into about half of the faulty convictions.

Eyewitness Testimony

Social scientists have known about the inherent weakness of eyewitness testimony for decades. Yet it continues to be the leading cause of wrongful convictions in America; it was a factor in 77 percent of those first 225 cases. Simple steps, such as making sure police who administer lineups have no knowledge of the case (since they can give subtle clues to witnesses, even unintentionally) and that witnesses are told that the actual perpetrator may not be among the photos included in a lineup, can go a long way toward improving accuracy. But such reforms also make it more difficult to win convictions, so many jurisdictions, under pressure from police and prosecutor groups, have been hesitant to embrace them.

False Confessions

Difficult as it may be to comprehend, people do confess to crimes they didn't commit. It happened in about one-quarter of the first 225 DNA exonerations. Confessions are more common among suspects who are minors or are mentally handicapped, but they can happen in other contexts as well, particularly after intense or abusive police interrogations.

In a candid 2008 op-ed piece for the *Los Angeles Times,* D.C. Police Detective Jim Trainum detailed how he unwittingly coaxed a false confession out of a 34-year-old woman he suspected of murder. She even revealed details about the crime that could only have been known to police investigators and the killer. But Trainum later discovered that the woman couldn't possibly have committed the crime. When he reviewed video of his interrogation, he realized that he had inadvertently provided

the woman with those very specific details, which she then repeated back to him when she was ready to confess.

Trainum concluded that all police interrogations should be videotaped, a policy that would not just discourage abusive questioning but also provide an incontrovertible record of how a suspect's confession was obtained. Here too, however, there has been pushback from some police agencies, out of fear that jurors may be turned off even by legitimate forms of questioning.

Jailhouse Informants

If you were to take every jailhouse informant at his word, you'd find that a remarkably high percentage of the people accused of felonies boast about their crimes to the complete strangers they meet in jail and prison cells. Informants are particularly valuable in federal drug cases, where helping a prosecutor obtain more convictions is often the only way to get time cut from a mandatory minimum sentence. That gives them a pretty good incentive to lie.

There is some disagreement over a prosecutor's duty to verify the testimony he solicits from jailhouse informants. In the 2006, Church Point, Louisiana, case of Ann Colomb, for example, Brett Grayson, an assistant U.S. attorney in Louisiana, put on a parade of jailhouse informants whose claims about buying drugs from Colomb and her sons were rather improbable, especially when the sum of their testimony was considered as a whole. According to defense attorneys I spoke with, when one attorney asked him if he actually believed what his informants were telling the jury, Grayson replied that it doesn't matter if he believes his witnesses; it only matters if the jury does. He expressed a similar sentiment in his closing argument.

After indicating that he isn't familiar with the Colomb case and isn't commenting on Grayson specifically, Josh Marquis says that sentiment is wrong. "A prosecutor absolutely has a duty to only put on evidence he believes is truthful," Marquis says. "And that includes the testimony you put on from informants."

In a 2005 study, the Center on Wrongful Convictions in Chicago found that false or misleading informant testimony was responsible for 38 wrongful convictions in death penalty cases.

The Professional Culture of the Criminal Justice System

In addition to the more specific causes of wrongful convictions listed above, there is a problem with the institutional culture among prosecutors, police officers, forensic analysts, and other officials. Misplaced incentives value high conviction rates more than a fair and equal administration of justice.

Prosecutors in particular enjoy absolute immunity from civil liability, even in cases where they manufacture evidence that leads to a wrongful conviction. The only time prosecutors can be sued is when they commit misconduct while acting as investigators—that is, while doing something police normally do. At that point they're subject to qualified immunity, which provides less protection than absolute immunity but still makes it difficult to recover damages.

Marquis says this isn't a problem. "Prosecutors are still subject to criminal liability," he says. "In fact, my predecessor here in Oregon was prosecuted for misconduct in criminal cases. State bars will also hold prosecutors accountable."

But criminal charges are few and far between, and prosecutors can make egregious mistakes that still don't rise to the level of criminal misconduct. Professional sanctions are also rare. A 2010 study by the Northern California Innocence Project found more than 700 examples between 1997 and 2009 in which a court had found misconduct on the part of a prosecutor in the state. Only six of those cases resulted in any disciplinary action by the state bar. A 2010 investigation of federal prosecutorial misconduct by *USA Today* produced similar results: Of 201 cases in which federal judges found that prosecutors had committed misconduct, just one resulted in discipline by a state bar association. Prosecutorial misconduct was a factor in about one-quarter of the first 225 DNA exonerations, but none of the prosecutors in those cases faced any significant discipline from the courts or the bar.

There is also a common misconception that appeals courts serve as a check on criminal justice abuse. It is actually rare for an appeals court to review the evidence in a criminal case. Appeals courts make sure trials abide by the state and federal constitutions and by state or federal rules of criminal procedure, but they almost never second-guess the conclusions of juries.

In a 2008 article published in the *Columbia Law Review*, the University of Virginia law professor Brandon L. Garrett looked at the procedural history of the first 200 cases of DNA exoneration. Of those, just 18 convictions were reversed by appellate courts. Another 67 defendants had their appeals denied with no written ruling at all. In 63 cases, the appellate court opinion described the defendant as guilty, and in 12 cases it referred to the "overwhelming" evidence of guilt. Keep in mind these were all cases in which DNA testing later proved actual innocence. In the remaining cases, the appeals courts either found the defendant's appeal without merit or found that the errors in the case were "harmless"—that is, there were problems with the case, but those problems were unlikely to have affected the jury's verdict due to the other overwhelming evidence of guilt.

"We've seen a lot of exoneration cases where, for example, the defendant raised a claim of ineffective assistance of counsel," says Peter Neufeld, co-founder of the Innocence Project of New York. "And in those cases, the appellate courts often found that the defense lawyer provided substandard representation. But they would then say that the poor lawyering didn't prejudice the case because the evidence of guilt was so overwhelming. Well, these people were later proven innocent! If you have a test that is frequently producing erroneous results,

there's either something wrong with the test, or there's something wrong with the way it's being implemented."

Life on the Outside

Paul House was diagnosed with multiple sclerosis in 2000, a year after the evidentiary hearing that would eventually lead to his release. But while House was convicted of Carolyn Muncey's murder less than a year after it happened, it took a decade after his conviction was called into serious question for House to get back home to Crossville. During those 10 years, the state's case continued to fall apart. So did House's body.

After the U.S. Supreme Court overturned House's conviction in 2006, Paul Phillips, the district attorney for Tennessee's 8th Judicial District and the man who prosecuted House in 1986, pushed ahead with plans to retry him. In December 2007, after a series of delays, Harry S. Mattice Jr., a U.S. district court judge in Knoxville, finally ordered the state to try House within 180 days or set him free. Those 180 days then came and went without House being freed, thanks to an extension granted by the 6th Circuit.

In another hearing held in May 2008, Phillips argued that House—who by that point couldn't walk or move his wheelchair without assistance—presented a flight risk. Later, Tennessee Associate Deputy Attorney General Jennifer Smith attempted to show that House presented a danger to the public because he was still capable of feeding himself with a fork, which apparently meant he was also capable of stabbing someone with one. House's bail was set at $500,000, later reduced to $100,000. In July 2008, an anonymous donor paid the bail, allowing House to finally leave prison.

That same month, Phillips told the Associated Press that he would send two additional pieces of biological evidence off for DNA testing: a hair found at the crime scene, and blood found under Carolyn Muncey's fingernails. House's defense team had asked to conduct its own testing of any untested biological evidence for years, but had been told that either there was no such evidence or, if there was, the state didn't know where it was. Philips told the A.P. that if the new tests didn't implicate House, he would drop the murder charge and allow House to go home. In February 2009 the results came back. They didn't implicate House, and in fact pointed to a third, unidentified man. In May of that year, Phillips finally dropped the charge. But he still wouldn't clear House's name, telling Knoxville's local TV station WATE, "There is very adequate proof that Mr. House was involved in this crime. We just don't know the degree of culpability beyond a reasonable doubt." (Phillips' office did not respond to my requests for comment.)

By the time House was diagnosed with M.S. in 2000, his symptoms were already severe, although it took his mother, and not a prison doctor, to notice something was wrong. "I was visiting him, and I brought along some microwave popcorn," Joyce House recalls. "He asked me to heat it up, and I said, 'No, you heat it up.' When he got up, he had to prop himself up and drag along the wall to get to the microwave. He couldn't even stand up straight." According to Joyce House, her son's doctors today say that the Tennessee prison system's failure to diagnose House's M.S. earlier—then treat it properly after it was diagnosed—may have taken years off his life. (M.S. is also exacerbated by stress.) The disease has also significantly diminished the quality of the life House has left.

Under Tennessee's compensation law for the wrongly convicted, if House is formally exonerated—and that's still a big if—he will be eligible for $50,000 for each year he was in prison, up to $1 million. But there's a catch. The compensation is given in annual $50,000 installments over 20 years. If House dies before then, the payments stop.

Most of the 27 states with compensation laws similarly pay the money off in installments. Last October, A.P. ran a story about Victor Burnette, a 57-year-old Virginia man who served eight years for a 1979 rape before he was exonerated by DNA testing in 2006. Burnette actually turned down the $226,500 the state offered in compensation in 2010 because he was offended by the stipulation that it be paid out over 25 years. Even after the DNA test confirmed his innocence, it took another three years for Burnette to officially be pardoned, which finally made him eligible for the money. The installment plans make it unlikely that many exonerees—especially long-timers, who are arguably the most deserving—will ever see full compensation for their years in prison.

Only about half the people exonerated by DNA testing so far have been compensated at all. Most compensation laws require official findings of actual innocence, which eliminates just about any case that doesn't involve DNA. Some states also exclude anyone who played some role in their own conviction, which would disqualify a defendant who falsely confessed, even if the confession was coerced or beaten out of them.

Paul House has yet another predicament ahead of him. Even if he does win an official exoneration, and even if he somehow lives long enough to receive all of his compensation, he'll have to lose his health insurance to accept it. House's medical care is currently covered by TennCare, Tennessee's Medicare program. If he accepts compensation for his conviction, he will be ineligible. His $50,000 per year in compensation for nearly a quarter century on death row will then be offset by a steep increase in what he'll have to pay for his medical care.

These odd, sometimes absurd predicaments aren't intentionally cruel. They just work out that way. Paul House's attorney Mike Pemberton points out that the prosecutors in these cases aren't necessarily evil, either. "Paul Phillips is an honorable man, and an outstanding trial attorney," Pemberton says. "But on this case he was wrong." Pemberton, who was once a prosecutor himself, says the job can lend itself to tunnel vision, especially once a prosecutor has won a conviction. It can be hard to let go. We have a system with misplaced incentives and very little accountability for state actors who make mistakes. That's a system ripe for bad outcomes.

When I ask Paul House why he thinks it has taken so long to clear his name, he starts to answer, then stammers, looks away, and retreats again to Oh well, his cue to move on because he has no answer.

That may be an understandable response from a guy with advanced M.S. who just spent two decades on death row. But for too long our national response to the increasing evidence that our justice system is flawed has been the same sort of resignation. DNA has only begun to show us where some of those flaws lie. It will take a strong public will to see that policymakers address them.

Critical Thinking

1. How are false confessions obtained?
2. Identify the pressures on prosecutors and the police to get convictions rather than the truth.
3. Why have these problems not been fixed already?

Internet References

Crime Times
    www.crime-times.org
 Sociosite
    www.topsite.com/goto/sociosite.net
Socioweb
    www.topsite.com/goto/socioweb.com
Sociology—Study Sociology Online
    http://edu.learnsoc.org
Sociology Web Resources
    www.mhhe.com/socscience/sociology/resources/index.htm

RADLEY BALKO (rbalko@reason.com) is a senior editor at Reason.

From *Reason Magazine*, July 2011, pp. 20–33. Copyright ©2011 by Reason Foundation, 3415 S. Sepulveda Blvd., Suite 400, Los Angeles, CA 90034. www.reason.com

Article　　　　Prepared by: Kurt Finsterbusch, *University of Maryland, College Park*

Cruel and Unusual

The True Costs of Our Prison System

ROBERT DEFINA AND LANCE HANNON

Learning Outcomes

After reading this article, you will be able to:

- Judge the Catholic bishops' pastoral statement criticizing the United States for an extremely high incarceration rate.

- Discern the political factors that made the incarceration rate so high.

- Evaluate the value of the principles of Catholic social teaching for addressing the problem.

A decade ago, in November 2000, the U.S. Conference of Catholic Bishops issued a pastoral statement titled *Responsibility, Rehabilitation, and Restoration: A Catholic Perspective on Crime and Criminal Justice.* Unapologetically critiquing a criminal-justice system focused primarily on punishment, the bishops called the American response to crime "a moral test for our nation and a challenge for our church."

Their statement chastised the United States for its "astounding" rate of incarceration, "six to twelve times higher than the rate of other Western countries," and went on to suggest changes that would make the system more humane and socially beneficial. "Putting more people in prison and, sadly, more people to death has not given Americans the security we seek," the bishops declared. "It is time for a new national dialogue on crime and corrections, justice and mercy, responsibility and treatment."

The backdrop to the bishops' pastoral was a dramatic rise in the incarceration rate. In the twenty years preceding their report, that rate rose steeply and steadily, more than tripling to 683 prisoners per 100,000 of the population—which meant 2 million people behind bars and a total bill to federal, state, and local governments of about $64 billion. Closer inspection of

the ranks of the imprisoned raised even more concerns. Prisons were increasingly admitting nonviolent criminals, especially those guilty of drug-related infractions. The prison population was increasingly made up of minorities: by 2000 about 60 percent of those imprisoned were either black or Hispanic. And Harvard sociologist Bruce Western noted that more than half of all African-American men who lack high-school diplomas were imprisoned by age thirty-four.

Scholars who studied the issue concluded that the prison buildup was not simply a response to rising crime: violent-crime rates in 2000, in fact, roughly equaled those of 1980, while property-crime rates were actually lower. The trend toward mass incarceration was rooted rather in a series of policy changes aimed at winning political favor by "getting tough on crime." These included mandatory sentencing, "three strikes and you're out" laws, and harsher rules for probation and parole. And so the same amount of crime yielded substantially more incarceration. Nor did the strategy of mass imprisonment contribute much toward keeping crime down. Even the most generous estimates suggested a relatively minor role in crime prevention; many studies showed that rates of violent crime were unaffected. Indeed, as we shall see, some evidence suggests that certain crimes might actually have increased as a result.

For the bishops a decade ago, the existing approaches to criminal justice were severely at odds with the church's scriptural, theological, and sacramental heritage. "A Catholic approach begins with the recognition that the dignity of the human person applies to both victim and offender," they wrote. "As bishops, we believe that the current trend of more prisons and more executions, with too little education and drug treatment, does not truly reflect Christian values and will not really leave our communities safer." The overriding emphasis on punishment, the harsh and dehumanizing conditions of prisons, the lack of help to prisoners attempting reentry into society: these and other failures of the system led the bishops to call for a new direction, one that emphasized restorative justice and reintegration while insisting on the well-being and fair treatment of both prisoners and their victims.

The system envisioned by the bishops offered prisoners reintegration into the community, including the opportunity for reconciliation with those harmed, even as it supported victim restitution. It rejected crudely punitive strategies, such as mandatory sentencing, that neglect the complex sources of crime and the particularities of an individual criminal's makeup. The bishops also called for better treatment within the prison walls, including expanded counseling, health care, education, and training to help emerging prisoners integrate successfully into society. They recommended that prisons be easily accessible to family, friends, and religious communities able to support the development and growth of prisoners. Finally, they reminded us of the community's responsibility to work toward reducing crime and helping those at risk of engaging in criminal activities.

These proposals added up to a progressive analysis of crime, punishment, and prevention, and it would be hard to argue against the bishops' prescriptions or the moral basis that underpinned them. A decade later, however, both the pastoral's criticisms and its suggestions seem all too limited. The criticism focused mainly on shortcomings in the condition and treatment of individual prisoners and victims. While these remain important concerns, recent research has highlighted serious detrimental effects that the justice system has on the broader communities from which prisoners come and to which they ultimately return. These community-level effects have added substantially to the individual-level problems the nation's prison policy has created. Recognizing these consequences will help lead to a broader and deeper critique than the one articulated in the pastoral—a critique, moreover, that points the way to a criminal-justice system more in line with the principles of Catholic social thought.

The bishops analyzed the effects of prisons using what Rutgers sociologist Todd Clear has called an "atomistic view." An atomistic view focuses on the individual prisoner—why he commits a crime, how he is treated within the criminal-justice system, and what happens to him once he is released. While such a view addresses the important issue of personal dignity, it mostly ignores the larger social fact that the individual prisoner is but one of over 2 million, and that those imprisoned come from geographically concentrated neighborhoods. A broader view discloses other problems. Imprisoning a large fraction of individuals from a particular community, it

turns out, can cause that community substantial harm—especially when that community was disadvantaged to begin with.

Recent studies have illuminated the many ways this harm can occur. To begin with, mass imprisonment removes spending power from a community, as most of those incarcerated are working at the time of their arrest and contributing significantly to their families' income. Furthermore, as sociologists Bruce Western and Devah Pager have demonstrated, incarceration significantly limits the earning capacity of ex-inmates through the erosion of their marketable skills, the loss of social networks, prison socialization into destructive behaviors, and, perhaps most important, the scarlet letter of a prison record. Ex-prisoners are barred from a large array of occupations in this country, ranging from emergency medicine to cosmetology; in thirty-seven states, employers are allowed to consider arrests *without conviction* when making hiring decisions. And loss of income is not limited to the incarcerated parent, but also afflicts the remaining parent, since childcare needs can significantly decrease the time available to find and keep a job. Research has consistently shown, moreover, that children with an incarcerated parent frequently suffer high levels of anxiety, shame, and depression; and attending to these needs forms a further obstacle to the remaining parent's participation in the labor force.

Such considerations reveal just how complex and multidimensional the impact of mass incarceration can be. At the community level, it disrupts social networks that bolster the chance for quality employment. The loss of an adult family member, especially one with years of experience in the legitimate labor market, reduces the "friend-of-a-friend" connections that aid employment. As sociologists Robert Sampson and Stephen Raudenbush point out, whole communities with high incarceration rates can become stigmatized, decreasing the likelihood that members will be hired, even those with no prison record. Other studies have suggested that mass incarceration disrupts a neighborhood's informal mechanisms of social support, as the constant churn of people in and out weakens bonds and diminishes collective identity. This in turn strains individual resources—as when parents who cannot rely on neighbors to look after children must spend money or forgo wages to do it themselves. The removal of adult breadwinners, meanwhile, eliminates role models important for young people. And the blatantly unequal and racialized use of incarceration can delegitimize governmental authority among youth and fuel an oppositional subculture in which mainstream activities such as work are devalued. These detrimental effects of concentrated incarceration on a community's norms and sense of collective efficacy may ultimately prevent residents from escaping what might otherwise be merely episodic poverty.

Another direct link to poverty is the increased prevalence of single-parent families. Not only does mass imprisonment shrink the pool of young men available for marriage, but the prison experience itself can make men less suitable for marriage. And single parenthood is a significant contributor to poverty and related social ills. As for released inmates, they face restricted access to the social-safety net. Several states, such as Texas and Missouri, deny them food stamps, public housing, and TANF, federal assistance for needy families. And the overhaul of the federal welfare system in 1996—the Personal Responsibility and Work Opportunity Reconciliation Act—included a lifetime ban on cash assistance and food stamps for anyone convicted of a drug offense. These rules not only impede the re-integration of ex-prisoners, but put the community as a whole at risk, especially children. Mass incarceration has also been associated with growing and serious community-health problems. Economists Steven Raphael and Michael Stoll, for example, have linked the prevalence of AIDS in poor communities to the transmission of the disease through sexual violence in prison. This in turn renders communities less able to deal with other crucial concerns.

Beyond all this lies a political dimension. Mass incarceration can exacerbate a community's long-term economic deprivation by politically disenfranchising those with the greatest stake in policies that might help lift people out of poverty. In forty-eight states, prisoners cannot vote. Many states disallow voting while on probation or parole, and a few states, like Florida, permanently disenfranchise those convicted of a felony. According to a study by the Sentencing Project and Human Rights Watch, as of 1998 3.9 million Americans—about one in fifty adults—had either temporarily or permanently lost their right to vote. A clear racial imbalance characterizes this loss; the study revealed that about one in seven black men had either temporarily or permanently lost the right to vote, and in several states, nearly one in four black men of voting age were *permanently* disenfranchised. To make matters worse, census procedures dictate that prisoners be counted not in their home communities, but in the jurisdiction where they are imprisoned. Since the areas where prisoners come from tend to be urban, diverse, and Democratic, while prisons are frequently located in rural, white, and Republican districts, high-incarceration communities suffer a sort of electoral double-whammy, with political power drained away from them and transferred to politically antithetical communities that receive greater representation because of their sizable, nonvoting inmate population. The end result is less legislative support for—and greater opposition to—a variety of progressive initiatives that could aid disadvantaged communities, including, for example, a boost in the statewide minimum wage.

Finally, as if all this weren't bad enough, it is clear that the harms done to a community's economy by mass incarceration are likely to be multiplied. In a vicious feedback loop, decreased spending caused by lost income due to incarceration results in fewer businesses being able to remain solvent. When businesses go under, additional residents lose their jobs and fall below the poverty line, depressing spending further. Crucial nonprofit institutions, such as community churches, can be negatively affected as well by the economic contraction. Because such institutions frequently provide goods and services that alleviate poverty, crime, and other social ills, their weakening can intensify the collateral consequences of mass incarceration.

Some observers have suggested that increased incarceration can benefit disadvantaged communities by removing socially disruptive young men. This idea has intuitive appeal, yet it loses force in the context of mass incarceration. While the removal of just a few "bad apples" might well have positive implications, in some communities more than a third of the population of young males is in prison; this is less like removing a few apples than like uprooting the whole tree. In such situations the negative effects will likely outweigh whatever positive effects might exist. Our own research indicates that mass incarceration in recent decades has plunged millions of Americans into poverty. Other studies suggest potentially criminogenic consequences of mass imprisonment, arising from the release into the community of large numbers of prisoners exposed to an isolating and sometimes violent prison environment. According to criminologists Lynn Vieraitis, Tomislav Kovandzic, and Thomas Marvell, imprisonment trends in the past few decades actually *increase* the incidence of various types of crime. And our own research suggests that any such crime-inducing effects of imprisonment can persist for many years.

In light of these manifest problems, we believe that Catholic Social Teaching (CST) should broaden its engagement with the criminal-justice system to include what we term "community justice." By community justice we mean the consideration of the community as an organic whole whose treatment should be subject to the demands of justice. Understanding communities this way is common for sociological analysis, but not perhaps for the kind of analysis typically used in CST. Yet with mass incarceration, it is simply not the case that the total damage equals the sum of individual harms. Rather, entire communities have been damaged, suffering perilous losses to their collective social, cultural, and physical capital.

This perspective opens up new questions and suggests new applications of CST to the criminal-justice system. Diminution of the *common good,* for instance, is much graver when entire communities are destroyed. The urgency of a *preferential option for the poor* is heightened when policies push millions more people into poverty. The *social nature of the person* and *solidarity* are violated more seriously when entire social networks and sets of norms are damaged. Barriers to *participation* are much greater when whole communities are stigmatized because of high levels of incarceration. Such perspectives both require and inform a broader, deeper critique of our penal system.

A community-justice lens can also help highlight the racial imbalance in mass imprisonment. Bruce Western and Loïc Wacquant have argued that policy initiatives, like the "War on Drugs," that have led to mass incarceration and the disproportionate incarceration of minorities constitute a reaction against the civil-rights movement. They represent, in other words, a new means of social control, in the tradition of such outlawed forms as blatant job discrimination, Jim Crow laws, and housing segregation, which effectively isolates members of a devalued social group and limits their access to valued resources. To the extent that this is accurate, criminal-justice policy directly violates several principles of CST, including the dignity of the person, the social nature of the person, participation, solidarity, and the universal destination of goods. Seen this way, mass incarceration isn't merely an ineffective system needing improvement. Rather, it is a sinful, repugnant, and disordered structure worthy of wholesale replacement.

W hat practical steps might be taken to bring this disordered system into line with Catholic principles? First and foremost, we need to incarcerate fewer people. One recent proposal by economists John Schmitt, Kris Warner, and Sarika Gupta argues that half of all nonviolent criminals could be removed from prison and put on probation or parole with no appreciable effect on public safety, at a savings of close to $17 billion—considerable resources for the common good, an especially attractive benefit for struggling state governments. Meaningful reductions in incarceration can also be achieved via judicious changes to parole and probation rules. Minor violations (such as lying about previous prison time on job applications) that can now land parolees back in jail, could be handled less punitively, keeping ex-inmates in the community. All in all, sociologist Todd Clear has suggested, the prison population could be cut in half by eliminating imprisonment for technical parole violations, trimming the length of parole supervision, and reducing prison sentences to those used twenty years ago.

Policies should be enacted to strengthen the efficacy of communities and their ability to exercise social control and offer social support. Foremost here are access to decent legitimate employment opportunities as well as to the childcare and transportation that facilitate working. Along these lines, the bipartisan Second Chance Act of 2008 suggests a heightened recognition of the problems of prisoner reentry and a new political willingness to do something about them. Signed by President George W. Bush and supported by President Barack Obama, the law authorizes federal grants for employment and housing assistance, drug and alcohol abuse treatment, and other services to reentering offenders. In addition, all restrictions on work should be scrutinized, and those not demonstrably necessary to community safety should be removed. States can also reconsider allowing arrests without convictions to be factored into employment decisions.

The voting rights of ex-prisoners and those on probation and parole should be guaranteed, not only to assure individual rights (as the bishops stressed), but to give reentering prisoners a tangible stake in their communities. They should also be given full access to the safety net, including the basic programs (such as food stamps and TANF) that are essential for low-income communities, especially children. Public programs should treat poor ex-prisoners as well as they treat nonpoor ex-prisoners. Today, while public housing is denied to ex-inmates, the mortgage-interest deduction, essentially a housing program for middle- and upper-class families, is not. This surely runs counter to the call for a preferential option for the poor.

The principles of Catholic Social Teaching have provided a useful framework for reflection and guidance in addressing countless social problems over the past century. The arena of criminal justice is no exception. For a decade, the bishops' pastoral has served as a powerful reminder that justice involves not only punishment but also the hard work of supporting the common good. As the bishops have pointed out, supporting the common good means helping the individual rejoin the community. And as we have stressed here, there must be a strong and vibrant community available to reintegrate with.

Sadly, in the ten years since the bishops' pastoral was published, the disturbing trends it addressed have only continued, with the latest data showing the 2008 incarceration rate reaching 753 per 100,000 of the U.S. population, at a total direct cost of about $75 billion. The trends in racial composition and the decreased severity of crimes meriting incarceration have continued as well. Meanwhile, the evidence for incarceration's crime-reducing effect has weakened considerably. These failures demand our renewed attention and effort.

We have tried here to broaden the view presented in the bishops' pastoral to recognize that incarceration on the scale seen in this country affects not only the individual but also the community at large, significantly amplifying poverty, crime, and other social pathologies. Analyses that fail to incorporate these community-level effects will continue to underestimate the harms caused by the current American approach to criminal justice. The principles of Catholic Social Teaching, on the other hand, can markedly improve what is clearly a broken system. Reconstructing the criminal-justice system in ways consistent with those principles will put us on a path toward respecting both the authentic development of the individual and the common good, and help us reverse an all-out assault on our most vulnerable communities.

Critical Thinking

1. Why has the criminal justice system been allowed to operate in such a way as to ruin millions of lives?
2. Fairly simple changes could cut the prison population in half. Analyze why they are not utilized.
3. Discuss both positive and negative impacts of treating prisoners as humans as the bishops recommend.

Internet References

Crime Times
www.crime-times.org
Sociosite
www.topsite.com/goto/sociosite.net
Socioweb
www.topsite.com/goto/socioweb.com
Sociology—Study Sociology Online
http://edu.learnsoc.org
Sociology Web Resources
www.mhhe.com/socscience/sociology/resources/index.htm

ROBERT DEFINA is professor of sociology at Villanova University and co-editor of the Journal of Catholic Social Thought. LANCE HANNON is associate professor of sociology at Villanova University. The authors' work was supported in part by a Veritas grant from Villanova University

Article
Prepared by: Kurt Finsterbusch, *University of Maryland, College Park*

Estimates of Cost of Crime

History, Methodologies, and Implications

JACEK CZABAŃSKI

Learning Outcomes

After reading this article, you will be able to:

- Discuss the complex issue of the total costs of crime.
- Understand the relative costs to victims, enforcement costs, and costs for trying to prevent crime.
- Compare the costs of street crime and white-collar crime.

There are some crimes that have been recognized everywhere and in any time. These crimes include traditional ones like murder, rape, assault, robbery, larceny, that is to say: inflicting harm to others.

Focusing my attention on traditional crimes only, I will avoid discussion about the proper limits of criminal law. It is worth noting, however, that costs of crime estimates are connected with the economic theory of law. According to the economic theory of law, the ultimate goal of law is to maximize social welfare, and criminal law is preferred to other means (like contract or tort law) under certain circumstances (see, for example, Posner 1985). Following Benthamic concept, the economic theory of law postulates that only harmful behavior should be made criminal. Harm is considered as a decrease in the individual's well-being.

Therefore, there is a class of behavior, namely victimless crimes, that poses particular problems for the economic analysis. Examples of this class include drug trade, prostitution, gambling, et cetera. The most basic economic assumption is that by exchange people can enhance their utility, but in the above mentioned examples that very process of exchange is forbidden by law. The fact that the exchange, potentially beneficial for both parties, is forbidden by society for whatever reason, suggests that there are some external effects that make society so attentive to this transaction. The conflict between private and public interest is clear in such circumstances and any relevant analysis of cost of these crimes has to weight these factors as well.

There is no one way that the costs of crime may be categorized. Generally, the costs of crime can be divided into three broad categories:

1. Costs of crime itself (pain and suffering, stolen/damaged property, health consequences for victims);
2. Costs of society's response to crime (costs of criminal justice system: police, prosecutors, judges, prisons, and other correctional facilities); and
3. Costs in anticipation of crime (costs of avoidance behavior and precautionary expenditures).

Total Cost of Crime

As was previously described, from the historic perspective the direct costs of crime estimates were the first methodology employed. Costs of law enforcement were easy to calculate so costs of police, prosecution, judges, and prisons and other institutions were included in all estimates. . . . But it was also very clear that these costs formed only one side of the equation. The very reason why society spends money on crime prevention is to lower crime and the burden associated with it. The economic consequences of crime were then estimated: Smith used an approximation of criminal gains as an equivalent of public losses due to crime; National Commission on Law Observance and Enforcement used available data on some crime prevention costs and used labor wages to calculate the value of time lost by criminals behind bars and law officers; President's Commission on Law Enforcement and Administration of Justice provided only loss of earnings due to homicide, but excluded all costs of pain and suffering. Moreover, the Report included costs of illegal activities measured as a total income for illegal goods and services—this shifted an accent from street crimes into organized and white-collars crimes.

What was certainly lacking in all these calculations was the comprehensive list of all (or at least the main) consequences of crime, particularly those that affect victims. Although some methods of valuation (e.g. property prices, happiness loss) also have tried to capture the total cost of crime, they have been unsuccessful in this attempt.

A total cost of crime calculation should include as many consequences of crime as possible, even if they were assessed with different methodologies. The point of reference is a hypothetical state of no crime. Therefore, these kinds of assessments do not answer the question of how much people would like to pay for crime reduction, but rather a question of what is the total burden of crime, compared to the ideal world without it.

While historically the first studies of crime were of this kind, they lacked too many important costs. Modern estimates of the total cost have tried to capture the whole picture.

Anderson included in his analyses a wide spectrum of costs:

Crime-induced production covers personal protection devices (guns, locks, safes, etc.), operation of correctional facilities, and drug trafficking. In the absence of crime, time, money and other resources would be used for other purposes.

Opportunity costs—the value of time of criminals which could have been devoted to legal activities instead. Similarly, the value of victims' time lost due to having been victimized.

Value of risk to life and health—this is the value people place on the risk that they will suffer injury or die due to crime.

Transfers—some crimes involve transfers of property, for example theft. However, according to standard economic reasoning, transfers are not considered to be a net loss to society.

Main Anderson's numerical estimates are reported below (Table 1).

The total burden of crime (net of transfers) was estimated at 1.1 trillion. But as high as it may appear, these estimates did not include all costs, for lack of data. Nevertheless, this collection of costs, limited by data availability, provokes one to asking many questions. For example, the biggest position in crime-induced production is drug trafficking. This amount was taken from the report of the President's Commission on Organized Crime and is simply an amount of money spent on the yearly consumption of drugs. But as was argued before, this can be hardly viewed as a cost of crime. The very fact that people willingly buy drugs stands as an argument for classifying it rather as social benefit than cost. While it is true that there are negative externalities connected with drug consumption (higher mortality rate, lower productivity, and so on), the same is true with many other human activities like alcohol and tobacco consumption, junk food consumption or extreme sports practicing. Moreover, it seems to be

Table 1   Total cost of crime in the US. 1999

Category	Cost (billion dollars)
Crime-induced production, including	397
Drug trafficking	161
Police protection	47
Corrections	36
Prenatal exposure to cocaine and heroin	28
Federal agencies	23
Judicial and legal services	19
Guards	18
Drug control	11
DUI costs to driver	10
Opportunity costs, including	130
Time spent securing assets	90
Criminals' lost work days	39
The value of risk to life and health	574
Value of lost life	440
Value of injuries	134
Transfers	603
Occupational fraud	204
Unpaid taxes	123
Health insurance fraud	109
Total burden	1,705
Net of transfers	1,102
Per capita (in dollars)	4,118

a pure transfer from a buyer to a seller, so it should instead be classified under that heading. In Anderson's study there are more inconsistencies like this: in the cost of driving under the influence, penalties and fees were included (another transfer), costs of exposure to cocaine and heroine were exaggerated and for no reason the costs of exposure to alcohol or tobacco were not included.

One of the most surprising components was the value of time lost on securing assets. This is mainly the value of time spent on locking, and unlocking doors. Anderson estimated that each adult spends 2 min a day locking and unlocking doors, and more than 2 min looking for keys.

Anderson also included such minor items, as anti-theft devices in libraries, but did not include such costs as pain and suffering of victims (only lost working days were included). He also did not include any estimates of fear of crime, which has an impact

Table 2   Total cost of crime in different countries

Country	Year	Total cost of crime (local currency)	Cost of crime as % of GDP	Source
US	1900	USD 600 m	2.9%	Smith (1901)
US	1930	USD 1 bn	1.1%	Report on the Cost of Crime and Criminal Justice in the United States (1931)
US	1965	USD 107 bn	14.9%	President's Commission on Law Enforcement and Administration of Justice (1967)
US	1993	USD 451 bn	6.8%	Miller et al. (1996)
England and Wales	1999	GBP 59 bn	6.5%	Brand and Price (2000)
US	1999	USD 1,102 bn	11.9%	Anderson (1999)
Australia	2002	AUD 31.8 bn	4.2%	Mayhew (2003)
England and Wales	2003	GBP 36.2 bn	3.5%	Dubourg et al. (2005) [only for households and individuals]
New Zealand	2003	NZD 9.1 bn	6.5%	Roper and Thompson (2006)

Note: GDP in current prices taken from the database of the International Monetary Fund: http://www.imf.org/external/pubs/ft/weo/2006/02/data/index.aspx, last accessed 30 November 2006.

not only on an individual's well-being, but also on his behavior. His estimates then are likely to understate the true impact of crime, even if his selection was highly arbitrary. The report also did not allow for differentiating between different categories of crimes, and he only estimated the total cost for all crimes. . . .

Nevertheless, calculations of the total cost of crime show that the burden of crime is enormous. Victimization studies confirm that a substantial part of society is victimized every year. The society's fear of crime is then understandable. . . .

Conclusions

. . . I have argued that the development of costs of crime estimates makes them a valuable, and indeed irreplaceable, tool in criminal law and crime policy. While the concept of monetizing pain and suffering, which are necessarily connected with crime, for many people seems unfeasible, and maybe even unreasonable, such calculations have many advantages over more intuitive approaches that have been in use so far.

Averting crimes has always been the aim of crime policy. The lack of reliable estimates as to the real benefits of averting crimes led to the biased perspective of the criminal justice system. Costs of the system were easily seen, as they were borne mainly by state budgets. At the same time, the benefits eluded quantification.

Lives lost, pain and suffering, costs of healthcare, property damaged and stolen—all these constitute direct costs of crime. Yet, this list is far from being comprehensive—behavioral

responses, changing patterns of life, counter-crime measures, and reduced quality of living all comprise another part of the costs of crime. And the emergence of the criminal justice system with its own costs of police, courts, and prisons make the final part of the total costs. The enormous burden that crime imposes on societies for long was as obvious as vaguely quantified. . . .

Critical Thinking

1. Assess how accurate the author's measures are in costing crime and its impacts.
2. If the costs of crime exceed a trillion dollars, should it be handled differently than it currently is handled?
3. What new perspectives does this article give you?

Internet References

Sociosite
www.topsite.com/goto/sociosite.net

Socioweb
www.topsite.com/goto/socioweb.com

Sociology—Study Sociology Online
http://edu.learnsoc.org

Sociology Web Resources
www.mhhe.com/socscience/sociology/resources/index.htm

Unit 3

UNIT

Prepared by: Kurt Finsterbusch, *University of Maryland, College Park*

Groups and Roles in Transition

Primary groups are small, intimate, spontaneous, and personal. In contrast, secondary groups are large, formal, and impersonal. Primary groups include the family, couples, gangs, cliques, teams, and small tribes or rural villages. Primary groups are the main sources that the individual draws upon in developing values and an identity. Secondary groups include most of the organizations and bureaucracies in a modern society, and carry out most of its instrumental functions. Often, primary groups are formed within secondary groups, such as a factory, school, or business. Urbanization, geographic mobility, centralization, bureaucratization, and other aspects of modernization have had an impact on the nature of groups, the quality of the relationships between people, and individual's feelings of belonging.

The family, in particular, has undergone radical transformation. The greatly increased participation of women in the paid-labor force and their increased careerism has led to severe conflicts for women between their work and family roles.

Article   Prepared by: Kurt Finsterbusch, *University of Maryland, College Park*

The Gay Guide to Wedded Bliss

Compared with straight marriages, research finds, same-sex unions tend to be happier, with less conflict, greater emotional intimacy, and more-equal sharing of chores and child-rearing. What gay and lesbian spouses can teach straight ones about living happily ever after.

LIZA MUNDY

Learning Outcomes

After reading this article, you will be able to:

- Assess more carefully the quality of gay/lesbian marriages or partnerships.

- Know the qualities of relationships that on average are critical to successful marriages.

- Better understand the changing role of homosexual relationships in American society.

It is more than a little ironic that gay marriage has emerged as the era's defining civil-right struggle even as marriage itself seems more endangered every day. Americans are waiting longer to marry: according to the U.S. Census Bureau, the median age of first marriage is 28 for men and 26 for women, up from 23 and 20, respectively, in 1950. Rates of cohabitation have risen swiftly and sharply, and more people than ever are living single. Most Americans still marry at some point, but many of those marriages end in divorce. (Although the U.S. divorce rate has declined from its all-time high in the late '70s and early '80s, it has remained higher than those of most European countries.) All told, this has created an unstable system of what the UCLA sociologist Suzanne Bianchi calls "partnering and repartnering," a relentless emotional and domestic churn that sometimes results in people forgoing the institution altogether.

Though people may be waiting to marry, they are not necessarily waiting to have children. The National Center for Family and Marriage Research has produced a startling analysis of data from the Census Bureau and the Centers for Disease Control and Prevention showing that women's median age when they have their first child is lower than their median age at first marriage. In other words, having children before you marry has become normal. College graduates enjoy relatively stable unions, but for every other group, marriage is collapsing. Among "middle American" women (those with a high-school degree or some college), an astonishing 58 percent of first-time mothers are unmarried. The old Groucho Marx joke—"I don't care to belong to any club that will have me as a member"—applies a little differently in this context: you might well ask why gays and lesbians want to join an institution that keeps dithering about whether to admit them even as the repo men are coming for the furniture and the fire marshal is about to close down the clubhouse.

Against this backdrop, gay-marriage opponents have argued that allowing same-sex couples to wed will pretty much finish matrimony off. This point was advanced in briefs and oral arguments before the Supreme Court in March, in two major same-sex-marriage cases. One of these is a constitutional challenge to a key section of the Defense of Marriage Act, the 1996 law that defines marriage as a union between a man and a woman, and bars the federal government from recognizing same-sex marriages. The other involves California's Proposition 8, a same-sex-marriage ban passed by voters in 2008 but overturned by a federal judge in 2010. Appearing before the high court in March, Charles J. Cooper, the lawyer defending the California ban, predicted that same-sex marriage would undermine traditional marriage by eroding "marital norms."

The belief that gay marriage will harm marriage has roots in both religious beliefs about matrimony and secular conservative concerns about broader shifts in American life. One prominent line of thinking holds that men and women have distinct roles to play in family life; that children need both a mother and a father, preferably biologically related to them; and that a central purpose of marriage is abetting heterosexual procreation. During the Supreme Court arguments over Proposition 8, Justice Elena Kagan asked Cooper whether the essence of his argument against gay marriage was that opposite-sex couples can procreate while same-sex ones cannot. "That's the essential thrust of our position, yes," replied Cooper. He also warned that "redefining marriage as a genderless institution could well lead over time to harms to that institution."

Threaded through this thinking is a related conviction that mothers and fathers should treat their union as "permanent and exclusive," as the Princeton professor Robert P. George and his co-authors write in the new book *What Is Marriage? Man and Woman: A Defense.* Marriage, seen this way, is a rigid institution that exists primarily for the rearing of children and that powerfully constrains the behavior of adults (one is tempted to call this the "long slog 'til death" view of marriage), rather than an emotional union entered into for pleasure and companionship between adults. These critics of gay marriage are, quite validly, worried that too many American children are being raised in unstable homes, either by struggling single parents or by a transient succession of live-in adults. They fear that the spread of gay marriage could help finally sever the increasingly tenuous link between children and marriage, confirming that it's okay for dads, or moms, to be deleted from family life as hedonic fulfillment dictates.

In mounting their defense, advocates of same-sex marriage have argued that gays and lesbians who wish to marry are committed to family well-being; that concern for children's welfare is a chief reason many do want to marry; that gay people are being discriminated against, as a class, in being denied rights readily available to any heterosexual. And to the charge that same-sex marriage will change marriage, they tend to argue that it will not—that married gays and lesbians will blend seamlessly with the millions of married straight Americans. "The notion that this group can somehow fundamentally change the institution of marriage—I find it difficult to wrap my head around," says Gary Gates, a demographer with the Williams Institute, a research center affiliated with the UCLA School of Law.

But what if the critics are correct, just not in the way they suppose? What if same-sex marriage does change marriage, but primarily for the better? For one thing, there is reason to think that, rather than making marriage more fragile, the boom of publicity around same-sex weddings could awaken among heterosexuals a new interest in the institution, at least for a time. But the larger change might be this: by providing a new model of how two people can live together equitably, same-sex marriage could help haul matrimony more fully into the 21st century. Although marriage is in many ways fairer and

more pleasurable for both men and women than it once was, it hasn't entirely thrown off old notions and habits. As a result, many men and women enter into it burdened with assumptions and stereotypes that create stress and resentment. Others, confronted with these increasingly anachronistic expectations—expectations at odds with the economic and practical realities of their own lives—don't enter into it at all.

Same-sex spouses, who cannot divide their labor based on preexisting gender norms, must approach marriage differently than their heterosexual peers. From sex to fighting, from child-rearing to chores, they must hammer out every last detail of domestic life without falling back on assumptions about who will do what. In this regard, they provide an example that can be enlightening to all couples. Critics warn of an institution rendered "genderless." But if a genderless marriage is a marriage in which the wife is not automatically expected to be responsible for school forms and child care and dinner preparation and birthday parties and midnight feedings and holiday shopping, I think it's fair to say that many heterosexual women would cry "Bring it on!"

Beyond that, gay marriage can function as a controlled experiment, helping us see which aspects of marital difficulty are truly rooted in gender and which are not. A growing body of social science has begun to compare straight and same-sex couples in an attempt to get at the question of what is female, what is male. Some of the findings are surprising. For instance: we know that heterosexual wives are more likely than husbands to initiate divorce. Social scientists have struggled to explain the discrepancy, variously attributing it to the sexual revolution; to women's financial independence; to men's failure to keep modern wives happy. Intriguingly, in Norway and Sweden, where registered partnerships for same-sex couples have been in place for about two decades (full-fledged marriage was introduced several years ago), research has found that lesbians are twice as likely as gay men to split up. If women become dissatisfied even when married to other women, maybe the problem with marriage isn't men. Maybe women are too particular. Maybe even women don't know what women want. These are the kinds of things that we will be able to tease out.

In the past few years, as support for same-sex marriage has gained momentum, advocates have been able to shift their strategy away from fighting bans on it (on the books in 38 states as of this writing) and toward orchestrating popular votes in its favor. In 2012, voters in Maine, Maryland, and Washington state passed measures legalizing same-sex marriage, joining the District of Columbia and the six states that had already legalized gay marriage via legislatures or courts. Similar measures are moving forward in four other states. In the coming weeks, the high court is expected to issue its rulings on gay marriage. After oral arguments in the two cases concluded, many Court observers predicted that the part of DOMA in question might well be struck down as a federal intrusion on states' ability to decide family law, thereby forcing the federal government to recognize the marriages of same-sex couples. As for Prop 8, any number of outcomes seem possible. The Court could decide that the case should not have been heard in the first place, given that the ban isn't being defended by California state officials but instead by the original supporters of the initiative. Such dismissal on "standing" could have the effect of legalizing same-sex marriage in California. Alternatively, the Court could deliver a narrow ruling (whether upholding or overturning the ban) that does not apply to every state. Among other feasible, if less likely, outcomes: the Court could use Prop 8 to declare all such bans unconstitutional, legalizing gay marriage everywhere.

Whatever happens with the high court, it seems likely that gay marriage will continue its spread through the land. So what happens, then, to the institution of marriage? The impact is likely to be felt near and far, both fleetingly and more permanently, in ways confounding to partisans on both sides.

Rules for a More Perfect Union

Not all is broken within modern marriage, of course. On the contrary: the institution is far more flexible and forgiving than it used to be. In the wake of women's large-scale entry into the workplace, men are less likely than they once were to be saddled with being a family's sole breadwinner, and can carve out a life that includes the close companionship of their children. Meanwhile, women are less likely to be saddled with the sole responsibility for child care and housework, and can envision a life beyond the stove top and laundry basket.

And yet for many couples, as Bianchi, the UCLA sociologist, has pointed out, the modern ideal of egalitarianism has proved "quite difficult to realize." Though men are carrying more of a domestic workload than in the past, women still bear the brunt of the second shift. Among couples with children, when both spouses work full-time, women do 32 hours a week of housework, child care, shopping, and other family-related services, compared with the 21 hours men put in. Men do more paid work—45 hours, compared with 39 for women—but still have more free time: 31 hours, compared with 25 for women. Betsey Stevenson and Justin Wolfers, economists and professors of public policy at the University of Michigan, have shown that happiness rates among women have dropped even as women have acquired more life options. One possible cause is the lingering inequity in male-female marriage: women's at-home workload can become so burdensome that wives opt out of the paid workforce—or sit at the office making mental lists of the chores they do versus the chores their husbands do, and bang their heads on their desks in despair.

Not that everything is easy for fathers in dual-earner couples, who now feel afflicted by work-life conflict in even greater numbers than their wives (60 percent of men in such couples say they experience this conflict, versus 47 percent of women, according to a 2008 study by the Families and Work Institute). And men face a set of unfair expectations all their own: the Pew Research Center found in 2010 that 67 percent of Americans still believe it's "very important" that a man be ready to support a family before getting married, while only 33 percent believe the same about women.

This burden, exacerbated by the economic realities facing many men today, has undoubtedly contributed to marriage's recent decline. As our economy has transitioned away from manufacturing and industry, men with a high-school education can no longer expect the steady, well-paying union jobs that formerly enabled many to support their families. Outdated assumptions that men should bring something to the table, and that this something should be money, don't help. Surveying their prospects, many working-class mothers reject marriage altogether, perhaps reasoning that they can support a child, but don't want a dependent husband.

It's not that people don't want to marry. Most never-married Americans say they still aspire to marriage, but many of them see it as something grand and out of reach. Getting married is no longer something you do when you are young and foolish and starting out; prosperity is not something spouses build together. Rather, marriage has become a "marker of prestige," as the sociologist Andrew Cherlin puts it—a capstone of a successful life, rather than its cornerstone. But while many couples have concluded that they are not ready for marriage, they have things backwards. It's not that they aren't ready for marriage; it's that marriage isn't ready for the realities of 21st-century life. Particularly for less affluent, less educated Americans, changing economic and gender realities have dismantled the old institution, without constructing any sort of replacement.

As we attempt to come up with a more functional model, research on same-sex unions can provide what Gary Gates of the Williams Institute calls an "important counterfactual." Although gays and lesbians cannot solve all that ails marriage, they seem to be working certain things out in ways straight couples might do well to emulate, chief among them a back-to-the-drawing-board approach to divvying up marital duties. A growing body of scholarship on household division of labor shows that in many ways, same-sex couples do it better.

This scholarship got its start in the late 1960s, with a brilliant insight by the sociologist Pepper Schwartz, then a doctoral candidate at Yale. Against a backdrop of cultural upheaval—including changes at the university, which had just begun to admit female undergraduates—gender was, Schwartz says, "all we thought about." Like many of her peers, she was keen to figure out what women were and what men were: which traits were biological and which social, and where there might be potential for transformational change. "It occurred to me," she says, that "a naturally occurring experiment" could shed light on these issues. Actually, two experiments: the rise of unmarried heterosexual cohabitation, and the growing visibility of gay and lesbian couples. If she surveyed people in three kinds of relationships—married; straight and cohabiting; and gay and cohabiting—and all showed similarity on some measures, maybe this would say something about both men and women. If the findings didn't line up, maybe this would say something about marriage.

After taking a teaching position at the University of Washington (where she remains a faculty member), Schwartz teamed up with a gay colleague, the late Philip Blumstein, to conduct just such a survey, zeroing in on the greater San Francisco, New York City, and Seattle metropolitan areas. It was a huge effort. Unmarried cohabiting couples were not yet easy to find, and gays and lesbians were so leery of being outed that when Schwartz asked a woman who belonged to a lesbian bridge group whether she could interview the other players about their relationships, the woman said, "We don't even talk about it ourselves." Schwartz and Blumstein collected responses to 12,000 questionnaires and conducted hundreds of interviews; at one point, they had 20 graduate students helping tabulate data. The project took about a decade, and resulted in a groundbreaking piece of sociology, the book *American Couples: Money, Work, Sex.*

What Schwartz and Blumstein found is that gay and lesbian couples were fairer in their dealings with one another than straight couples, both in intent and in practice. The lesbians in the study were almost painfully egalitarian—in some cases putting money in jars and splitting everything down to the penny in a way, Schwartz says, that "would have driven me crazy." Many unmarried heterosexual cohabitators were also careful about divvying things up, but lesbian couples seemed to take the practice to extremes: "it was almost like 'my kitty, your litter.'" Gay men, like lesbians, were more likely than straight couples to share cooking and chores. Many had been in heterosexual marriages, and when asked whether they had helped their wives with the housework in those prior unions, they usually said they had not. "You can imagine," Schwartz says, "how irritating I found this."

There were still some inequities: in all couples, the person with the higher income had more authority and decision-making power. This was least true for lesbians; truer for heterosexuals; and most true for gay men. Somehow, putting two men together seemed to intensify the sense that "money talks," as Schwartz and Blumstein put it. They could not hope to determine whether this tendency was innate or social—were men naturally inclined to equate resources with power, or had our culture ingrained that idea in them?—but one way or another,

the finding suggested that money was a way men competed with other men, and not just a way for husbands to compete with their wives. Among lesbians, the contested terrain lay elsewhere: for instance, interacting more with the children could be, Schwartz says, a "power move."

Lesbians also tended to discuss things endlessly, achieving a degree of closeness unmatched by the other types of couples. Schwartz wondered whether this might account for another finding: over time, sex in lesbian relationships dwindled—a state of affairs she has described as "lesbian bed death." (The coinage ended up on Schwartz's Wikipedia page, to her exasperation: "There are other things that I wish I were famous around.") She posits that lesbians may have had so much intimacy already that they didn't need sex to get it; by contrast, heterosexual women, whose spouses were less likely to be chatty, found that "sex is a highway to intimacy." As for men, she eventually concluded that whether they were straight or gay, they approached sex as they might a sandwich: good, bad, or mediocre, they were likely to grab it.

RULE 1: Negotiate in advance who will empty the trash and who will clean the bathroom.

Other studies have since confirmed Schwartz and Blumstein's findings that same-sex couples are more egalitarian. In 2000, when Vermont became the first state to legalize same-sex civil unions, the psychologist Esther Rothblum saw an opportunity to explore how duties get sorted among a broad swath of the same-sex population. Rothblum, now at San Diego State University, is herself a lesbian and had long been interested in the relationships and mental health of lesbians. She also wanted to see how legal recognition affected couples.

As people from around the country flocked to Vermont to apply for civil-union licenses, Rothblum and two colleagues got their names and addresses from public records and asked them to complete a questionnaire. Then, they asked each of the civil-union couples to suggest friends in same-sex couples who were not in civil unions, and to identify a heterosexual sibling who was married, and wrote those people asking them to participate. This approach helped control for factors like background and upbringing among the subjects. The researchers asked people to rate, on a scale of one to nine, which partner was more likely to do the dishes, repair things around the house, buy groceries. They asked who was more likely to deal with the landlord, punish the children, call the plumber, drive the kids to appointments, give spontaneous hugs, pay compliments. They also asked who was more likely to appreciate the other person's point of view during an argument.

They found that, even in the new millennium, married heterosexual couples were very likely to divide duties along old-fashioned gender lines. Straight women were more likely than lesbians to report that their partner paid the mortgage or the rent and the utility bills, and bought groceries, household appliances, even the women's clothing. These wives were also more likely to say they did the bulk of the cooking, vacuuming, dishes, and laundry. Compared with their husbands, they were far, far more likely to clean the bathroom. They were also more likely than their husbands to perform "relationship maintenance" such as showing affection and initiating serious conversations. When Rothblum and her colleagues held the heterosexual husbands up against the gay men, they found the same pattern. The straight guys were more likely to take care of the lawn, empty the trash, and make household repairs than their partners. They were the ones to fix drinks for company and to drive when the couple went out. They cooked breakfast reasonably often, but not dinner. On all these measures and more, the same-sex couples were far more likely to divide responsibilities evenly. This is not to say that the same-sex couples split each duty half-and-half. One partner might do the same chore regularly, but because there was no default assignment based on gender, such patterns evolved organically, based on preferences and talents.

Rothblum's observations are borne out by the couples I interviewed for this piece. "I'm a better cook, so I take on most of that responsibility," said Seth Thayer, who lives in a small coastal town in Maine. His husband, Greg Tinder, "is a better handyman." Others spoke of the perils of lopsided relationships. Chris Kast, a Maine newlywed, told me that he and his husband, Byron Bartlett, had both been married to women. In Bartlett's first marriage, it was tacitly assumed that he would take out the garbage. Now the two men divide tasks by inclination. "I'm more of a Felix Ungar—I notice when something's dirty—but we both clean," Kast said. "With Chris and I," Bartlett added, "we have to get *everything* done." Isabelle Dikland, a Washington, D.C., business consultant who is married to Amy Clement, a teacher, told me about a dinner party she recently attended with a group of mostly straight parents. Dikland and Clement, who had just had a second daughter, were extolling the virtues of having two children. The straight mother they were talking with seemed dubious, "if we had a second kid, guess who would do all the work," she told them. "I'd have to give up my career; I'm already doing everything." The woman glanced surreptitiously at her husband, at which point Dikland "dropped the subject really quickly."

RULE 2: When it comes to parenting, a 50–50 split isn't necessarily best.

Charlotte J. Patterson, a psychologist at the University of Virginia, has arresting visual evidence of the same egalitarianism at work in parenting: compared with husband-and-wife pairs, she has found, same-sex parents tend to be more cooperative and mutually hands-on. Patterson and a colleague, Rachel Farr, have conducted a study of more than 100 same-sex and

heterosexual adoptive parents in 11 states and the District of Columbia; it is among the first such studies to include gay fathers. As reported in an article in a forthcoming issue of the journal *Child Development,* the researchers visited families in their homes, scattered some toys on a blanket, invited the subjects to play with them any way they chose, and videotaped the interactions. "What you see is what they did with that blank slate," Patterson says. "One thing that I found riveting: the same-sex couples are far more likely to be in there together, and the opposite-sex couples show the conventional pattern—the mom more involved, the dad playing with Tinkertoys by himself." When the opposite-sex couples did parent simultaneously, they were more likely to undermine each other by talking at cross-purposes or suggesting different toys. The lesbian mothers tended to be egalitarian and warm in their dealings with one another, and showed greater pleasure in parenting than the other groups did. Same-sex dads were also more egalitarian in their division of labor than straight couples, though not as warm or interactive as lesbian moms. (Patterson says she and her colleagues may need to refine their analysis to take into account male ways of expressing warmth.)

By and large, all of the families studied, gay and straight alike, were happy, high functioning, and financially secure. Each type of partner—gay, straight; man, woman—reported satisfaction with his or her family's parenting arrangement, though the heterosexual wife was less content than the others, invariably saying that she wanted more help from her husband. "Of all the parents we've studied, she's the least satisfied with the division of labor," says Patterson, who is in a same-sex partnership and says she knows from experience that deciding who will do what isn't always easy.

Even as they are more egalitarian in their parenting styles, same-sex parents resemble their heterosexual counterparts in one somewhat old-fashioned way: a surprising number establish a division of labor whereby one spouse becomes the primary earner and the other stays home. Lee Badgett, an economist at the University of Massachusetts at Amherst, told me that, "in terms of economics," same-sex couples with children resemble heterosexual couples with children much more than they resemble childless same-sex couples. You might say that gay parents are simultaneously departing from traditional family structures and leading the way back toward them.

In his seminal book *A Treatise on the Family,* published in 1981, the Nobel Prize-winning economist Gary Becker argued that "specialization," whereby one parent stays home and the other does the earning, is the most efficient way of running a household, because the at-home spouse enables the at-work spouse to earn more. Feminists, who had been fighting for domestic parity, not specialization, deplored this theory, rightly fearing that it could be harnessed to keep women at home. Now the example of gay and lesbian parents might give us all permission to relax a little: maybe sometimes it really is easier when one parent works and the other is the supplementary or nonearning partner, either because this is the natural order of things or because the American workplace is so greedy and unforgiving that something or somebody has to give. As Martha Ertman, a University of Maryland law professor, put it to me, many families just function better when the same person is consistently "in charge of making vaccinations happen, making sure the model of the World War II monument gets done, getting the Christmas tree home or the challah bought by 6 o'clock on Friday." The good news is that the decision about which parent plays this role need not have anything to do with gender.

More surprising still, guess who is most likely to specialize. Gay dads. Using the most recent Census Bureau data, Gary Gates found that 32 percent of married heterosexual couples with children have only one parent in the labor force, compared with 33 percent of gay-male couples with children. (Lesbians also specialize, but not at such high rates, perhaps because they are so devoted to equality, or perhaps because their earnings are lower—women's median wage is 81 percent that of men—and not working is an unaffordable luxury.) While the percentage point dividing gay men from straight couples is not statistically significant, it's intriguing that gay dads are as likely as straight women to be stay-at-home parents.

Gay men's decisions about breadwinning can nonetheless be fraught, as many associate employment with power. A study published in the *Journal of GLBT Family Studies* in 2005 by Stephanie Jill Schacher and two colleagues found that when gay men do specialize, they don't have an easy time deciding who will do what: some stay-at-home dads perceived that their choice carried with it a loss in prestige and stature. As a result, gay men tended to fight not over who got to stay home, but over who didn't have to. "it's probably the biggest problem in our relationship," said one man interviewed for that study. Perhaps what Betty Friedan called "the problem that has no name" is inherent in child-rearing, and will always be with us.

RULE 3: Don't want a divorce? Don't marry a woman.

Three years after they first gathered information from the couples who received licenses in Vermont, Esther Rothblum and her colleagues checked back to evaluate the condition of their relationships. Overall, the researchers found that the quality of gay and lesbian relationships was higher on many measures than that of the straight control group (the married heterosexual siblings), with more compatibility and intimacy, and less conflict.

Which is not to say same-sex couples don't have conflict. When they fight, however, they fight fairer. They can even fight funny, as researchers from the University of Washington and the University of California at Berkeley showed in an article published in 2003, based on a study of couples who were

navigating potentially tense interactions. Recruiting married straight couples as well as gays and lesbians in committed relationships, the researchers orchestrated a scenario in which one partner had to bring up an area of conflict to discuss with the other. In same-sex couples, the partner with the bone to pick was rated "less belligerent and less domineering" than the straight-couple counterpart, while the person on the receiving end was less aggressive and showed less fear or tension. The same-sex "initiator" also displayed less sadness and "whining," and more affection, joy, and humor. In trying to make sense of the disparity, the researchers noted that same-sex couples valued equality more, and posited that the greater negativity of straight couples "may have to do with the standard status hierarchy between men and women." Which perhaps boils down to something like this: straight women see themselves as being less powerful than men, and this breeds hostility.

When it comes to conflict, a crucial variable separates many gay and lesbian couples from their straight counterparts: children. As Rothblum points out, for married heterosexual parents, happiness tends to be U-shaped: high at the beginning of marriage, then dipping to a low, then high again. What happens in that low middle is child-rearing. Although the proportion of gay and lesbian couples with children is increasing, same-sex couples are still less likely than straight couples to be parents. Not all research comparing same-sex and married straight couples has done an adequate job of controlling for this important difference. One that did, a 2008 study in the *Journal of Family Psychology,* looked at couples during their first 10 years of cohabitation. It found that childless lesbians had a higher "relationship quality" than their child-free gay-male and heterosexual counterparts. And yet a 2010 study in the same journal found that gay-male, lesbian, and straight couples alike experienced a "modest decline in relationship quality" in the first year of adopting a child. As same-sex couples become parents in greater numbers, they could well endure some of the same strife as their straight peers. It remains to be seen whether the different parenting styles identified by Charlotte Patterson might blunt some of the ennui of child-rearing.

As for divorce, the data are still coming in. A 2006 study of Sweden and Norway found higher dissolution rates among same-sex couples in registered partnerships than among married straight people. Yet in the United States, a study by the Williams Institute has found that gay unions have lower dissolution rates than straight ones. It is simply too soon to tell with any certainty whether gay marriages will be more or less durable in the long run than straight ones. What the studies to date do (for the most part) suggest is this: despite—or maybe because of—their perfectionist approach to egalitarianism, lesbian couples seem to be more likely to break up than gay ones. Pepper Schwartz noted this in the early 1980s, as did the 2006 study of same-sex couples in Sweden and Norway, in which researchers speculated that women may have a "stronger general sensitivity to the quality of relationships." Meaning maybe women are just picky, and when you have two women, you have double the pickiness. So perhaps the real threat to marriage is: women.

The Contagion Effect

Whatever this string of studies may teach us about marriage and gender dynamics, the next logical question becomes this: Might such marriages do more than merely inform our understanding of straight marriage—might their attributes trickle over to straight marriage in some fashion?

In the course of my reporting this year in states that had newly legalized same-sex marriage, people in the know—wedding planners, officiants, fiancés and fiancées—told me time and again that nuptial fever had broken out around them, among gay and straight couples alike. Same-sex weddings seemed to be bestowing a new frisson on the idea of getting hitched, or maybe restoring an old one. At the Gay and Lesbian Wedding Expo in downtown Baltimore, just a few weeks after same-sex marriage became legal in Maryland, Drew Vanlandingham, who describes himself as a "wedding planner designer," was delighted at how business had picked up. Here it was, January, and many of his favorite venues were booked into late summer—much to the consternation, he said, of his straight brides. "They're like, 'I better get a move on!'" It was his view that in Maryland, both teams were now engaged in an amiable but spirited race to the altar.

Ministers told me of wedding booms in their congregations. In her years as the pastor of the Unitarian church in Rockville, Maryland, Lynn Strauss said she had grown accustomed to a thin wedding roster: some years she might perform one or two services; other years, none. But this year, "my calendar is full of weddings," she said. "Two in March, one in April, one in May, one in September, one in October—oh, and one in July." Three were same-sex weddings, but the rest were heterosexual. When I attended the church's first lesbian wedding, in early March, I spoke with Steve Greene and Ellen Rohan, who had recently been married by Strauss. It was Steve's third marriage, Ellen's second. Before he met Ellen, Steve had sworn he would never marry again. Ellen said the arrival of same-sex marriage had influenced their feelings. "Marriage," she said simply, "is on everyone's mind."

Robert M. Hardies, who is a pastor at the Unitarian All Souls Church in Washington, D.C., and who is engaged to be married to his longtime partner and co-parent, Chris Nealon, told me that he has seen "a re-enchantment of marriage" among those who attend same-sex ceremonies: "Straight folks come to [same-sex] weddings, and I watch it on their face—there's a feeling that this is really special. Suddenly marriage is sexy again." We could chalk these anecdotes up to the human desire to witness love that overcomes obstacles—the same desire behind all romantic comedies, whether Shakespeare's or Hollywood's. But could something a bit less romantic also be at work?

There is some reason to suppose that attitudes about marriage could, in fact, be catching. The phenomenon known as "social contagion" lies at the heart of an increasingly prominent line of research on how our behavior and emotions affect the people we know. One famous example dates from 2008, when James H. Fowler and Nicholas A. Christakis published a study showing that happiness "spreads" through social networks. They arrived at this conclusion via an ingenious crunching of data from a long-running medical study involving thousands of interconnected residents—and their children, and later their grandchildren—in Framingham, Massachusetts. "Emotional states can be transferred directly from one individual to another," they found, across three degrees of separation. Other studies have shown that obesity, smoking habits, and school performance may also be catching.

Most relevant, in a working paper that is under submission to a sociology journal, the Brown University political scientist Rose McDermott, along with her co-authors, Fowler and Christakis, has identified a contagion effect for divorce. Divorce, she found, can spread among friends. She told me that she also suspects that tending to the marriages of friends can help preserve your own. McDermott says she readily sees how marriage could itself be contagious. Intriguingly, some of the Scandinavian countries where same-sex unions have been legal for a decade or more have seen a rise, not a fall, in marriage rates. In response to conservative arguments that same-sex marriage had driven a stake through the heart of marriage in northern Europe, the Yale University law professor William N. Eskridge Jr. and Darren Spedale in 2006 published an analysis showing that in the decade since same-sex partnerships became legal, heterosexual marriage rates had increased 10.7 percent in Denmark, 12.7 percent in Norway, and 28.8 percent in Sweden. Divorce rates had dropped in all three countries. Although there was no way to prove cause and effect, the authors allowed, you could safely say that marriage had not been harmed.

So let's suppose for a moment that marital behavior is catching. How, exactly, might it spread? I found one possible vector of contagion inside the Washington National Cathedral, a neo-Gothic landmark that towers watchfully over the Washington, D.C., skyline. The seat of the bishop of an Episcopal diocese that includes D.C. and parts of Maryland, the cathedral is a symbol of American religious life, and strives to provide a spiritual home for the nation, frequently hosting interfaith events and programs. Presiding over it is the Very Reverend Gary Hall, an Episcopal priest and the cathedral's dean. Earlier this year, Hall announced that the cathedral would conduct same-sex weddings, a declaration that attracted more attention than he expected. Only people closely involved with the church and graduates of the private schools on its grounds can marry there. Even so, it is an influential venue, and Hall used the occasion to argue that same-sex couples offer an image of "radical" equality that straight couples can profitably emulate. He believes, moreover, that their example can be communicated through intermediaries like him: ministers and counselors gleaning insights from same-sex couples, and transmitting them, as it were, to straight ones. Hall says that counseling same-sex couples in preparation for their ceremonies has already altered the way he counsels men and women.

"I have a list of like 12 issues that people need to talk about that cause conflict," said Hall, who is lanky, with short gray hair and horn-rims, and who looks like he could be a dean of pretty much anything: American literature, political philosophy, East Asian studies. As we talked in his office one morning this spring, sunlight poured through a bank of arched windows onto an Oriental rug. Over the years, he has amassed a collection of cheesy 1970s paperbacks with names like *Open Marriage* and *Total Woman*, which he calls "books that got people into trouble." The dean grew up in Hollywood, and in the 1990s was a priest at a church in Pasadena where he did many same-sex blessings (a blessing being a ceremony that stops short of legal marriage). He is as comfortable talking about Camille Paglia and the LGBT critique of marriage as he is about Holy Week. He is also capable of saying things like "The problem with genital sex is that it involves us emotionally in a way that we're not in control of."

When Hall sees couples for premarital preparation, he gives them a list of hypothetical conflicts to take home, hash out, and report back on. Everybody fights, he tells them. The people who thrive in marriage are the ones who can handle disagreement and make their needs known. So he presents them with the prime sticking points: affection and lovemaking; how to deal with in-laws; where holidays will be spent; outside friendships. He talks to them about parenting roles, and chores, and money—who will earn it and who will make decisions about it.

Like Esther Rothblum, he has found that heterosexual couples persist in approaching these topics with stereotypical assumptions. "You start throwing out questions for men and women: 'Who's going to take care of the money?' And the guy says, 'That's me.' And you ask: 'Who's responsible for birth control?' And the guy says, 'That's her department.'" By contrast, he reports, same-sex couples "have thought really hard about how they're going to share the property, the responsibilities, the obligations in a mutual way. They've had to devote much more thought to that than straight couples, because the straight couples pretty much still fall back on old modes."

Now when Hall counsels heterosexuals, "I'm really pushing back on their patriarchal assumptions: that the woman's got to give up her career for the guy; that the guy is going to take care of the money." Every now and then, he says, he has

a breakthrough, and a straight groom realizes that, say, contraception is his concern too. Hall says the same thing is happening in the offices of any number of pastors, rabbis, and therapists. "You're not going to be able to talk to heterosexual couples where there's a power imbalance and talk to a homosexual couple where there is a power mutuality," and not have the conversations impact one another. As a result, he believes there will be changes to marriage, changes that some people will find scary. "When [conservatives] say that gay marriage threatens my marriage, I used to say, 'That's ridiculous.' Now I say, 'Yeah, it does. It's asking you a crucial question about your marriage that you may not want to answer: If I'm a man, am I actually sharing the duties and responsibilities of married life equally with my wife?' Same-sex marriage gives us another image of what marriage can be."

Hall argues that same-sex marriage stands to change even the wedding service itself. For a good 1,000 years, he notes, the Christian Church stayed out of matrimony, which was primarily a way for society to regulate things like inheritance. But ever since the Church did get involved, the wedding ceremony has tended to reflect the gender mores of the time. For example, the Book of Common Prayer for years stated that a wife must love, honor, and obey her husband, treating him as her master and lord. That language is long gone, but vestiges persist: the tradition of the father giving away the bride dates from an era when marriage was a property transfer and the woman was the property. In response to the push for same-sex marriage, Hall says, the General Convention, the governing council of the entire Episcopal Church, has devised a liturgy for same-sex ceremonies (in most dioceses, these are blessings) that honors but alters this tradition so that both spouses are presented by sponsors.

"The new service does not ground marriage in a doctrine of creation and procreation," Hall says. "It grounds marriage in a kind of free coming-together of two people to live out their lives." A study group has convened to look at the Church's teachings on marriage, and in the next couple of years, Hall expects, the General Convention will adopt a new service for all Episcopal weddings. He is hopeful that the current same-sex service will serve as its basis.

The legalization of same-sex marriage is likely to affect even members of churches that have not performed such ceremonies. Delman Coates, the pastor of Mt. Ennon Baptist, a predominantly African American mega-church in southern Maryland, was active in his state's fight for marriage equality, presenting it to his parishioners as a civil-rights issue. The topic has also led to some productive, if difficult, conversations about "what the Scriptures are condemning and what they're confirming." In particular, he has challenged his flock over what he calls the "typical clobber passages": certain verses in Leviticus, Romans, and elsewhere that many people interpret as condemnations of homosexuality. These discussions are part of a long-standing effort to challenge people's thinking about other passages having to do with divorce and premarital sex—issues many parishioners have struggled with at home. Coates preaches that what the Bible is condemning is not modern divorce, but a practice, common in biblical times, whereby men cast out their wives for no good reason. Similarly, he tells them that the "fornication" invoked is something extreme—rape, incest, prostitution. He does not condone illicit behavior or familial dissolution, but he wants the members of his congregation to feel better about their own lives. In exchanges like these, he is making gay marriage part of a much larger conversation about the way we live and love now.

Gay marriage's ripples are also starting to be felt beyond churches, in schools and neighborhoods and playgroups. Which raises another question: Will gay and lesbian couples be peacemakers or combatants in the "mommy wars"—the long-simmering struggle between moms who stay at home and moms who work outside it? If you doubt that straight households are paying attention to same-sex ones, consider Danie, a woman who lives with her husband and two children in Bethesda, Maryland. (Danie asked me not to use her last name out of concern for her family's privacy.) Not long after she completed a master's degree in Spanish linguistics at Georgetown University, her first baby was born. Because her husband, Jesse, works long hours as a litigator, she decided to become a full-time parent—not an easy decision in work-obsessed Washington, D.C. For a while, she ran a photography business out of their home, partly because she loves photography but partly so she could assure people at dinner parties that she had paying work. Whenever people venture that women who work outside the home don't judge stay-at-home moms, Danie thinks: *Are you freaking kidding me?*

She takes some comfort, however, in the example of a lesbian couple with whom she is friendly. Both women are attorneys, and one stays home with their child. "Their life is exactly the same as ours," Danie told me, with a hint of vindication. If being a stay-at-home mother is "good enough for her, then what's my issue? She's a huge women's-rights activist." But while comparing herself with a lesbian couple is liberating in some ways, it also exacerbates the competitive anxiety that afflicts so many modern mothers. The other thing about these two mothers, Danie said, is that they are so relaxed, so happy, so present. Even the working spouse manages to be a super-involved parent, to a much greater extent than most of the working fathers she knows. "I'm a little bit obsessed with them," she says.

Related to this is the question of how gay fatherhood might impact heterosexual fatherhood—by, for example, encouraging the idea that men can be emotionally accessible, logistically capable parents. Will the growing presence of gay dads in some communities mean that men are more often included in the endless e-mail chains that go to parents of preschoolers and birthday-party invitees? As radically as fatherhood has changed in recent decades, a number of antiquated attitudes about dads have proved strangely enduring: Rob Hardies, the pastor at All Souls, reports that when his partner, Chris, successfully folded a stroller before getting on an airplane with their son, Nico, he was roundly congratulated by passersby, as if he had solved a difficult mathematical equation in public. So low are expectations for fathers, even now, that in Stephanie Schacher's study of gay fathers and their feelings about care-giving, her subjects reported that people would see them walking on the street with their children and say things like "Giving Mom a break?" Hardies thinks that every time he and Chris take their son to the playground or to story hour, they help disrupt this sort of thinking. He imagines moms seeing a man doing this and gently—or maybe not so gently—pointing it out to their husbands. "Two guys somehow manage to get their act together and have a household and cook dinner and raise a child, without a woman doing all the work," he says. Rather than setting an example that fathers don't matter, gay men are setting an example that fathers do matter, and that marriage matters, too.

The Sex Problem

When, in the 1970s and early 1980s, Pepper Schwartz asked couples about their sex lives, she arrived at perhaps her most explosive finding: non-monogamy was rampant among gay men, a whopping 82 percent of whom reported having had sex outside their relationship. Slightly more than one-third of gay-male couples felt that monogamy was important; the other two-thirds said that monogamy was unimportant or that they were neutral on the topic. In a funny way, Schwartz says, her findings suggested that same-sex unions (like straight ones) aren't necessarily about sex. Some gay men made a point of telling her they loved their partners but weren't physically attracted to them. Others said they wanted to be monogamous but were unsupported in that wish, by their partner, gay culture, or both.

Schwartz believes that a move toward greater monogamy was emerging among gay men even before the AIDS crisis. Decades later, gay-male couples are more monogamous than they used to be, but not nearly to the same degree as other kinds of couples. In her Vermont research, Esther Rothblum found that 15 percent of straight husbands said they'd had sex outside their relationship, compared with 58 percent of gay men in civil unions and 61 percent of gay men who were partnered but not in civil unions. When asked whether a couple had arrived at an explicit agreement about extra-relational sex, a minuscule 4 percent of straight husbands said they'd discussed it with their partner and determined that it was okay, compared with 40 percent of gay men in civil unions and 49 percent of gay men in partnerships that were not legally recognized. Straight women and lesbians, meanwhile, were united in their commitment to monogamy, lesbians more so than straight women: 14 percent of straight wives said they had sex outside their marriage, compared with 9 percent of lesbians in civil unions and 7 percent of lesbians who were partnered but not in civil unions.

The question of whether gays and lesbians will change marriage, or vice versa, is at its thorniest around sex and monogamy. Private behavior could well stay private: when she studied marriage in the Netherlands, Lee Badgett, the University of Massachusetts economist, found that while many same-sex couples proselytize about the egalitarianism of their relationships, they don't tend to promote non-monogamy, even if they practice it. Then again, some gay-rights advocates, like the writer and sex columnist Dan Savage, argue very publicly that insisting on monogamy can do a couple more harm than good. Savage, who questions whether most humans are cut out for decades of sex with only one person, told me that "monogamy in marriage has been a disaster for straight couples" because it has set unrealistic expectations. "Gay-male couples are much more likely to be realistic about what men are," he said. Savage's own marriage started out monogamous; the agreement was that if either partner cheated, this would be grounds for ending the relationship. But when he and his husband decided to adopt a child, Savage suggested that they relax their zero-tolerance policy on infidelity. He felt that risking family dissolution over such an incident no longer made sense. His husband later suggested they explicitly allow each other occasional dalliances, a policy Savage sees as providing a safety valve for the relationship. If society wants marriage to be more resilient, he argues, we must make it more "monagamish."

This is, to be sure, a difficult argument to win: a husband proposing non-monogamy to his wife on the grounds that it is in the best interest of a new baby would have a tough time prevailing in the court of public opinion. But while most gay-marriage advocates stop short of championing Savage's "wiggle room," some experts say that gay men are better at talking more openly about sex. Naveen Jonathan, a family therapist and a professor at Chapman University, in California, says he sees many gay partners hammer out an elaborate who-can-do-what-when sexual contract, one that says, "These are the times and the situations where it's okay to be non-monogamous, and these are the times and the situations where it is not." While some straight couples have deals of their own, he finds that for the most part, they simply presume monogamy. A possible downside of this assumption: straight couples are far less likely than gay men to frankly and routinely discuss sex, desire, and the challenges of sexual commitment.

Other experts question the idea that most gay males share a preference for non-monogamous relationships, or will in the long term. Savage's argument that non-monogamy is a safety valve is "very interesting, but it really is no more than a claim," says Justin Garcia, an evolutionary biologist at the Kinsey Institute for Research in Sex, Gender, and Reproduction. Garcia points out that not all men are relentlessly sexual beings, and not all men want an open relationship, "in some ways, same-sex couples are healthier—they tend to have these negotiations more," he says. But negotiating can be stressful: in many cases, Garcia notes, one gay partner would prefer to be monogamous, but gives in to the other partner.

So which version will prevail: non-monogamous marriage, or marriage as we conventionally understand it? It's worth pointing out that in the U.S., same-sex unions are slightly more likely between women, and non-monogamy is not a cause women tend to champion. And some evidence suggests that getting married changes behavior: William Eskridge and Darren Spedale found that in the years after Norway, Sweden, and Denmark instituted registered partnerships, many same-sex couples reported placing a greater emphasis on monogamy, while national rates of HIV infections declined.

Sex, then, may be one area where the institution of marriage pushes back against norms that have been embraced by many gay couples. Gary Hall of the National Cathedral allows that in many ways, gay relationships offer a salutary "critique" of marriage, but argues that the marriage establishment will do some critiquing back. He says he would not marry two people who intended to be non-monogamous, and believes that monogamy will be a "critical issue" in the dialogue between the gay community and the Church. Up until now, he says, progressive churches have embraced "the part of gay behavior that looks like straight behavior," but at some point, churches also have to engage gay couples whose behavior doesn't conform to monogamous ideals. He hopes that, in the course of this give-and-take, the church ends up reckoning with other ongoing cultural changes, from unmarried cohabitation to the increasing number of adults who choose to live as singles. "How do we speak credibly to people about their sexuality and their sexual relationships?" he asks. "We really need to rethink this."

So yes, marriage will change. Or rather, it will change again. The fact is, there is no such thing as traditional marriage. In various places and at various points in human history, marriage has been a means by which young children were betrothed, uniting royal houses and sealing alliances between nations. In the Bible, it was a union that sometimes took place between a man and his dead brother's widow, or between one man and several wives. It has been a vehicle for the orderly transfer of property from one generation of males to the next; the test by which children were deemed legitimate or bastard; a privilege not available to black Americans;

something parents arranged for their adult children; a contract under which women, legally, ceased to exist. Well into the 19th century, the British common-law concept of "unity of person" meant a woman became her husband when she married, giving up her legal standing and the right to own property or control her own wages.

Many of these strictures have already loosened. Child marriage is today seen by most people as the human-rights violation that it is. The Married Women's Property Acts guaranteed that a woman could get married and remain a legally recognized human being. The Supreme Court's decision in *Loving v. Virginia* did away with state bans on interracial marriage. By making it easier to dissolve marriage, no-fault divorce helped ensure that unions need not be lifelong. The recent surge in single parenthood, combined with an aging population, has unyoked marriage and child-rearing. History shows that marriage evolves over time. We have every reason to believe that same-sex marriage will contribute to its continued evolution.

The argument that gays and lesbians are social pioneers and bellwethers has been made before. Back in 1992, the British sociologist Anthony Giddens suggested that gays and lesbians were a harbinger of a new kind of union, one subject to constant renegotiation and expected to last only as long as both partners were happy with it. Now that these so-called harbingers are looking to commit to more-binding relationships, we will have the "counterfactual" that Gary Gates talks about: we will be better able to tell which marital stresses and pleasures are due to gender, and which are not.

In the end, it could turn out that same-sex marriage isn't all that different from straight marriage. If gay and lesbian marriages are in the long run as quarrelsome, tedious, and unbearable; as satisfying, joyous, and loving as other marriages, we'll know that a certain amount of strife is not the fault of the alleged war between men and women, but just an inevitable thing that happens when two human beings are doing the best they can to find a way to live together.

Critical Thinking

1. Do you think that gay marriages should be legally treated as equal to heterosexual marriages?

2. Why or why not are gay marriages a threat to heterosexual marriages?

3. What "rules" should help improve marriages?

Internet References

Marriage and Family Therapy
www.aamft.org/index_nm.asp

Sociosite
www.topsite.com/goto/sociosite.net

Socioweb
www.topsite.com/goto/socioweb.com

Sociology—Study Sociology Online
http://edu.learnsoc.org

Sociology Web Resources
www.mhhe.com/socscience/sociology/resources/index.htm

LIZA MUNDY is a BERNARD L. SCHWARTZ Fellow at the New America Foundation and the author of *The Richer Sex: How the New Majority of Female Breadwinners Is Transforming Our Culture*.

Article   Prepared by: Kurt Finsterbusch, *University of Maryland, College Park*

US Women Make Strides Toward Equality, But Work Remains

Mia Bush

Learning Outcomes

After reading this article, you will be able to:

- Understand the progress toward equality that women have made in the United States in the past century.

- Explain why the United States ranks only 28th among countries today on gender equality.

- Understand why women are poorly represented in business leadership.

The beginnings of International Women's Day—a mass protest by thousands of women in New York City seeking better pay and working conditions, and the right to vote—have evolved into a day to take stock of the progress made toward gender equality as well as issues that still need to be addressed.

The United Nations views gender equality—the view that women and men have equal value and should be afforded equal treatment—as a human right.

Yet despite a more than 100-year history for International Women's Day, discrimination against women and girls continues worldwide in the form of gender-based violence and discrimination.

US Ranking

The United States has made huge strides since that first march in 1908: women won the right to vote, they make up about half of the workforce and they now earn a higher percentage of college degrees than men, among other things.

However, the United States rates 28th of the 145 countries in an annual world ranking of equality for women.

The World Economic Forum "Global Gender Gap Report 2015" bases its equality ranking on economic, educational, health-based, and political indicators.

The report, which was first published in 2006, shows progress has been made in the past decade, yet inequalities remain. In fact, it notes the gender gap has closed only 4 percent in the past 10 years, and at that rate, it would take 118 years to reach parity.

Iceland ranks No. 1 in the report, a position it has held for the past seven years. The Scandinavian countries—Norway, Sweden, and Finland—as well as Ireland round out the top five countries. At the lower end, Yemen ranks as the least equal country for women.

Wages, Politics

The U.S. fell eight places in 2015, with the report citing a slight drop in wage equality for similar work and fewer women in leading government positions.

While former Secretary of State Hillary Clinton is a frontrunner in the Democratic presidential nominating race this year, the United States, with women holding just 26.1 percent of high government positions, ranks 29th in the world, according to a U.N. report, "Women in Politics: 2015."

It fares worse regarding congressional seats. The United States ranks 73rd—tying with Panama—with women holding just 19.3 percent of the seats in the U.S. Congress—84 in the House and 20 in the Senate.

While the United States does well regarding three criteria of the gender gap report, "the political representation of women in this country is abysmal," Keshet Bachan, a girl's empowerment expert in Washington, DC, told VOA.

"Just for comparison, Rwanda's female representation to their [parliament] is over 60 percent, and in the Netherlands it's almost 40 percent," Bachan said. "We've never had a female president, which further drops our score."

Leadership in Business

The lack of gender equality extends to women in positions of leadership in U.S. businesses as well.

Just 20 years ago, there were no female CEOs of Fortune 500 companies, according to the Pew Research Center. In January 2015, Pew counted 26 women—5.2 percent—serving as CEOs of such companies.

However, women held nearly 17 percent of positions on company boards, according to 2013 data, up from nearly 10 percent in 1995.

In November 2014, women accounted for nearly half of the U.S. workforce—47 percent. The number of working women 16 and older steadily grew for three decades, increasing from 39 percent in 1965 to 60 percent in 1999, Pew found. But the number fell to 57 percent by November 2014.

Education has been proven to be a strong equalizer between men and women, yet globally, nearly half a billion women cannot read and 62 million girls are denied an education, according to UNICEF.

However, education is an area where U.S. women have surpassed men. Since the 1990s, women have outnumbered men in college enrollment and completion rates, a Pew study found in 2013. Thirty-seven percent of women ages 25–29 had at least a bachelor's degree, compared with 30 percent of men the same age, according to Pew.

College Degrees

Women are also more likely to continue in education after receiving a bachelor's degree: in 2012, women earned 60 percent of all master's degrees and 51 percent of all doctorates; in 2013, women earned 36 percent of master of business administration degrees, according to the Pew study.

However, despite the gains in education, a gender wage gap persists and is even wider for minority women.

The median weekly earnings for full-time female workers were about 80.4 percent of men's earnings, according to fourth-quarter 2015 statistics by the U.S. Department of Labor.

In 2014, African-American women were paid 63 percent of what White men were paid, while Hispanic women were paid just 54 percent, according to a survey by the American Association of University Women (AAUW), a group that advocates for equity and education for women and girls.

In 1979, U.S. women earned about 62 percent as much as men in the same position, the Department of Labor said.

AAUW's report, "The Simple Truth About the Gender Pay Gap," found the wage gap has narrowed in the past 30 years due largely to more women furthering their education and entering the workforce.

Nationwide, the pay gap was smallest in Washington, DC, where women were paid 90 percent of what men were paid in 2015, according to the American Community Survey, the ongoing statistical survey by the U.S. Census Bureau. The pay gap was largest in Louisiana, where women were paid 65 percent of what men were paid.

Advances Made

In one of his first acts in office in 2009, President Barack Obama signed into law the Lilly Ledbetter Fair Pay Act, which prohibits sex-based wage discrimination. However, Congress has not passed the Paycheck Fairness Act, which would make it easier for women to challenge wage disparities.

"We've made strides in closing the pay gap, but we could do more," Bachan said, referring to a report earlier this month by researchers at Accenture that said becoming adept at digital technology would help women close the gender gap in the workplace. "So that's the good news," she said.

"The bad news is that women's health in the U.S. is under constant threat, especially their access to comprehensive sexual and reproductive health and family planning. The campaign against Planned Parenthood, and the way states like Texas are making it harder for women to access abortion clinics. These are direct threats to our ability to make informed choices freely about whether, when, and how many children we want to have," Bachan said.

"In terms of international laws, this is a basic minimum standard, and yet in the U.S. it's so highly politicized it's constantly being undermined," she told VOA.

Twenty years ago, a global gathering organized by the United Nations yielded what many consider a defining moment in the ongoing fight for gender equality.

Hillary Clinton, who was then the first lady of the United States, took the stage in Beijing and, in a 19-min address, laid out a simple but soaring equation. "Human rights are women's rights and women's rights are human rights, once and for all," she said as applause erupted.

Her speech—delivered September 5, 1995, at the U.N. Fourth World Conference on Women—distilled the concerns brought forward by 5,000 official delegates and at least as many other participants.

Conference History

They challenged limits on women's and girls' education and health care, including reproductive health. Disparities in economic security, wages, and inheritance rights. Violence against women, from domestic abuse to female circumcision to human trafficking.

This fourth women's conference made history, 20 years after the first, by securing the pledges of 189 world leaders to help females attain equality. Leaders committed to an action plan setting benchmarks and ensuring that women have "a full and equal share in economic, social, cultural and political decision-making" in public and private life.

"There was anticipation. There was excitement, too," recalled former U.S. Representative Connie Morella, who had led a small, bipartisan congressional delegation to the conference.

The Republican said she "felt the eyes of the world needed to look at what was happening to women . . . . I knew that my sisters in other parts of the world needed to have the protections I needed to have. In most instances, they needed them even more."

As Clinton noted in her 1995 remarks: "What we are learning around the world is that if women are healthy and educated, their families will flourish. If women are free from violence, their families will flourish. If women have a chance to work and earn as full and equal partners in society, their families will flourish. And when families flourish, communities and nations do as well."

"That is why every woman, every man, every child, every family, and every nation on this planet does have a stake in the discussion"—and in reaching those goals, she said.

Bachan is also optimistic that the goal of gender equality can be reached.

"The biggest win we could see is in encouraging more girls and young women to study science, technology, engineering, and math subjects and enter the tech industry. The stereotypes that discourage girls from studying engineering or mathematics are changing rapidly," she said, adding it is also up to tech companies to eliminate bias in their hiring practices.

"At the very end of that pipeline we still need companies to be more female friendly," Bachan said. "It's still very much a tech-bro space which alienates women. I'm optimistic, though, given the rise of girls and women in this industry, and looking to other sectors like law or female doctors, where we've seen huge increases in female representation in the past few decades means it can be done."

International Women's Day was first observed in 1909, but it wasn't observed by the United Nations until 1975. It's now celebrated in more than 25 countries around the world, from Afghanistan to Russia.

In 1981, the U.S. Congress established National Women's History Week to be commemorated the second week of March, expanding the observation to a women's history month in 1987.

Events have taken place in the days leading up to Tuesday's official day of recognition, when events are scheduled throughout the United States and the world.

Critical Thinking

1. Explain why the US women in government is barely above the world average.

2. Understand the role of education in improving gender equality.

3. Why have these problems not been fixed already?

Internet References

Global Gender Gap Report
 reports.weforum.org/global-gender-gap-report-2016/rankings/

Sociology—Study Sociology Online
 http://edu.learnsoc.org/

Sociology Web Resources
 http://www.mhhe.com/socscience/sociology/resources/index.htm

Sociosite
 http://www.topsite.com/goto/sociosite.net

Socioweb

 http://www.topsite.com/goto/socioweb.com

Article   Prepared by: Kurt Finsterbusch, *University of Maryland, College Park*

Houston Rising

Why the Next Great American Cities Aren't What You Think

JOEL KOTKIN

Learning Outcomes

After reading this article, you will be able to:

- Understand the attractiveness to their residents of the moderately large cities compared to the very largest cities.

- Discuss the different views on the appropriate type of city for the future.

- Discuss the critical functions that cities provide to the national and international economies.

America's urban landscape is changing, but in ways not always predicted or much admired by our media, planners, and pundits. The real trend-setters of the future—judged by both population and job growth—are not in the oft-praised great "legacy" cities like New York, Chicago, or San Francisco, but a crop of newer, more sprawling urban regions primarily located in the Sun Belt and, surprisingly, the resurgent Great Plains.

While Gotham and the Windy City have experienced modest growth and significant net domestic out-migration, burgeoning if often disdained urban regions such as Houston, Dallas-Ft. Worth, Charlotte, and Oklahoma City have expanded rapidly. These low-density, car-dominated, heavily suburbanized areas with small central cores likely represent the next wave of great American cities.

There's a whole industry led by the likes of Harvard's Ed Glaeser, my occasional sparring partner Richard Florida and developer-funded groups like CEOs for Cities, who advocate for old-style, high-density cities, and insist that they represent the inevitable future.

But the numbers tell a different story: the most rapid urban growth is occurring outside of the great, dense, highly developed and vastly expensive old American metropolises.

An aspirational city, by definition, is one that people and industries migrate to improve their economic prospects and achieve a better relative quality of life. In the 19th and early 20th centuries, this aspirational spirit was epitomized by cities such as New York and Chicago and then in the decades after World War Two by Los Angeles, which for many years was the fastest-growing big city in the high-income world.

Until the 1970s, the country's established big cities were synonymous with aspiration—where the jobs and opportunities for broad portions of the population abounded. But as the financial markets took on an oversized role in the American economy and manufacturing receded, the cost of living in the nation's oldest metropolises shot up far faster than the median income there—and Americans have turned elsewhere now that, as Virginia Postrel wrote in an important essay on the nation's growing economic wall, "the promise of a better life that once drew people of all backgrounds to rich places like New York and [coastal] California now applies only to an educated elite—because rich places have made housing prohibitively expensive."

Like the great legacy cities during their now long-past adolescent and at times ungainly growth spurts, today's aspirational cities often meet with little approval from travelers from other, older cities. A 19th-century Swedish visitor to Chicago described it as "one of the most miserable and ugly cities" in North America. New York, complained the French Consul in 1810, was a city where the inhabitants had "in general no mind for anything but business"; later Bostonian Ralph Waldo Emerson, granted Gotham's entrepreneurial supremacy only to explain that his more cultured "little city" was "appointed" by destiny to "lead the civilization of North America."

Los Angeles, most of whose early-20th-century migrants came from the Midwest, became a favorite object of scorn from sophisticates. William Faulkner in the 1930s described the city of angels as "the plastic asshole of the world." As the first great city built largely around the automobile, mainstream urbanists detested it; their icon Jane Jacobs called it "a vast blind-eyed reservation."

A half century later, today's aspirational urban centers suffer similarly poor reputations among urbanists, planners and journalists. One *New York Post* reporter recently described Houston as "brutally ugly" while new urbanists like Andres Duany relegate the region to a netherworld inhabited by car-centric cities such as Phoenix and Atlanta.

Yet over the past decade the 25 fastest-growing cities have been mostly such urbanist "assholes"—Raleigh, Austin, Houston, San Antonio, Las Vegas, Orlando, Dallas-Fort Worth, Charlotte, and Phoenix. Despite hopeful claims from density advocates that the Great Recession and the housing bust ended this trend, the latest census data shows that Americans have continued choosing places that are affordable enough to offer opportunity, and space.

One common article of faith among mainstream urbanists, at least when they stop to note this growth at all, is that these cities grow mainly because they are cheap and can house the unskilled. But in reality many of these metropolitan areas are also leading the nation in growing their number of well-educated arrivals. Houston, Charlotte, Raleigh, Las Vegas, Nashville, and San Antonio, for example, experienced increases in the number of college-educated residents of nearly 40 percent or more over the decade, roughly twice the level of growth as in "brain centers" such as Boston, San Francisco, San Jose (Silicon Valley), or Chicago. Atlanta, Houston, and Dallas each have added about 300,000 college grads in the past decade, more than greater Boston's pickup of 240,000 or San Francisco's 211,000.

Once considered backwaters, these Sunbelt cities are quietly achieving a critical mass of well-educated residents. They are also becoming major magnets for immigrants. Over the past decade, the largest percentage growth in foreign-born population has occurred in sunbelt cities, led by Nashville, which has doubled its number of immigrants, as have Charlotte and Raleigh. During the first decade of the 21st century, Houston attracted the second-most new, foreign-born residents, some 400,000, of any American city—behind only much larger New York and slightly ahead of Dallas-Ft. Worth, but more than three times as many as Los Angeles. According to one recent Rice University study, Census data now shows that Houston has now surpassed New York as the country's most racially and ethnically diverse metropolis.

Why are these people flocking to the aspirational cities, that lack the hip amenities, tourist draws, and cultural landmarks of the biggest American cities? People are still far more likely to buy a million dollar *pied à terre* in Manhattan than to do so in Oklahoma City. Like early-20th-century Polish peasants who came to work in Chicago's factories or Russian immigrants, like my grandparents, who came to New York to labor in the rag trade, the appeal of today's smaller cities is largely economic. The foreign born, along with generally younger

educated workers, are canaries in the coal mine—singing loudest and most frequently in places that offer both employment and opportunities for upward mobility and a better life.

Over the decade, for example, Austin's job base grew 28 percent, Raleigh's by 21 percent, Houston by 20 percent, while Nashville, Atlanta, San Antonio, and Dallas-Ft. Worth saw job growth in the 14 percent range or better. In contrast, among all the legacy cities, only Seattle and Washington D.C.—the great economic parasite—have created jobs faster than the national average of roughly 5 percent. Most did far worse, with New York and Boston 20 percent *below* the norm; big urban regions including Philadelphia, Los Angeles, and, despite the current tech bubble, San Francisco have created essentially *zero* new jobs over the decade.

Another common urban legend maintains these areas lag in terms of higher-wage employment, lacking the density essential for what boosters like Glaeser and Florida describe as "knowledge-intensive cities." Defenders of traditional cities often cite Santa Fe Institute research that they say links innovation with density—but actually does nothing of the kind. Rather, that research suggests that *size,* not compactness, constitutes the decisive factor. After all, it's hard to define Silicon Valley, still the nation's premier innovation region, as anything other than large, sprawling, and overwhelmingly suburban in form.

Size does matter and many of the fastest growth areas are themselves large enough to sport a major airport, large corporate presences and other critical pieces of economic infrastructure. The largest gains in GDP (PDF) in 2011 were in Houston, Dallas and, surprisingly, resurgent greater Detroit (and that despite its shrinking urban core). None of these areas are characterized by high density yet their income growth was well ahead of Seattle, San Francisco, or Boston, and more than twice that of New York, Washington, or Chicago.

But in fact neither density nor size necessarily determine which regions generate new high-end jobs. The growth in STEM—or science-technology-engineering and mathematics-related—employment in Houston, Raleigh, Nashville, Austin, and Las Vegas surpassed that in San Francisco, Los Angeles, Boston, or New York. One reason: most STEM jobs are not found in fashionable fields like designing social media or videogames but in more prosaic activities tied to medicine, manufacturing, agriculture and (horror of horrors) natural resource extraction, including fossil fuel energy. In this sense, technology reflects the definition of the French sociologists Marcel Mauss as "a traditional action made effective."

This pattern also extends to growth in business and professional services, the nation's biggest high-wage job category. Since 2000, Houston, Dallas-Fort Worth, Charlotte, Austin and Raleigh expanded their number of such jobs by twenty percent or more—twice the rate as greater New York, the longtime business-service capital, while Chicago and San Jose actually lost jobs in this critical category.

Finally there is the too often neglected topic of real purchasing power—that a dollar in New York doesn't go nearly as far as one in Atlanta, for example. My colleague Mark Schill at the Praxis Strategy group has calculated the average regional paycheck, adjusted for cost of living. Houston led the pack in real median pay in, and seven of the 10 cities with the highest adjusted salary were aspirational ones (the exceptions were San Jose-Silicon Valley, Seattle, and the greater Detroit region). Portland, Los Angeles, New York, and San Diego all landed near the bottom of the list.

Conventional urbanists—call them density nostalgists—continue to see the future in legacy cities that, as the University of Washington demographer Richard Morrill notes, were built out before the dominance of the car, air-conditioning and with them the prevalence of suburban lifestyles.

Looking forward, it is simply presumptuous and ahistorical to dismiss the fast-growing regions as anti-cities, as 60s-era urbanists did with places like Los Angeles. When tradition-bound urbanists hope these sprawling young cities choke on their traffic and exhaust fumes, or from rising energy costs, they are reflecting the classic prejudice of city-dwellers of established urban centers toward upstarts.

The reality is that most urban growth in our most dynamic, fastest-growing regions has included strong expansion of the suburban and even exurban fringe, along with a limited resurgence in their historically small inner cores. Economic growth, it turns out, allows for young hipsters to find amenable places before they enter their 30s, and affordable, more suburban environments nearby to start families.

This urbanizing process is shaped, in many ways, by the late development of these regions. In most aspirational cities, close-in neighborhoods often are dominated by single-family houses; it's a mere 10 or 15 minute drive from nice, leafy streets in Ft. Worth, Charlotte, or Austin to the urban core. In these cities, families or individuals who want to live near the center can do so without being forced to live in a tiny apartment.

And in many of these places, the historic underdevelopment in the central district, coupled with job growth, presents developers with economically viable options for higher-density housing as well. Houston presents the strongest example of this trend. Although nearly 60 percent of Houston's growth over the decade has been more than 20 miles outside the core, the inner ring area encompassed within the loop around Interstate 610 has also been growing steadily, albeit at a markedly slower rate. This contrasts with many urban regions, where close-in areas just beyond downtowns have been actually *losing* population.

Even as Houston has continued to advance outwards, the region has added more multiunit buildings over the past decade than more populous New York, Los Angeles or Chicago. With its economy growing faster and producing wealth faster than any other region in the country, urban developers there usually do not need subsidies or planning dictates to be economically viable.

Modern urban culture also is spreading in the Bayou City. In what has to be a first, my colleagues at Forbes recently ranked Houston as America's "coolest city," citing not only its economy, but its thriving arts scene and excellent restaurants. Such praise may make some of us, who relish Houston's unpretentious nature, a little nervous—but it shows that hip urbanism can co-exist with rapidly expanding suburban development.

And Houston's not the only proverbial urban ugly duckling having an amenity makeover. Oklahoma City has developed its central "Bricktown" into a centerpiece for arts and entertainment. Ft. Worth boasts its own, cowboy-themed downtown, along with fine museums, while its rival Dallas, in typical Texan fashion, boasts of having the nation's largest arts district.

More important still, both for families and outdoor-oriented singles, both cities are developing large urban park systems. At an expense of $30 million, Raleigh is nearing the completion of its Neuse River Greenway Trail, a 28-mile trail through the forested areas of Raleigh. Houston has plans for a series of bayou-oriented green ways. For its part, Dallas is envisioning a vast new 6,000 acre park system, along the Trinity River that will dwarf New York's 840-acre Central Park.

To be sure, there's no foreseeable circumstance in which these cities will challenge Paris or Buenos Aires, New York, or San Francisco as favored destinations for those primarily motivated by aesthetics that are largely the result of history. Nor are they likely to become models of progressive governance, as poverty and gaps in medical coverage become even more difficult problems for elected officials without a well-entrenched ultra-wealthy class to cull resources from.

Finally, they will not become highly dense, apartment cities—as developers and planners insist they "should." Instead the aspirational regions are likely to remain dominated by a suburbanized form characterized by car dependency, dispersion of job centers, and single-family homes. In 2011, for example, twice as many single-family homes sold in Raleigh as condos and townhouses combined. The ratio of new suburban to new urban housing, according to the American Community Survey, is 10 to 1 in Las Vegas and Orlando, 5 to 1 in Dallas, 4 to 1 in Houston and 3 to 1 in Phoenix.

Pressed by local developers and planners, some aspirational cities spend heavily on urban transit, including light rail. To my mind, these efforts are largely quixotic, with transit accounting for five percent or less of all commuters in most systems. The Charlotte Area Transit System represents less a viable means of commuting for most residents than what could be called Manhattan infrastructure envy. Even urban-planning model Portland, now with five radial light rail lines and a population now growing largely at its fringes, carries a smaller portion of commuters on transit than before opening its first line in 1986.

But such pretentions, however ill-suited, have always been commonplace for ambitious and ascending cities, and are hardly a reason to discount their prospects. Urbanistas need to wake up, start recognizing what the future is really looking like and search for ways to make it work better. Under almost any imaginable scenario, we are unlikely to see the creation of regions with anything like the dynamic inner cores of successful legacy cities such as New York, Boston, Chicago or San Francisco. For better or worse, demographic and economic trends suggest our urban destiny lies increasingly with the likes of Houston, Charlotte, Dallas-Ft. Worth, Raleigh and even Phoenix.

The critical reason for this is likely to be missed by those who worship at the altar of density and contemporary planning dogma. These cities grow primarily because they do what cities were designed to do in the first place: help their residents achieve their aspirations—and that's why they keep getting bigger and more consequential, in spite of the planners who keep ignoring or deploring their ascendance.

Critical Thinking

1. What types of residents make for the best cities?

2. How are planners at odds with residents in terms of what they favor?

3. Over one-half of the world is urban. What is the future of cities and why?

Internet References

Sociosite
www.topsite.com/goto/sociosite.net

Socioweb
www.topsite.com/goto/socioweb.com

Sociology—Study Sociology Online
http://edu.learnsoc.org

Sociology Web Resources
www.mhhe.com/socscience/sociology/resources/index.htm

Article   Prepared by: Kurt Finsterbusch, *University of Maryland, College Park*

Have Smartphones Destroyed a Generation?

More comfortable outline than out playing, postmillennials are safer, physically, than adolescents have ever been. But they are on the brink of a mental health crisis.

JEAN M. TWENGE

Learning Outcomes

After reading this article, you will be able to:

- Discuss social media's impact on generational differences.

- Discuss both the positive and negative social effects of smartphones.

- Discuss how teen independence expresses itself in different generations.

ONE DAY last summer, around noon, I called Athena, a 13-year-old who lives in Houston, TX. She answered her phone—she's had an iPhone since she was 11—sounding as if she'd just woken up. We chatted about her favorite songs and TV shows, and I asked her what she likes to do with her friends. "We go to the mall," she said. "Do your parents drop you off?," I asked, recalling my own middle-school days, in the 1980s, when I'd enjoy a few parent-free hours shopping with my friends. "No—I go with my family," she replied. "We'll go with my mom and brothers and walk a little behind them. I just have to tell my mom where we're going. I have to check in every hour or every 30 minutes."

Those mall trips are infrequent—about once a month. More often, Athena and her friends spend time together on their phones, unchaperoned. Unlike the teens of my generation, who might have spent an evening tying up the family landline with gossip, they talk on Snapchat, the smartphone app that allows users to send pictures and videos that quickly disappear. They make sure to keep up their Snapstreaks, which show how many days in a row they have Snapchatted with each other. Sometimes they save screenshots of particularly ridiculous pictures of friends. "It's good blackmail," Athena said. (Because she's a minor, I'm not using her real name.) She told me she'd spent most of the summer hanging out alone in her room with her phone. That's just the way her generation is, she said. "We didn't have a choice to know any life without iPads or iPhones. I think we like our phones more than we like actual people."

I've been researching generational differences for 25 years, starting when I was a 22-year-old doctoral student in psychology. Typically, the characteristics that come to define a generation appear gradually, and along a continuum. Beliefs and behaviors that were already rising simply continue to do so. Millennials, for instance, are a highly individualistic generation, but individualism had been increasing since the Baby Boomers turned on, tuned in, and dropped out. I had grown accustomed to line graphs of trends that looked like modest hills and valleys. Then, I began studying Athena's generation.

Around 2012, I noticed abrupt shifts in teen behaviors and emotional states. The gentle slopes of the line graphs became steep mountains and sheer cliffs, and many of the distinctive characteristics of the millennial generation began to disappear. In all my analyses of generational data—some reaching back to the 1930s—I had never seen anything like it.

At first, I presumed these might be blips, but the trends persisted, across several years and a series of national surveys. The changes weren't just in degree, but in kind. The biggest difference between the millennials and their predecessors was in how they viewed the world; teens today differ from the millennials not just in their views but in how they spend their time. The experiences they have every day are radically different from those of the generation that came of age just a few years before them.

What happened in 2012 to cause such dramatic shifts in behavior? It was after the Great Recession, which officially lasted from 2007 to 2009 and had a starker effect on millennials trying to find a place in a sputtering economy. But it was exactly the moment when the proportion of Americans who owned a smartphone surpassed 50 percent.

THE MORE I pored over yearly surveys of teen attitudes and behaviors, and the more I talked with young people like Athena, the clearer it became that theirs is a generation shaped by the smartphone and by the concomitant rise of social media. I call them iGen. Born between 1995 and 2012, members of this generation are growing up with smartphones, have an Instagram account before they start high school, and do not remember a time before the Internet. The millennials grew up with the web as well, but it wasn't ever-present in their lives, at hand at all times, day and night. iGen's oldest members were early adolescents when the iPhone was introduced, in 2007, and high-school students when the iPad entered the scene, in 2010. A 2017 survey of more than 5,000 American teens found that three out of four owned an iPhone.

The advent of the smartphone and its cousin the tablet was followed quickly by hand-wringing about the deleterious effects of "screen time." But the impact of these devices has not been fully appreciated, and goes far beyond the usual concerns about curtailed attention spans. The arrival of the smartphone has radically changed every aspect of teenagers' lives, from the nature of their social interactions to their mental health. These changes have affected young people in every corner of the nation and in every type of household. The trends appear among teens poor and rich; of every ethnic background; in cities, suburbs, and small towns. Where there are cell towers, there are teens living their lives on their smartphone.

To those of us who fondly recall a more analog adolescence, this may seem foreign and troubling. The aim of generational study, however, is not to succumb to nostalgia for the way things used to be; it's to understand how they are now. Some generational changes are positive, some are negative, and many are both. More comfortable in their bedrooms than in a car or at a party, today's teens are physically safer than teens have ever been. They're markedly less likely to get into a car accident and, having less of a taste for alcohol than their predecessors, are less susceptible to drinking's attendant ills.

Psychologically, however, they are more vulnerable than millennials were: rates of teen depression and suicide have skyrocketed since 2011. It's not an exaggeration to describe iGen as being on the brink of the worst mental health crisis in decades. Much of this deterioration can be traced to their phones.

Even when a seismic event—a war, a technological leap, and a free concert in the mud—plays an outsize role in shaping a group of young people, no single factor ever defines a generation. Parenting styles continue to change, as do school curricula and culture, and these things matter. But the twin rise of the smartphone and social media has caused an earthquake of a magnitude we've not seen in a very long time, if ever. There is compelling evidence that the devices we've placed in young people's hands are having profound effects on their lives—and making them seriously unhappy.

IN THE EARLY 1970s, the photographer Bill Yates shot a series of portraits at the Sweetheart Roller Skating Rink in Tampa, FL. In one, a shirtless teen stands with a large bottle of peppermint schnapps stuck in the waistband of his jeans. In another, a boy who looks no older than 12 poses with a cigarette in his mouth. The rink was a place where kids could get away from their parents and inhabit a world of their own, a world where they could drink, smoke, and make out in the backs of their cars. In stark black-and-white, the adolescent Boomers gaze at Yates's camera with the self-confidence born of making your own choices—even if, perhaps especially if, your parents wouldn't think they were the right ones.

Fifteen years later, during my own teenage years as a member of Generation X, smoking had lost some of its romance, but independence was definitely still in. My friends and I plotted to get our driver's license as soon as we could, making DMV appointments for the day we turned 16 and using our newfound freedom to escape the confines of our suburban neighborhood. Asked by our parents, "When will you be home?," we replied "When do I have to be?"

But the allure of independence, so powerful to previous generations, holds less sway over today's teens, who are less likely to leave the house without their parents. The shift is stunning: 12th-graders in 2015 were going out less often than *eighth-graders* did as recently as 2009.

Today's teens are also less likely to date. The initial stage of courtship, which Gen Xers called "liking" (as in "Ooh, he likes you!"), kids now call "talking"—an ironic choice for a generation that prefers texting to actual conversation. After two teens have "talked" for a while, they might start dating. But only about 56 percent of high-school seniors in 2015 went out on dates; for Boomers and Gen Xers, the number was about 85 percent.

The decline in dating tracks with a decline in sexual activity. The drop is the sharpest for ninth-graders, among whom the number of sexually active teens has been cut by almost 40 percent since 1991. The average teen now has had sex for the first time by the spring of 11th grade, a full year later than the average Gen Xer. Fewer teens having sex has contributed to what many see as one of the most positive youth trends in recent years: The teen birth rate hit an all-time low in 2016, down 67 percent since its modern peak, in 1991.

Even driving, a symbol of adolescent freedom inscribed in American popular culture, from *Rebel Without a Cause* to *Ferris Bueller's Day Off*, has lost its appeal for today's teens. Nearly all Boomer high-school students had their driver's license by the spring of their senior year; more than one in four teens today still lack one at the end of high school. For some, mom and dad are such good chauffeurs that there's no urgent need to drive. "My parents drove me everywhere and never complained, so I always had rides," a 21-year-old student in San Diego told me. "I didn't get my license until my mom told me I had to because she could not keep driving me to school." She finally got her license six months after her 18th birthday. In conversation after conversation, teens described getting their license as something to be nagged into by their parents—a notion that would have been unthinkable to previous generations.

Independence isn't free—you need some money in your pocket to pay for gas, or for that bottle of schnapps. In earlier eras, kids worked in great numbers, eager to finance their freedom or prodded by their parents to learn the value of a dollar. But iGen teens aren't working (or managing their own money) as much. In the late 1970s, 77 percent of high-school seniors worked for pay during the school year; by the mid-2010s, only 55 percent did. The number of eighth-graders who work for pay has been cut in half. These declines accelerated during the Great Recession, but teen employment has not bounced back, even though job availability has.

Of course, putting off the responsibilities of adulthood is not an iGen innovation. Gen Xers, in the 1990s, were the first to postpone the traditional markers of adulthood. Young Gen Xers were just about as likely to drive, drink alcohol, and date as young Boomers had been, and more likely to have sex and get pregnant as teens. But as they left their teenage years behind, Gen Xers married and started careers later than their Boomer predecessors had.

Gen X managed to stretch adolescence beyond all previous limits: Its members started becoming adults earlier and finished becoming adults later. Beginning with millennials and continuing with iGen, adolescence is contracting again—but only because its onset is being delayed. Across a range of behaviors—drinking, dating, and spending time unsupervised—18-year-olds now act more like 15-year-olds used to, and 15-year-olds more like 13-year-olds. Childhood now stretches well into high school.

Why are today's teens waiting longer to take on both the responsibilities and the pleasures of adulthood? Shifts in the economy, and parenting, certainly play a role. In an information economy that rewards higher education more than early work history, parents may be inclined to encourage their kids to stay home and study rather than to get a part-time job. Teens, in turn, seem to be content with this homebody arrangement—not because they're so studious, but because their social life is lived on their phone. They don't need to leave home to spend time with their friends.

If today's teens were a generation of grinds, we'd see that in the data. But eighth-, 10th-, and 12th-graders in the 2010s actually spend less time on homework than Gen X teens did in the early 1990s. (High-school seniors headed for four-year colleges spend about the same amount of time on homework as their predecessors did.) The time that seniors spend on activities such as student clubs and sports and exercise has changed little in recent years. Combined with the decline in working for pay, this means iGen teens have more leisure time than Gen X teens did, not less.

So what are they doing with all that time? They are on their phone, in their room, alone and often distressed.

ONE OF THE IRONIES of iGen life is that despite spending far more time under the same roof as their parents, today's teens can hardly be said to be closer to their mothers and fathers than their predecessors were. "I've seen my friends with their families—they don't talk to them," Athena told me. "They just say 'Okay, okay, whatever' while they're on their phones. They don't pay attention to their family." Like her peers, Athena is an expert at tuning out her parents so she can focus on her phone. She spent much of her summer keeping up with friends, but nearly all of it was over text or Snapchat. "I've been on my phone more than I've been with actual people," she said. "My bed has, like, an imprint of my body."

In this, too, she is typical. The number of teens who get together with their friends nearly every day dropped by more than 40 percent from 2000 to 2015; the decline has been especially steep recently. It's not only a matter of fewer kids partying; fewer kids are spending time simply hanging out. That's something most teens used to do: nerds and jocks, poor kids and rich kids, C students and A students. The roller rink, the basketball court, the town pool, and the local necking spot—they've all been replaced by virtual spaces accessed through apps and the web.

You might expect that teens spend so much time in these new spaces because it makes them happy, but most data suggest that it does not. The Monitoring the Future survey, funded by the National Institute on Drug Abuse and designed to be nationally representative, has asked 12th-graders more than 1,000 questions every year since 1975 and queried eighth- and 10th-graders since 1991. The survey asks teens how happy they are and also how much of their leisure time they spend on various activities, including nonscreen activities such as in-person social interaction and exercise, and, in recent years, screen activities such as using social media, texting, and browsing the web. The results could not be clearer: Teens who spend more time than average on screen activities are more likely to be unhappy, and those who spend more time than average on nonscreen activities are more likely to be happy.

There's not a single exception. All screen activities are linked to less happiness, and all nonscreen activities are linked to more happiness. Eighth-graders who spend 10 or more hours a week on social media are 56 percent more likely to say they're unhappy than those who devote less time to social media. Admittedly, 10 h a week is a lot. But those who spend six to nine hours a week on social media are still 47 percent more likely to say they are unhappy than those who use social media even less. The opposite is true of in-person interactions. Those who spend an above-average amount of time with their friends in person are 20 percent less likely to say they're unhappy than those who hang out for a below-average amount of time.

If you were going to give advice for a happy adolescence based on this survey, it would be straightforward: Put down the phone, turn off the laptop, and do something—anything—that does not involve a screen. Of course, these analyses don't unequivocally prove that screen time *causes* unhappiness; it's possible that unhappy teens spend more time online. But recent research suggests that screen time, in particular social-media use, does indeed cause unhappiness. One study asked college students with a Facebook page to complete short surveys on their phone over the course of 2 weeks. They'd get a text message with a link five times a day and report on their mood and how much they'd used Facebook. The more they'd used Facebook, the unhappier they felt, but feeling unhappy did not subsequently lead to more Facebook use.

Social-networking sites like Facebook promise to connect us to friends. But the portrait of iGen teens emerging from the data is one of a lonely, dislocated generation. Teens who visit social-networking sites every day but see their friends in person less frequently are the most likely to agree with the statements "A lot of times I feel lonely," "I often feel left out of things," and "I often wish I had more good friends." Teens' feelings of loneliness spiked in 2013 and have remained high since.

This doesn't always mean that, on an individual level, kids who spend more time online are lonelier than kids who spend less time online. Teens who spend more time on social media also spend more time with their friends in person, on average—highly social teens are more social in both venues, and less social teens are less so. But at the generational level, when teens spend more time on smartphones and less time on in-person social interactions, loneliness is more common.

So is depression. Once again, the effect of screen activities is unmistakable: The more time teens spend looking at screens, the more likely they are to report symptoms of depression. Eighth-graders who are heavy users of social media increase their risk of depression by 27 percent, while those who play sports, go to religious services, or even do homework more than the average teen cut their risk significantly.

Teens who spend three hours a day or more on electronic devices are 35 percent more likely to have a risk factor for suicide, such as making a suicide plan. (That's much more than the risk related to, say, watching TV.) One piece of data that indirectly but stunningly captures kids' growing isolation, for good and for bad: Since 2007, the homicide rate among teens has declined, but the suicide rate has increased. As teens have started spending less time together, they have become less likely to kill one another, and more likely to kill themselves. In 2011, for the first time in 24 years, the teen suicide rate was higher than the teen homicide rate.

Depression and suicide have many causes; too much technology is clearly not the only one. And the teen suicide rate was even higher in the 1990s, long before smartphones existed. Then again, about four times as many Americans now take antidepressants, which are often effective in treating severe depression, the type most strongly linked to suicide.

WHAT'S THE CONNECTION between smartphones and the apparent psychological distress this generation is experiencing? For all their power to link kids day and night, social media also exacerbate the age-old teen concern about being left out. Today's teens may go to fewer parties and spend less time together in person, but when they do congregate, they document their hangouts relentlessly—on Snapchat, Instagram, and Facebook. Those not invited to come along are keenly aware of it. Accordingly, the number of teens who feel left out has reached all-time highs across age groups. Like the increase in loneliness, the upswing in feeling left out has been swift and significant.

This trend has been especially steep among girls. Forty-eight percent more girls said they often felt left out in 2015 than in 2010, compared with 27 percent more boys. Girls use social media more often, giving them additional opportunities to feel excluded and lonely when they see their friends or classmates getting together without them. Social media levy a psychic tax on the teen doing the posting as well, as she anxiously awaits the affirmation of comments and likes. When Athena posts pictures to Instagram, she told me, "I'm nervous about what people think and are going to say. It sometimes bugs me when I don't get a certain amount of likes on a picture."

Girls have also borne the brunt of the rise in depressive symptoms among today's teens. Boys' depressive symptoms increased by 21 percent from 2012 to 2015, while girls' increased by 50 percent—more than twice as much. The rise in suicide, too, is more pronounced among girls. Although the rate increased for both sexes, three times as many 12- to 14-year-old girls killed themselves in 2015 as in 2007, compared with twice as many boys. The suicide rate is still higher for boys, in part because they use more lethal methods, but girls are beginning to close the gap.

These more dire consequences for teenage girls could also be rooted in the fact that they're more likely to experience cyber-bullying. Boys tend to bully one another physically, while girls are more likely to do so by undermining a victim's social status or relationships. Social media give middle- and high-school girls a platform on which to carry out the style of aggression they favor, ostracizing and excluding other girls around the clock.

Social-media companies are of course aware of these problems, and to one degree or another have endeavored to prevent cyberbullying. But their various motivations are, to say the least, complex. A recently leaked Facebook document indicated that the company had been touting to advertisers its ability to determine teens' emotional state based on their on-site behavior, and even to pinpoint "moments when young people need a confidence boost." Facebook acknowledged that the document was real, but denied that it offers "tools to target people based on their emotional state."

In July 2014, a 13-year-old girl in North Texas woke to the smell of something burning. Her phone had overheated and melted into the sheets. National news outlets picked up the story, stoking readers' fears that their cellphone might spontaneously combust. To me, however, the flaming cellphone wasn't the only surprising aspect of the story. *Why*, I wondered, *would anyone sleep with her phone beside her in bed?* It's not as though you can surf the web while you're sleeping. And who could slumber deeply inches from a buzzing phone?

Curious, I asked my undergraduate students at San Diego State University what they do with their phone while they sleep. Their answers were a profile in obsession. Nearly all slept with their phone, putting it under their pillow, on the mattress, or at the very least within arm's reach of the bed. They checked social media right before they went to sleep, and reached for their phone as soon as they woke up in the morning (they had to—all of them used it as their alarm clock). Their phone was the last thing they saw before they went to sleep and the first thing they saw when they woke up. If they woke in the middle of the night, they often ended up looking at their phone. Some used the language of addiction. "I know I shouldn't, but I just can't help it," one said about looking at her phone while in bed. Others saw their phone as an extension of their body—or even like a lover: "Having my phone closer to me while I'm sleeping is a comfort."

It may be a comfort, but the smartphone is cutting into teens' sleep: Many now sleep less than seven hours most nights. Sleep experts say that teens should get about nine hours of sleep a night; a teen who is getting less than seven hours a night is significantly sleep deprived. Fifty-seven percent more teens were sleep deprived in 2015 than in 1991. In just the four years from 2012 to 2015, 22 percent more teens failed to get seven hours of sleep.

The increase is suspiciously timed, once again starting around when most teens got a smartphone. Two national surveys show that teens who spend three or more hours a day on electronic devices are 28 percent more likely to get less than seven hours of sleep than those who spend fewer than three hours, and teens who visit social-media sites every day are 19 percent more likely to be sleep deprived. A meta-analysis of studies on electronic device use among children found similar results: Children who use a media device right before bed are more likely to sleep less than they should, more likely to sleep poorly, and more than twice as likely to be sleepy during the day.

Electronic devices and social media seem to have an especially strong ability to disrupt sleep. Teens who read books and magazines more often than the average are actually slightly less likely to be sleep deprived—either reading lulls them to sleep, or they can put the book down at bedtime. Watching TV for several hours a day is only weakly linked to sleeping less. But the allure of the smartphone is often too much to resist.

Sleep deprivation is linked to myriad issues, including compromised thinking and reasoning, susceptibility to illness, weight gain, and high blood pressure. It also affects mood: People who don't sleep enough are prone to depression and anxiety. Again, it's difficult to trace the precise paths of causation. Smartphones could be causing lack of sleep, which leads to depression, or the phones could be causing depression, which leads to lack of sleep. Or some other factor could be causing both depression and sleep deprivation to rise. But the smartphone, its blue light glowing in the dark, is likely playing a nefarious role.

The correlations between depression and smartphone use are strong enough to suggest that more parents should be telling their kids to put down their phone. As the technology writer Nick Bilton has reported, it's a policy some Silicon Valley executives follow. Even Steve Jobs limited his kids' use of the devices he brought into the world.

What's at stake isn't just how kids experience adolescence. The constant presence of smartphones is likely to affect them well into adulthood. Among people who suffer an episode of depression, at least half become depressed again later in life. Adolescence is a key time for developing social skills; as teens spend less time with their friends face-to-face, they have fewer opportunities to practice them. In the next decade, we may see more adults who know just the right emoji for a situation, but not the right facial expression.

I realize that restricting technology might be an unrealistic demand to impose on a generation of kids so accustomed to being wired at all times. My three daughters were born in 2006, 2009, and 2012. They're not yet old enough to display the traits of iGen teens, but I have already witnessed firsthand just how ingrained new media are in their young lives. I've observed my toddler, barely old enough to walk, confidently swiping her way through an iPad. I've experienced my 6-year-old asking for her own cellphone. I've overheard my 9-year-old discussing the latest app to sweep the fourth grade. Prying the phone out of our kids' hands will be difficult, even more so than the quixotic efforts of my parents' generation to get their kids to turn off MTV and get some fresh air. But more seems to be at stake in urging teens to use their phone responsibly, and there are benefits to be gained even if all we instill in our children is the importance of moderation. Significant effects on both mental health and sleep time appear after two or more hours a day on electronic devices. The average teen spends about two and a half hours a day on electronic devices. Some mild boundary-setting could keep kids from falling into harmful habits.

In my conversations with teens, I saw hopeful signs that kids themselves are beginning to link some of their troubles to their ever-present phone. Athena told me that when she does spend time with her friends in person, they are often looking at their device instead of at her. "I'm trying to talk to them about something, and they don't actually look at my face," she said. "They're looking at their phone, or they're looking at their Apple Watch." "What does that feel like, when you're trying to talk to somebody face-to-face and they're not looking at you?," I asked. "It kind of hurts," she said. "It hurts. I know my parents' generation didn't do that. I could be talking about something super important to me, and they wouldn't even be listening."

Once, she told me, she was hanging out with a friend who was texting her boyfriend. "I was trying to talk to her about my family, and what was going on, and she was like, 'Uh-huh, yeah, whatever.' So I took her phone out of her hands and I threw it at my wall."

I couldn't help laughing. "You play volleyball," I said. "Do you have a pretty good arm?" "Yep," she replied.

Critical Thinking

1. Why do smartphones contribute to mental health problems?
2. How do you feel about the comment that "she'd spent most of the summer hanging out alone in her room with her phone'?
3. Explain how relating on devices may reduce the development of social skills.

Internet References

Sociology—Study Sociology Online
http://edu.learnsoc.org/

Sociology Web Resources
http://www.mhhe.com/socscience/sociology/resources/index.htm

Sociosite
http://www.topsite.com/goto/sociosite.net

Socioweb
http://www.topsite.com/goto/socioweb.com

Unit 4

UNIT

Prepared by: Kurt Finsterbusch, *University of Maryland, College Park*

Stratification and Social Inequalities

People are ranked in many different ways—by physical strength, education, wealth, or other characteristics. Those who are rated highly often have power over others, special status, and prestige. These differences among people constitute their life chances—the probability that an individual or group will be able to obtain the valued and desired goods in a society. These differences are referred to as stratification, the system of structured inequalities in social relationships. In most industrialized societies, income is one of the most important divisions among people. Karl Marx described stratification in terms of class rather than income. For him, social class referred mainly to two distinct groups: those who control the means of production and those who do not. This difference results in great differences in income, wealth, power, status, privileges, and opportunities.

Article   Prepared by: Kurt Finsterbusch, *University of Maryland, College Park*

Why Are Men Dropping Out of Work?

MICHAEL HOUT

Learning Outcomes

After reading this article, you will be able to:

- Understand both Eberstadt's thesis and Hout's counter thesis about men dropping out of work.

- Understand how important men's work is to men's egos.

- Understanding what is included and what is excluded in statistics helps properly interpret them.

America's working man has taken a pounding over the course of the past half-century. According to the most recent data available, 15 percent of men in their prime working years (between 25 and 54) had no job—5 percent were unemployed and 10 percent were neither working nor looking for work. Fifty years earlier, in the summer of 1966, only 5 percent of men in that age range had no job. Most of the decline in male employment took place relatively recently, during the Great Recession, when men's prime-age employment fell 8 percentage points, from 88 percent in the spring of 2007 to 80 percent in December 2009. Since the bottom of the recession, prime-age men have regained 5 percentage points, reaching 85 percent employed in the most recent data.

Nicholas Eberstadt, a demographer at the American Enterprise Institute, sees this as an "invisible crisis" that urgently needs the nation's attention. Eberstadt's rhetoric runs high, but he is right to bring attention to employment trends. American culture measures men's contributions to society in proportion to how hard they work, and most Americans embrace the idea that men's worth is tied up in what they do for a living. Meanwhile, public policy insists on work. Laid-off workers in most states have to produce evidence of job applications in order to collect their unemployment insurance; mothers have to agree to look for employment when they apply for welfare (Temporary Assistance for Needy Families). With this kind of cultural and

policy pressure, it is shocking to learn that 10 percent of prime-age men were neither at work nor looking for work in the fall of 2016. Whether they are idle, injured, criminal, or merely working under the table, they are more numerous than just a decade ago and deserving of public attention for what it tells us about our economy and society.

The question of why more men are jobless is a variant of "Did they jump or were they pushed?" The answer is far from obvious. Job growth had been robust for most of the past three years, clearing out the "discouraged workers" of the Great Recession. That suggests many jobless men "jumped." Eberstadt thinks so. He believes the choices were voluntary and uses words like "hiding," "flight," and "idle" in provocative chapter titles, padding his argument with several dubious statistical comparisons. For example, he compares employment among 20- to 64-year-olds in 1930 and 1940 with their employment in 2016, arguing that work rates for men are lower today than in the Great Depression. But far more 20- to 24-year-olds are now enrolled in college, and employer provided pensions and Social Security enable more 55- to 64-year-old men to retire early. We can't assume men prefer to be idle.

Illness and injury may contribute to joblessness among men of prime working age. The economist Alan B. Krueger estimates that 43 percent of prime-age men who were out of the labor force struggled with what they described as "poor" or "fair" health, 34 percent had a condition that interfered with daily activity or cognitive functioning, and 18 percent had more than one such condition. Half reported pain; 43 percent were taking pain medications.

Two other factors, recessions and incarceration, are critical to the case that prime-age men have been pushed out of work. According to my own research, hard times have been harder on men than women at least since the 1970s. The American economy has suffered seven recessions since 1970. Predictably, American men's prime-age employment has fallen during each one. Although most men have returned to work after each recession, men's employment has not returned all the way to prerecession levels, even during the longest growth periods. Each succeeding recession has dropped men's employment a little lower.

Mass incarceration has added to men's work woes. Men disappear from the data while in prison, but their struggles upon release contribute to the trends that Eberstadt discusses. Ex-felons face grim odds in the job market. Rebuilding a life after prison would be daunting if employers were merely indifferent; most employers aggressively weed out ex-felons. Men returning from prison face background checks and scrutiny when they are lucky enough to get a callback from a prospective employer. Eberstadt walks the reader through the difficulties in estimating the scope and scale of this problem. He then concludes that mass incarceration accounts for both why the United States has a higher proportion of prime-age men out of the labor force than other countries do and why American men's labor force participation has fallen more than American women's since 2000. The analysis is interesting, but to me it works strongly against Eberstadt's view that men are fleeing work. Discrimination against ex-felons is a push factor. The more the aftermath of incarceration matters, the less likely it is that out of work men need new incentives to seek employment. Perhaps they need remedial education or training. They almost certainly need advocacy and legal protection.

How Do Men Without Work Survive? Most Rely on Family

How do men without work survive? Most rely on family. Their employed wives, cohabiting partners, and sometimes even grown children support them. Many get benefits from federal and state programs, but the government does not know how many do so. Each program keeps records, but since the records are not linked, the government and researchers have a hard time estimating how many men get benefits from multiple sources or how many men are left out of all programs. This is the strongest and most original part of Eberstadt's book.

Eberstadt asserts that falling employment reduced economic growth, exacerbated inequality, and increased public debt. I think he has the first two backward. Fleeing workers did not precipitate recessions; recessions pushed those men out of the workforce. Inequality did not come from voluntary pay reductions by idle men; it came about because capital now reaps the rewards of whatever growth occurs. And disability programs, which replace only a fraction of the wages sick and hurt men have lost, are not a major factor in public debt. Manual work in the service economy damages joints, backs, and heads just as manual work in the higher paid industrial past did. If there

is fraud, find it and prosecute it. But if not, employers' and employees' contributions to Social Security disability insurance should be raised to meet the needs of the disabled.

Public policy should offer incentives to those who have left work and a path back to legitimate employment for those blocked by a criminal record or discrimination. The best incentives are a choice of jobs and rising pay. Until recently, the U.S. economy created about 200,000 jobs a month while wages stagnated. These trends increased prime-age men's employment ratio from 81 percent in September 2009 to 85 percent in October 2016, according to the Bureau of Labor Statistics. Unemployed men (those without a job and looking for work) found employment, but prime-age men's labor force participation fell slightly from 90 percent in September 2009 to 89 percent in October 2016. The increases have all been so recent that we can only say that they did not immediately increase labor force participation.

As states release more men from prison, both ex-felons and would-be employers will need a way to come together. Opening the gates and setting the former inmates free will not, by itself, create demand for their labor. Matching men released from prison with employers willing to hire them will be a challenge. Most prisoners have only a high-school education or less. While some earn credentials in prison, most will need a way to demonstrate that they are ready, willing, and able to work, and a third party to vet them.

When Eberstadt gets to his policy recommendations, his often-original book gets conventional and familiar. He pushes tax and benefit cuts and is vague on the path that might lead from tax cuts to higher employment. The argument is too thin to convince anyone who does not already believe in tax cuts as an all-purpose fix. Evidence from a state where tax cuts worked would help here. My casual reading suggests that Kansas's crumbling state economy contradicts his argument, as does California's ongoing boom. Cutting benefits could spur men who are faking disabilities to seek work, I suppose. But Eberstadt shows no evidence that men on disability are cheating. If they are suffering as much as Krueger's data indicate, cutting benefits would harm men who need help without changing employment trends.

Eberstadt is right to point to a serious issue, but to make progress, we need to calibrate the scope and scale of the problem correctly. A 10-point drop in men's prime-age employment ratio from a historic peak is consequential, but hardly the "death of work."

Eberstadt and I are demographers. We write with numbers and think our graphs are pictures. We can talk to each other in this language. But when I read the data, specific people come to my mind. One is a guy who, in the 1990s, hoped to ride the dot-com boom to a six-figure income. Obsessive computer coding led to overmedication and, now, disability checks. The other is a neighbor who fought in the first Iraq War. He leans on his walker down by the bodega and talks to any passerby who will listen. People-you-know is a lousy sample, but their stories make me doubt that men out of work chose their path.

We have to respond to falling employment among working-age men, but we cannot rely on the usual prescriptions. The idle among them need incentives, the injured need care, and the formerly incarcerated need just one employer willing to give them a break—and maybe some legal protection to make that break more likely.

Critical Thinking

1. Site some work requirements for welfare recipients.
2. How do men survive without work?
3. Explain how jobs, unemployment, and the economy work together.

Internet References

Sociology—Study Sociology Online
    http://edu.learnsoc.org/

Sociology Web Resources
    http://www.mhhe.com/socscience/sociology/resources/index.htm

Sociosite
    http://www.topsite.com/goto/sociosite.net

Socioweb
    http://www.topsite.com/goto/socioweb.com

Article   Prepared by: Kurt Finsterbusch, *University of Maryland, College Park*

The State of Poverty in America

PETER EDELMAN

Learning Outcomes

After reading this article, you will be able to:

- Understand the extent of poverty in America and the two basic poverty problems this article identifies.

- Know the progress that has been made against poverty and the major policies and developments that have created this progress.

- Understand the differences between persistent and temporary poverty and the appropriate policies for each.

The problem is worse than we thought, but we can solve it.

We have two basic poverty problems in the United States. One is the prevalence of low-wage work. The other concerns those who have almost no work.

The two overlap.

Most people who are poor work as much as they can and go in and out of poverty. Fewer people have little or no work on a continuing basis, but they are in much worse straits and tend to stay poor from one generation to the next.

The numbers in both categories are stunning.

Low-wage work encompasses people with incomes below twice the poverty line—not poor but struggling all the time to make ends meet. They now total 103 million, which means that fully one-third of the population has an income below what would be $36,000 for a family of three.

In the bottom tier are 20.5 million people—6.7 percent of the population—who are in deep poverty, with an income less than half the poverty line (below $9,000 for a family of three). Some 6 million people out of those 20.5 million have no income at all other than food stamps.

These dire facts tempt one to believe that there may be some truth to President Ronald Reagan's often-quoted declaration that "we fought a war against poverty and poverty won." But

that is not the case. Our public policies have been remarkably successful. Starting with the Social Security Act of 1935, continuing with the burst of activity in the 1960s, and on from there, we have made great progress.

We enacted Medicaid and the Children's Health Insurance Program, and many health indicators for low-income people improved. We enacted food stamps, and the near-starvation conditions we saw in some parts of the country were ameliorated. We enacted the Earned Income Tax Credit and the Child Tax Credit, and the incomes of low-wage workers with children were lifted. We enacted Pell grants, and millions of people could afford college who otherwise couldn't possibly attend. We enacted Supplemental Security Income and thereby raised the income floor for elderly and disabled people whose earnings from work didn't provide enough Social Security. There is much more—housing vouchers, Head Start, child-care assistance, and legal services for the poor, to name a few. The Obama administration and Congress added 16 million people to Medicaid in the Affordable Care Act, appropriated billions to improve the education of low-income children, and spent an impressive amount on the least well-off in the Recovery Act.

All in all, our various public policies kept a remarkable 40 million people from falling into poverty in 2010—about half because of Social Security and half due to the other programs just mentioned. To assert that we fought a war against poverty and poverty won because there is still poverty is like saying that the Clean Air and Clean Water acts failed because there is still pollution.

Nonetheless, the level of poverty in the nation changed little between 1970 and 2000 and is much worse now. It was at 11.1 percent in 1973—the lowest level achieved since we began measuring—and after going up sharply during the Reagan and George H.W. Bush years, went back down during the 1990s to 11.3 percent in 2000, as President Bill Clinton left office.

Why didn't it fall further? The economics have been working against us for four decades, exacerbated by trends in family composition. Well-paying industrial jobs disappeared to other countries and to automation. The economy grew, but the fruits of the growth went exclusively to those at the top. Other jobs replaced the ones lost, but most of the new jobs paid much less. The wage of the median-paying job barely grew—by one measure going up only about 7 percent over the 38 years from 1973 to 2011. Half the jobs in the country now pay less than $33,000 a year, and a quarter pay less than the poverty line of $22,000 for a family of four. We have become a low-wage economy to a far greater extent than we realize.

Households with only one wage-earner—typically those headed by single mothers—have found it extremely difficult to support a family. The share of families with children headed by single mothers rose from 12.8 percent in 1970 to 26.2 percent in 2010 (and from 37.1 percent in 1971 to 52.8 percent in 2010 among African Americans). In 2010, 46.9 percent of children under 18 living in households headed by a single mother were poor.

The percentage of people in deep poverty has doubled since 1976. A major reason for this rise is the near death of cash assistance for families with children. Welfare has shrunk from 14 million recipients (too many, in my view) before the Temporary Assistance for Needy Families law (TANF) was enacted in 1996 to 4.2 million today, just 1.5 percent of the population. At last count, Wyoming had 607 people on TANF, or just 2.7 percent of its poor children. Twenty-six states have less than 20 percent of their poor children on TANF. The proportion of poor families with children receiving welfare has shrunk from 68 percent before TANF was enacted to 27 percent today.

What's the agenda going forward? The heart of it is creating jobs that yield a living income. Restoring prosperity, ensuring that the economy functions at or near full employment, is our most powerful anti-poverty weapon. We need more, though—a vital union sector and a higher minimum wage, for two. We also need work supports—health care, child care, and help with the cost of housing and postsecondary education. These are all income equivalents—all policies that will contribute to bringing everyone closer to having a living income.

There's a gigantic problem here, however: We look to be headed to a future of too many low-wage jobs. Wages in China, India, and other emerging economies may be rising, but we can't foresee any substantial increase in the prevailing wage for many millions of American jobs. That means we better start talking about wage supplements that are much bigger than the Earned Income Tax Credit. We need a dose of reality about the future of the American paycheck.

The second big problem is the crisis—and it is a crisis—posed by the 20 million people at the bottom of the economy.

We have a huge hole in our safety net. In many states, TANF and food stamps combined don't even get people to half of the poverty line, and a substantial majority of poor families don't receive TANF at all.

Even worse, we have destroyed the safety net for the poorest children in the country. Seven million women and children are among the 20.5 million in deep poverty. One in four children in a household headed by a single mother is in deep poverty. We have to restore the safety net for the poorest of the poor.

Getting serious about investing in our children—from prenatal care and early-childhood assistance on through education at all levels—is also essential if we are to achieve a future without such calamitous levels of poverty. In addition, we must confront the destruction being wrought by the criminal-justice system. These are poverty issues and race issues as well. The schools and the justice system present the civil-rights challenges of this century.

Combining all of the problems in vicious interaction is the question of place—the issues that arise from having too many poor people concentrated in one area, whether in the inner city, Appalachia, the Mississippi Delta, or on Indian reservations. Such places are home to a minority of the poor, but they include a hugely disproportionate share of intergenerational and persistent poverty. Our most serious policy failing over the past four-plus decades has been our neglect of this concentrated poverty. We have held our own in other respects, but we have lost ground here.

Finally, we need to be much more forthright about how much all of this has to do with race and gender. It is always important to emphasize that white people make up the largest number of the poor, to counter the stereotype that the face of poverty is one of color. At the same time, though, we must face more squarely that African Americans, Latinos, and Native Americans are all poor at almost three times the rate of whites and ask why that continues to be true. We need as a nation to be more honest about who it is that suffers most from terrible schools and the way we lock people up. Poverty most definitely cuts across racial lines, but it doesn't cut evenly.

There's a lot to do.

Critical Thinking

1. Why is there so much poverty in America when America used to claim that it was the richest nation in the world?

2. How much do prejudice, bias, blaming the victim, and other attitudinal factors factor into the poverty problem?

3. Does America have a safety net? Is there a hole in the safety net?

Internet References

Sociosite

www.topsite.com/goto/sociosite.net

Socioweb

www.topsite.com/goto/socioweb.com

Sociology—Study Sociology Online

http://edu.learnsoc.org

Sociology Web Resources

www.mhhe.com/socscience/sociology/resources/index.htm

Article   Prepared by: Kurt Finsterbusch, *University of Maryland, College Park*

The End of Welfare as I Knew It

How Temporary Assistance for Needy Families Failed the Test of the Great Recession

Diana Spatz

Learning Outcomes

After reading this article, you will be able to:

- Determine what TANF has accomplished.

- Determine what TANF has not accomplished.

- Identify administrative problems of the current welfare system.

I'll always remember the day President Clinton signed Temporary Assistance to Needy Families (TANF), or welfare reform, into law. It was August 1996, and I was reading the morning paper in Barstow, California, completing the last leg of a cross-country road trip I'd taken with my daughter to celebrate my finishing school. Having just earned my bachelor's degree from the University of California, Berkeley, I would finally earn enough to get my family off welfare—and out of poverty—for good. As I read the news that the Personal Responsibility and Work Opportunity Reconciliation Act had become law, I hung my head and cried. I felt like I'd crossed a bridge just as it collapsed behind me, and worried what would become of mothers who remained trapped on the other side.

Since 1996, politicians have bragged about passing welfare reform. Even House Speaker John Boehner recently praised TANF as a bipartisan success. But successful at what? If kicking low-income children and their families off welfare is the measure, then TANF was a huge success. States were given bonuses for reducing their caseloads rather than reducing poverty. As long as families were off the rolls, it didn't matter how or why. Studies show that parents were ten times more likely to get cut off welfare because of punitive sanctions than because they got jobs paying enough to "income off." In many states, "full family"

sanctions cut low-income children off welfare along with their parents. Under the "work first" mantra, TANF caseloads plummeted by almost 70 percent, as nearly 9 million low-income parents and children were purged from the national welfare rolls by 2008. Given the four goals of TANF—promoting low-wage work, encouraging marriage, reducing caseloads and curtailing out-of-wedlock births—these outcomes are no surprise. But if the measure of success is poverty reduction, TANF has failed.

To start, its restrictions on postsecondary education and training—the most effective pathway out of poverty for parents on welfare—make earning a bachelor's degree nearly impossible. Even earning an associate degree is difficult. "Any job is a good job" was the slogan emblazoned on the walls of county welfare agencies across the country, as tens of thousands of low-income mothers were made to quit college to do up to thirty-five hours per week of unpaid "workfare": sweeping streets, picking up trash in parks and cleaning public restrooms in exchange for benefits as low as $240 a month.

Contrary to "welfare queen" stereotypes, like most welfare mothers, I worked first. Work wasn't the problem; it was the nature of the work—low-wage, dead-end jobs with no benefits and little chance for advancement—that kept families like mine on the welfare rolls. Investing in my education enabled me to break that cycle and earn a solid upper-middle-class income. I now pay three times more in taxes than I used to earn working full time in a low-wage, dead-end job.

This trajectory is what motivated mothers like Rya Frontera and Melissa Johnson to pursue nursing degrees, despite being sanctioned: having their families' cash grants cut off and losing childcare and transportation assistance when they refused to quit school. Whereas mothers in "work first" programs earn less than $9,000 a year, after completing her BS in nursing Melissa graduated off welfare to a career-path job as a registered nurse making

$90,000 a year. Similarly, Rya is now a full-time nurse with full benefits working for Kaiser. Not only are they off welfare permanently; both women are filling a crucial labor market need, as our nation faces a nursing shortage with no end in sight. Isn't that how welfare should work?

It is also time to end the arbitrary rules under TANF that imposed a lifetime limit of sixty months for receiving benefits, and that allowed states to enact shorter time limits. It took me ten years to overcome a lifetime of physical, emotional and sexual abuse; depression; and post-traumatic stress disorder, one or more of which have been experienced by most mothers on welfare as girls or adults—or in my case, both. In California—home to one-third of welfare families nationally—the experience of "timed off" families clearly challenges the notion that five years is enough; TANF's work-first emphasis relegated many parents to low-wage jobs that didn't pay enough to get their families off welfare, let alone out of poverty. Consequently, in 2003 the vast majority of parents in California's CalWORKs program who reached their sixty-month limit were working and playing by the rules when they timed off welfare for the rest of their lives. And this year, like many states, California shortened its lifetime limit to forty-eight months in response to budget shortfalls, despite having the second-highest unemployment rate in the country. As a result, 22,500 parents were permanently cut off the welfare rolls on July 1.

Ashley Proctor, a young single mother in Oakland, was doing her thirty-two-hour weekly work requirement when she timed off. Her benefits were cut to a "child only" grant of $320 per month. "My son and I are sleeping on a friend's sofa," she says. "On the weekends I take him to our storage unit so he can play with his toys." That's better than what mothers faced in other states, where time limits as short as twenty-one months were enacted. How unfortunate that Congress, in its infinite wisdom, didn't put a time limit on poverty instead.

While states like California curtailed much-needed benefits, under welfare reform billions in federal funds were invested in unproven "marriage promotion" programs to marry poor women off the welfare rolls. Never mind that in some of California's most populous counties in 2003, most timed-off parents were already in two-parent families where one was working. And in a cruel twist, while billions were spent on marriage promotion programs that were mandatory for the states, the Family Violence Option let states choose whether to provide domestic violence services in their TANF programs, including waivers of time limits and welfare-to-work rules. Furthermore, although research shows that women who receive welfare experience domestic violence at double the rate of all American women, not a dime in federal funding was provided for family violence services. Even in California,

which adopted the FVO, studies show that as many as 80 percent of CalWORKs mothers are domestic violence victims. Of these, less than 1 percent get family violence counseling and services, and less than one-quarter of 1 percent get waivers from welfare work requirements that could save their lives.

This includes mothers like Felicia Jones, whom my agency, Low-Income Families' Empowerment Through Education, or LIFETIME, was helping when she went into hiding after her ex threatened to kill her and their children. While on the run, Felicia got a notice of a mandatory welfare-to-work appointment, which had been scheduled on the same day and time as the hearing for her restraining order. When she called to say she couldn't make the appointment, her caseworker said she couldn't help her and hung up the phone, and later sanctioned Felicia for missing that appointment. Despite my urging, Felicia was too afraid to request a state appeals hearing and later disappeared. To this day, I don't know what happened to her and her children.

Fifteen years of welfare reform, and what do we have to show for it? Poverty is at its highest level in nearly twenty years. The number of children living in deep poverty—in families with income less than 50 percent of the poverty line—is at its highest level in thirty-five years. The unemployment rate for single mothers, who represent 90 percent of parents in the welfare system, has nearly doubled, to a twenty-five-year high. Welfare rolls are rising for the first time since TANF was passed, despite efforts by states to tighten time limits and make it harder for families to get help. In Georgia, for example, families applying for TANF have faced "wait periods" before they can get cash assistance—the welfare equivalent of a poll tax or literacy test—with caseworkers offering to send children into foster care or put them up for adoption to ease the burden. Consequently, since 2002 Georgia increased TANF spending on child welfare–related services by 245 percent. According to Clare Richie, a senior policy analyst with the Georgia Budget and Policy Institute, the state now spends more on adoption services and foster care (58 percent) than it does on assistance to families.

This trend is alarming to people like Georgia State Senator Donzella James, who has been getting calls from constituents whose children are being taken away by the Department of Family and Child Services, the state's welfare agency. "One woman told me, 'I'm not a bad mother. I'm just unemployed,'" she said. Similarly, Arizona, Rhode Island and Texas spend nearly half their TANF block grants on child welfare–related services. One has to wonder if this was the plan all along, given the proposal by Newt Gingrich, who was House speaker when TANF was created, to use orphanages to reduce the welfare rolls.

The Great Recession was the first true test of welfare reform during an economic downturn, and TANF failed the grade miserably. The proof is in the numbers: in 1995 the old welfare program served at least eight out of every ten low-income children, including mine. Today TANF serves only two out of every ten poor children nationwide. In passing TANF, Congress and Bill Clinton made good on their promise to "end welfare as we know it." It's time to end welfare reform as we know it instead.

Critical Thinking

1. Poverty is at its highest level in nearly twenty years. Does that mean that TANF has failed?

2. Why are welfare rolls now rising?

3. Does TANF address the incentives problem of welfare?

Internet References

Sociosite
www.topsite.com/goto/sociosite.net

Socioweb
www.topsite.com/goto/socioweb.com

Sociology—Study Sociology Online
http://edu.learnsoc.org

Sociology Web Resources
www.mhhe.com/socscience/sociology/resources/index.htm

DIANA SPATZ is executive director of LIFETIME, a statewide organization of low-income parents in California who are pursuing postsecondary education and training as their pathway out of poverty.

Article   Prepared by: Kurt Finsterbusch, *University of Maryland, College Park*

Emmett and Trayvon

How Racial Prejudice in America Has Changed in the Last Sixty Years

Elijah Anderson

Learning Outcomes

After reading this article, you will be able to:

- Understand how racial prejudice has substantially changed in the past sixty years.
- Assess the remaining problems of racism and how they might be addressed.
- Note how the ghetto plays a significant role in racial prejudice today.

Separated by a thousand miles, two state borders, and nearly six decades, two young African American boys met tragic fates that seem remarkably similar today: both walked into a small market to buy some candy; both ended up dead.

The first boy is Emmett Till, who was fourteen years old in the summer of 1955 when he walked into a local grocery store in Money, Mississippi, to buy gum. He was later roused from bed, beaten brutally, and possibly shot by a group of white men who later dumped his body in a nearby river. They claimed he had stepped out of his place by flirting with a young white woman, the wife of the store's owner. The second boy is Trayvon Martin, who was seventeen years old late last winter when he walked into a 7-Eleven near a gated community in Sanford, Florida, to buy Skittles and an iced tea. He was later shot to death at close range by a mixed-race man, who claimed Martin had behaved suspiciously and seemed out of place. The deaths of both boys galvanized the nation, drew sympathy and disbelief across racial lines, and, through the popular media, prompted a reexamination of race relations.

In the aftermath of Martin's death last February, a handful of reporters and columnists, and many members of the general public, made the obvious comparison: Trayvon Martin, it seemed, was the Emmett Till of our times. And while that comparison has some merit—the boys' deaths are similar both in some of their details and in their tragic outcome—these killings must also be understood as the result of very different strains of racial tension in America. The racism that led to Till's death was embedded in a virulent ideology of white racial superiority born out of slavery and the Jim Crow codes, particularly in the Deep South. That sort of racism hinges on the idea that blacks are an inherently inferior race, a morally null group that deserves both the subjugation and poverty it gets.

The racial prejudice that led to Trayvon Martin's death is different. While it, too, was born of America's painful legacy of slavery and segregation, and informed by those old concepts of racial order—that blacks have their "place" in society—it in addition reflects the urban iconography of today's racial inequality, namely the black ghetto, a uniquely urban American creation. Strikingly, this segregation of the black community coexists with an ongoing racial incorporation process that has produced the largest black middle class in history, and that reflects the extraordinary social progress this country has made since the 1960s. The civil rights movement paved the way for blacks and other people of color to access public and professional opportunities and spaces that would have been unimaginable in Till's time.

While the sort of racism that led to Till's death still exists in society today, Americans in general have a much more nuanced, more textured attitude toward race than anything we've seen before, and usually that attitude does not manifest in overtly hateful, exclusionary, or violent acts. Instead, it manifests in pervasive mindsets and stereotypes that all black people start from the inner-city ghetto and are therefore stigmatized by their association with its putative amorality, danger, crime, and poverty. Hence, in public a black person is burdened with a negative presumption that he must disprove before he can establish mutually trusting relationships with others.

Most consequentially, black skin, and its association with the ghetto, translates into a deficit of credibility as black skin is conflated with lower-class status. This deficit impacts poor blacks of the ghetto one way and middle-class black people another. While middle-class blacks may be able to successfully disabuse others of their negative presumptions, lower-class blacks may not. For instance, all blacks, particularly "ghetto-looking" young men, are at risk of enduring yet another "stop and frisk" from the police as well as suspicion from potential employers, shopkeepers, and strangers on the street. Members of the black middle class and black professionals can usually pass inspection and withstand such scrutiny; many poorer blacks cannot. And many blacks who have never stepped foot in a ghetto must repeatedly prove themselves as non-ghetto, often operating in a provisional status, in the workplace or, say, a fancy restaurant, until they can convince others—either by speaking "white" English or by demonstrating intelligence, poise, or manners—that they are to be trusted, that they are not "one of those" blacks from the ghetto, and that they deserve respect. In other words, a middle-class black man who is, for instance, waiting in line for an ATM at night will in many cases be treated with a level of suspicion that a middle-class white man simply does not experience.

But this pervasive cultural association—black skin equals the ghetto—does not come out of the blue. After all, as a result of historical, political, and economic factors, blacks have been confined in the ghetto. Today, with persistent housing discrimination and the disappearance of manufacturing jobs, America's ghettos face structural poverty. In addition, crime and homicide rates within those communities are high, young black men are typically the ones killing one another, and ghetto culture, made iconic by artists like Tupac Shakur, 50 Cent, and the Notorious B.I.G., is inextricably intertwined with blackness.

As a result, in America's collective imagination the ghetto is a dangerous, scary part of the city. It's where rap comes from, where drugs are sold, where hoodlums rule, and where The Wire might have been filmed. Above all, to many white Americans the ghetto is where "the black people live," and thus, as the misguided logic follows, all black people live in the ghetto. It's that pervasive, if accidental, fallacy that's at the root of the wider society's perceptions of black people today. While it may be true that everyone who lives in a certain ghetto is black, it is patently untrue that everyone who is black lives in a ghetto. Regardless, black people of all classes, including those born and raised far from the inner cities and those who've never been in a ghetto, are by virtue of skin color alone stigmatized by the place.

I call this idea the "iconic ghetto," and it has become a powerful source of stereotype, prejudice, and discrimination in our society, negatively defining the black person in public. In some ways, the iconic ghetto reflects the old version of racism that led to Till's death. In Till's day, a black person's "place" was in the field, in the maid's quarters, or in the back of the bus. If a black man was found "out of his place," he could be punished, jailed, or lynched. In Martin's day—in our day—a black person's "place" is in the ghetto. If he is found "out of his place," like in a fancy hotel lobby, on a golf course, or, say, in an upscale community, he can be treated with suspicion, avoided, pulled over, frisked, arrested—or worse.

Trayvon Martin's death is an example of how this more current type of racial stereotyping works. While the facts of the case are still under investigation, from what is known it seems fair to say that George Zimmerman, Martin's killer, saw a young black man wearing a hoodie and assumed he was from the ghetto and therefore "out of place" in the Retreat at Twin Lakes, Zimmerman's gated community. Until recently, Twin Lakes was a safe, largely middle-class neighborhood. But as a result of collapsing housing prices, it has been witnessing an influx of renters and a rash of burglaries. Some of the burglaries have been committed by black men. Zimmerman, who is himself of mixed race (of Latino, black, and white descent), did not have a history of racism, and his family has claimed that he had previously volunteered handing out leaflets at black churches protesting the assault of a homeless black man. The point is, Zimmerman did not shoot and kill Martin because he hates black people. It seems that he put a gun in his pocket and followed Martin after making the assumption that Martin's black skin and choice of dress meant that he was from the ghetto, and therefore up to no good; he was a threat. And that's an important distinction.

Zimmerman acted brashly and was almost certainly motivated by assumptions about young black men, but he did not act brutally out of hatred for Martin's race. That does not make Zimmerman's actions excusable, but it does make his actions understandable in a way that Till's murderers' heinous brutality is not.

The complex racially charged drama that led to Martin's death is indicative of both our history and our rapid and uneven racial progress as a society. While there are no longer clear demarcations separating blacks and whites in social strata, there have been major racial changes that do just that. It's no longer uncommon to see black people in positions of power, in boardrooms, universities, hospitals, and judges' chambers, but we must also face the reality that poverty, unemployment, and incarceration still break down along racial lines.

This situation fuels the iconic ghetto, including a prevalent assumption among many white Americans, even among some progressive whites who are not by any measure traditionally racist, that there are two types of blacks: those residing in the ghetto, and those who appear to have played by the rules and become successful. In situations in which black people encounter strangers, many often feel they have to prove as quickly as possible that they belong in the latter category in order to be accepted and treated with respect. As a result of this pervasive dichotomy—that there are "ghetto" and "non-ghetto" blacks—many middle-class blacks actively work to separate and distance themselves from the popular association of their race with the ghetto by deliberately dressing well or by spurning hip-hop, rap, and ghetto styles of dress. Similarly, some blacks, when interacting with whites, may cultivate an overt, sometimes unnaturally formal way of speaking to distance themselves from "those" black people from the ghetto.

But it's also not that simple. Strikingly, many middle-class black young people, most of whom have no personal connection with the ghetto, go out of their way in the other direction, claiming the ghetto by adopting its symbols, including styles of dress, patterns of speech, or choice of music, as a means of establishing their authenticity as "still Black" in the largely white middle class; they want to demonstrate they have not "sold out." Thus, the iconic ghetto is, paradoxically, both a stigma and a sign of authenticity for some American blacks—a kind of double bind that beleaguers many middle-class black parents.

Despite the significant racial progress our society has made since Till's childhood, from the civil rights movement to the reelection of President Obama, the pervasive association of black people with the ghetto, and therefore with a certain social station, betrays a persistent cultural lag. After all, it has only been two generations since schools were legally desegregated, five decades since blacks and whites started drinking from the same water fountains. If Till were alive today, he'd remember when restaurants had "White Only" entrances and when stories of lynchings peppered the New York Times. He'd also remember the Freedom Riders, Martin Luther King Jr., and the Million Man March. He'd remember when his peers became generals and justices, and when a black man, just twenty years his junior, became president of the United States. He would have been seventy-three—had he lived.

Critical Thinking

1. What is the role of generational change in the changes in race relations?

2. What are some of the best ways for people to reduce their negative racial attitudes?

3. What role has the election of a black president had in reducing or increasing racial prejudice?

Internet References

Sociosite
www.topsite.com/goto/sociosite.net

Socioweb
www.topsite.com/goto/socioweb.com

Sociology—Study Sociology Online
http://edu.learnsoc.org

Sociology Web Resources
www.mhhe.com/socscience/sociology/resources/index.htm

ELIJAH ANDERSON is the William K. Lanman Jr. Professor of Sociology at Yale University. His latest book is *The Cosmopolitan Canopy: Race and Civility in Everyday Life.*

Anderson, Elijah. From *Washington Monthly,* January/February 2013. Copyright ©2013 by Washington Monthly Publishing, LLC, 1319 F St. NW, Suite 710, Washington, DC 20004. (202) 393–5155. Reprinted by permission. www.washingtonmonthly.com

Article   Prepared by: Kurt Finsterbusch, *University of Maryland, College Park*

Free and Equal in Dignity and LGBT Rights

HILLARY RODHAM CLINTON

Learning Outcomes

After reading this article, you will be able to:

- Evaluate the significance of the Universal Declaration of Human Rights that the United Nations passed in 1948 without a negative vote.

- Understand the progress on human rights that has occurred since the declaration.

- Identify the critical issues that are involved in extending the declaration to LGBT equality.

Good evening, and let me express my deep honor and pleasure at being here. I want to thank Director General Tokayev and Ms. Wyden along with other ministers, ambassadors, excellencies, and UN partners. This weekend, we will celebrate Human Rights Day, the anniversary of one of the great accomplishments of the last century.

Beginning in 1947, delegates from six continents devoted themselves to drafting a declaration that would enshrine the fundamental rights and freedoms of people everywhere. In the aftermath of World War II, many nations pressed for a statement of this kind to help ensure that we would prevent future atrocities and protect the inherent humanity and dignity of all people. And so the delegates went to work. They discussed, they wrote, they revisited, revised, rewrote, for thousands of hours. And they incorporated suggestions and revisions from governments, organizations and individuals around the world.

At three o'clock in the morning on December 10th, 1948, after nearly two years of drafting and one last long night of debate, the president of the UN General Assembly called for a vote on the final text. Forty-eight nations voted in favor; eight abstained; none dissented. And the Universal Declaration of Human Rights was adopted. It proclaims a simple, powerful idea: All human beings are born free and equal in dignity and rights. And with the declaration, it was made clear that rights are not conferred by government; they are the birthright of all people. It does not matter what country we live in, who our leaders are, or even who we are. Because we are human, we therefore have rights. And because we have rights, governments are bound to protect them.

In the 63 years since the declaration was adopted, many nations have made great progress in making human rights a human reality. Step by step, barriers that once prevented people from enjoying the full measure of liberty, the full experience of dignity, and the full benefits of humanity have fallen away. In many places, racist laws have been repealed, legal and social practices that relegated women to second-class status have been abolished, the ability of religious minorities to practice their faith freely has been secured.

In most cases, this progress was not easily won. People fought and organized and campaigned in public squares and private spaces to change not only laws, but hearts and minds. And thanks to that work of generations, for millions of individuals whose lives were once narrowed by injustice, they are now able to live more freely and to participate more fully in the political, economic, and social lives of their communities.

Now, there is still, as you all know, much more to be done to secure that commitment, that reality, and progress for all people. Today, I want to talk about the work we have left to do to protect one group of people whose human rights are still denied in too many parts of the world today. In many ways, they are an invisible minority. They are arrested, beaten, terrorized, even executed. Many are treated with contempt and violence by their fellow citizens while authorities empowered to protect them look the other way or, too often, even join in the abuse. They are denied opportunities to work and learn, driven from their homes and countries, and forced to suppress or deny who they are to protect themselves from harm.

I am talking about gay, lesbian, bisexual, and transgender people, human beings born free and given bestowed equality and dignity, who have a right to claim that, which is now one of the remaining human rights challenges of our time. I speak about this subject knowing that my own country's record on human rights for gay people is far from perfect. Until 2003, it was still a crime in parts of our country. Many LGBT Americans have endured violence and harassment in their own lives, and for some, including many young people, bullying and exclusion are daily experiences. So we, like all nations, have more work to do to protect human rights at home.

Now, raising this issue, I know, is sensitive for many people and that the obstacles standing in the way of protecting the human rights of LGBT people rest on deeply held personal, political, cultural, and religious beliefs. So I come here before you with respect, understanding, and humility. Even though progress on this front is not easy, we cannot delay acting. So in that spirit, I want to talk about the difficult and important issues we must address together to reach a global consensus that recognizes the human rights of LGBT citizens everywhere.

The first issue goes to the heart of the matter. Some have suggested that gay rights and human rights are separate and distinct; but, in fact, they are one and the same. Now, of course, 60 years ago, the governments that drafted and passed the Universal Declaration of Human Rights were not thinking about how it applied to the LGBT community. They also weren't thinking about how it applied to indigenous people or children or people with disabilities or other marginalized groups. Yet in the past 60 years, we have come to recognize that members of these groups are entitled to the full measure of dignity and rights, because, like all people, they share a common humanity.

This recognition did not occur all at once. It evolved over time. And as it did, we understood that we were honoring rights that people always had, rather than creating new or special rights for them. Like being a woman, like being a racial, religious, tribal, or ethnic minority, being LGBT does not make you less human. And that is why gay rights are human rights, and human rights are gay rights.

It is violation of human rights when people are beaten or killed because of their sexual orientation, or because they do not conform to cultural norms about how men and women should look or behave. It is a violation of human rights when governments declare it illegal to be gay, or allow those who harm gay people to go unpunished. It is a violation of human rights when lesbian or transgendered women are subjected to so-called corrective rape, or forcibly subjected to hormone treatments, or when people are murdered after public calls for violence toward gays, or when they are forced to flee their

nations and seek asylum in other lands to save their lives. And it is a violation of human rights when life-saving care is withheld from people because they are gay, or equal access to justice is denied to people because they are gay, or public spaces are out of bounds to people because they are gay. No matter what we look like, where we come from, or who we are, we are all equally entitled to our human rights and dignity.

The second issue is a question of whether homosexuality arises from a particular part of the world. Some seem to believe it is a Western phenomenon, and therefore people outside the West have grounds to reject it. Well, in reality, gay people are born into and belong to every society in the world. They are all ages, all races, all faiths; they are doctors and teachers, farmers and bankers, soldiers and athletes; and whether we know it, or whether we acknowledge it, they are our family, our friends, and our neighbors.

Being gay is not a Western invention; it is a human reality. And protecting the human rights of all people, gay or straight, is not something that only Western governments do. South Africa's constitution, written in the aftermath of Apartheid, protects the equality of all citizens, including gay people. In Colombia and Argentina, the rights of gays are also legally protected. In Nepal, the supreme court has ruled that equal rights apply to LGBT citizens. The Government of Mongolia has committed to pursue new legislation that will tackle anti-gay discrimination.

Now, some worry that protecting the human rights of the LGBT community is a luxury that only wealthy nations can afford. But in fact, in all countries, there are costs to not protecting these rights, in both gay and straight lives lost to disease and violence, and the silencing of voices and views that would strengthen communities, in ideas never pursued by entrepreneurs who happen to be gay. Costs are incurred whenever any group is treated as lesser or the other, whether they are women, racial, or religious minorities, or the LGBT. Former President Mogae of Botswana pointed out recently that for as long as LGBT people are kept in the shadows, there cannot be an effective public health program to tackle HIV and AIDS. Well, that holds true for other challenges as well.

The third, and perhaps most challenging, issue arises when people cite religious or cultural values as a reason to violate or not to protect the human rights of LGBT citizens. This is not unlike the justification offered for violent practices towards women like honor killings, widow burning, or female genital mutilation. Some people still defend those practices as part of a cultural tradition. But violence toward women isn't cultural; it's criminal. Likewise with slavery, what was once justified as sanctioned by God is now properly reviled as an unconscionable violation of human rights.

In each of these cases, we came to learn that no practice or tradition trumps the human rights that belong to all of us. And this holds true for inflicting violence on LGBT people, criminalizing their status or behavior, expelling them from their families and communities, or tacitly or explicitly accepting their killing.

Of course, it bears noting that rarely are cultural and religious traditions and teachings actually in conflict with the protection of human rights. Indeed, our religion and our culture are sources of compassion and inspiration toward our fellow human beings. It was not only those who've justified slavery who leaned on religion, it was also those who sought to abolish it. And let us keep in mind that our commitments to protect the freedom of religion and to defend the dignity of LGBT people emanate from a common source. For many of us, religious belief and practice is a vital source of meaning and identity, and fundamental to who we are as people. And likewise, for most of us, the bonds of love and family that we forge are also vital sources of meaning and identity. And caring for others is an expression of what it means to be fully human. It is because the human experience is universal that human rights are universal and cut across all religions and cultures.

The fourth issue is what history teaches us about how we make progress towards rights for all. Progress starts with honest discussion. Now, there are some who say and believe that all gay people are pedophiles, that homosexuality is a disease that can be caught or cured, or that gays recruit others to become gay. Well, these notions are simply not true. They are also unlikely to disappear if those who promote or accept them are dismissed out of hand rather than invited to share their fears and concerns. No one has ever abandoned a belief because he was forced to do so.

Universal human rights include freedom of expression and freedom of belief, even if our words or beliefs denigrate the humanity of others. Yet, while we are each free to believe whatever we choose, we cannot do whatever we choose, not in a world where we protect the human rights of all.

Reaching understanding of these issues takes more than speech. It does take a conversation. In fact, it takes a constellation of conversations in places big and small. And it takes a willingness to see stark differences in belief as a reason to begin the conversation, not to avoid it.

But progress comes from changes in laws. In many places, including my own country, legal protections have preceded, not followed, broader recognition of rights. Laws have a teaching effect. Laws that discriminate validate other kinds of discrimination. Laws that require equal protections reinforce the moral imperative of equality. And practically speaking, it is often the case that laws must change before fears about change dissipate.

Many in my country thought that President Truman was making a grave error when he ordered the racial desegregation of our military. They argued that it would undermine unit cohesion. And it wasn't until he went ahead and did it that we saw how it strengthened our social fabric in ways even the supporters

of the policy could not foresee. Likewise, some worried in my country that the repeal of "Don't Ask, Don't Tell" would have a negative effect on our armed forces. Now, the Marine Corps Commandant, who was one of the strongest voices against the repeal, says that his concerns were unfounded and that the Marines have embraced the change.

Finally, progress comes from being willing to walk a mile in someone else's shoes. We need to ask ourselves, "How would it feel if it were a crime to love the person I love? How would it feel to be discriminated against for something about myself that I cannot change?" This challenge applies to all of us as we reflect upon deeply held beliefs, as we work to embrace tolerance and respect for the dignity of all persons, and as we engage humbly with those with whom we disagree in the hope of creating greater understanding.

A fifth and final question is how we do our part to bring the world to embrace human rights for all people including LGBT people. Yes, LGBT people must help lead this effort, as so many of you are. Their knowledge and experiences are invaluable and their courage inspirational. We know the names of brave LGBT activists who have literally given their lives for this cause, and there are many more whose names we will never know. But often those who are denied rights are least empowered to bring about the changes they seek. Acting alone, minorities can never achieve the majorities necessary for political change.

So when any part of humanity is sidelined, the rest of us cannot sit on the sidelines. Every time a barrier to progress has fallen, it has taken a cooperative effort from those on both sides of the barrier. In the fight for women's rights, the support of men remains crucial. The fight for racial equality has relied on contributions from people of all races. Combating Islamaphobia or anti-Semitism is a task for people of all faiths. And the same is true with this struggle for equality.

Conversely, when we see denials and abuses of human rights and fail to act, that sends the message to those deniers and abusers that they won't suffer any consequences for their actions, and so they carry on. But when we do act we send a powerful moral message. Right here in Geneva, the international community acted this year to strengthen a global consensus around the human rights of LGBT people. At the Human Rights Council in March, 85 countries from all regions supported a statement calling for an end to criminalization and violence against people because of their sexual orientation and gender identity.

At the following session of the Council in June, South Africa took the lead on a resolution about violence against LGBT people. The delegation from South Africa spoke eloquently about their own experience and struggle for human equality and its indivisibility. When the measure passed, it became the first-ever UN resolution recognizing the human rights of gay people worldwide. In the Organization of American States this year, the Inter-American Commission on Human Rights created a unit on the rights of LGBT people, a step toward what we hope will be the creation of a special rapporteur.

Now, we must go further and work here and in every region of the world to galvanize more support for the human rights of the LGBT community. To the leaders of those countries where people are jailed, beaten, or executed for being gay, I ask you to consider this: Leadership, by definition, means being out in front of your people when it is called for. It means standing up for the dignity of all your citizens and persuading your people to do the same. It also means ensuring that all citizens are treated as equals under your laws, because let me be clear—I am not saying that gay people can't or don't commit crimes. They can and they do, just like straight people. And when they do, they should be held accountable, but it should never be a crime to be gay.

And to people of all nations, I say supporting human rights is your responsibility too. The lives of gay people are shaped not only by laws, but by the treatment they receive every day from their families, from their neighbors. Eleanor Roosevelt, who did so much to advance human rights worldwide, said that these rights begin in the small places close to home—the streets where people live, the schools they attend, the factories, farms, and offices where they work. These places are your domain. The actions you take, the ideals that you advocate, can determine whether human rights flourish where you are.

And finally, to LGBT men and women worldwide, let me say this: Wherever you live and whatever the circumstances of your life, whether you are connected to a network of support or feel isolated and vulnerable, please know that you are not alone. People around the globe are working hard to support you and to bring an end to the injustices and dangers you face. That is certainly true for my country. And you have an ally in the United States of America and you have millions of friends among the American people.

The Obama Administration defends the human rights of LGBT people as part of our comprehensive human rights policy and as a priority of our foreign policy. In our embassies, our diplomats are raising concerns about specific cases and laws, and working with a range of partners to strengthen human rights protections for all. In Washington, we have created a task force at the State Department to support and coordinate this work. And in the coming months, we will provide every embassy with a toolkit to help improve their efforts. And we have created a program that offers emergency support to defenders of human rights for LGBT people.

This morning, back in Washington, President Obama put into place the first U.S. Government strategy dedicated to combating human rights abuses against LGBT persons abroad. Building on efforts already underway at the State Department and across the government, the President has directed all U.S. Government agencies engaged overseas to combat the criminalization of LGBT status and conduct, to enhance efforts to protect vulnerable LGBT refugees and asylum seekers, to ensure that our foreign assistance promotes the protection of LGBT rights, to enlist international organizations in the fight against discrimination, and to respond swiftly to abuses against LGBT persons.

I am also pleased to announce that we are launching a new Global Equality Fund that will support the work of civil society organizations working on these issues around the world. This fund will help them record facts so they can target their advocacy, learn how to use the law as a tool, manage their budgets, train their staffs, and forge partnerships with women's organizations and other human rights groups. We have committed more than $3 million to start this fund, and we have hope that others will join us in supporting it.

The women and men who advocate for human rights for the LGBT community in hostile places, some of whom are here today with us, are brave and dedicated, and deserve all the help we can give them. We know the road ahead will not be easy. A great deal of work lies before us. But many of us have seen firsthand how quickly change can come. In our lifetimes, attitudes toward gay people in many places have been transformed. Many people, including myself, have experienced a deepening of our own convictions on this topic over the years, as we have devoted more thought to it, engaged in dialogues and debates, and established personal and professional relationships with people who are gay.

This evolution is evident in many places. To highlight one example, the Delhi High Court decriminalized homosexuality in India two years ago, writing, and I quote, "If there is one tenet that can be said to be an underlying theme of the Indian constitution, it is inclusiveness." There is little doubt in my mind that support for LGBT human rights will continue to climb. Because for many young people, this is simple: All people deserve to be treated with dignity and have their human rights respected, no matter who they are or whom they love.

There is a phrase that people in the United States invoke when urging others to support human rights: "Be on the right side of history." The story of the United States is the story of a nation that has repeatedly grappled with intolerance and inequality. We fought a brutal civil war over slavery. People from coast to coast joined in campaigns to recognize the rights of women, indigenous peoples, racial minorities, children, people with disabilities, immigrants, workers, and on and on. And the march toward equality and justice has continued. Those who advocate for expanding the circle of human rights were and are on the right side of history, and history honors them. Those who tried to constrict human rights were wrong, and history reflects that as well.

I know that the thoughts I've shared today involve questions on which opinions are still evolving. As it has happened so many times before, opinion will converge once again with the truth, the immutable truth, that all persons are created free and equal in dignity and rights. We are called once more to make real the words of the Universal Declaration. Let us answer that call. Let us be on the right side of history, for our people, our nations, and future generations, whose lives will be shaped by the work we do today. I come before you with great hope and confidence that no matter how long the road ahead, we will travel it successfully together. Thank you very much.

Critical Thinking

1. Do you agree with Hillary Clinton that the Universal Declaration of Human Rights should apply to LGBT people?

2. What actions does Clinton advocate at this time?

3. Where is the Obama Administration on this issue?

Internet References

Sociosite
www.topsite.com/goto/sociosite.net

Socioweb
www.topsite.com/goto/socioweb.com

Sociology—Study Sociology Online
http://edu.learnsoc.org

Sociology Web Resources
www.mhhe.com/socscience/sociology/resources/index.htm

Clinton, Hillary Rodham. From speech delivered at Palais des Nations, Geneva, Switzerland, December 6, 2011.

Unit 5

UNIT

Prepared by: Kurt Finsterbusch, *University of Maryland, College Park*

Social Institutions: Issues, Crises, and Changes

Social institutions are the building blocks of social structure. They accomplish the important tasks of society—for example, regulation of reproduction, socialization of children, production and distribution of economic goods, law enforcement and social control, and organization of religion and other value systems. Social institutions are not rigid arrangements; they reflect changing social conditions. Institutions generally change slowly. At the present time, however, many of the social institutions in the United States and in many other parts of the world are in crisis and are undergoing rapid change. Eastern European countries are literally transforming their political and economic institutions. Economic institutions, such as stock markets, are becoming truly international, and when a major country experiences a recession, many other countries feel the effects. In the United States, major reform movements are active in political, economic, family, medical, and educational institutions.

Article   Prepared by: Kurt Finsterbusch, *University of Maryland, College Park*

A Fitful Union: What the Founders Wrought?

JAMES T. KLOPPENBERG

Learning Outcomes

After reading this article, you will be able to:

- Provide an explanation for the 2016 election outcome as the outcome of traditional political ideas and forces.

- Throughout our history, many Americans have an animosity toward federal authority and toward federal government.

- Understand the political developments today by understanding the forces enshrined in the constitutions of the states and the federal government.

To the state governments, by contrast, the "founders" gave all but unlimited authority to regulate citizens by invoking "police power," or "coercion," which Gerstle traces to the traditions of civic republicanism and English common law. [. . .]incompatible defenses of liberty, on the one hand, and reliance on coercion, on the other hand, "bound together from the earliest days of the republic," have coexisted uneasily ever since. If we understand it instead as setting in motion a dynamic framework of self-government—a "living" set of rules that can be altered not only by the dramatic step of amending the Constitution but also reshaped incrementally, by juries and city councils, by state legislatures and district courts, and by the endless struggles fought between the executive, legislative, and judicial branches of the federal government as well as between the national and state governments—we will see instead that our challenges are those always facing a democracy.

Hatred is as American as apple pie. Progressives who are struggling to understand the catastrophic result of the 2016 presidential election should return to American history. A candidate who proudly trumpeted his disdain for women, African

Americans, Mexicans, Muslims, gays, and the disabled, and who wore his lack of experience in public office as a badge of honor, struck many Americans as unfit as well as unqualified for the presidency. Yet that candidate tapped into some of the most venerable traditions in our nation's past, traditions that have survived the attacks of the past six decades. Now that many self-styled conservatives are openly embracing such traditions, progressives—including the majority of voters who preferred Hillary Clinton—must face facts. Our past is alive. As Ta-Nehisi Coates has put it, "racism is heritage."

In his ambitious study of governance in U.S. history, the distinguished American historian Gary Gerstle shows that Americans have distrusted each other ever since they forged a single nation from states that considered themselves as independent of each other as they were of Great Britain. That suspicion has manifested itself in an apparent contradiction that Gerstle probes in Liberty and Coercion: The Paradox of American Government from the Founding to the Present (Princeton University Press, $36, 472 pp.). Whereas the U.S. Constitution gave limited authority to the central government, state governments reserved much more robust and too-seldom appreciated "police powers," long exercised by English authorities, that justified not only economic regulation but regimes of "surveillance" constraining the freedoms ostensibly guaranteed by the Bill of Rights.

A venerable tradition of animosity toward federal authority has animated foes of a stronger national government. Antifederalists opposed ratifying the Constitution. Flinty frontiersmen ignored demands that they respect Indian treaties. Jacksonians denigrated the nationalism (and antislavery activism) of their foes. Self-proclaimed "redeemers" thwarted post-Civil War attempts to end White supremacy in the former Confederacy. More recently, that animosity blunted or rolled back New Deal and Great Society programs, and it lives on among Tea Party activists who denounce Barack Obama as a socialist dictator.

The conflict between those who tried to empower the central government and those who fought to contain it, Gerstle insists, has defined American political history. The federal government, enfeebled by the Tenth Amendment, failed to consolidate temporary expansions of its authority in potentially "transformative" moments such as the Civil War, the New Deal, and the 1960s. Instead, in an effort to sidestep the states' dogged opposition, the federal government was forced into "improvisational" maneuvers, inadequate to establish the legitimacy of progressive social and economic reforms, as it tried vainly either to use the courts, enlist the states, or cooperate with private partners to reach its goals.

Many observers have tried to explain why contemporary conservatives, pledged to oppose the federal government and all its works, nevertheless insist that state governments outlaw abortion and gay marriage, secure the right to pray in school and carry assault rifles in malls, and impose strict regulations on who can work (under what conditions) and who can vote. Gerstle finds the answer to that apparent contradiction in Americans' peculiar fear of centralized power and their confidence in the authority of the states. This is a deeply pessimistic account of U.S. history. Changes that have led to greater freedom and equality, in Gerstle's view, are ultimately futile improvisations that violate the Constitution. Resistance to those changes is grounded solidly in the police powers reserved for the states.

My two reservations concerning Gerstle's provocative argument should not be taken as dissent from the praise the book has earned. Given that so much of Gerstle's case turns on his conception of the eighteenth-century origins of the "liberal" federal government and the limits placed on it by the "founders," his brief and schematic interpretation of that period offers a misleadingly straightforward account of devilishly complicated developments. When he gets to the nineteenth and especially the twentieth century, this author of two outstanding books, one on industrial labor and another on race and nationalism, and co-editor of two well-known essay collections, is on much more solid ground. For readers who want to know what the scholarly community thinks about the past two centuries of U.S. political history, Liberty and Coercion is a reliable and comprehensive guide.

Gerstle's overall argument, though, depends on a distinction that I consider problematic. He attributes the safeguards against a powerful national government—safeguards built into the Constitution—to the prevailing eighteenth-century "liberal" mistrust of centralized authority and Americans' commitment to securing liberty. To the state governments, by contrast, the "founders" gave all but unlimited authority to regulate citizens

by invoking "police power," or "coercion," which Gerstle traces to the traditions of civic republicanism and English common law. Thus, incompatible defenses of liberty, on the one hand, and reliance on coercion, on the other, "bound together from the earliest days of the republic," have coexisted uneasily ever since.

As historians have been pointing out for three decades, however, the split between "liberal" and "republican" ideas on which Gerstle's interpretation depends is a figment of the scholarly imagination. Those who wrote the state constitutions and the U.S. Constitution were the same people. They were not liberals obsessed with rights at one moment, then republicans focused on civic duties at another. The original state constitutions emerged in a flurry of writing during the period from 1775 to 1780; many delegates to the Constitutional Convention in Philadelphia in 1787, and to the state ratifying conventions that adopted the Constitution, had framed those documents. As John Adams wrote in the Massachusetts Constitution that he drafted in 1780, "government is instituted for the common good, for the protection, safety, prosperity, and happiness of the people and not for the profit, honor, or private interest of any one man, family, or class of men." The plan being adopted by Massachusetts was "Locke, Sidney, and Rousseau and de Mably reduced to practice."

Neither Adams nor Thomas Jefferson nor James Madison distinguished between the "liberal" Locke and the "republican" Rousseau, or between individual liberty and government coercion. Notwithstanding their real disagreements, all the members of the founding generation believed that individual rights must be exercised within the boundaries of laws written by representatives of the people themselves. That shared commitment to popular sovereignty, not a schizoid or incoherent yearning for unbounded freedom and unlimited surveillance, made the state constitutions and the U.S. Constitution emblems of the world's first democratic revolution. The architects of these founding documents, with very few exceptions (Alexander Hamilton, who wanted bankers to govern and the president to serve for life, comes to mind), prized equality and decentralization because they judged concentrated political power a threat to self-government. They also feared concentrated economic power, which is among the reasons that they thought the rich should pay more in taxes than the poor.

These God-fearing men, whether Deists or conventional Protestant Christians, knew they were flawed creatures incapable of establishing, once and for all, the delicate equilibrium between freedom and obligation, which explains the provision for amendments. They aimed to secure for citizens a wide array of liberties bounded by laws that would develop, over time, as a result of deliberations in sites ranging from town meetings and state legislatures to the Congress, and from local jury rooms to the Supreme Court. Gerstle concedes that references to the principle undergirding the states' police power, "salus populi," the people's welfare, "did slip in" to the Preamble of the Constitution and Article 1, Section 8. I believe instead that those references to the obligations shouldered by state and national government alike to "promote the general welfare" were central to all these founding documents and the reason why, despite the Antifederalists' anxieties, the Constitution was ratified by the states.

Although the founders did value rights, they also valued justice. They differed, though, about how both rights and justice—both liberty and coercion—should be secured, and for whom. From the earliest squabbling about whether to form a single nation until today, race and ethnicity have been among the most important issues underlying those disagreements. Whether the question was the survival of indigenous peoples, the immigration of Germans to the colony of Pennsylvania (Benjamin Franklin disparaged them as "Palatine boors"), or the suitability for citizenship of women, Catholics, Jews, Muslims, Asians, Latinos, or, most persistently, African Americans, disputes concerning federal or state authority stemmed from the unwillingness of many White Protestant Americans to accept as their equals people unlike themselves. Beneath the masquerade of battles over local or state control, I believe, lay struggles over White male supremacy. Although Gerstle understands that persistent animosity as well as any American historian, he chooses not to emphasize the persistence of racism or sexism in this book. In the wake of this year's presidential election, the consequences of those traditions loom larger.

The heart of Liberty and Coercion is a series of eight superb chapters dealing with the battles fought to establish and expand the power of the national government against forces defending two different oligarchies, those entrenched in the states and those spawned in the ever-rising tide of capitalism. Gerstle shows the stutter-step establishment of national authority, as the United States spread across the continent, and eventually around the world, by means of land distribution, post offices, local militias, and ultimately the nation's military forces. Usually that expansion occurred through cloaked partnerships with entrepreneurs, ranging from nineteenth-century railroad, banking, and industrial tycoons to those who used generous government funding to create the military-industrial complex in the region now known as the Sunbelt. All these champions of "private enterprise" profited handsomely from federal largesse, even though their shrill attacks on "big government" veiled their feeding at the public trough.

Along the way, Gerstle catalogues various measures adopted by state governments to regulate economic activity, many of which he labels "progressive," and others regulating religious belief, alcohol consumption, and sexual behavior, which he dubs "regressive." Although those categories are less stable

historically than Liberty or Coercion suggests, a generation of legal historians has puzzled over the fact that states undertook much more robust forms of regulation than did the federal government. Gerstle contends that the explanation lies in the Constitution's original shackling of federal authority. Yet debates over the role of government, at every level, have been at the heart of U.S. politics and law from the beginning: Federalists and Jeffersonian Republicans in the 1790s, Whigs and the Jackson Party in the 1830s, and, since 1860, Republicans and Democrats have all battled nonstop over the purpose and the proper scope of government, within the states as well as between the states and the federal government. The outcomes have varied; the struggle continues.

Gerstle argues that the fault line between states and nation has shaped our political history, but that emphasis leads him to understate the extent to which there has been, and continues to be, tension between the tectonic plate of the Southern states and the rest of the nation. Parties enjoying greater strength in the North showed stronger support for the rights of indigenous peoples, internal improvements, antislavery agitation, compulsory education, unionization of labor, social-welfare programs, and, in more recent decades, struggles to secure equal rights for African Americans, women, the disabled, and LGBTQ people. Of course, opposition to all those causes was never limited to one region, as the election reminded us, and the hardy band of Southern progressives cannot be ignored. Yet again and again, the strongest opposition to what Gerstle (and most readers of Commonweal) would consider forward-thinking legislation concerning agriculture, industrial relations, civil liberties, and especially the rights of minorities has come not just from "the states" but from particular states: those of the former Confederacy and its latter-day cultural outposts further west.

Those who view the expansion of the central government as the most effective way to advance an egalitarian agenda have often emphasized the transformative role of war. Although Gerstle agrees that the scope and scale of federal power expanded by necessity during wartime, he terms that expansion a "mirage." Opponents dismantled most of the improvised initiatives once peace returned, except after WWII, when the Cold War justified military spending on an unprecedented scale for an apparently endless time. In 1944, Franklin Roosevelt laid out ambitious plans for a postwar social-welfare state as generous as any of those created in Northern Europe. That agenda came to nothing, though, when southern Democrats made clear that they would never support programs that would have extended benefits to all citizens, Black as well as White. Gerstle shows brilliantly how and why New Deal efforts to assist struggling farmers and industrial workers, efforts that substantially shrank the gap between the richest and poorest Americans, ended up benefiting primarily the most organized and (relatively) affluent sectors of agriculture and labor. A fine chapter on the 1960s shows that enforcing civil rights and anti-poverty legislation required "breaking the power of the states," but he minimizes the extent to which the states that had to be "broken" clustered in the former Confederacy.

That campaign for equality and inclusiveness sparked a "conservative revolt" that has dominated American politics since the 1970s. Confronted with a flurry of federal regulations, the states reasserted their authority to resist the power of the central government with the significant exceptions of military spending and initiatives to police citizens' drug use and sexual behavior. Conservatives began to insist, in the face of the longest period of sustained economic growth in U.S. history and a steady decline in inequality, that government regulations and the steeply progressive income tax put in place in the 1930s had stifled initiative and productivity. They embarked on a campaign to reverse the central decisions of the Warren Court by demanding a return to what they conjured up as the "original meaning" of the Constitution. Under the leadership of President Ronald Reagan, they challenged the power of organized labor, slashed taxes, and campaigned against increases in the minimum wage, ostensibly out of renewed reverence for a "free market" that, as Liberty and Coercion makes abundantly clear, was always thoroughly regulated, albeit frequently in the interest of those who howled about preserving the freedom of contract.

Gerstle illuminates the novelty of recent conservatism by spotlighting President Dwight Eisenhower's March 15, 1954, address on Americans' civic duty to pay their fair share of taxes in order to expand Social Security and unemployment insurance, improve the nation's housing stock, and provide health care for all. The political center of gravity has shifted dramatically, in part due to the Reagan revolution and in part due to Jimmy Carter's and Bill Clinton's embrace of deregulation. President Obama's Affordable Care Act, as Gerstle points out, was modeled on the health-care law enacted in Massachusetts under Governor Mitt Romney. This plan, relying on private insurance exchanges, was conceived as a Republican Party alternative to the single-payer system that Hillary Clinton proposed in 1993. By 2010, all taxes—and all public–private partnerships—were being condemned as threats to Americans' freedom. By 2016, that refrain was being repeated endlessly, particularly by a real-estate developer who boasted about his shrewd and (so far at least) successful evasion of federal income taxes.

Among the fascinating features of Liberty and Coercion is Gerstle's analysis of the rise of political parties and the relation between partisanship and corruption. The founders neglected to address the necessity of funding elections because, as Gerstle acknowledges, they deemed parties inimical to the civic virtue necessary for popular government. If the common good, not the interest of any particular group, was to be every statesman's aim, then parties were dangerous, as Washington warned in his Farewell Address. Yet because of the vast size of the nation and the decentralization of political authority, Gerstle argues, the nation immediately split into factions, and electioneering was thus bound to be an expensive proposition. The founders' naïve unwillingness to provide for public funding spelled disaster. Private money inevitably seeped through even the tiniest cracks in the dams that "elite reformers"—a phrase that appears five times in less than two pages—have tried again and again to erect to stop corruption from flooding the political process. The fault lay, Gerstle insists, with "the deficiencies of the Constitution" rather than "the moral deficiencies of individual men." Perhaps because those "moral deficiencies" are so hard to overlook right now, that judgment seems debatable.

What is to be done? This reviewer was surprised that Gerstle endorses the view, for decades associated with the most conservative legal scholars but now embraced by some on the left as well, that the limits placed on the federal government by the Constitution render most forms of economic regulation unconstitutional. Moreover, decisions rendered by the Warren Court, based on the principle of substantive due process, are said to impinge illegitimately on the states' authority. Efforts to limit the influence of money in politics are dismissed as hopeless. So if we want to bolster the imperiled labor movement, shrink the widening gap between rich and poor, and secure the rights of minorities, Gerstle concludes, we must amend the Constitution. Because the founders really did intend "to limit and fragment federal power," and because they really did fail to give "the federal government a power to act for the good and welfare of the commonwealth," we must undo what they did. I disagree, and I believe that both John Adams and James Madison, the much misunderstood darlings of many conservatives today, would disagree as well.

Although I doubt there are differences that make a difference between Gerstle's vision of social democracy and my own, my second disagreement with the analysis offered in Liberty and Coercion centers on how we should understand the Constitution. Ever since the Progressive era, generations of reformers and scholars, some influenced by philosophical pragmatism and others informed by the best historical research on the founding period, have insisted on the idea of a "living Constitution," a charter that the founders understood would have to change and develop along with the nation itself. Partisans of that view, including constitutional scholars such as Jack Rakove and Akhil Amar, dismiss the idea of originalism as incoherent. The Constitution was a compromise forged by individuals from starkly different regions—slave and free— who cherished different ideals of what the United States should become. The document ratified by the states embodied the compromises they had to make in order to satisfy their fellow delegates. Many of the ideas it contains, particularly those about women and non-Whites but also those about many other aspects of the world we inhabit–including but not limited to ideas about economic regulation, religious, and ethnic pluralism, and the diversity of choices people can legitimately make about how they want to live their lives—no longer conform to the shared understandings of most Americans.

If we enshrine the Constitution in a glass case said to contain its "original meaning," we embalm it. If we understand it instead as setting in motion a dynamic framework of self-government—a "living" set of rules that can be altered not only by the dramatic step of amending the Constitution but also reshaped incrementally, by juries and city councils, by state legislatures and district courts, and by the endless struggles fought between the executive, legislative, and judicial branches of the federal government as well as between the national and state governments—we will see instead that our challenges are those always facing a democracy. We must make persuasive arguments for what we believe, we must elect those who share our convictions, and we must abide by the decisions they make whether we like it or not.

Seldom in U.S. history has our nation faced a choice as stark as that of 2016. Particularly in light of the result, we must resist the idea that nothing short of amending the Constitution is adequate. Our future will be shaped, as our past has been, by our democratic process, imperfect and in need of reform as it always is. We must build with the tools we have. We must resist the temptation to see the perfect as the enemy of the good, as so many of those who voted for Barack Obama but failed to vote at all in 2016 evidently did. Gary Gerstle has given us a masterful overview of the dynamics that have shaped American politics, including the persistent struggle between the states and the federal government. Anyone who shares Gerstle's conviction that our democracy should be moving toward greater equality and inclusion, and who seeks a clearer understanding of what we are up against as we work toward those ideals, should read Liberty and Coercion.

Critical Thinking

1. Do you agree with Kloppenberg that the history of the United States constantly involves the struggle between freedom and rights on the one hand and law and order and regulations on the other hand?

2. Have regulations gone too far in the United States?

3. Do you agree with Kloppenberg that "hatred is as American as apple pie"?

Internet References

Sociology—Study Sociology Online
　　http://edu.learnsoc.org/

Sociology Web Resources
　　http://www.mhhe.com/socscience/sociology/resources/index.htm

Sociosite
　　http://www.topsite.com/goto/sociosite.net

Socioweb
　　http://www.topsite.com/goto/socioweb.com

James T. Kloppenberg, Charles Warren Professor of American History at Harvard, is the author of Toward Democracy: The Struggle for Self-Rule in European and American Thought (Oxford) and Reading Obama: Dreams, Hope, and the American Political Tradition (Princeton).

Article

Prepared by: Kurt Finsterbusch, *University of Maryland, College Park*

Is Capitalism in Crisis? Latest Trends of a System Run Amok

Capitalism has always been a highly irrational socioeconomic system, but the constant drive for accumulation has especially run amok in the age of high finance, privatization and globalization.

C. J. POLYCHRONIOU

Learning Outcomes

After reading this article, you will be able to:

- Understand why corporate capitalism came back so well from the financial meltdown of 2008.

- Explain how the capital classes of the developed countries responded to the declining rate of profits of the 1970s.

- Identify the virtues and vices of capitalism.

Having survived the financial meltdown of 2008, corporate capitalism and the financial masters of the universe have made a triumphant return to their "business as usual" approach: They are now savoring a new era of wealth, even as the rest of the population continues to struggle with income stagnation, job insecurity, and unemployment.

This travesty was made possible in large part by the massive US government bailout plan that essentially rescued major banks and financial institutions from bankruptcy with taxpayer money (the total commitment on the part of the government to the bank bailout plan was over $16 trillion). In the meantime, corporate capitalism has continued running recklessly to the precipice with regard to the environment, as profits take precedence not only over people but over the sustainability of the planet itself.

Capitalism has always been a highly irrational socioeconomic system, but the constant drive for accumulation has especially run amok in the age of high finance, privatization, and globalization.

Today, the question that should haunt progressive-minded and radical scholars and activists alike is whether capitalism itself is in crisis, given that the latest trends in the system are working perfectly well for global corporations and the rich, producing new levels of wealth and increasing inequality. For insights into the above questions, I interviewed David M. Kotz, professor of economics at the University of Massachusetts at Amherst and author of *The Rise and Fall of Neoliberal Capitalism* (Harvard University Press, 2015).

C. J. Polychroniou: David, corporate capitalism and the masters of the universe have bounced back quite nicely from the global financial crisis of 2008. Is this an indication of the system's resilience, or do we need to think about larger considerations, such as the trajectory of the class struggle in the contemporary world, the role of ideology, and the power of the state?

David M. Kotz: The severe phase of the economic and financial crisis ended in the summer of 2009. By then the banks had been bailed out and the Great Recession ended, as production stopped falling and began to rise in North America and Europe. As you say, since then profits have recovered quite well. However, normal capitalist economic expansion has not resumed, but instead, global capitalism has been stuck in stagnation.

Stagnation means no economic growth or very slow economic growth. Stagnation has afflicted most of the developed countries since 2010, with some countries, such as Greece, still in a severe depression. US GDP growth has averaged only 2.1 percent per year since the bottom of the Great Recession in 2009. That is by far the slowest expansion following a recession since the end of World War II. Even mainstream economists, such as Lawrence Summers and Paul Krugman, have recognized that the economy is stuck in a severe stagnation.

In the United States, the official unemployment rate has fallen to a low level, but that is due to millions of people being dropped from the official labor force as a result of giving up looking for work after finding none for a long period. Most of the new jobs pay low wages and provide little or no job security. Meanwhile, the rich continue to get still richer.

The long-lasting stagnation has brought stagnating wages and worsening job opportunities. This creates a severe problem for capitalism, even with rising corporate profits and growing wealth for the top 1 percent. This problem has an ideological and a political dimension. While capitalism always brings a high degree of inequality, it is tolerable for those holding the short end of the stick as long as living standards are rising and job opportunities are good for most people. A long period of stagnation delegitimizes the existing system. As growing numbers of people turn against "the system" and the elites who run it, a political crisis develops. The bourgeois democracy that normally acts to stabilize capitalism turns into a source of instability, as anti-establishment parties and candidates start winning elections.

What do you consider to be the latest and most critical trends in the workings of capitalism in the 21st century?

Not only has capitalism failed to bring economic progress in this century, it has brought worsening conditions for the majority. The reason for this is rooted in the transformation of capitalism around 1980, when the post-World War II "regulated capitalism" was rapidly replaced by "neoliberal capitalism." Regulated capitalism arose mainly because of the serious challenge to capitalism from socialist and communist movements around the world and from the Communist Party-ruled states after World War II. The new regulated capitalism was based on capital–labor compromise. It led to the construction of welfare states, state regulation of business, and trade union–led rising wages and more stable jobs for working people.

In the 1970s, regulated capitalism entered a period of economic crisis indicated by a long decline in the rate of profit in the United States and Western Europe. The capitalist classes of the developed countries responded by abandoning the capital–labor compromise, attacking the trade union movement, lifting state regulation of business and banking, and making drastic cuts in the welfare state and in the various forms of social provision. This gave us the neoliberal form of capitalism.

The neoliberal transformation resolved the economic crisis of the 1970s from the viewpoint of capital, as profits began to rise again. That transformation freed the banks from state regulation, setting off the process of financialization. It rewrote the rules of the global system, promoting an increasingly globally integrated world economy.

Every form of capitalism eventually enters a phase of structural crisis, and in 2008 the superficial stability of neoliberal capitalism gave way to severe economic and financial crisis.

Neoliberal capitalism gave rise to some 25 years of relatively stable economic conditions after 1980, although economic growth was slower than it had been in the preceding period. Capitalists became much richer, but the promised benefits for the majority never emerged. After 1980, working people's wages and job conditions steadily worsened through 2007. However, as long as the economy expanded at a reasonable rate, it was difficult to challenge neoliberalism. Every form of capitalism eventually enters a phase of structural crisis, and in 2008, the superficial stability of neoliberal capitalism gave way to severe economic and financial crisis, followed by stagnation.

We live in the age of the financialization of the planet, in which financial institutions and markets are expanding. In what ways does financialization increase capitalism's inherent tendencies toward economic dependence, inequality, and exploitation?

Starting in the late 1980s, a trend of financialization began, meaning a growing role for financial markets, financial institutions, and financial motives in the economy. This is not the first period of financialization in capitalist history, financialization also developed in the late 19th century and in the 1920s. It is an inherent tendency in capitalism, which is released in periods of loose regulation of the financial sector, but it has been halted and even reversed when the state or other institutions have intervened to block or reverse it, as occurred after 1900 and again after the 1930s. Contemporary financialization is a product of deregulation of the financial sector along with the effects of neoliberal ideology and other features of neoliberalism.

Since 2008, the trend in financialization has been mixed. There is an ongoing political struggle over financial regulation in the United States. The giant banks have so far faced some restrictions on their ability to engage in highly risky and predatory activities, although other financial institutions continue to pursue such activities. Some major nonfinancial corporations, such as General Electric, have abandoned their financial divisions to concentrate on manufacturing and other nonfinancial activities.

Whether financialized or not, capitalism itself brings rising exploitation and worsening inequality, unless it is restrained by states, trade unions, and other institutions. The financialization of capitalism accentuates the tendency toward rising inequality by promoting new forms of profit-making and generating huge fortunes for unproductive actors, as we have seen in recent decades. The most important determinant of the trend in inequality is the relative power of capital versus labor. The neoliberal transformation of capitalism empowered capital and weakened labor, which has enabled employers to drive down wages, while CEO salaries skyrocketed.

If the degree of financialization stops growing or even declines, inequality would not decline as long as capitalism retains its neoliberal form. Only in a closely regulated form of capitalism, based on capital–labor compromise, has inequality actually declined, as in the post-World War II decades.

Do you think that income and wealth inequality levels pose a legitimization crisis for capitalism in the 21st century? I ask this question in light of the rise and decline of the Occupy movement and other recent efforts to steer contemporary societies toward a more rational and humane social order.

Growing oppression and suffering has made millions of people receptive to the socialist critique of capitalism.

There is indeed a legitimization crisis for the dominant world system at this time, as discussed above. However, there is a political and ideological struggle over how to define the dominant system and the direction of change that is needed. Leftists and socialists understand that the dominant world system is capitalism, and they have targeted the 1 percent, that is, the capitalists. This was evident in the Occupy movement and other left-wing upsurges around the world since 2010–2011. The growing oppression and suffering has made millions of people, especially the young, receptive to the socialist critique of capitalism.

However, various extreme right-wing groups have also ridden the wave of anger at the discredited ruling class, with greater success than the left at this time. The right-wing response has taken the form of right-wing repressive nationalism, which targets an ill-defined "elite," which it promises to replace. Right-wing nationalism blames the problems of ordinary people on religious, ethnic, and national minorities . . . It portrays the ruling elite as weak-kneed "liberals" who are afraid to confront the scapegoated groups. It offers a strongman ruler who will vanquish the scapegoated groups and restore an imagined past glory of the nation.

The recent trend of political polarization is not surprising in a period of long-lasting structural crisis of capitalism that takes the form of stagnation. Such a crisis can be resolved in only three ways: One, the emergence of a right-wing nationalist statist regime; two, a period of progressive reform of capitalism based on capital–labor compromise; three, a transition beyond capitalism to socialism.

The last stagnation of capitalism, in the 1920s, gave rise to all three directions of change. Right-wing nationalist regimes in the form of fascism arose in Germany, Italy, Spain, and Japan. Progressive reform of capitalism took place in France, Scandinavia, and the United States and after World War II throughout Western Europe. And a state socialist regime was consolidated in the USSR and new ones arose in East-Central Europe and Asia.

Today, the labor and socialist movements are historically weak. This increases the likelihood of the rise of right-wing nationalist regimes. The Trump presidency is an example. Some view the Trump presidency as one more neoliberal, finance-backed regime, but in my view, this is not the case . . .

If the labor and socialist movements can grow sufficiently which is possible under the current conditions of delegitimized capitalism then the other two directions of change become possible. The growing mass support for Jeremy Corbyn in Britain and for Bernie Sanders in the United States illustrates the possibility of a shift toward at least progressive reform of capitalism in the short run and, in the longer run, for socialist transition to eventually move onto the political agenda. Thus, this period holds great dangers, as well as great opportunities, for the left and for social and economic progress.

In discussions among economists today, the economic and social devastation experienced by so many communities here and around the world is attributed either to automation or trade policy and their impact on employment. Is automation or trade policy the real issue, or capitalism itself?

Neither automation nor trade policy is by itself the root of the trends that have wreaked so much destruction on working people and their communities. Capitalism always brings technological change, and the long-run trend in capitalism has been toward increasing global economic interactions. However, in some periods, the regulation of capitalism has held the most destructive tendencies at bay by limiting inequality and creating new good jobs that replace those lost to automation and trade. Labor productivity rose faster under postwar regulated capitalism and global trade and investment grew rapidly, but at the same time, a large part of the working class held stable jobs with rising wages in that period, resulting from the power of labor in that form of capitalism.

Under neoliberal capitalism, so far technological change has been slower than it was under regulated capitalism, measured by the growth in labor productivity, while global economic integration has accelerated. The negative results for working people come from the overwhelming power of capital in this period, which has enabled the capitalists to seize all of the benefits of increased labor productivity, while the largely unregulated global marketplace forces workers of all countries to compete with one another.

Thus, the real cause of the current high level of suffering is neoliberal capitalism. While regulated capitalism is less oppressive to working people, it is a highly contradictory form of capitalism that is bound to be eventually dismantled by the capitalists. Like every form of capitalism, it is based on exploitation of labor, as well as generating many related problems, such as imperialism and the destruction of the natural environment.

Do you foresee capitalism's unquestionable ingenuity eventually providing a solution to climate change, or is the

planet doomed without a transition to an economic system that is based on sustainable growth and socialist economics?

There is a sharp debate on the left about whether irreversible global climate change can be averted within capitalism or only through a transition to a postcapitalist system. Those arguing for the former position stress the likelihood that capitalism will not be superseded in time to avert disastrous consequences from rising temperatures, while claiming that strong state action based on popular mobilization can do the job through some combination of incentives and penalties for corporations. They further argue that the promotion of investment in sustainable technologies within capitalism can provide a path to economic progress for working people while containing the rise in global temperatures.

Those who believe climate disaster cannot be averted under capitalism argue that the profitability of the very technologies that are causing global climate change is bound to prevent timely action, as capital uses its power to protect its profits. They claim that neither incentives nor penalties can be effective when confronted with the huge profits to be made by capitalist firms from the use of the atmosphere as a free waste disposal system.

The advantages of a socialist planned economy for overcoming the threat of disastrous global climate change are undeniable. Socially owned enterprises operating in a planned economy could be instructed to pursue climate sustainability as the number one priority, which would be far more effective than trying to restrain profit-seeking enterprises from doing what is most profitable for them.

Stopping the rise in temperatures short of a tipping point requires a rapid restructuring of the transportation, power, and production systems of the world economy, and economic planning is the best way, and possibly the only way, to carry out such a task. Few economists remember that after the Japanese bombed Pearl Harbor in 1941, the US government, facing the need to rapidly restructure the peacetime economy to a war economy, suspended the market for the duration and set up a system of central planning. The results were highly successful, soon producing the ships, planes, tanks, and other weapons and food and clothing needed to win the war, while incidentally finally bringing the Great Depression to an end.

The serious threat to civilization from looming global climate change gives one more reason for the need to replace capitalism with socialism.

Socialism has many advantages over any form of capitalism. I believe the serious threat to civilization from looming global climate change gives one more reason for the need to replace capitalism with socialism. The building of a strong socialist movement, in this time of opportunity for the left, is an urgent priority. It is essential if we are to defeat the threat of right-wing nationalism. It is the only way to build a sustainable economy for the long run.

At the same time, socialists are obligated to contribute to the solution of urgent social problems while we are working for the replacement of capitalism. It is primarily through the process of mass struggles for reform that people are radicalized and come to realize the need for system change. We should support all reforms that can slow the rise in global temperatures, even if only for a time. It is possible to build a movement to replace capitalism and at the same time engage in the struggle to pull capitalism away from the global temperature tipping point.

Critical Thinking

1. What have been the consequences of the long-lasting stagnation that followed the recession of 2008?

2. What are the differences between regulated capitalism and neoliberal capitalism?

3. What are the consequences of the financialization of capitalism?

Internet References

Sociology—Study Sociology Online
  http://edu.learnsoc.org/
Sociology Web Resources
  http://www.mhhe.com/socscience/sociology/resources/index.htm
Sociosite
  http://www.topsite.com/goto/sociosite.net
Socioweb
  http://www.topsite.com/goto/socioweb.com

C.J. POLYCHRONIOU is a political economist/political scientist who has taught and worked in universities and research centers in Europe and the United States. His main research interests are in European economic integration, globalization, the political economy of the United States, and the deconstruction of neoliberalism's politico-economic project.

Article   Prepared by: Kurt Finsterbusch, *University of Maryland, College Park*

The Boom Was a Blip: Getting Used to Slow Growth

Ruchir Sharma

Learning Outcomes

After reading this article, you will be able to:

- Understand the role of depopulation, deleveraging, and deglobalization in slower economic growth since 2009.
- Understand the causes of the new economic trends.
- Explain the populist movement.

The global recovery from the Great Recession of 2009 has just entered its eighth year and shows few signs of fading. That should be cause for celebration. But this recovery has been an underwhelming one. Throughout this period, the global economy has grown at an average annual pace of just 2.5 percent—a record low when compared with economic rebounds that took place in the decades after World War II. Rather than rejoicing, then, many experts are now anxiously searching for a way to push the world economy out of its low-growth trap. Some economists and investors have placed their hopes on populists such as U.S. President Donald Trump, figuring that if they can make their countries' economies grow quickly again, the rest of the world might follow along.

Given how long the global economy has been in the doldrums, however, it's worth asking whether the forces slowing growth are merely temporary. Although economists and business leaders complain that a 2.5 percent global growth rate is painfully slow, prior to the 1800s, the world's economy never grew that fast for long; in fact, it never topped 1 percent for a sustained period. Even after the Industrial Revolution began in the late eighteenth century, the average global growth rate rarely exceeded 2.5 percent. It was only with the massive baby boom following World War II that the global economy grew

at an average pace close to 4 percent for several decades. That period was an anomaly, however—and should be recognized as such.

The causes of the current slowdown can be summed up as the Three Ds: depopulation, deleveraging, and deglobalization. Between the end of World War II and the financial crisis of 2008, the global economy was supercharged by explosive population growth, a debt boom that fueled investment and boosted productivity, and an astonishing increase in cross-border flows of goods, money, and people. Today, all three trends have begun to sharply decelerate: families are having fewer children than they did in the early postwar years, banks are not expanding their lending as they did before the global financial crisis, and countries are engaging in less cross-border trade.

In an ideal world, political leaders would recognize this new reality and dial back their ambitions accordingly. Instead, many governments are still trying to push their economies to reach unrealistic growth targets. Their desperation is understandable, for few voters have accepted the new reality either. Indeed, many recent elections have punished establishment politicians for failing to do more, and some have brought to the fore populists who promise to bring back the good times.

This growing disconnect between the political mood and the economic reality could prove dangerous. Anxious to please angry publics, a number of governments have launched radical policy experiments designed to revive economic growth and increase wages, or to at least spread the wealth more equitably—even though such plans are likely to fail, since they often rely on heavy spending that is liable to drive up deficits and spark inflation, leading to boom-and-bust swings. Even worse, some leaders are trying to use nationalism—by scapegoating foreigners or launching military adventures—to divert the public's attention from the economy altogether.

Depopulation, deleveraging, and deglobalization need not hurt everyone; in fact, they will benefit certain classes of countries, companies, and people. To respond properly to these trends, governments need to plan for them and to manage public expectations. So far, however, few leaders have shown the ability—or even the inclination—to recognize the new economic reality.

More or Less

The emergence of the Three Ds represents an epochal reversal in the story of global development, which for decades prior to the Great Recession was a tale of more: more people, more borrowing, and more goods crossing borders. To understand why the plot took such an unexpected turn, it's helpful to consider the roots of each trend.

Depopulation was already under way prior to the economic meltdown. During the postwar baby boom, the annual rate of growth in the global population of working-age people nearly doubled, from 1 percent in the mid-1950s to over 2 percent by 1980. This directly boosted economic growth, which is a simple function of how many people are joining the workforce and how rapidly their productivity is increasing. By the 1980s, however, signs that the boom would fade had begun to appear, as women in many countries began to bear fewer children, in part because of the spread of contraception. As a result, the annual growth rate of the global working-age population started to fall in stages, with a sharp drop after 2005. By 2016, it had dropped all the way back to just 1 percent. In the United States, growth in the working-age population declined from 1.2 percent in the early years of this century to just 0.3 percent in 2016—the lowest rate since the UN began recording this statistic in 1951.

The UN now predicts that worldwide, population growth rates will continue to decline through 2025 and beyond. Such long-term forecasts, which are based on a relatively simple combination of birth and death rates, have an excellent track record. And the economic implications of that trend are clear: every percentage point decline in working-age population growth shaves an equally large chunk off the GDP growth rate.

In the 1950s and 1960s, the baby boom provided a massive boost to the global economy, as did increases in productivity rooted in large measure in technological advances. As productivity growth slowed in the subsequent decades; however, easy money started to take its place as an economic spur. Beginning in the early 1980s, central banks began to win the war on inflation, which allowed them to lower interest rates dramatically. Until that point, borrowing and economic growth had moved in tandem, as is the norm in a capitalist system; for decades, global debt had grown in line with global GDP. But as falling interest rates lowered the cost of borrowing to near zero, debt surged from 100 percent of global GDP in the late 1980s to 300 percent by 2008. Although some of this borrowed money was wasted on speculation, much of it went to fuel business activity and economic growth.

Then came the global financial crisis. Regulations issued in its wake limited the risks that United States and European banks could take both in their domestic markets and overseas. In 2008, global capital flows—which are dominated by bank loans—stood at 16 percent of global GDP.

Today, those flows hover at around 2 percent of global GDP—back to where they were in the early 1980s. Meanwhile, many private borrowers and lenders have been paralyzed by "debt phobia," which has prevented new lending despite the fact that interest rates are at record lows. The only country where borrowing has continued to grow rapidly is China, which did not develop a fear of debt because it remained insulated from the financial crisis in 2008. But globally, since interest rates can hardly drop any further, a new debt boom is extremely unlikely.

Globalization is not likely to revive quickly, either. The last time that cross-border flows of money and people slowed down was in 1914, at the onset of World War I. It took three decades for that decline to hit bottom, and then another three decades for flows to recover their prewar peaks. Then, in the early 1980s, many countries began to open their borders, and for the next three decades, the volume of cross-border trade doubled, from the equivalent of 30 percent of global GDP in 1980 to 60 percent in 2008. For many countries, export industries were by far the fastest-growing sector, lifting the overall growth rate of the economy.

In the wake of the recession, however, consumers have cut back on spending, and governments have started erecting barriers to goods and services from overseas. Since 2008, according to the Centre for Economic Policy Research's Global Trade Alert, the world's major economies have imposed more than 6,000 barriers to protect themselves from foreign competition, including "stealth" measures designed to dodge trade agreements. Partly as a result of such policies, international trade has fallen back to the equivalent of 55 percent of global GDP. This trend is likely to continue as populists opposed to globalization move to further restrict the movement of goods and people. Witness, for example, one of Trump's first moves in office: killing the Trans-Pacific Partnership (TPP), a 12-nation deal that was designed by Trump's predecessor to assure that American-style free-market rules would govern trade in Asia.

Welcome to the Desert of the Real

Depopulation, deleveraging, and deglobalization have become potent obstacles to growth and should prompt policy makers in countries at all levels of development to redefine economic success, lowering the threshold for what counts as strong annual

GDP growth by a full percentage point or two. Poorer countries tend to grow faster, because they start from a lower base. In countries with average annual incomes of less than $5,000, such as Indonesia, a GDP growth rate of more than 7 percent has historically been considered strong, but that number should come down to 5 percent. For countries with average annual incomes of between $5,000 and $15,000, such as China, 4 percent GDP growth should be considered relatively robust. For developed nations such as the United States, with average annual incomes above $25,000, anything over 1.5 percent should be seen as healthy.

This is the new reality of economic success. Yet few, if any, leaders understand or accept it. Given the constraints imposed by the Three Ds, the economies of China, India, Peru, the Philippines, Poland, and the United States are all growing at what should be considered healthy rates. Yet few citizens or policy makers in those countries seem satisfied with the status quo. In India, where the economy is now growing at a pace between 5 percent and 6 percent, according to independent estimates, elites still fantasize about hitting 8 percent or 9 percent and becoming the next China. The actual China, meanwhile, is still taking on ever more debt in an effort to keep its growth rate above 6 percent. And in the United States, Trump has talked of somehow getting the already fully developed U.S. economy to grow at 4 percent, 5 percent, or even 6 percent a year.

Such rhetoric is creating an expectations gap. No region of the world is growing as fast as it was before 2008, and none should expect to. In 2007, at the peak of the precrisis boom, the economies of 65 countries—including a number of large ones, such as Argentina, China, India, Nigeria, Russia, and Vietnam—grew at annual rates of 7 percent or more. Today, just six economies are growing at that rate, and most of those are in small countries such as Côte d'Ivoire and Laos. Yet the leaders of many emerging-market countries still see 7 percent annual GDP growth as the benchmark for success.

The Populist Moment

"What's wrong with ambition?" some might object. The answer is that pushing an economy to sustain speeds beyond its potential is like persistently gunning a car's engine: it may sound cool, but eventually the motor will burn out. And if buyers are promised a muscle car but find themselves stuck in a broken-down family sedan, they will turn on the dealer.

In the last year, numerous leaders once considered rising stars, such as Mexico's Enrique Peña Nieto and Italy's Matteo Renzi, have seen their approval ratings tumble and, in Renzi's case, have been forced out of office after their reform plans failed to deliver as promised. Normally, incumbent politicians enjoy an advantage on Election Day, but not during antiestablishment revolts, such as the one occurring now. In 2009, in the 50 most populous democracies, the governing party won 90 percent of elections at the national level. Since then, the success rate of ruling parties has fallen steadily, to just 40 percent last year.

The beneficiaries of this shift have often been populist and nationalist leaders who have cast doubt on the central tenets of the liberal postwar order. Figures such as Trump, Prime Minister Theresa May in the United Kingdom, and the right-wing leader Marine Le Pen in France have encouraged people to question the so-called Washington consensus—that is, the belief that there is an intrinsic link between global free markets and rising prosperity—which was an article of faith in the United States and other Western countries for decades.

Many of these same politicians promise more muscular leadership in the name of promoting their countries' interests, and publics have shown themselves to be increasingly open to such appeals. The World Values Survey polled citizens of 30 large countries in the late 1990s and then again in the first five years of the current decade, asking, among other things, whether "having a strong leader who does not have to bother with parliament and elections" would be good for their country. In 25 of the surveyed countries, the share of people who said they would prefer authoritarian rule to democracy rose. The figure increased by 11 percentage points in the United States, 24 percentage points in Russia, and 26 points in India, where the number now stands at a stunning 70 percent. Even more striking, the decline in support for democracy was sharper among young people than among the old.

Many leaders are responding to this shift by embracing protectionist policies and by intervening more aggressively in markets. One of the main reasons for British voters' surprising 2016 decision to leave the EU was a popular desire, whipped up by populists, to "retake control" of national borders and trade policy. Now, the Washington consensus is under attack even in Washington. In the name of his "America first" agenda, Trump has begun publicly demanding that private companies build with U.S.-sourced materials and threatening to change the tax code to explicitly favor exports over imports. This willingness to scrap postwar economic orthodoxy has extended into emerging markets as well. Although Indian Prime Minister Narendra Modi was once a darling of the free-market crowd, he has recently begun to defy its preferences, most recently by deciding to withdraw 86 percent of the paper currency in circulation in India, virtually overnight, as a way to punish wealthy tax dodgers.

Such policies stand little chance of accomplishing the larger goal: bringing back a period of broad prosperity. Indeed, populist experiments will likely do more harm than good, in part by threatening the victory in the war on inflation that governments won in the 1980s and have sustained ever since, as tighter central bank policies have combined with intensifying international competition to put a lid on prices. If countries pursue insular, protectionist policies, decreased foreign competition will likely remove that lid. Populist proposals to boost growth by increasing government spending could also push prices up, especially if the economy is already running close to full capacity, as it is in the United States right now. That is why expectations for U.S. inflation have risen markedly since Trump took office.

Populist spending might indeed drive up growth for a year or so, but it would come at the expense of higher deficits and rising inflation. That would force central banks to raise interest rates faster than expected, triggering a downturn. Trump's call for significant new spending on roads and bridges has proved broadly popular, but the timing is all wrong.

The U.S. economy is already in the eighth year of a recovery, which means the need for stimulus spending has passed. And the Trump plan would push the U.S. budget deficit, which is already at unprecedented levels, even higher. At this stage, Washington should be building a surplus money—it will need when the next recession inevitably hits. But the idea of saving for a rainy day seems quaint at a time when disgruntled voters are demanding an economic revival. The U.S. economy is already growing in line with its potential rate of 1.5–2 percent, yet most politicians seem to share the public's disappointment and eagerness for more.

Winners and Losers

The slowdown in global flows of goods, money, and people has affected more than just national politics and policy-making: it has also rearranged the international balance of economic power. Before 2008, emerging economies sought to export their way to prosperity. But that model has become less effective as the competitive edge once enjoyed by major exporters, such as South Korea and Taiwan, has begun to shift to countries that can grow by selling to their own large domestic markets, such as Indonesia or Poland.

At the same time, countries that got ahead by specializing in outsourced labor will probably see their advantage dwindle. India has seen cities such as Bangalore emerge as incubators of the country's rising middle class, spurred by opportunities at global outsourcing firms. The same goes for the Philippines, where call centers did not exist at the turn of the millennium but have exploded into a $22 billion industry employing more than one million people. As globalization retreats, however, outsourcing is likely to decline, and Trump's tax plans, designed to bring companies and jobs back to the United States, will accelerate this shift.

Economic advantages are also moving away from big multinationals and toward smaller, domestically focused companies that rely less on exporting goods and importing or outsourcing labor. As borders tighten and it becomes harder to fill positions

with foreign employees, workers in developed economies such as the United States will gain more bargaining power. For much of the postwar era, the share of U.S. national income that went to workers declined, in large part because many companies cut labor costs by shifting jobs abroad. Meanwhile, the share of national income going to corporate profits rose steadily, to a peak of 10 percent in 2012. Since then, however, the corporate share has started to drop and the workers' share has begun inching up.

Border restrictions and aggressive government intervention in markets are nonetheless likely to slow the global economy. Reduced competition tends to undermine productivity, one of the key drivers of growth. As leaders attempt to grab a greater share of the global pie for their countries, their combined efforts will wind up shrinking the pie itself.

I'm a Survivor

So what will happen when populists and nationalists fail to deliver faster growth? One might expect everything to come crashing down around them. In fact, history shows that canny populists can survive such outcomes. But the tactics they tend to use often stoke international instability, as the cases of Russia and Turkey demonstrate.

When Russian President Vladimir Putin came to power in 2000, his basic promise was that he would make Russia great again by reviving its economy. Thanks largely to rising prices for Russia's top exports, oil and gas, average annual income increased 10-fold over the next decade, to the equivalent of $15,000. Putin reaped the benefits, basking in unprecedented levels of public support. But in 2014, energy prices collapsed, setting off a recession, and average annual income fell to just $9,000. Putin suddenly seemed politically vulnerable.

To deflect attention from the downturn, Putin embarked on a series of foreign adventures: invading and annexing Crimea, fomenting a pro-Russian insurrection in eastern Ukraine, and launching a military intervention to support the embattled Assad regime in Syria. By playing the nationalism card and casting himself as the hero of a campaign to restore Russian prestige and power, Putin has avoided suffering the fate of so many other establishment politicians. Despite Russia's continued economic struggles, his approval rating remains above 80 percent.

Like Putin, Turkish President Recep Tayyip Erdogan is also well into his second decade in power despite the fact that he presides over a sputtering economy. Erdogan's ideas about economics are distinctly unconventional: he has claimed, for example, that raising interest rates—a standard antidote to inflation—is in fact a cause of inflation. Turkey faces a crippling mix of rising deficits, accelerating inflation, and slow growth. Yet the latest polls put Erdogan's approval rating at close to 70 percent, in part because Erdogan has managed to convince many Turks that the United States and the EU are the masterminds of a conspiracy to weaken Turkey. When military officers launched a coup attempt against him last year, Erdogan claimed that the plot was "written abroad," and members of his government accused the CIA and the FBI of involvement—an accusation that Washington denies but that most Turks believe, according to polls.

This trick—diverting attention from economic troubles by launching foreign adventures or by scapegoating foreign cabals and enemies within—is as old as politics. But Putin's and Erdogan's success with such tactics will only make other leaders more willing to take similar measures when they find themselves unable to deliver on promises of renewed prosperity. The resulting wave of nationalist antagonism and aggression will stoke geopolitical tensions, especially at a time when Washington's commitment to upholding the liberal international order seems to be wavering.

The New Normal

Not all the effects of the Three Ds will be negative; the trends will produce some winners, such as countries whose economies are less reliant on international trade and firms that deal primarily with domestic markets. A slower-growing, less globalized economy might also raise middle-class wages in developed economies, which might in turn halt or even reverse the increase in income inequality that many nations have experienced in recent decades. Such gains will prove fleeting, however, if leaders and policy makers refuse to accept the new normal.

There are some steps that governments can take to dampen the impact of the Three Ds. Although attempts to reverse the long-term decline in birth rates, such as offering women "baby bonuses," have proved largely futile, governments can offer more women and elderly people incentives to enter or reenter the workforce. They can also open doors to immigrants. But doing so will be at best politically impractical at a time of rising nativism. And working-age populations are falling so sharply that women, senior citizens, and immigrants can make up for only a small portion of the looming labor shortage.

The same basic math applies to deglobalization: at a time when global trade talks have stalled and regional trade deals are dying on the vine, countries can try to boost trade by cutting bilateral deals—but this will only partly counteract the global antitrade trend. And the rise of populists will continue pushing mainstream politicians to be wary of any trade deals: before beginning her 2016 presidential campaign, former U.S. Secretary of State Hillary Clinton had called the TPP "the gold standard" for trade deals; once primary season started, she withdrew her support for the agreement in response to antitrade populism in the Democratic Party's base.

The obstacles to reviving the postwar debt boom are even more daunting. The financial crisis of 2008 led to new regulations and new restrictions on lending and made big banks an easy target for populists of all stripes, limiting the room to maneuver for policy makers and financial firms alike. And global debt, although stable, is already quite high, at around 300 percent of GDP. That means that, even if policy makers wanted to do so, it would be politically difficult and perhaps economically destabilizing to trigger a new period of debt expansion.

If political leaders can't summon the words or the courage to explain this slow-growth world to a demanding public, they can at least avoid overpromising on growth and eschew unorthodox policy experiments to achieve it. Some traditional economic policies, such as well-designed tax cuts and deregulation, could help increase productivity and lift growth rates at the margin. But the gains from such policies are unlikely to add up to much. No country will be able to avoid the constraints on growth posed by the Three Ds; the time has come to prepare for life in a post-miracle world.

Critical Thinking

1. Why was the recovery from the great recession of 2009 so slow?

2. Why do most countries' leaders not recognize the new economic realities?

3. Will populist movements bring back stronger growth?

Internet References

Sociology—Study Sociology Online
http://edu.learnsoc.org/

Sociology Web Resources
http://www.mhhe.com/socscience/sociology/resources/index.htm

Sociosite
http://www.topsite.com/goto/sociosite.net

Socioweb
http://www.topsite.com/goto/socioweb.com

Sharma, Ruchir. "The Boom Was a Blip: Getting Used to Slow Growth," *Foreign Affairs*, May 2017. Copyright ©2017 by Council on Foreign Relations. Used with permission.

Article   Prepared by: Kurt Finsterbusch, *University of Maryland, College Park*

The Return of Monopoly

With Amazon on the rise and a business tycoon in the White House, can a new generation of Democrats return the party to its trust-busting roots?

MATT STOLLER

Learning Outcomes

After reading this article, you will be able to:

- Understand the extent of monopoly today.

- Understand the price we pay for the increasing monopolization of the economy.

- Understand why the Democratic Party must lead the fight against growing monopolization.

On July 15, 2015, Amazon marked the twentieth anniversary of its founding with a "global shopping event" called Prime Day. Over the next 24 hours, starting at midnight, the company offered special discounts every 10 min to the 44 million users of Amazon Prime, its members-only benefit program. The event was astonishingly successful: Amazon made 34 million Prime sales that day, nearly 20 percent more than it had on Black Friday, the traditional post-Thanksgiving buying bonanza. The company received almost 400 orders per second—all on a single, ordinary day in the middle of summer.

Prime Day is now an annual event; last year it marked the largest sales day in Amazon's history. The sale has become a secular holiday, akin in its economic wallop and social ubiquity to Super Bowl Sunday or the Fourth of July. Today, nearly half of the nation's households are enrolled in Prime. That's more Americans than go to church every month. More than own a gun. And more than voted for either Donald Trump or Hillary Clinton last November.

The rise of Amazon, and its overwhelming market dominance, has accelerated the collapse of traditional retail outlets. Amazon's stock has risen by 300 percent since 2012, and Wall Street analysts have compiled a "Death by Amazon" index to track the retail companies most likely to be killed off by the online giant. This year alone, three retail stalwarts—Walmart, JCPenney, and Rite Aid—plan to shutter or sell off nearly 1,200 stores, and nearly 90,000 Americans have been thrown out of work since October. One of every 11 jobs is tied to shopping centers, which generate $151 billion in sales taxes each year. All of which is rapidly being lost to a single company. In June, Amazon announced its largest-ever acquisition, paying $13.4 billion to buy the Whole Foods grocery chain. Such is the power of the "everything store" and its "one-click ordering."

Amazon did not come to dominate the way we shop because of its technology. It did so because we let it. Over the past three decades, the U.S. government has permitted corporate giants to take over an ever-increasing share of the economy. Monopoly—the ultimate enemy of free-market competition—now pervades every corner of American life: every transaction we make, every product we consume, every news story we read, every piece of data we download. Eighty percent of seats on airplanes are sold by just four airlines. In 2015, the number of major health insurers shrank from five to just three. CVS and Walgreens have a virtual lock on the drugstore and pharmacy business. A private equity firm in Brazil controls roughly half of the U.S. beer market. The chemical giant Monsanto is able to dictate when and how farmers plant its seeds. Google and Facebook control nearly 75 percent of the $73 billion market in digital advertising. Most communities have one cable company to choose from, one provider of electricity, one gas company. Economic power, in fact, is more concentrated than ever: According to a study published earlier this year, half of all publicly traded companies have disappeared over the past four decades.

Monopoly can sometimes seem like a good thing. When Walmart first began to take over the retail industry, for example,

Americans embraced its "everyday low prices." Mom-and-pop stores on Main Street may have been going out of business, but the savings at the new Walmart were just too good to resist.

But the lower prices offered by monopolies come at a steep cost. A corporate giant like Amazon is able to use its economic advantage to eliminate jobs, drive down wages, dictate favorable terms to its suppliers, and even set the price the postal service is permitted to charge for the privilege of delivering its packages. In 2012, Amazon bought a robotics company that automates warehouse labor and then blocked its competitors from using the technology. If robots are going to take all our jobs, Amazon wants to make sure it owns all the robots.

Then, there's the way Amazon exploits the conflicts of interest inherent in its business model. Writing in the Yale Law Journal in January, policy analyst Lina Khan recounts the case of an independent merchant who used Amazon to sell Pillow Pets, a line of pillows modeled on NFL mascots. Sales were booming—until the merchant noticed that Amazon had begun offering the exact same product on its own, right before the holidays. Undercut by Amazon, which gave its own Pillow Pets featured placement on the site, the merchant's sales plummeted. Khan calls this "the antitrust paradox." As one merchant observed, "You can't really be a high-volume seller online without being on Amazon, but sellers are very aware of the fact that Amazon is also their primary competitor."

Increasing concentration of ownership has also led to unprecedented levels of corporate crime. In case after case, courts in Europe and the United States have ruled that giant companies are operating as "cartels," engaging in illegal conspiracies among themselves to divide up their turf. As a result, they have been able to fix the price of almost everything in the economy: antibiotics and other life-saving medication, fees on credit card transactions, essential commodities like cell-phone batteries and electric cables and auto parts, the rates companies pay to exchange foreign currency, even the interest rates on the municipal bonds that cities and towns rely on to build schools and libraries and nursing homes. A single price-fixing scandal by the world's largest banks—fixing the global interest rates known as libor—involved more than $500 trillion in financial instruments.

But the price we pay for increasing monopolization goes far beyond such corporate rip-offs. Monopoly increases income inequality by concentrating wealth in major cities: St. Louis, for example, has lost a long roster of hometown companies to mergers and acquisitions, including Anheuser-Busch, TWA, Ralston Purina, May Department Stores, A. G. Edwards, and Panera Bread. Rural America has been especially hard hit, as local stores and family farms have been "disrupted" by giant supermarket chains, seed companies, fertilizer giants, meat processors, and grain traders. And don't blame automation: Corporate America's investments in workplace technology

have plunged by 30 percent over the past 30 years. Even robots are subject to the power of monopoly.

What drives monopolization is not business know-how or technological innovation, but public policy—a political environment that permits or even enables an investor like Jeff Bezos to engage in a massive accumulation of economic power. Not that long ago in America, no company as large and destructive as Amazon would have been allowed to exist. Preventing and breaking up such corporate behemoths, in fact, was at the very center of the Democratic Party's agenda. "Private monopolies are indefensible and intolerable," the party's platform declared in 1900. "They are the most efficient means yet devised for appropriating the fruits of industry to the benefit of the few at the expense of the many."

In the late 1970s, however, the Democrats began to abandon the idea that big is bad. Over the past four decades, the party has stood by as giant supermarket chains replaced local grocery stores and Too Big to Fail banks replaced local lenders. As monopolies broke up unions and drove down wages, Democrats increasingly came to rely on campaign contributions from the very corporations that were consolidating their control over the American economy. The Obama administration, like the Bush administration before it, declined to bring a single major monopolization suit against U.S. companies. Even The Washington Post, that exemplar of political opposition to Donald Trump, is now owned by Jeff Bezos. Dissent, brought to you by monopolists.

But with Republicans in control of all three branches of government, and with the big business ethos espoused by Hillary Clinton in tatters, Democrats may finally be returning to their anti-monopoly roots. Leaders within the party are once again looking to the aggressive antitrust movement launched during the Progressive era and extended through the New Deal, which propelled America into three of its greatest decades of rising prosperity and economic equality. The question now is: Can Democrats find a way to rechannel the popular outrage unleashed by Trump, and to repurpose the party's traditional opposition to monopoly in the age of Amazon?

DEMOCRATS SCORED THEIR first major victory against corporate monopolies during the presidential election of 1912. That year, two candidates ran on platforms that called for placing major restrictions on companies that attempted to dominate the market and thwart competition. Teddy Roosevelt, running on the third-party "Bull Moose" ticket, believed that monopolies were inevitable and in some ways even virtuous, and that the government should simply oversee them to make sure they operated in the public interest. Woodrow Wilson, the Democrat, took a different approach: He argued that monopolies are a fundamental threat to political liberty, and that the government should attack and disperse them to protect democracy from the corrupting influence of economic concentration. After his election, Wilson went on to lay the foundation for the government's anti-monopoly apparatus. He established federal oversight of corporate mergers, set up the Federal Reserve System to rein in Wall Street, and created the Federal Trade Commission to protect free commerce from anticompetitive business practices. Most important of all, perhaps, he placed Louis Brandeis on the Supreme Court.

Brandeis, who had cemented his reputation as "the people's lawyer" during his six-year crusade to prevent banker J. P. Morgan from monopolizing New England's railroads, was the chief intellectual architect of the New Deal. In 1933, just days after Franklin Roosevelt was inaugurated, Brandeis issued a stirring dissent in *Liggett v. Lee*, which struck down a Florida law designed to protect local businesses from out-of-state chains. Reading from the bench, Brandeis blamed the Great Depression on "the gross inequality in the distribution of wealth and income which giant corporations have fostered." The government, he argued, had the right to regulate the "concentration of wealth and power" if it threatened the public welfare. Antitrust, as Brandeis saw it, wasn't about protecting consumers—it was a way to safeguard democracy.

At the time, Brandeis was incredibly influential as a public intellectual; a reissue of his 1914 book, Other People's Money, which detailed how "trusts" were harming the economy, had become a best seller. He not only influenced FDR, who had swept into the White House on a wave of anti-monopoly sentiment, he placed his disciples within the administration. Roosevelt's coalition combined both Brandeisians and Bull Moosers, who waged a fierce intraparty battle over how Democrats should manage the economy. During the first years of the New Deal, the Bull Moose side held sway and even suspended many of the existing antitrust laws. But starting in 1935, with the Second New Deal, Brandeis's faction gained the upper hand and began to take apart the centralized power of corporate monopolies. The Robinson–Patman Act protected local retailers from the onslaught of chain stores such as A&P, the Walmart of its time, while the Glass–Steagall Act prevented Wall Street from gambling with other people's money.

Democrats also unleashed the largest and most aggressive wave of antitrust prosecution in American history. Thurman Arnold, FDR's head of antitrust enforcement, cracked down on some of the country's biggest corporations and trade associations, from General Motors and Alcoa to the American Medical Association and the Associated Press, which were engaged in price fixing and other anticompetitive activities. Rather than railing against monopoly in political terms, Arnold was careful to present himself as an impartial "cop on the beat," a nonpartisan prosecutor using the courts to defend the bedrock American principle of economic competition. By 1942, he was widely considered the most popular figure of the New Deal, alongside J. Edgar Hoover.

The anti-monopoly principle that Arnold and Brandeis established—the idea that economic power should be decentralized and spread into many hands—became the basis of a new social contract. For the next three decades, the federal government largely permitted big business only in segments of the economy that required scale and technical know-how, such as cars, chemicals, and steel. Labor unions made sure that workers were treated fairly, while stores, farms, and banks remained relatively small and under local control. The government also prevented electric utilities, phone companies, airlines, and other "natural monopolies" from diversifying into other businesses, and forced them to offer everyone the same services at the same price. Productivity boomed, and America entered a golden age of egalitarian prosperity, with a large and expanding middle class.

By the late 1960s, however, the social contract had come under attack from both the right and the left. At the University of Chicago, the emerging group of conservative thinkers known as the Chicago School, which produced economists and lawyers such as Milton Friedman, George Stigler, and Robert Bork, rebelled against what they perceived as the socialism of the New Deal. What was needed, they argued, was less government intervention in the marketplace. In 1982, spurred by the theories of Friedman and Bork, Ronald Reagan gutted the federal government's enforcement of antitrust laws, unleashing a massive merger boom in everything from airlines, retail, and oil to packaged goods and manufacturing.

Scholars on the left had also begun to question the antitrust achievements of the New Deal. The historian Richard Hofstadter argued that the anti-monopoly faction of the Democratic Party grew out of the "status anxiety" of the working class, paving the way for McCarthyism. The economist John Kenneth Galbraith, meanwhile, theorized that big business serves as a benevolent, "countervailing power" against the excesses of big labor and big government. His analysis of A&P, the monopoly supermarket chain broken up by Brandeis and the New Dealers, argued that large, concentrated businesses are actually good for consumers because they drive down prices—the same argument made today in support of Amazon. "New Democrats" like Gary Hart, Paul Tsongas, Michael Dukakis, and Bill Clinton moved the party even further from its anti-monopoly roots, embracing concentration, which supposedly offered efficiency and low prices, as a boon to the economy.

In 1992, Clinton removed antitrust language from the Democratic platform and began bashing bank regulators. Once in office, he gutted anti-monopoly restrictions on broadcasters, laying the groundwork for the media concentration that brought us Fox News and Rush Limbaugh. He touched off an unprecedented wave of consolidation in the defense industry; since Clinton took office, the number of "prime" defense contractors has plummeted from 300 to only five. He also repealed the Glass-Steagall Act, which had been erected during the New Deal to separate big banks and investment firms, and moved power into shadow markets free from regulation. The result was the worldwide economic collapse of 2008, brought on by the megabanks and insurance giants created in the wake of the repeal of Glass–Steagall.

Barack Obama, who took office at the height of the financial crisis, was presented with a historic opportunity to reassert the government's role in preventing and breaking up dangerous monopolies. Instead, he argued that the megabanks that Democrats had unleashed on the marketplace were now so central to the economy that they could never be dismantled. Such thinking indicates just how far Democrats have retreated from the trust-busting days of Brandeis, who authored an influential book called The Curse of Bigness. In the view of centrists like Obama, bigness is no longer a menace to society—it's essential to the efficient functioning of the entire economy.

Under Obama, the Justice Department prosecuted only one banker involved in the collapse of the financial system, opting instead for negotiated settlements and inconsequential fines. Federal regulators likewise stood by and did nothing as corporate giants like Facebook and Google and Amazon asserted a staggering level of control over America's digital platforms. Even Obama's signature policy wound up increasing concentration: The Affordable Care Act kicked off a wave of consolidation among hospitals, pharmaceutical companies, and health insurers. Since 2008, there have been more than $10 trillion in mergers, as corporate giants went on a consolidation spree to buy up competitors and expand their dominance in the marketplace. In 2015, the year before Trump was elected, America set a record for the most mergers in a year.

The Democratic Party's about-face on monopolies wasn't just bad for citizens and communities—it led to the disintegration of the party itself. In 1994, two years into Bill Clinton's first term, Democrats lost control of the House of Representatives, which it had held more or less continuously since 1930. Today, Republicans not only control all three branches of the federal government, they also hold majorities in 32 state legislatures, along with the governorships of 33 states. As monopolization has returned in full force, the Democrats now hold less power at the state and local level than they have at any point since the 1920s—the very decade that sparked the rise of the chain store and the onset of the Great Depression. By turning their back on the Progressive-era philosophy of Brandeis and his fellow reformers, Democrats have effectively rendered themselves indistinguishable from pro-business Republicans. "Today, while liberals and conservatives may argue about the size and scope of the federal government," anti-monopoly activist Stacy Mitchell has observed, "support for breaking up and dispersing economic power finds expression in neither of the major parties."

IN MAY, DEMOCRATS gathered for an "ideas conference" at the Center for American Progress in Washington, DC. The daylong event was widely seen as the first audition for 2020, as prominent Democrats lined up to try out for the lead role of presidential candidate. But when Senator Elizabeth Warren stepped up to give the conference's keynote address, she delivered an antitrust speech that would have been right at home at a meeting of FDR's brain trust. "We can crack down on anticompetitive mergers and existing monopolies," Warren assured the approving crowd. "We can break up the big banks."

It was unusually direct language, even for such a liberal gathering. For the first time in nearly half a century, Democrats appear poised to restore monopoly power to the center of their agenda. Beginning with Occupy Wall Street and the populist campaign of Bernie Sanders, and accelerating since the wave of nationalist victories from Brexit to Donald Trump, Democrats are undergoing a generational shift in how they understand the economy, away from the pro-trust accommodations of the Clinton–Obama years and toward the Brandeisian interventions that preceded them.

Warren is now the leader of the emerging Brandeisian wing of the Democratic Party. In 2015, she called for reimposing Glass–Steagall, the powerful anti-monopoly law passed during the New Deal to separate investment and commercial banking. In a speech last year, she directly criticized her party's pro-monopoly stance. "Some people argue that concentration can be good, because big profits encourage competitors to get into the game," she said. "This is the perfect stand-on-your-head-and-the-world-looks-great argument. The truth is pretty basic—markets need competition, now." Since then, Warren has cosponsored a bill to bypass the monopoly on hearing aids by making them available over the counter, sought greater transparency in fees charged by airlines, and worked to block the proposed merger of Time Warner and AT&T.

Other Democrats are also leading the charge against monopolies. Senator Al Franken has used his seat on the Judiciary Committee to help block the Comcast–Time Warner merger and has sought to restrict conflicts of interest in the credit-rating industry. Three Democratic congressmen—Ro Khanna, Rick Nolan, and Mark Pocan—are setting up a caucus to focus on questions of monopoly. And a new family-farm group led by Joe Maxwell, the former lieutenant governor of Missouri, is being organized to take on rural monopolies like Monsanto and meat-processing giant JBS. Even moderate Democrats are being forced to recognize the threat posed by monopoly. "The American people intuitively understand that there's too much concentration in this country," Senator Amy Klobuchar, the ranking Democrat on the antitrust subcommittee, declared in March. "Tackling concentrations of power is a linchpin to a healthy economy and democracy." So far, though, Klobuchar has offered only a few modest reforms that would help federal regulators better analyze proposed mergers and acquisitions.

In the current climate, Democrats oppose antitrust measures at their own peril. During a recent debate over the budget resolution, Klobuchar and Bernie Sanders introduced a proposal to allow the importation of prescription drugs, a measure designed to introduce competition into the pharmaceutical marketplace and reduce prices. Several Democrats, including Senator Cory Booker, worked with the Republicans to vote the measure down. Grassroots reformers responded by sending out e-mail alerts, and Booker was deluged by comments from angry voters. A month later, Booker and Sanders proposed a joint bill to allow prescription drug imports.

Even big business itself is rising up against the monopolistic power wielded by the Big Three: Google, Facebook, and Amazon. All three companies profit from the anticompetitive nature of their business models. Google and Facebook not only control massive content empires, they own the large advertising networks that monetize that content. Amazon is simultaneously a giant retailer, a marketplace for other retailers, and a producer of goods and services. It charges different people different prices for the same items, and it manipulates what gets shown to users through control of the Buy button on its site. So the Big Three's rivals are starting to fight back. Yelp has accused Google of stealing its content to build a shopping site, then manipulating search results to direct users there. News Corp recently accused Google of creating a "dysfunctional and socially destructive" environment for journalism by profiting from fake news. Oracle is financing a Google Transparency Project to expose the company's political influence.

What is emerging, slowly but surely, is a new agenda—one that could once again make tackling the power of monopolies a core component of what it means to be a Democrat. Americans recognize that corporate consolidation doesn't just undercut freedom in the marketplace—it undercuts the economic equality and free flow of information on which our political system depends. "If we will not endure a king as a political power," Senator John Sherman argued in 1890, advocating for the antitrust law that bears his name, "we should not endure a king over the production, transportation, and sale of any of the necessaries of life. If we would not submit to an emperor, we should not submit to an autocrat of trade." Unchecked monopoly power, in short, is simply not compatible with democracy.

To succeed at breaking up today's economic overlords, Democrats must pursue three related approaches to antitrust. First, they must stop monopoly before it happens. That means using the antitrust authority of the federal government to crack down on mergers. "Monopoly is made by acquisition," notes Jonathan Taplin, the author of Move Fast and Break Things: How Facebook, Google, and Amazon Cornered Culture and Undermined Democracy. "Google buying AdMob and DoubleClick, Facebook buying Instagram and WhatsApp, Amazon buying, to name just a few, Audible, Twitch, Zappos, and Alexa. At a minimum, these companies should not be allowed to acquire other major firms, like Spotify or Snapchat." When it comes to stopping mergers and acquisitions, Democrats should become far more aggressive.

Second, Democrats should work to rebuild structural barriers to monopoly in a wide range of industries, as they did in the 1930s with Glass-Steagall in banking. A content distributor like AT&T should not be allowed to buy a content provider like Time Warner. Online ad companies should be barred from owning browsers and ad blockers. And Amazon should not operate as both a marketplace and a competitor within that marketplace. It's one thing, say, to run a big trucking company—but if you're allowed to own the highway itself, other truckers won't stand a chance.

Third, Democrats should move to split up or neutralize the power of corporations that have the ability to dominate and control entire realms of commerce. Amazon has forced publishers to offer it steep discounts on books, Monsanto is organizing the genetics behind much of our food supply, and the Cleveland Clinic exerts power over doctors throughout northeast Ohio. Such monopolies must either be regulated aggressively or broken up.

What is most needed is a new way of understanding how our political economy works, and for whom. Democrats, at last, are beginning to see the need to aggressively restructure the marketplace and decentralize both economic and political power. To win elections on an anti-monopoly platform, however, the party must abandon its penchant for technocratic prescriptions and frame its new agenda in broadly inspirational terms. Here again, they should take a page from Brandeis and the reformers of the Progressive era, who couched their opposition to monopoly in terms of economic common sense and bedrock American values, like competition and community and democracy. To oppose monopoly, by definition, is to support an independent citizenry against financial autocracy—and few things are more American than that. Antitrust means protecting the family farm from Monsanto, free speech from Facebook, the community from Citibank.

Economic power, as Supreme Court Justice William Douglas observed in a 1952 landmark case against Big Steel, "should be scattered into many hands so that the fortune of the people will not be dependent on the whim or caprice, the political prejudices, the emotional stability of a few self-appointed men." The philosophy of antitrust, he explained, "is founded on a theory of hostility to the concentration in private hands of power so great that only a government of the people should have it." As the Trump presidency, a government of the minority, implodes in scandals of its own making, those who voted for him will join the millions of other Americans searching for genuine solutions to the political chaos and economic inequality that is fueled by corporate monopolies. This is the challenge facing the Democratic Party. The goal is not just to oust Trump, but to address the dangerous concentrations of power that drove so many citizens to vote for him in the first place.

Critical Thinking

1. As Amazon expands what contracts?
2. What are the prospects of trust busting?
3. Should economic power be decentralized and spread to many entities?

Internet References

Sociology—Study Sociology Online
http://edu.learnsoc.org/

Sociology Web Resources
http://www.mhhe.com/socscience/sociology/resources/index.htm

Sociosite
http://www.topsite.com/goto/sociosite.net

Socioweb
http://www.topsite.com/goto/socioweb.com

Article   Prepared by: Kurt Finsterbusch, *University of Maryland, College Park*

Hard at Work in the Jobless Future

JAMES H. LEE

Learning Outcomes

After reading this article, you will be able to:

- Consider how automation and innovation that produce so many economic benefits could also produce very negative outcomes.

- Understand how important work is for peoples' self-respect, purpose, and functioning.

- Contemplate how the relations between the haves and the have-nots would change with very high unemployment.

Futurists have long been following the impacts of automation on jobs—not just in manufacturing, but also increasingly in white-collar work. Those in financial services, for example, are being lost to software algorithms, intelligent computers, and robotics.

Terms used for this phenomenon include "off-peopling" and "othersourcing." As Jared Weiner of Weiner, Edrich, Brown recently observed, "Those jobs are not going to return—they can be done more efficiently and error-free by intelligent software."

In the investment business (in which I work), we are seeing the replacement of financial analysts with quantitative analytic systems, and floor traders with trading algorithms. Mutual funds and traditional portfolio managers now compete against ETFs (exchange-traded funds), many of which offer completely automated strategies.

Industries that undergo this transformation don't disappear, but the number of jobs that they support changes drastically. Consider the business of farming, which employed half the population in the early 1900s but now provides just 3% of all jobs. The United States is still a huge exporter of food; it is simply a far more efficient food producer now in terms of total output per farm worker.

In an ideal world, jobs would be plentiful, competitive, and pay well. Most job opportunities have two of these qualities but not all three.

Medicine, law, and finance are jobs that are both competitive and pay well. Retail, hospitality, and personal services are competitive but pay low wages. Unions often ensure that jobs pay well and are plentiful, only to later find that those jobs and related industries are no longer competitive.

Since 1970, manufacturing jobs as a percentage of total employment have declined from a quarter of payrolls to less than 10%. Some of this decline is from outsourcing, some is a result of othersourcing. Those looking for a rebound in manufacturing jobs will likely be disappointed. These jobs will probably not be replaced—not in the United States and possibly not overseas, either.

This is all a part of the transition toward a postindustrial economy.

Jeff Dachis, Internet consulting legend and founder of Razorfish, coined the phrase "everything that can be digital, will be." To the extent that the world becomes more digital, it will also become more global. To the extent that the economy remains physical, business may become more local.

The question is, what is the future of work, and what can we do about it? Here are some ideas.

The Future of Work: Emerging Trends

Work will always be about finding what other people want and need, and then creating practical solutions to fulfill those desires. Our basic assumptions about how work gets done are what's changing. It's less about having a fixed location and schedule and more about thoughtful and engaged activity. Increasingly, this inspiration can happen anytime, anyplace.

Jobs are disappearing, but there's still a future for work. An investment manager looks at how automation and information technology are changing the economic landscape and forcing workers to forge new career paths beyond outdated ideas about permanent employment.

There is a blurring of distinctions among work, play, and professional development. The ways that we measure productivity will be less focused on time spent and more about the value of the ideas and the quality of the output. People are also going to have a much better awareness of when good work is being done.

The old model of work provided an enormous level of predictability. In previous eras, people had a sense of job security and knew how much they would earn on a monthly basis. This gave people a certain sense of confidence in their ability to maintain large amounts of debt. The consumer economy thrived on this system for more than half a century. Location-based and formal jobs will continue to exist, of course, but these will become smaller slices of the overall economy.

The new trends for the workplace have significantly less built-in certainty. We will all need to rethink, redefine, and broaden our sources of economic security. To the extent that people are developing a broader range of skills, we will also become more resilient and capable of adapting to change.

Finally, we can expect that people will redefine what they truly need in a physical sense and find better ways of fulfilling their needs. This involves sharing and making smarter use of the assets we already have. Businesses are doing the same.

The outcome could be an economy that balances the needs between economic efficiency and human values.

Multitasking Careers

In *Escape from Cubicle Nation* (Berkley Trade, 2010), career coach Pamela Slim encourages corporate employees to start a "side hustle" to try out new business ideas. She also recommends having a side hustle as a backup plan in the event of job loss. This strategy is not just for corporate types, and Slim says that "it can also be a great backup for small business owners affected by shifting markets and slow sales."

She says that an ideal side hustle is money-making activity that is doable, enjoyable, can generate quick cash flow, and does not require significant investment. Examples that she includes are businesses such as Web design, massage, tax preparation, photography, and personal training.

The new norm is for people to maintain and develop skill sets in multiple simultaneous careers. In this environment, the ability to learn is something of a survival skill. Education never stops, and the line between working and learning becomes increasingly blurred.

After getting her PhD in gastrointestinal medicine, Helen Samson Mullen spent years working for a pharmaceutical company—first as a medical researcher and then as an independent consultant. More recently, she has been getting certifications for her career transition as a life coach. Clinical project management is now her "side hustle" to bring in cash flow while she builds her coaching business. Meanwhile, she's also writing a book and manages her own Web site. Even with so many things happening at once, Helen told me that "life is so much less crazy now than it was when I was consulting. I was always searching for life balance and now feel like I'm moving into harmony." Her husband, Rob, is managing some interesting career shifts of his own, and is making a lateral move from a 22-year career in pharmaceuticals to starting his own insurance agency with State Farm.

Fixed hours, fixed location, and fixed jobs are quickly becoming a thing of the past for many industries, as opportunities become more fluid and transient. The 40-hour workweek is becoming less relevant as we see more subcontractors, temps, freelancers, and self-employed. The U.S. Government Accountability Office estimates that these "contingent workers" now make up a third of the workforce. Uncertain economics make long-term employment contracts less realistic, while improvements in communications make it easier to subcontract even complex jobs to knowledge workers who log in from airports, home offices, and coffee shops.

Results-Only Workplace Environments

Imagine an office where meetings are optional. Nobody talks about how many hours they worked last week. People have an unlimited amount of vacation and paid time off. Work is done anytime and anywhere, based entirely on individual needs and preferences. Finally, employees at all levels are encouraged to stop doing anything that is a waste of their time, their customers' time, or the company's time.

There is a catch: Quality work needs to be completed on schedule and within budget.

Sound like a radical utopia? These are all basic principles of the Results Only Work Environment (ROWE), as pioneered by Cali Ressler and Jody Thompson while they were human resource managers for Best Buy.

It's "management by objective" taken to a whole new level, Ressler and Thompson write in their book, *Why Work Sucks and How to Fix It* (Portfolio, 2008).

Best Buy's headquarters was one of the first offices to implement the ROWE a little over five years ago, according to Ressler and Thompson. The movement is small, but growing. The Gap Outlet, Valspar, and a number of Minneapolis-based municipal departments have implemented the strategy. Today, 10,000 employees now work in some form of ROWE.

Employees don't even know if they are working fewer hours (they no longer count them), but firms that have adopted the practice have often shown significant improvements in productivity.

"Thanks to ROWE, people at Best Buy are happier with their lives and their work," Ressler and Thompson write in their book. "The company has benefited, too, with increases in productivity averaging 35% and sharp decreases in voluntary turnover rates, as much as 90% in some divisions."

Interestingly enough, the process tends to reveal workers who do not produce results, causing involuntary terminations to creep upward. ROWE managers learn how to treat their employees like responsible grown-ups. There is no time tracking or micromanagement.

"The funny thing is that once employees experience a ROWE they don't want to work any other way," they write. "So employees give back. They get smarter about their work because they want to make sure they get results. They know that if they can deliver results then in exchange they will get trust and control over their time."

Co-Working

There are now more alternatives to either working at home alone or being part of a much larger office. Co-working spaces are shared work facilities where people can get together in an officelike environment while telecommuting or starting up new businesses.

"We provide space and opportunity for people that don't have it," Wes Garnett, founder of The coIN Loft, a co-working space in Wilmington, Delaware, told me.

Getting office space in the traditional sense can be an expensive proposition—with multiyear leases, renovation costs, monthly utilities. "For $200 [a month], you can have access to presentation facilities, a conference room, and a dedicated place to work." And coIN Loft offers day rates for people with less-frequent space needs.

According to Garnett, more people are going to co-working spaces as "community centers for people with ideas and entrepreneurial inclinations." He explains that co-working spaces provide a physical proximity that allows people to develop natural networks and exchange ideas on projects.

"We all know that we're happier and more productive together, than alone" is the motto for nearby Independents Hall in Philadelphia.

Co-working visas enable people to choose from among 200 locations across the United States and in three dozen other countries.

Silicon Colleagues

Expert systems such as IBM's Watson are now "smarter" than real people—at least on the game show *Jeopardy*. It was a moment in television history when Watson decimated previous human champions Ken Jennings and Brad Rutter on trivia questions, which included categories such as "Chicks Dig Me."

IBM's Watson is a software-based knowledge system with unusually robust voice recognition. IBM has stated that its initial markets for the technology are health care, financial services, and customer relations. In the beginning, these systems will work side-by-side with human agents, whispering in their ear to prompt them with appropriate questions and answers that they might not have considered otherwise. In the next decade, they may replace people altogether in jobs that require simple requests for information.

"It's a way for America to get back its call centers," futurist Garry Golden told me. He sees such expert systems reaching the workplace in the next two to three years.

Opting Out

A changing economy is causing people to rethink their priorities. In a recent survey by Ogilvy and Mather, 76% of respondents reported that they would rather spend more time with their families than make more money.

Similarly, the Associated Press has reported that less than half of all Americans say they are happy with their jobs.

Given the stresses of the modern workplace, it is not surprising that more people are simply "opting out" of the workforce. Since 1998, there has been a slight decline in the labor force participation rate—about 5% for men and 3% for women. This trend may accelerate once extensions to unemployment benefits expire. Some of these people are joining the DIY movement, and others are becoming homesteaders.

A shift back toward one-income households can happen when the costs of taxes, commuting, and child care consume a large portion of earnings. People who opt out are not considered unemployed, as they are no longer actively looking for paid work. Their focus often reflects a shift in values toward other activities, such as raising kids, volunteer work, or living simply. This type of lifestyle is often precarious and carries risks, two factors that can be mitigated through public policy that extends the social safety net to better cover informal working as well as formal employment. But this way of life also carries rewards and is becoming a more and more attractive option for millions of people.

The Future of Work, Personified

Justin Caggiano is a laid-back rock-climbing guide whom my wife and I met during our last vacation in the red canyons of Moab, Utah. He's also been guiding rafters, climbers, and hikers for the past six years.

We watched Justin scramble up the side of a hundred-foot natural wall called The Ice Cream Parlor, a nearby climbing destination that earned its name from keeping shaded and cool in the morning despite the surrounding desert. His wiry frame allowed him to navigate the canyon cliffs and set up the safety ropes in a fraction of the time that it took us to make the same climb later that day.

Justin's rock-climbing skills easily translated into work as an arborist during the off-season, climbing up trees and then cutting them from the top down to prevent damage to nearby buildings. Since graduating from college six years ago, he has also worked as an artisanal baker, a carpenter, and a house painter. This makes him something of a down-to-earth renaissance man.

His advice is "to be as flexible as you can—and work your tail off."

It's an itinerant lifestyle for Justin, who frequently changes his location based on the season, work, and nearby climbing opportunities. Rather than committing to a single employer, he pieces together jobs wherever he can find them. His easygoing personality enables him to connect with people and find new opportunities when they become available.

In the winter, he planned to stay with a friend who is building a house, trading help with carpentry and wiring in exchange for free rent. He's been living on a shoestring for a while now, putting away money every year. Longer term, he'd like to develop all of the skills that he needs to build his own home and then pay for land and materials entirely with savings from his bank account. He plans to grow fruit trees and become somewhat self-sufficient. After that time, he says, "I'll work when I'm needed, and live the debt-free, low-cost lifestyle when I'm older."

Our concept of work is getting reworked. A career used to be a ladder of opportunities within a single company. For the postwar generation, the concept of "lifetime employment" was a realistic expectation. My father worked for 40 years at DuPont as a research scientist and spent almost all of that time at a sprawling complex called the Experimental Station. Most of my friends' parents had similar careers. Over time, they were gradually promoted and moved up the corporate ladder. At best, it was a steady progression. At worst, they found their careers stuck in neutral.

The baby boomers had a somewhat different career trajectory. They still managed to have a single career, but it more closely resembled a lattice than a ladder. After working for an employer for five to 10 years, they might find a better opportunity elsewhere and continue their climb. The successful ones cultivated networks at related businesses and continually found better opportunities for themselves.

The career path for younger generations more closely resembles a patchwork quilt, as people attempt to stitch together multiple jobs into something that is flexible and works for them. In today's environment, they sometimes can't find a single job that is big enough to cover all of their expenses, so, like Justin, they find themselves working multiple jobs simultaneously. Some of these jobs might match and be complementary to existing skills, while others may be completely unrelated.

The future of work is less secure and less stable than it was. For many of us, our notions of employment were formed by the labor environment of the later twentieth century. But the reality of jobless working may be more in line with our values. If we can build support systems to benefit workers, wherever they are and whether they be formally employed or not, then we may be able to view the changes sweeping across society as opportunities to return to a fuller, more genuine, and more honest way of life.

Justin's lesson is applicable to all of us; there's a difference between earning a living and making a life.

Justin Caggiano, a rock climber who shows how flexibility and hard work can lead to success even without a steady job.

Critical Thinking

1. What does Lee mean by the "jobless future"?
2. What will happen in America if unemployment rates are very high for a long time?
3. If many workers are redundant, how should the work world be reorganized?

Internet References

Sociosite
www.topsite.com/goto/sociosite.net

Socioweb
www.topsite.com/goto/socioweb.com

Sociology—Study Sociology Online
http://edu.learnsoc.org

Sociology Web Resources
www.mhhe.com/socscience/sociology/resources/index.htm

JAMES H. LEE is an investment manager in Wilmington, Delaware, and a blogger for *THE FUTURIST* magazine.

Lee, James H. Originally published in the March/April 2012 issue of *The Futurist*. Copyright ©2012 by World Future Society, Bethesda, MD. Used with permission via Copyright Clearance Center.

Article   Prepared by: Kurt Finsterbusch, *University of Maryland, College Park*

The Case for Less

Is abundance really the solution to our problems?

TIM WU

Learning Outcomes

After reading this article, you will be able to:

- Appreciate the blessings of abundance but also appreciate the benefits of some constraints.

- Evaluate whether abundance makes us insatiable and causes the loss of some of our self-control.

- See the danger of excessive consumption that drives indebtedness and materialism but be able to distinguish appropriate consumption.

"The future is better than you think" is the message of Peter Diamandis's and Steven Kotler's book *Abundance: The Future Is Better Than You Think.* Despite a flat economy and intractable environmental problems, Diamandis and his journalist co-author are deeply optimistic about humanity's prospects. "Technology," they say, "has the potential to significantly raise the basic standards of living for every man, woman, and child on the planet. . . . Abundance for all is actually within our grasp."

This is a lively book, and it provides an interesting, if uncritical, survey of developments across a range of technologies. We find Craig Venter, the man who sequenced the human genome, sailing around the world looking for algae that can be engineered to emit jet fuel. We explore "vertical farms," which extend the methods perfected by pot growers to entire buildings full of crops. (Imagine Manhattan growing corn.) And in their section on "the almighty stem cell," the authors suggest a future in which the replacing of our organs is not dissimilar to installing a new muffler.

But Diamandis, a space entrepreneur and the co-founder of "Singularity University," is ultimately more interested in our attitude toward the future than in scientific details. He fears that humanity is biologically wired to be pessimistic, and that it therefore cannot appreciate the capacity of "exponential technologies" (those that improve at an exponential rate) to solve humanity's problems. By 2035, Diamandis claims, most of humanity's problems can be solved: we can reach "an end to most of what ails us." Those who doubt the truth of such a proposition are the avatars of "moaning pessimism," who suffer from cognitive defects that prevent them from seeing the truth. The "linear brain," Diamandis says, cannot "comprehend our exponential rate of progress."

A book that preaches the "good news" of humanity's redemption in 2035 may bring to mind more explicitly religious works. Skeptics may call it religion for geeks, where exponential technologies replace Yahweh as the Great Provider. Others may dismiss the book as a species-wide extrapolation from *The Power of Positive Thinking,* where cynicism is humanity's downfall.

But the book is not so easily discounted, for it accurately reflects an important tradition that has driven American technologists since the time of Henry Ford, if not earlier. *Abundance* pretends to be contrarian, and it once might have been, but today it mainly reaffirms a view of society already deeply embedded in much of America's technological elite, especially in Silicon Valley.

That view is simple to state. Humanity's fundamental problem comes down to scarcity—not having enough of what we need and want. We need food, water, new shoes, new gadgets, and so on, and we suffer when we do not have them. That problem can and will be solved by technology, or—at an individual level—by buying or otherwise gaining access to the objects of our desires. Once our needs are met, we can all live happily ever after. As Diamandis puts it, we must imagine "a world where everyone's days are spent dreaming and doing, not scrapping and scraping."

Optimism is a useful motivational tool, and I see no reason to argue with Diamandis about the benefits of maintaining a sunny disposition. I also agree with both Diamandis and the *New Testament* that we may worry about the future more than necessary. Still, all this does not eliminate the need to ask whether the abundance program that Diamandis prescribes is actually right for humanity.

The unhappy irony is that Diamandis prescribes a program of "more" exactly at a point when a century of similar projects have begun to turn on us. To be fair, his ideas are most pertinent to the poorer parts of the world, where many suffer terribly from a lack of the basics. But in the rich and semi-rich parts of the world, it is a different story. There we are starting to see just what happens when we reach surplus levels across many categories of human desire, and it isn't pretty. The unfortunate fact is that extreme abundance—like extreme scarcity, but in different ways—can make humans miserable. Where the abundance project has been truly successful, it has created a new host of problems that are now hitting humanity.

The worldwide obesity epidemic is our most obvious example of this "flip" from problems of scarcity to problems of surplus. Even a few decades ago, the idea of fatness as a public health problem would have seemed ridiculous. Yes, there have always been fat people, but as the scholar Benjamin Caballero writes, as late as the 1930s most nations still just wanted larger citizens. "The military and economic might of countries," he observes, "was critically dependent on the body size and strength of their young generations, from which soldiers and workers were drawn."

Today the statistics on obesity are so outrageous that they seem almost unbelievable. The Centers for Disease Control find that 69 percent of American adults are overweight, and half that number obese or extremely obese. The suffering caused by extreme or morbid obesity is horrifying. Millions of people around the world (nearly seven million in the United States) have trouble moving, and may often stop breathing during sleep, and are prone to ghastly skin infections within the folds of fat, and may be unable to have sex because of hormonal imbalances or because the flab just gets in the way. While no one wants to starve, it is actually hard to say whether it is worse to be malnourished or extremely obese.

There is no single cause for obesity, but the sine qua non for it is plenty of cheap, high-calorie foods. And such foods, of course, are the byproduct of our marvelous technologies of abundance, many of them celebrated in Diamandis's book. They are the byproducts of the "Green Revolution," brilliant techniques in industrial farming and the genetic modification of crops. We have achieved abundance in food, and it is killing us.

Consider another problem with no precise historical equivalent: "information overload." For most of history, humans have mainly been in a state of information scarcity. During the War of 1812, between Britain and the United States, hundreds of soldiers died during the battle of New Orleans because no one had yet heard that the war was over. People died for no reason other than want of good information. But today we sometimes have too much information, and phrases such as "Internet addiction" describe people who are literally unable to stop consuming information even though it is destroying their lives. Consider the case of a Hawaii man named Craig Smallwood who, in 2010, sued the developer of an online game named *Lineage II* for failing to warn him of its addictive qualities. Claiming that he played twenty thousand hours over five years (more than ten hours a day), Smallwood said that the game left him "unable to function independently in usual daily activities."

That is a bizarre extreme, of course; but many of us suffer from milder versions of information overload. Nicolas Carr, in *The Shallows,* made a persuasive case that the excessive availability of information has begun to re-program our brains, creating serious issues for memory and attention span. Where people were once bored, we now face too many entertainment choices, creating a strange misery aptly termed "the paradox of choice" by the psychologist Barry Schwartz. We have achieved the information abundance that our ancestors craved, and it is driving us insane.

Scarce credit—the inability of individuals to borrow money—has long been regarded by economists as among the principal obstacles to economic growth. Hence the "credit revolution" of the twentieth century—a series of inventions that made credit abundant and easily available not just to institutions but also to any individual consumer. Fannie Mae was a clever invention of the 1930s, designed to make it easier for banks to lend money to people who wanted to buy homes. The last century yielded an amazing range of new credit technologies that we now take for granted, such as credit cards, electronic payment systems, and the securitization of mortgages. These inventions, until recent years, managed at long last to make enormous amounts of personal credit available to nearly everyone.

Abundant credit is surely a blessing and essential to economic growth. Yet anyone who reads a newspaper cannot fail to be aware of the systemic downsides. Americans were once known as thrifty; today, personal debt is a leading source of misery. There are more than 1.1 billion credit cards in the United States, and a survey last year suggested that 24 percent of Americans have not just more debt, but more credit card debt, than savings. The amount of household debt held in the United States is about $11.3 trillion, comparable to the amount of government debt held by the public, $12 trillion. The result is that, despite greater actual wealth than ever before, and more access to credit, it is not uncommon for Americans to feel desperate and poor, like the indebted servitors of centuries past.

Those are the personal consequences. At a wider level, a century of technological abundance has failed in its promise to solve problems of disparity, and has actually exacerbated inequalities. While it cannot be denied that the inventions of the last half-century have done much to increase the size of the pie, they have also done much less to distribute it, particularly since the 1970s. The mathematics of more means that the potential for relative disparity has increased. Those with less do have more than before—but relative disparity, or feeling much poorer than others, is a different kind of problem. More of everything has simply made possible disparity on a different scale.

None of this should be taken to downplay the triumphs of the great abundance project of the last century. In the rich parts of the world, most do not fear starvation or a lack of the basics, for perhaps the first time in human history. That is nothing to overlook. Yet it has also many side effects and unintended consequences that we are just beginning to understand fully. If the old world of scarcity yielded a mass population that was hungry, bored, and impoverished, our current surpluses lead to a population that is fat, in debt, overwhelmed, and swamped with too much stuff.

This very idea that too much of what we want can be a bad thing is hard to accept. It seems like a problem that is nice to have: surely we would rather have too much than too little. The miserable in Dickens's times—malnourished, impoverished, overworked—had the right to blame social conditions and demand change. But in today's richer world, if you are overweight, in debt, and overwhelmed, there is no one to blame but yourself. Go on a diet, stop watching cable, and pay off your credit card—that's the answer. In short, we think of scarcity problems as real, and surplus problems as matters of self-control.

That may account for the current popularity of books designed to help readers control themselves. The most interesting among them is *Willpower: Rediscovering the Greatest Human Strength,* by Roy Baumeister and John Tierney, which was explicitly written as a response to the challenges of our times. "People feel overwhelmed because there are more temptations than ever," Baumeister and Tierney argue. "You can put off any job by checking e-mail or Facebook, surfing gossip sites, or playing a video game," not to mention the lure of "alcohol, tobacco, Cinnabons, and cocktail waitresses."

Willpower offers observations, backed by scientific studies, that cannot fail to be fascinating to anyone who has ever wondered where the last hour went. The authors suggest that one's willpower is less an abstraction and more like an actual muscle that must be trained and can fail. The book's most profound sections describe a phenomenon that they call "ego depletion," a state of mental exhaustion where bad decisions are made. It turns out that being forced to make constant decisions is what causes ego depletion. So if willpower is a muscle, making too many decisions in one day is the equivalent of blowing out your hamstrings with too many squats.

The best advice that the authors of *Willpower* offer is this: yes, you can improve your powers of self-control, but don't expect too much. Rather, they recommend avoiding situations that cause ego-depletion altogether. And here is where we find the link between *Abundance* and *Willpower.*

Over the last century, mainly through the abundance project, we have created a world where avoiding constant decisions is nearly impossible. We have created environments that are designed to destroy our powers of self-control by creating constant choices among abundant options. The path of least resistance leads to a pile of debt, a fat body, and an enormous cable bill; strenuous daily efforts are required to avoid that fate. The result is a negative feedback loop: we have more than ever, and therefore need more self-control than ever, but the abundance we've created destroys our ability to resist. It is a setup that Sisyphus might have actually envied.

One possible solution is to double-down on the self-control, and train ourselves to better resist temptation and stick with the program. But, as even Baumeister and Tierney admit, there are good reasons to suspect that relying on willpower alone will not work in an environment designed to destroy it. For, as Baumeister and Tierney make clear, self-control is highly fallible at the best of times. A German study found that using willpower to resist a specific temptation failed half the time. (And those were Germans!) Humans have tested and tried self-control in the face of temptation, and it has repeatedly been found wanting. After decades of dieting and good nutrition, Americans are fatter than ever. And the authors of *Willpower* make the reason clear: we have created conditions that exhaust our willpower, more or less guaranteeing failure.

Moreover, the development of extreme self-control can have some unpleasant side-effects. Baumeister and Tierney don't discuss anorexia nervosa, but they do concede that willpower's greatest twentieth-century advocate was Hitler, and that his greatest propaganda film was named *Triumph of the Will.* Self-control is no doubt the first line of defense in an age of abundance. But if surviving in modern times takes the iron will of a Nazi stormtrooper, perhaps we should ask why we made things this way in the first place.

It is time, as Baumeister and Tierney would agree, to think systematically about the human environments that we are creating with technological powers only imagined by previous generations. At this point, using our powers to create still more of everything—the prescription of *Abundance*—is simply to add fuel to the fire. It is time to take seriously the problems of overload and excess as collective, social challenges, even though they may be our own creations.

When facing a systemic challenge, the classic answer is to deploy government, as the representative of the people. Measures such as New York City's proposed ban on large bottles of soda is exactly such a measure. It is a good start, but there are limits as to what government can do and to what Americans will accept as solutions dictated by elected officials. It is challenging for centralized institutions to manage such subtle matters as information overload and lack of time.

The fact is that our technology industries do far more to determine how we live on a daily basis than government does. For that reason, it is increasingly the duty of the technology industry and the technologists to take seriously the challenge of human overload, and to give it as much attention as the abundance project. It is the first great challenge for post-scarcity thinkers.

Consider that the most successful tech companies of the twentieth century were instruments of abundance, firms such as Archer Daniels Midland, General Motors, and Procter & Gamble. Those firms and their technologies will not disappear. But many of the most successful firms of the twenty-first will be different. They will be augmenters of human will, engineers of self-management, and agents of more effective self-control. Their mission is to liberate humans from the sufferings created by too much.

If I am right, then the future of technology will be different than the one forecast in *Abundance*. Using the technologies that Diamandis describes, there will indeed be, as he says, much more of everything by 2035. But that will be only one side of the picture—the producers, who will generate more and more of what humans crave. On the other side will be the technologies of self-control, which seek to augment humanity's powers to deal with too many choices and with too much of what we want. It may sound crazy, but our technologies are always extensions of ourselves, and humans are strange and conflicted creatures.

So advanced are our technological powers that we will be increasingly trying to create access to abundance and to limit it at the same time. Sometimes we must create both the thesis and the antithesis to go in the right direction. We have spent the last century creating an abundance that exceeds any human scale, and now technologists must turn their powers to controlling our, or their, creation.

Critical Thinking

1. Does wealth produce character defects?

2. Why do most religious teachings warn about the conflict between wealth and spirituality? "You cannot serve both God and money."

3. Consider how environmental limits and deterioration justify consuming less.

Internet References

Sociosite
www.topsite.com/goto/sociosite.net

Socioweb
www.topsite.com/goto/socioweb.com

Sociology—Study Sociology Online
http://edu.learnsoc.org

Sociology Web Resources
www.mhhe.com/socscience/sociology/resources/index.htm

TIM WU is a professor at Columbia Law School and the author, most recently, of *The Master Switch: The Rise and Fall of Information Empires* (Knopf).

Article   Prepared by: Kurt Finsterbusch, *University of Maryland, College Park*

Why For-Profit Education Fails: Moguls' Good Intentions Too Often Betray Them

JONATHAN A. KNEE

Learning Outcomes

After reading this article, you will be able to:

- Understand what are the main motives behind the for-profit efforts in education.

- Point out when educational-business can be the most successful.

Earlier this year, LeapFrog Enterprises, the educational-entertainment business, sold itself for $1 a share. The deal came several months after LeapFrog received a warning from the New York Stock Exchange that it would be delisted if the value of its stock did not improve, a disappointing end to the public life of a company that had the best-performing IPO of 2002.

LeapFrog was one of the very last remaining of the dozens of investments made by Michael Milken through his ambitiously named Knowledge Universe. Founded in 1996 by Milken and his brother, Lowell, with the software giant Oracle's CEO, Larry Ellison, as a silent partner, Knowledge Universe aspired to transform education. Its founders intended it to become, in Milken's phrase, "the pre-eminent for-profit education and training company," serving the world's needs "from cradle to grave."

Knowledge Universe businesses included early childhood learning centers, for-profit K-12 schools, online M.B.A. programs, IT-training services for working professionals, and more. Milken's penchant for secrecy makes a comprehensive assessment impossible—most of the businesses were privately held and some were sold to private buyers for undisclosed sums. But of the companies about which there is public information, most, like LeapFrog, ended badly. Education remains untransformed.

Milken was far from alone in the belief that education could be revolutionized through radical new business models. In 2012, the media mogul Rupert Murdoch and the former New York City schools chancellor Joel Klein established the Amplify division within News Corp. At the time of his initial investment, Murdoch described K-12 education as "a $500 billion sector in the United States alone that is waiting desperately to be transformed." Their idea was to overturn the way children were taught in public schools by integrating technology into the classroom. Although inspirational, the idea entailed competing with a series of multibillion-dollar global leaders in educational hardware, software, and curriculum development. After several years and more than $1 billion, with no serious prospect of ever turning a profit, Murdoch and Klein sold their venture for scrap value to Laurene Powell Jobs, Steve Jobs's widow, last year.

Indeed, over the past couple of decades, a veritable who's who of investors and entrepreneurs has seen an opportunity to apply market discipline or new technology to a sector that often seems to shun both on principle. Yet as attractive and intuitive as these opportunities seemed, those who pursued them have, with surprising regularity, lost their shirts. JP Morgan backed Edison Schools' ill-conceived effort to outsource public education in the late 1990s and saw the business lose 90 percent of its value during its four years as a public company; Goldman Sachs was one of many private-equity firms that came up empty after betting on the inevitable ascendance of for-profit universities; the billionaire Ronald Perelman shut down his futuristic

K-12 educational-technology company, GlobalScholar, after spending $135 million and concluding that the software was faulty and a "mirage"; by the time the hedge-fund titan John Paulson was able to sell the last of his stake in Houghton Mifflin Harcourt, in 2015, he had likely lost hundreds of millions financing the company's misguided mission to remake textbook publishing.

Not all financial investments in education end badly, but the number that have is notable, as are the magnitudes of the fiascos, in stark contrast to the successes of many of these same investors in other domains. The precise sources of failure in each instance are diverse, as are the educational subsectors targeted and the approaches pursued. But what many share is the sweeping nature of their ambition.

YOU CAN SEE this ambition in both the scale and the scope that many of these ventures sought out—often simultaneously. Scale can be an important driver of sustainable profitability, but it is striking just how many for-profit educational ventures—particularly those centered on bricks-and-mortar educational services—have confused scale, which is a relative concept, with absolute size. For services like day care and classroom education, local or regional density of operations can be advantageous, because it enables efficient management of personnel (by far the largest cost), the sharing of fixed expenses like marketing, and sometimes even pricing power. The benefits of a national footprint are seldom as obvious. Yet it is national scale that many ventures have sought. For example, Milken's effort to roll up many of the nation's day care centers began in 1998 and reached its zenith with the $1 billion purchase of KinderCare in 2005. The inherently local nature of this business, however, ensured that its profitability did not improve as it grew larger. When Milken finally sold the business last year, he received less than what he'd paid for his day care acquisitions over the previous 17 years.

Scope, meanwhile, can be the enemy of scale, particularly when pursued at the same time. Spreading investments across a variety of segments can impede the achievement of scale in any of them and also scatter the attention of executives. Time and again in education, big-name investors have launched companies with the broadest ambitions, only to be undone by more-focused players. For example, an early Milken investment wisely targeted a growing population of families who wanted to homeschool their children and were increasingly eligible for public funding through distance-learning charter schools. The business, founded in 1999 and called K12, managed the technology, teaching, and curriculum needed to deliver the full educational experience to kids online. The problem was that Milken wanted to do more than provide a technology-enabled service or run a profitable business; he wanted to transform education by also delivering an entirely new, proprietary, all-digital curriculum.

A competing business, Connections Academy, started later but decided to concentrate on perfecting its technology service and simply adapting the best of existing curricula to its digital environment. Even at a fraction of the size of K12, Connections Academy had a higher profit margin, and five years ago, it sold for a price far higher than K12's current valuation. Today, K12's stock trades at a price far below that of its 2007 IPO.

There is reason to suspect that ego has played a meaningful role in many of these investments. What else, for instance, could explain the consistent fascination with business models that hinge on relationships with elite universities? Great universities have a number of exceptional qualities, but they are not good organizations with which to partner. They are generally much more interested in protecting their exclusivity than in growing, and their bureaucratic decision-making leads them to act slowly and cautiously. These inclinations serve them just fine: Exclusivity and reputation are essentially self-perpetuating for top schools, as reflected in how rarely university rankings change significantly. But that also means the outcome of any commercial arrangements the universities enter into are likely to be lopsided in the schools' favor.

An extreme example of this unhealthy preoccupation with the most-selective institutions is a Milken-backed business originally called Knowledge University, which agreed to finance the expensive development of online-M.B.A. course material and then share revenues, largely in exchange for simply being able to mention its association with institutions like Columbia, Stanford, and the University of Chicago. When Columbia Business School, where I am a co-director of the media-and-technology program, signed its deal with the company—which guaranteed a minimum payment of $20 million over five years—my colleague Bruce Greenwald was quoted as being supportive because the deal "looked like money for nothing." It was, and the company eventually pivoted to another business model (and then collapsed in the face of a federal civil fraud lawsuit). The carcass of the business was sold to K12 for a nominal amount.

YET DESPITE THE FACT that ego and the drive for status are inseparable from many of these ventures, and that they are for-profit enterprises, my own study of these businesses and the people behind them strongly suggests a genuine—and in many cases intense—desire by the founders and investors to improve education. That desire is often associated with deep-seated beliefs about what is wrong with the current system. The evidence suggests that the intensity of desire and belief can cloud the judgment of even the most sophisticated investor. The pursuit of high-minded ideals and the belief that the status quo is so bad that it can't be hard to improve upon causes many investors to devalue execution—yet execution is particularly crucial to the survival of organizations that take on overly broad mandates.

Should anyone care that a bunch of very rich people have failed in these ventures? In fact, this should matter to anyone concerned about education. That failure, repeated so consistently, has given credible fodder to people who resist the active participation of for-profit enterprises in the educational sphere. But that sphere will always comprise public and private, nonprofit and for-profit institutions, and for-profit businesses play an essential role. Public-sector funding is subject to political whims, and the nonprofit sector's funding sources are also typically uncertain. Advocates of for-profit education often understandably emphasize the role that market forces play in improving quality and efficiency. But the most constructive role the for-profit segment may play is in providing a unique level of stability to the educational ecosystem when (and only when) it establishes sustainable business models.

Regardless of whether investors try to do well by doing good, with respect to the operation of for-profit ventures, one basic fact is incontrovertible: One cannot do good for very long if the business does not do well enough to survive. The possibility of doing good would expand exponentially if more investors and managers shifted their attention toward the question of what qualities are most important in building a successful educational franchise.

The greatest educational-business successes have come from a series of targeted, incremental steps forward within tightly defined markets. Recent examples include a business based on plagiarism detection; another that provides tools to high-school students and guidance counselors for college and career selection; and another that delivers day care and early learning programs sponsored by employers. It is no coincidence that Laurene Powell Jobs insisted that News Corp radically contract the scope of Amplify's operations before she agreed to buy the company. Since the purchase, she has continued to spin off marginally related businesses and has greatly narrowed the subject-matter and grade-level focus—targeting middle-school reading, for instance. It is precisely the exit of Amplify's two original visionaries—Murdoch and Klein—that has created the possibility of a successful and socially beneficial future for the company.

As frustrating as they may be to education investors, modest, incremental successes can serve as both a platform and a stimulus for broader transformations to come. Without a sustainable business model, however, even the most inspired investors and entrepreneurs will ultimately only build a legacy of disillusionment.

Critical Thinking

1. Why do so many for-profit education businesses fail?
2. Do you agree with Knee that for-profit enterprises can make valuable contributions to education?
3. Why do for-profit enterprises want to enter the field of education?

Internet References

Sociology—Study Sociology Online
　http://edu.learnsoc.org/
Sociology Web Resources
　http://www.mhhe.com/socscience/sociology/resources/index.htm
Sociosite
　http://www.topsite.com/goto/sociosite.net
Socioweb
　http://www.topsite.com/goto/socioweb.com

Jonathan A. Knee is a professor of practice at Columbia Business School and a senior adviser at Evercore Partners.

Article   Prepared by: Kurt Finsterbusch, *University of Maryland, College Park*

Noam Chomsky on How the United States Developed Such a Scandalous Health System

C. J. POLYCHRONIOU

Learning Outcomes

After reading this article, you will be able to:

- Discuss most of the health-care issues.
- Explain why the United States is an outlier in the provision of free health care among developed nations.
- Describe other rights that the US refuses to agree to.

In the following excerpt, originally published at Truthout in January 2017, shortly before Donald Trump's inauguration, Chomsky discusses the historical and political factors that have created and maintained such a shamefully profit-driven health system in the United States.

C. J. Polychroniou: Article 25 of the UN Universal Declaration on Human Rights (UDHR) states that the right to health care is indeed a human right. Yet, it is estimated that close to 30 million Americans remain uninsured even with the 2010 Patient Protection and Affordable Care Act (ACA) in place. What are some of the key cultural, economic, and political factors that make the United States an outlier in the provision of free health care?

Noam Chomsky: First, it is important to remember that the United States does not accept the Universal Declaration of Human Rights—though in fact the UDHR was largely the initiative of Eleanor Roosevelt, who chaired the commission that drafted its articles, with quite broad international participation.

The UDHR has three components, which are of equal status: civil–political, socioeconomic, and cultural rights. The United States formally accepts the first of the three, though it has often violated its provisions. The US pretty much disregards the third. And to the point here, the United States has officially and strongly condemned the second component, socioeconomic rights, including Article 25.

Opposition to Article 25 was particularly vehement in the Reagan and Bush I years. Paula Dobriansky, deputy assistant secretary of state for human rights and humanitarian affairs in these administrations, dismissed the "myth" that "economic and social rights constitute human rights," as the UDHR declares. She was following the lead of Reagan's UN Ambassador Jeane Kirkpatrick, who ridiculed the myth as "little more than an empty vessel into which vague hopes and inchoate expectations can be poured." Kirkpatrick thus joined Soviet Ambassador Andrei Vyshinsky, who agreed that it was a mere "collection of pious phrases." The concepts of Article 25 are "preposterous" and even a "dangerous incitement," according to Ambassador Morris Abram, the distinguished civil rights attorney who was US Representative to the UN Commission on Human Rights under Bush I, casting the sole veto of the UN Right to Development, which closely paraphrased Article 25 of the UDHR. The Bush II administration maintained the tradition by voting alone to reject a UN resolution on the right to food and the right to the highest attainable standard of physical and mental health (the resolution passed 52-1).

Rejection of Article 25, then, is a matter of principle. And also a matter of practice. In the OECD ranking of social justice, the United States is in 21th place of the 31, right above Greece, Chile, Mexico, and Turkey. This is happening in the richest country in world history, with incomparable advantages. It was quite possibly already the richest region in the world in the eighteenth century.

In extenuation of the Reagan–Bush–Vyshinsky alliance on this matter, we should recognize that formal support for the UDHR is all too often divorced from practice.

US dismissal of the UDHR in principle and practice extends to other areas. Take labor rights. The United States has failed to ratify the first principle of the International Labour Organization Convention, which endorses "Freedom of Association and Protection of the Right to Organise." An editorial comment in the *American Journal of International Law* refers to this provision of the International Labour Organization Convention as "the untouchable treaty in American politics." US rejection is guarded with such fervor, the report continues, that there has never even been any debate about the matter. The rejection of International Labour Organization Conventions contrasts dramatically with the fervor of Washington's dedication to the highly protectionist elements of the misnamed "free trade agreements," designed to guarantee monopoly pricing rights for corporations ("intellectual property rights"), on spurious grounds. In general, it would be more accurate to call these "investor rights agreements."

Comparison of the attitude toward elementary rights of labor and extraordinary rights of private power tells us a good deal about the nature of American society.

Furthermore, US labor history is unusually violent. Hundreds of US workers were being killed by private and state security forces in strike actions, practices unknown in similar countries. In her history of American labor, Patricia Sexton—noting that there are no serious studies—reports an estimate of 700 strikers killed and thousands injured from 1877 to 1968, a figure which, she concludes, may "grossly understate the total casualties." In comparison, one British striker was killed since 1911.

As struggles for freedom gained victories and violent means became less available, business turned to softer measures, such as the "scientific methods of strike breaking" that have become a leading industry. In much the same way, the overthrow of reformist governments by violence, once routine, has been displaced by "soft coups" such as the recent coup in Brazil, though the former options are still pursued when possible, as in Obama's support for the Honduran military coup in 2009, in near isolation. Labor remains relatively weak in the United States in comparison to similar societies. It is constantly battling even for survival as a significant organized force in the society, under particularly harsh attack since the Reagan years.

All of this is part of the background for the US departure in health care from the norm of the OECD, and even less privileged societies. But there are deeper reasons why the United States is an "outlier" in health care and social justice generally. These trace back to unusual features of American history. Unlike other developed state capitalist industrial democracies,

the political economy and social structure of the United States developed in a kind of tabula rasa. The expulsion or mass killing of Indigenous nations cleared the ground for the invading settlers, who had enormous resources and ample fertile lands at their disposal, and extraordinary security for reasons of geography and power. That led to the rise of a society of individual farmers, and also, thanks to slavery, substantial control of the product that fueled the industrial revolution: cotton, the foundation of manufacturing, banking, commerce, retail for both the United States and Britain, and less directly, other European societies. Also relevant is the fact that the country has actually been at war for 500 years with little respite, a history that has created "the richest, most powerful and ultimately most militarized nation in world history," as scholar Walter Hixson has documented.

For similar reasons, American society lacked the traditional social stratification and autocratic political structure of Europe, and the various measures of social support that developed unevenly and erratically. There has been ample state intervention in the economy from the outset—dramatically in recent years—but without general support systems.

As a result, US society is, to an unusual extent, business-run, with a highly class-conscious business community dedicated to "the everlasting battle for the minds of men." The business community is also set on containing or demolishing the "political power of the masses," which it deems as a serious "hazard to industrialists" (to sample some of the rhetoric of the business press during the New Deal years, when the threat to the overwhelming dominance of business power seemed real).

Here is yet another anomaly about US health care: According to data by the Organization for Economic Cooperation and Development (OECD), the United States spends far more on health care than most other advanced nations, yet Americans have poor health outcomes and are plagued by chronic illnesses at higher rates than the citizens of other advanced nations. Why is that?

US health-care costs are estimated to be about twice the OECD average, with rather poor outcomes by comparative standards. Infant mortality, for example, is higher in the United States than in Cuba, Greece, and the EU generally, according to CIA figures.

As for reasons, we can return to the more general question of social justice comparisons, but there are special reasons in the health-care domain. To an unusual extent, the US health-care system is privatized and unregulated. Insurance companies are in the business of making money, not providing health care, and when they undertake the latter, it is likely not to be in the best interests of patients or to be efficient. Administrative costs are far greater in the private component of the health-care system than in Medicare, which itself suffers by having to work through the private system.

Comparisons with other countries reveal much more bureaucracy and higher administrative costs in the US privatized system than elsewhere. One study of the United States and Canada a decade ago, by medical researcher Steffie Woolhandler and associates, found enormous disparities, and concluded that "Reducing U.S. administrative costs to Canadian levels would save at least $209 billion annually, enough to fund universal coverage." Another anomalous feature of the US system is the law banning the government from negotiating drug prices, which leads to highly inflated prices in the United States as compared with other countries. That effect is magnified considerably by the extreme patent rights accorded to the pharmaceutical industry in "trade agreements," enabling monopoly profits. In a profit-driven system, there are also incentives for expensive treatments rather than preventive care, as strikingly in Cuba, with remarkably efficient and effective health care.

Why aren't Americans demanding—not simply expressing a preference for in survey polls—access to a universal health-care system?

They are indeed expressing a preference, over a long period. Just to give one telling illustration, in the late Reagan years 70 percent of the adult population thought that health care should be a constitutional guarantee, and 40 percent thought it already was in the Constitution since it is such an obviously legitimate right. Poll results depend on wording and nuance, but they have quite consistently, over the years, shown strong and often large majority support for universal health care—often called "Canadian-style," not because Canada necessarily has the best system, but because it is close by and observable. The early ACA proposals called for a "public option." It was supported by almost ⅔ of the population, but was dropped without serious consideration, presumably as part of a compact with financial institutions. The legislative bar to government negotiation of drug prices was opposed by 85 percent, also disregarded—again, presumably, to prevent opposition by the pharmaceutical giants. The preference for universal health care is particularly remarkable in light of the fact that there is almost no support or advocacy in sources that reach the general public and virtually no discussion in the public domain.

The facts about public support for universal health care receive occasional comment, in an interesting way. When running for president in 2004, Democrat John Kerry, the *New York Times* reported, "took pains . . . to say that his plan for expanding access to health insurance would not create a new government program," because "there is so little political support for government intervention in the health care market in the United States." At the same time, polls in the *Wall Street Journal, Businessweek, the Washington Post* and other media found overwhelming public support for government guarantees to everyone of "the best and most advanced health care that technology can supply."

But that is only public support. The press reported correctly that there was little "political support" and that what the public wants is "politically impossible"—a polite way of saying that the financial and pharmaceutical industries will not tolerate it, and in American democracy, that's what counts.

Returning to your question, it raises a crucial question about American democracy: Why isn't the population "demanding" what it strongly prefers? Why is it allowing concentrated private capital to undermine necessities of life in the interests of profit and power? The "demands" are hardly utopian. They are commonly satisfied elsewhere, even in sectors of the US system. Furthermore, the demands could readily be implemented even without significant legislative breakthroughs. For example, by steadily reducing the age for entry to Medicare.

The question directs our attention to a profound democratic deficit in an atomized society, lacking the kind of popular associations and organizations that enable the public to participate in a meaningful way in determining the course of political, social, and economic affairs. These would crucially include a strong and participatory labor movement and actual political parties growing from public deliberation and participation instead of the elite-run candidate-producing groups that pass for political parties. What remains is a depoliticized society in which a majority of voters (barely half the population even in the super-hyped presidential elections, much less in others) are literally disenfranchised, in that their representatives disregard their preferences, while effective decision-making lies largely in the hands of tiny concentrations of wealth and corporate power, as study after study reveals.

The prevailing situation reminds us of the words of America's leading twentieth-century social philosopher, John Dewey, much of whose work focused on democracy and its failures and promise. Dewey deplored the domination by "business for private profit through private control of banking, land, industry, reinforced by command of the press, press agents and other means of publicity and propaganda" and recognized that "Power today resides in control of the means of production, exchange, publicity, transportation and communication. Whoever owns them rules the life of the country," even if democratic forms remain. Until those institutions are in the hands of the public, he continued, politics will remain "the shadow cast on society by big business."

This was not a voice from the marginalized far left, but from the mainstream of liberal thought.

Turning finally to your question again, a rather general answer, which applies in its specific way to contemporary western democracies, was provided by David Hume over 250 years ago, in his classic study *Of the First Principles of Government*. Hume found nothing more surprising than to see the easiness with which the many are governed by the few; and to observe the implicit submission with which men resign their own sentiments and passions to those of their rulers. When we enquire by what means this wonder is brought about, we shall find that as Force is always on the side of the governed, the governors have nothing to support them but opinion. 'Tis therefore, on opinion only that government is founded; and this maxim extends to the most despotic and most military governments, as well as to the most free and most popular.

Implicit submission is not imposed by laws of nature or political theory. It is a choice, at least in societies such as ours, which enjoys the legacy provided by the struggles of those who came before us. Here power is indeed "on the side of the governed," if they organize and act to gain and exercise it. That holds for health care and for much else.

Critical Thinking

1. Why is the United States ranked 27th in the OECD ranking of social justice?
2. Why do high health-care costs in the United States not result in good health care?
3. Why are Americans not demanding a universal health-care system?

Internet References

Sociology—Study Sociology Online
  http://edu.learnsoc.org/
Sociology Web Resources
  http://www.mhhe.com/socscience/sociology/resources/index.htm
Sociosite
  http://www.topsite.com/goto/sociosite.net
Socioweb
  http://www.topsite.com/goto/socioweb.com

C. J. POLYCHRONIOU is a political economist/political scientist who has taught and worked in universities and research centers in Europe and the United States. His main research interests are in European economic integration, globalization, the political economy of the United States, and the deconstruction of neoliberalism's politico-economic project.

Article Prepared by: Kurt Finsterbusch, *University of Maryland, College Park*

A Thousand Years Young

An "anti-aging activist" identifies the medical and biochemical advances that could eventually eliminate all the wear and tear that our bodies and minds suffer as we grow old. Those who undergo continuous repair treatments could live for millennia, remain healthy throughout, and never fear dying of old age.

AUBREY DE GREY

Learning Outcomes

After reading this article, you will be able to:

- Understand that Aubrey de Grey's approach to life extension is to constantly rejuvenate the body as it deteriorates.

- Assuming that de Grey is right, consider how people would change their lifestyles.

- Understand the many specific treatments that would together greatly extend life.

L et me first say very explicitly: I don't work on longevity. I work on health. People are going to live longer as a result of the therapies I will describe, but extended longevity is a side effect—a consequence of keeping people healthy. There is no way in hell that we are going to keep people alive for a long time in a frail state. People will live longer only if we succeed in keeping them healthy longer.

The problem of aging is unequivocally humanity's worst medical problem. Roughly 100,000 people worldwide die every day of it, and there's an awful lot of suffering that happens before you die. But I feel that the defeat of aging in the foreseeable future is a realistic proposition. We will have medicine that will get aging under control to the same level that we now have most infectious diseases under control.

This article will describe what aging is, what regenerative medicine is, and what the various alternative approaches are to combat aging and postpone the ill health of old age. I'll then go into the details of the approach that I feel we need to take and what my expectations are for the future.

Regenerative medicine is any medical intervention that seeks to restore some part of the body—or the whole body—to how

it was before it suffered some kind of damage. It could be damage that happened as the result of an acute injury, such as spinal cord damage. But it could also be damage that accumulated as a chronic condition over a long period of time.

Aging is a side effect of being alive in the first place. *Metabolism* is the word that biologists use to encompass all the aspects of being alive—all the molecular and cellular and systemic processes that keep us going from one day to the next and from one year to the next.

Ongoing lifelong side effects of metabolism—i.e., *damages*—are created throughout life. For whatever reason, damage is not repaired when it occurs. So damage accumulates. For a long time, the amount of damage is tolerable, and the metabolism just carries on. But eventually, damage becomes sufficiently extensive that it gets in the way of metabolism. Then metabolism doesn't work so well, and *pathologies*—all the things that go wrong late in life, all the aspects of age-related ill health—emerge and progress.

Geriatrics versus Gerontology

Traditionally, there have been two themes within the study of aging that aim to actually do something about this process. One is the *geriatrics* approach, which encompasses pretty much everything that we have today in terms of medical treatments for the elderly.

The geriatrics approach is all about the pathology. It focuses on old people in whom the pathologies are already emerging, and strives to slow down their progression so that it takes longer for those pathologies to reach a life-threatening stage.

The *gerontology* approach, on the other hand, says that prevention is better than cure. This approach assumes that it will be more effective to dive in at an earlier point in the chain of events and clean up metabolism so that it creates these various types of damage at a slower rate than it naturally would. The effect would be to postpone the age at which damage reaches the level of abundance that is pathogenic.

The two approaches both sound pretty promising, but they're really not. The problem with the geriatrics approach is that aging is awfully chaotic, miserable, and complicated. There are many things that go wrong with people as they get older, and they tend to happen at much the same time. These problems interact, exacerbating each other, and damage accumulates. Even later in life, as damage continues to accumulate, the pathologies of old age become progressively more and more difficult to combat.

The geriatric approach is thus intervening too late in the chain of events. It's better than nothing, but it's not much better than nothing.

So that leaves us with the gerontology approach. Unfortunately, the gerontology approach has its own problem: Metabolism is complicated. What we know about how metabolism works is completely dwarfed by the utterly astronomical amount that we *don't* know about how metabolism works. We have no prospect whatsoever of being able to interfere in this process in a way that does not simply do more harm than good.

A Maintenance Approach

There are some Volkswagen Bugs that are 50 years old or more and still running. And the reason is because those VW Bugs have been extraordinarily well maintained. If you maintain your car only as well as the law requires, then it will only last 15 years or so. But if you do a lot more, then you can do a lot better. Maintenance works.

Now what does that tell us about the human body? Well, quite a lot, because the human body is a machine. It's a really complicated machine, but it's still a machine. So there is a third way of combating aging by postponing age-related ill health. This is the *maintenance* approach. We go in and periodically repair the damage that metabolism creates, so as to prevent that damage from accumulating and reaching the level that causes the pathology of old age to emerge and to progress.

Maintenance is a much more promising approach than either geriatrics or gerontology. First, the maintenance approach is preemptive, so it doesn't have this problem of this downward spiral of the geriatrics approach.

Second, the maintenance approach avoids the problem of the gerontology approach because it does not attempt to intervene with metabolism; we merely fix up the consequences. In other words, we let metabolism create these various types of damage at the rate that it naturally does, and then repair the damages before they cause pathology. We can get away with not understanding very much at all about how metabolism creates damage. We just have to characterize the damage itself and figure out ways to repair it.

That's pretty good news, but it gets better. It also turns out that damage is simpler than its causes or its consequences. All the phenomena that qualify as damage can be classified into one of seven major categories:

- Junk inside cells.
- Junk outside cells.
- Too few cells.
- Too many cells.
- Chromosome mutations.
- Mitochondria mutations.
- Protein cross-links.

By "junk inside cells," I am referring to the molecular byproducts of normal biologic processes that are created in the cell and that the cell, for whatever reason, does not have the machinery to break down or to excrete. Those byproducts simply accumulate, and eventually the cell doesn't work so well. That turns out to be the main cause of cardiovascular disease and of macular degeneration.

"Junk outside cells" means things like senile plaques in Alzheimer's disease. This creates the same molecular damage, but in this case it is in the spaces between cells.

"Too few cells" simply means cells are dying and not being automatically replaced by the division of other cells. This is the cause of Parkinson's disease, the particular part of the brain in which neurons happen to die more rapidly than in most parts of the brain and they're not replaced. When there are too few of them, that part of the brain doesn't work so well.

But here's the really good news. We actually have a pretty good idea how to fix all of these types of damage. Here is the same list of types of damage, and on the right is the set of approaches that I feel are very promising for fixing them:

Damage	Treatment
Junk inside cells	transgenic microbial hydolases
Junk outside cells	Phagocytosis by immune stimulation
Too few cells (cell loss)	cell therapy
Too many cells (death-resistant cells)	suicide genes and immune stimulation
Chromosome mutations	telomerase/ALT gene deletion plus periodic stem-cell reseeding
Mitochondria mutations	allotopic expression of 13 proteins
Protein cross-links	AGE-breaking molecules and enzymes

Stem-cell therapy replaces those cells that the body cannot replace on its own. That includes joint degeneration and muscular-skeletal problems. For example, arthritis ultimately comes from the degeneration of the collagen and other extracellular material in the joints, which happens as a result of insufficient regeneration of that tissue.

The SENS Foundation: Doing Something About Aging

I'm the chief officer of a 501(c)3 public charity based in California. The mission of the SENS Foundation is to develop, promote, and enable widespread access to regenerative medicine as solutions to the disabilities and diseases of aging.

Is there any competition in this work? Are other people trying other things? The short answer is, Not really. There are other people, of course, looking at ways to postpone aging and age-related ill health. But regenerative medicine is really the only game in town when we're talking about serious postponement of age-related ill health. And the SENS Foundation really is the hub of that concept.

We are a charity, so if you are a billionaire, please see me! But of course it's not just money we need. We need people's time and expertise. If you're a biologist, work on relevant things. Write to us and ask us for advice about what to work on, because we need more manpower in this area. If you're a conference organizer, have me to speak. If you're a journalist, come and interview me. It's all about getting the word out.

—*Aubrey de Grey*

Details: The SENS Foundation, www.sens.org; e-mail foundation @sens.org.

For some other medical conditions, such as Alzheimer's, we need to restore the functions of those cells that are already there by getting rid of the garbage accumulating outside them. Toward that purpose, there are phase-three clinical trials for the elimination of senile plaques in the brains of Alzheimer's patients. This is a technology using vaccination that we at the SENS Foundation are extending to the elimination of other types of extracellular garbage.

In fact, we now have an enormous amount of detail about how we're going to reverse each of the seven categories of age-related damage, so that's why I feel that my estimates of how long it's going to take to get there are likely to be borne out accurately.

Case in Point: Cleaning the Cellular Garbage

I'm going to talk about one example: the garbage that accumulates inside cells. I'm going to explain what *transgenic microbial hydrolases* are.

White blood cells, called macrophages, sweep along a healthy adult's artery walls to clean up miscellaneous detritus,

typically lipo protein particles that were transporting cholesterol around the body from one place to another and that got stuck in the artery wall. Macrophages are very good at coping with cholesterol, but they are not so good at coping with certain derivatives of cholesterol, such as oxysterols. These contaminants end up poisoning macrophages. The macrophages become unable even to cope with native cholesterol, and then they themselves break down, lodging in the artery walls. This is the beginning of an atherosclerotic plaque. The results are cardiovascular disease, heart attacks, or strokes. In the eye, this phenomenon causes macular degeneration.

To combat this problem, we might adapt bioremediation technology from environmental decontamination. The technology that is used to break down pollutants in the environment could be adapted for biomedical purposes, breaking down the body's contaminants.

If we could apply this bioremediation process to our own cells, we could combat the initial process that turns young people into old people in the first place. A very simple idea. The question is, does it work? Bioremediation for getting rid of pollutants works really well: It's a thriving commercial discipline.

There are a number of oxidized derivatives of cholesterol, but the nastiest in abundance and toxicity is 7-ketocholesterol—public enemy number one in atherosclerosis. We have tried "feeding" it to many different strains of bacteria. Most of them can't do anything with it, but we've found two strains of bacteria that gorge themselves on it. After only 10 days, the material is completely gone.

The next step is to figure out how these bacteria are able to do this from a genetic basis. From there, we could try to turn 7-ketocholesterol back into native cholesterol. But there are other steps that we can use—remember that I said we're looking to avoid the problem of things neither being broken down nor excreted. There are modifications that we can make to compounds that are toxic that simply promote their excretion rather than promoting their degradation.

So that's all pretty good news. But don't get me wrong. This is really hard. This is a very ambitious, long-term. project. The processes we hope to develop must work in vivo. What we are seeking is a truly definitive, complete cure for cardiovascular disease and for other pathologies caused by the accumulation of molecular garbage inside cells.

Escape Velocity: From Longevity To Immortality?

I do not claim that any of the work I've just described is going to be a "cure" for aging. I claim, rather, that it's got a good chance of adding 30 years of extra healthy life to people's lives. I call that *robust human rejuvenation*. And 30 years is better than nothing, but it sure does not equate to defeating aging completely. So what's the rest of my story?

The rest of the story is that it's not something that's going to work just on people who haven't been conceived yet. It's stuff that is going to work on people who are already middle-aged or older when the therapies arrive.

This is fundamentally what it all comes down to. The maintenance approach is so cool because repairing damage buys time.

At age zero, people start off with not much damage. Time goes on, they age, damage accumulates, reserve is depleted, and eventually, they get down to a certain point—the frailty threshold—and that's when pathologies start to happen. Then they're not long for this world.

Now take someone who is in middle age. You have therapies that are pretty good, but not perfect, at fixing the damage. They can be rejuvenated, but not all the way. These therapies do not reduce the rate at which damage is created. Aging happens at the normal rate.

Then we reapply the same therapies again and again. But consider that the interval between the first and second applications of these therapies to some particular individual may be 15 to 20 years. That's a long time in biomedical technology, and it means that the person is going to get new and improved therapies that will not only fix the types of damage that they could fix 15 years previously, but also fix some types of damage that they could not fix 15 years previously.

So after the second rejuvenation, our hero is not only more thoroughly rejuvenated than he would be if he'd gotten the old therapies, but he's actually more rejuvenated than he was when he got the old therapies, even though at that point he was chronologically younger. Now we see this phenomenon where we don't hit diminishing returns on additional therapies. People over the long term will be getting progressively younger as they're getting chronologically older. They'll remain far away from reaching the frailty threshold, however long that they live. They will only be subjected to the risks of death and ill health that affect young adults. They never become more susceptible to ill health simply as a result of having been born a long time ago.

There's some minimum rate at which we have to improve the comprehensiveness of these therapies in order for the general trend in increased life span to be upwards rather than downwards. And that minimum rate is what I call *longevity escape velocity*. It's the rate at which these rejuvenation therapies need to be improved in terms of comprehensiveness following that first step—the first-generation therapies that give robust human regeneration—in order to stay one step ahead of the problem and to outpace the accumulation of damage that they cannot yet repair.

So is it realistic? Are we likely actually to reach longevity escape velocity and to maintain it? We are. Consider powered flight as an illustrated example: There are very big differences between fundamental breakthroughs and incremental refinements of those breakthroughs. Fundamental breakthroughs are very hard to predict. Mostly people think they're not going to happen right up until they already have happened.

Incremental refinements, meanwhile, are very much more predictable. Leonardo da Vinci probably thought he was only a couple of decades away from getting off the ground. He was wrong. But once the Wright brothers got there, progress was ridiculously rapid. It only took 24 years for someone to fly solo across the Atlantic (that was Lindbergh), 22 more years until the first commercial jet liner, and 20 more years until the first supersonic airlines.

Can we actually give more direct evidence that we are likely to achieve longevity escape velocity? I believe that we can.

An Age-Busting Virtuous Cycle

A few years ago I worked with others on a computer simulation of the aging process to see what the impact would be of these interventions coming in at a realistic schedule. We started by imagining a population of adults who were all born in 1999. Everyone is alive at age zero and almost everyone survives until age 50 or 60, at which point they start dropping like flies; hardly anyone gets beyond 100.

Next, we imagined another population whose intrinsic risk of death at any given age is the same as for the first, but who are receiving these therapies. But they only start receiving them when they are already 80 years old. That population's survival rate will actually mostly coincide with the first population's survival rate, because obviously half the population or so is dead by age 80 and those who are still living are already in a reasonably bad way.

But what if population number two started getting these therapies 10 years earlier, when they're only 70? Initially, the same story is the case—there is not a lot of benefit. But gradually, the therapies get the upper hand. They start to impose genuine rejuvenation on these people so that they become biologically younger and less likely to die. Some of them reach 150, by which time they have very little chance of dying of *any* age-related cause. Eventually, there is exactly no such risk.

And if they're 60 years old when the therapies begin? Then almost half of them will get to that point. So we calculated, group by group.

Here's the real kicker: I was ludicrously over-pessimistic in the parameters that I chose for this simulation. I said that we would assume that the therapy would only be doubled in their efficacy every 42 years. Now, 42 years: That's the difference between Lindbergh's *Spirit of St. Louis* and the *Concorde!* But even then, we unambiguously see longevity escape velocity.

So it's inescapable. If and when we do succeed in developing these rejuvenation therapies that give us those first couple of decades more of health and the postponement of age-related ill health, then we will have done the hard part. The sky is the limit after that.

Here is what it means. At the moment, the world record for life span is 122. We won't be getting anyone who is 150 until such time as we do develop these technologies that give us robust human rejuvenation. But we will have done the hard part, so people not much younger than that will be able to escape aging indefinitely, living even to age 1,000.

A thousand is not pulled out of the air. It's simply the average age—plus or minus a factor of two—that people would live to if we already didn't have aging, if the only risks of death were the same risks that currently afflict young adults in the Western world today.

Should we be developing these therapies? We are ignorant about the circumstances within which humanity of the future will be deciding whether to use these technologies or not. It could actually be a no-brainer that they will want to use them. And if we have prevented them from using them by not developing them in time, then future generations won't be very happy. So it seems to me that we have a clear moral obligation to develop these technologies so as to give humanity of the future the choice. And the sooner, the better.

Critical Thinking

1. Would you like to live 1,000 years? Aubrey de Grey says that the technology will be developed to make that happen for you or your grandchildren.
2. What would be the impacts on social life and society if healthy life extended for hundreds of years?
3. Why is de Grey's message largely ignored by the media?

Internet References

Sociosite
www.topsite.com/goto/sociosite.net

Socioweb
www.topsite.com/goto/socioweb.com

Sociology—Study Sociology Online
http://edu.learnsoc.org

Sociology Web Resources
www.mhhe.com/socscience/sociology/resources/index.htm

AUBREY DE GREY is a biomedical gerontologist and chief science officer of the SENS Foundation (www.sens.org). He is the author (with Michael Rae) of *Ending Aging* (St. Martin's Press, 2007) and editor-in-chief of the journal *Rejuvenation Research*. This article draws from his presentation at WorldFuture 2011 in Vancouver.

Article　　Prepared by: Kurt Finsterbusch, *University of Maryland, College Park*

American Religion Has Never Looked Quite Like It Does Today

Based on these trends, the future of religion in America probably isn't a church.

ANTONIA BLUMBERG

Learning Outcomes

After reading this article, you will be able to:

- Describe the changing religious scene in America.
- Identify some of the ideas and practices that have changed over the years.
- Describe the situation historically of non-Christian faiths in the United States.

Nearly a century after German philosopher Friedrich Nietzsche first proclaimed "God is dead," TIME magazine released a controversial cover on its April 8, 1966 edition with the related provocative question: "Is God dead?"

Both Nietzsche and TIME were exploring the prominence of God in people's lives, and whether religiosity was on the decline in the society. Fifty years later, religion experts are still grappling with that question, though the context has drastically changed.

By many measures, religious practice and affiliation has greatly declined in the United States in the last 50 years. And yet spirituality, religion's free-spirited sibling, appears to be as strong—if not stronger—than ever.

Here's a look at some of the ways religious practice and belief have changed in the United States the last 50 years, and the trends that may continue to evolve:

Belief in God Has Wavered

In 1966, some 98 percent of Americans said they believed in God, according to a Gallup survey. When Gallup and Pew Research surveyed Americans in 2014, the number had dropped to 86 percent and 89 percent, respectively. Among the youngest adults surveyed by Pew, those born between 1990 and 1996, the share of believers was just 80 percent. Some researchers argue that the number has decreased simply because Americans are more comfortable now than they were in the 60s admitting that they don't believe in God.

Christianity Has Declined

In 1948, Gallup found that about 91 percent of Americans identified as Christian. That number took a big dip in subsequent decades and continues to decline in recent years. From 2007 to 2014 alone, the percentage of Americans who identified as Christian fell from 78.4 percent to 70.6 percent.

A New "Religious" Group Has Emerged

Nearly one in three Americans under 35 today are religiously unaffiliated, meaning they do not identify with any formal religious group. As a whole, these "nones" comprise the second largest religious group in the United States behind evangelical Protestants.

Spirituality Has Taken Center Stage

The term "spiritual but not religious" has emerged in recent years to describe how more and more Americans identify. Yes, religious affiliation has declined. But feelings of spiritual peace and well-being? Wonder about the universe? Both have significantly increased in the last decade across religious and nonreligious groups. Even among the unaffiliated and those who say religion isn't particularly important to them, spiritual sentiment is strong and growing. And more than half of atheists say they regularly feel a sense of awe and wonder. Between 2007 and 2014, the percentage of atheists who said they felt a deep sense of wonder about the universe on a weekly basis rose a full 17 points from 37 percent to 54 percent.

The Importance of Religion in Americans' Lives Has Shifted

In 2007, 56 percent of Americans said religion was very important in their lives. Measures of this question from the 1950s and 1960s showed that at that time, over 70 percent of Americans said religion was very important in their daily lives.

Church Attendance Has Declined

In a 1937 Gallup Poll, 73 percent of Americans said they were church members. That percentage fell to around 70 percent in the 1960s and 1970s. By the 2000s, that number hovered around 60 percent.

More Women Are Entering the Clergy

In many Christian and Jewish congregations, the number of clergywomen has greatly increased. According to data from the Association of Theological Schools, women today make up about a third of all seminary students. Thirty years ago, women made up less than a fifth of seminary students. This is due in large part to the fact that it wasn't until after World War II that many of the larger and more prominent denominations started allowing women's ordination. The United Methodist Church and what would later become the Presbyterian Church USA ordained their first women ministers in 1965. The Evangelical Lutheran Church in America, Reform Judaism, and the Episcopal Church followed their lead in the early 1970s.

The Religious Right Got Organized

Contrary to popular belief, it was segregation—and not abortion—that mobilized the religious right in the 1960s and 1970s. In a series of court cases, Paul Weyrich, a religious conservative political activist, worked to organize evangelicals around segregation as an issue of "religious freedom." A 1971 ruling in *Green v. Connally* upheld that racially discriminatory private schools could not receive tax exemption "for charitable, educational institutions, and persons making gifts to such schools." Weyrich and others tried to fight this by saying that because private schools received no federal funding, the government couldn't tell them how to operate (i.e., they could continue discriminating against African American applicants.) Sound familiar? Prior to the 1970s, the relationship between evangelical Christians and the Republican party was negligible. In 2016, it's hard to imagine a Republican party without its evangelical voting bloc.

We Entered an Era of Interfaith Engagement

In 1965, the Catholic Church took a huge step for interfaith relations by publishing a document that acknowledged the divine origin of all human beings. In the decades after, interfaith engagement exploded in the United States, with the founding of countless organizations and conferences dedicated to multi-faith dialogue. The Council for a Parliament of the World's Religions formed in 1988 in the spirit of the first interfaith convention that occurred a century earlier, and groups like Interfaith Power & Light and Interfaith Youth Core emerged to usher in a new millennium of interfaith work.

Non-Christian Faiths Have Grown

Islam, Hinduism, and a number of other non-Christian faiths have risen in the United States in recent years. This change in the face of American religion might be partially a result of the Immigration and Naturalization Act of 1965, which led to an influx of immigrants from India and other countries with large Hindu and Muslim populations. Pew Research predicts that by 2050, Muslims will surpass Jews as the second largest organized religious group after Christians. Hindus are also projected to rise from 0.7 percent of the U.S. population to 1.2 percent in 2050. Members of "other religions" (a category that includes Sikhs, Wiccans, and Unitarian Universalists) are also expected to continue growing.

Islamophobia Has Risen Sharply

Anti-Muslim sentiment is not a new phenomenon in the United States. For the first half of the 20th-century American courts frequently denied citizenship to Muslims and those perceived to be Muslim, according to legal scholar Khaled A Beydoun.

But many feel that Islamophobia has risen in recent decades, especially in the aftermath of the September 11 attacks. In the last few years, anti-Muslim aggression has taken a disturbing turn, with new incidents being reported weekly.

Advocacy Agencies Were Established for Frequently Targeted Religious Groups

The Council on American-Islamic Relations, or CAIR, was founded in 1994 as an "organization that challenges stereotypes of Islam and Muslims." The Sikh Coalition was formed in the aftermath of the terrorist attacks of September 11, 2001 and ensuing violence toward the country's Sikh population. The Hindu American Foundation, an advocacy organization for the Hindu American community, was founded in 2003. Lady Liberty League, an organization that fights for religious freedom for Wiccans, pagans, and other nature religion practitioners, formed in 1985. And the list goes on.

The Spirituality Marketplace Exploded

From spiritual gurus, to self-help books, to wellness retreats, the market for spirituality in the United States has perhaps never been so robust. The self-help industry, which often include[s] alternative modes of spirituality along with motivational books and life coaching, brings in $13 billion a year in the form of books, retreats, classes, and more. In the last 50 years, modern spiritual gurus like Deepak Chopra, Dr. Andrew Weil, Ram Dass, Eckhart Tolle, Oprah Winfrey, Byron Katie, Marianne Williamson, and countless others emerged with a new prescription for well-being. Yoga became a $27 billion industry with more than 20 million practitioners in the U.S. Meditation and mindfulness were quick to follow, gaining fans among major companies like Google, General Mills, Aetna, and Goldman Sachs.

The New Atheists Became a Religion unto Themselves

Nonbelievers have always been part of the American demographic, but atheists and humanists have perhaps never been as organized, prominent, and vocal as they are today. Though many of the largest organizations, like American Atheists, American Humanist Association, and Freedom from Religion Foundation, were established decades ago, the New Atheists emerged in the 2000s with a righteous, anti-religious fervor. Spearheaded by prominent British atheists Richard Dawkins and Christopher Hitchens, as well as American atheist Sam Harris, the New Atheists have gained a large following eager to read their books, watch their debates and attend their conventions.

Megachurches Have Gained Popularity

In 1960, there were just a handful of churches that might be described as "megachurches," those with a charismatic senior minister, an active social outreach ministry and at least 2,000 people attending every weekend. As of 2012, there were roughly 1,600 megachurches in the United States.

Americans Aren't Necessarily Sticking with the Religion in Which They Were Raised

Pew Research found in 2014 that between 34 percent and 42 percent of American adults currently have a religious identity different from the one in which they were raised. (The number depends on whether Protestantism is treated as a single religious group or as three different traditions—evangelical Protestantism, mainline Protestantism, and historically Black Protestantism.) Eighteen percent of Americans who were raised in a religion are now unaffiliated, compared with just 4 percent who have moved in the other direction.

Spirituality Found a Home Online

With the advent of computers, mobile apps, and the Internet, faith has gone increasingly high-tech. To access spiritual teachings and communities we need look no further than our cell phones. Pew Research found in a 2014 survey that some 20 percent of Americans shared their faith online in a given week. Sixty-one percent of millennials reported seeing others share their faith online. From Instagram accounts to podcasts to YouTube channels, there are more ways than ever to find and share spirituality.

The Neopagan Goddess Movement Emerged

Although famous 20th-century occultists Aleister Crowley and Gerald Gardner had already died by 1966, the U.S. goddess movement was still yet to fully blossom. In the decades that followed, American pagan authors Starhawk and Margot Adler both published seminal works on the nature religion; priestess Selena Fox started Circle Sanctuary; the Covenant of the Goddess was founded; many different traditions were established; and the first pagan seminary opened its doors.

At the heart of American faith's evolution is what religion journalist Krista Tippett calls a "proliferation of ways to engage spiritual practice." Yes, you'll still find Bibles in hotel rooms, but you'll also see yoga and meditation rooms in some airports and Muslim prayer spaces on many college campuses. What it means to be spiritual—and how that looks in practice—is rapidly changing and diversifying. But rather than diminishing Americans' faith, this transformation is also crystallizing certain core values, like service, community, and connection to something greater than ourselves.

Critical Thinking

1. How the role of women in churches has changed over the years?
2. How dynamic is the current religious situation in the United States?

3. How do you explain the Pew Research founding in a 2014 survey that some 20 percent of Americans shared their faith online in a given week?

Internet References

Sociology—Study Sociology Online
  http://edu.learnsoc.org/

Sociology Web Resources
  http://www.mhhe.com/socscience/sociology/resources/index.htm

Sociosite
  http://www.topsite.com/goto/sociosite.net

Socioweb
  http://www.topsite.com/goto/socioweb.com

Unit 6

UNIT

Prepared by: Kurt Finsterbusch, *University of Maryland, College Park*

Social Change and the Future

Fascination with the future is an enduring theme in literature, art, poetry, and religion. Human beings are anxious to know if tomorrow will be different from today, and in what ways it might differ. Coping with change has become a top priority in the lives of many. One result of change is stress. When the future is uncertain and the individual appears to have little control over what happens, stress can be a serious problem. On the other hand, stress can have positive effects on people's lives if they can perceive changes as challenges and opportunities.

Article   Prepared by: Kurt Finsterbusch, *University of Maryland, College Park*

Full Planet, Empty Plates

Food is the new oil. Land is the new gold.

LESTER R. BROWN

Learning Outcomes

After reading this article, you will be able to:

- Critique Brown's thesis that the world is facing a growing food crisis.

- Review the arguments for environmental limits and subsequent food production limits. Review the arguments against environmental limits.

- Assess the potential for technology to take care of the food problem while taking into account the failure of technology to noticeably increase food production in the past two decades.

Problems in a Hot and Hungry World

In the early spring of 2012, U.S. farmers were on their way to planting some 96 million acres in corn, the most in 75 years. A warm early spring got the crop off to a great start. Analysts were predicting the largest corn harvest on record.

The corn plant is as sensitive as it is productive. Thirsty and fast-growing, it is vulnerable to both extreme heat and drought. At elevated temperatures, the corn plant, which is normally so productive, goes into thermal shock. As spring turned into summer, the thermometer began to rise across the Corn Belt. In the St. Louis, Missouri area, the southern Corn Belt, the temperature climbed to a record 105 degrees Fahrenheit or higher 11 days in a row. The corn crop failed.

Over a span of weeks, we saw how the more extreme weather events that come with climate change can affect food security.

The United States is the leading producer and exporter of corn, the world's feed grain. At home, corn accounts for four-fifths of the U.S. grain harvest. Internationally, the U.S. corn crop exceeds China's rice and wheat harvests combined. Among the big three grains—corn, wheat, and rice—corn is now the leader, with production well above that of wheat and nearly double that of rice.

The U.S. Great Drought of 2012 has raised corn prices to the highest level in history. The world price of food, which has already doubled over the last decade, is slated to climb higher, ushering in a new wave of food unrest. This year's corn crop shortfall will accelerate the transition from the era of abundance and surpluses to an era of chronic scarcity. As food prices climb, the worldwide competition for control of land and water resources is intensifying.

In this new world, access to food is replacing access to oil as an overriding concern of governments. Food is the new oil, land is the new gold. Welcome to the new geopolitics of food.

For Americans who spend only 9 percent of their income on food, the doubling of food prices is not a big deal. But for those who spend 50–70 percent of their income on food, it is a serious matter. There is little latitude for them to offset the price rise simply by spending more. They must eat less.

A recent survey by Save the Children shows that 24 percent of families in India now have foodless days. For Nigeria, the comparable figure is 27 percent. For Peru, it is 14 percent. In a hungry world, hunger often has a child's face. Millions of children are dangerously hungry, some too weak to walk to school. Many are physically and mentally stunted.

Even as hunger spreads, farmers are facing new challenges on both sides of the food equation. On the demand side, there have been two sources of demand growth. The oldest of these is population growth. Each year the world adds nearly 80 million people. Tonight there will be 219,000 people at the dinner table who were not there last night, many with empty plates. Tomorrow night, the next night, and on.

The second source of growing demand for grain is consumers moving up the food chain. As incomes rise, people eat more grain-intensive livestock and poultry products. Today, with incomes rising fast in emerging economies, there are at least 3 billion people moving up the food chain. The largest single concentration of these new meat eaters is in China, which now consumes twice as much meat as the United States.

Now there is a third source of demand for grain: the automobile. In 2011, the United States harvested nearly 400 million tons of grain. Of this, 127 million tons (32 percent) went to ethanol distilleries to fuel cars.

This growing demand for grain has boosted the annual increase in world grain consumption from 20 million tons a year a decade ago to 45 million tons a year today.

On the supply side, farmers continue to wrestle with the age-old threat of soil erosion. Some 30 percent of the world's cropland is losing productive topsoil far faster than nature can replace it. Two huge new dust bowls are forming, one in Northwestern China and the other in Central Africa.

Beyond the loss of topsoil, three new challenges are emerging on the production front. One, aquifers are being depleted and irrigation wells are starting to go dry in 18 countries that together contain half the world's people. Two, in some of the more agriculturally advanced countries, rice and wheat yields per acre, which have been rising steadily for several decades, are beginning to plateau. And three, the Earth's temperature is rising, threatening to disrupt world agriculture in ways that can only be described as scary.

Among the countries where water tables are falling and aquifers are being depleted are the big three grain producers—China, India, and the United States. In India 175 million people are being fed with grain produced by overpumping. The comparable number for China is 130 million. In the United States, the irrigated area is shrinking in leading farm states with rapid population growth such as California and Texas as aquifers are depleted and irrigation water is diverted to cities.

After several decades of rising grain yields, some of the more agriculturally advanced countries are hitting limits that were not widely anticipated. Rice yields in Japan, a pioneer in raising yields, have not increased for 17 years. In both Japan and South Korea, yields have plateaued at just under 5 tons per hectare. (1 hectare = 2.47 acres.) China's rice yields are now closely approaching those of Japan and may also soon plateau.

A similar situation exists with wheat yields. In France, Germany, and the United Kingdom—the three leading wheat producers in Western Europe—there has been no rise for more than a decade. Other countries will soon be hitting their limits for grain yields.

The newest challenge confronting farmers is global warming. The massive burning of fossil fuels is increasing the level of carbon dioxide in the atmosphere, raising the Earth's temperature and disrupting climate. Historically when there was an extreme weather event—an intense heat wave or a drought—things would likely be back to normal by the next harvest. Now with the climate in flux, there is no "norm" to return to.

For each 1-degree-Celsius rise in temperature above the optimum during the growing season farmers can expect at least a 10-percent decline in grain yields. A study of the effect of temperature on corn and soybean yields in the United States found that a 1-degree-Celsius rise in temperature reduced yields 17 percent. If the world continues with business as usual, failing to address the climate issue, the Earth's temperature during this century could easily rise by 6 degrees Celsius (11 degrees Fahrenheit).

The effect of high temperature on food production is on full display in the United States where the summer drought and heat that covered much of the country, including most of the Corn Belt, will reduce the U.S. corn harvest by 30 percent or more.

As food supplies tighten, the geopolitics of food is fast overshadowing the geopolitics of oil. The first signs of trouble came in 2007, when world grain production fell behind demand. Grain and soybean prices started to climb, doubling by mid-2008. In response, many exporting countries tried to curb rising domestic food prices by restricting exports. Among them were Russia and Argentina, two leading wheat exporters. Viet Nam, the world's number two rice exporter, banned exports entirely in the early months of 2008.

With key suppliers restricting or banning exports, importing countries panicked. Fearing they might not be able to buy needed grain from the market, some of the more affluent countries, led by Saudi Arabia, China, and South Korea, then took the unusual step of buying or leasing land long term in other countries on which to grow food for themselves. These land acquisitions have since grown rapidly in number. Most of them are in Africa. Among the principal destinations for land hunters are Ethiopia, Sudan, and South Sudan, each of them countries that cannot feed the people who live there; millions of people are being sustained with food donations from the U.N. World Food Program.

As of mid-2012, hundreds of land acquisition deals had been negotiated or were under negotiation, some of them exceeding a million acres. A 2011 World Bank analysis of these "land grabs" reported that at least 140 million acres were involved—an area that exceeds the cropland devoted to corn and wheat combined in the United States. This onslaught of land acquisitions has become a land rush as governments, agribusiness firms, and private investors seek control of land wherever they can find it. Such acquisitions also typically involve water rights, meaning that land grabs potentially affect downstream countries as well.

For instance, any water extracted from the upper Nile River basin to irrigate newly planted crops in Ethiopia, Sudan, or South Sudan will now not reach Egypt, upending the delicate water politics of the Nile by adding new countries that Egypt must compete with for water. Egypt already has to import a great deal of grain.

The potential for conflict is high. Many of the land deals have been made in secret, and much of the time the land involved was already being farmed by villagers when it was sold or leased. Often those already farming the land were neither consulted nor even informed of the new arrangements. And because there typically are no formal land titles in many developing-country villages, the farmers who lost their land have had little support for bringing their cases to court.

Time is running out. The world may be much closer to an unmanageable food shortage—replete with soaring food prices, spreading food unrest, and ultimately political instability—than most people realize.

Solutions ~ Saving Civilization is not a Spectator Sport

On the demand side of the food equation, there are four pressing needs—to stabilize world population, eradicate poverty, reduce excessive meat consumption, and reverse biofuels policies that encourage the use of food, land, or water that could otherwise be used to feed people. We need to press forward on all four fronts at the same time.

The first two goals are closely related. Indeed, stabilizing population depends on eliminating poverty. Even a cursory look at population growth rates shows that the countries where population size has stabilized are virtually all high-income countries. On the other side of the coin, nearly all countries with high population growth rates are on the low end of the global economic ladder.

Shifting to smaller families has many benefits. For one, there will be fewer people at the dinner table. It comes as no surprise that a disproportionate share of malnutrition is found in larger families.

At the other end of the food spectrum, a large segment of the world's people are consuming animal products at a level that is unhealthy and contributing to obesity and cardiovascular disease. The good news is that when the affluent consume less meat, milk, and eggs, it improves their health. When meat consumption falls in the United States, as it recently has, this frees up grain for direct consumption. Moving down the food chain also lessens pressure on the Earth's land and water resources. In short, it is a win-win-win situation.

Another initiative, one that can quickly lower food prices, is the cancellation of biofuel mandates. There is no social justification for the massive conversion of food into fuel for cars. With plug-in hybrids and all-electric cars coming to market that can run on local wind-generated electricity at a gasoline-equivalent cost of 80¢ per gallon, why keep burning costly fuel at four times the price?

On the supply side of the food equation, we face several challenges, including stabilizing climate, raising water productivity, and conserving soil. Stabilizing climate is not easy, but it can be done if we act quickly. It will take a huge cut in carbon emissions, some 80 percent within a decade, to give us a chance of avoiding the worst consequences of climate change. This means a wholesale restructuring of the world energy economy.

The easiest way to do this is to restructure the tax system. The market has many strengths, but it also has some dangerous weaknesses. It readily captures the direct costs of mining coal and delivering it to power plants. But the market does not incorporate the indirect costs of fossil fuels, such as the costs to society of global warming. Sir Nicholas Stern, former chief economist at the World Bank, noted that climate change was the product of a massive market failure.

The goal of restructuring taxes is to lower income taxes and raise carbon taxes so that the cost of climate change and other indirect costs of fossil fuel use are incorporated in market prices. If we can get the market to tell the truth, the transition from coal and oil to wind, solar, and geothermal energy will move very fast. If we remove the massive subsidies to the fossil fuel industry, we will move even faster.

Although this energy transition may seem farfetched, it is moving ahead, and at an exciting pace in some countries. For example, four states in northern Germany now get at least 46 percent of their electricity from wind. For Denmark, the figure is 26 percent. In the United States, both Iowa and South Dakota now get one fifth of their electricity from wind farms. Solar power in Europe can now satisfy the electricity needs of some 15 million households. Kenya now gets one fifth of its electricity from geothermal energy. And Indonesia is shooting for 9,500 megawatts of geothermal generating capacity by 2025, which would meet 56 percent of current electricity needs.

In addition to the carbon tax, we need to reduce dependence on the automobile by upgrading public transportation worldwide to European standards. The world has already proved that passenger rail systems can be electric. As we shift from traditional oil-powered engines to plug-in hybrids and all-electric cars, we can substitute electricity from renewable sources for oil. In the meantime, as the U.S. automobile fleet, which peaked in 2008, shrinks, U.S. gasoline use will continue the decline of recent years. This decline, in the country that consumes more gasoline than the next 16 countries combined, is a welcome new trend.

Along with stabilizing climate, another key component to avoiding a breakdown in the food system is to raise water productivity. This begins with agriculture, simply because 70 percent of all water use goes to irrigation. The least efficient irrigation technologies are flood and furrow irrigation. Sprinkler irrigation, using the center-pivot systems that are widely seen in the crop circles in the western U.S. Great Plains, and drip irrigation are far more efficient. The advantage of drip irrigation is that it applies water very slowly at a rate that the plants can use, losing little to evaporation. It simultaneously raises yields and reduces water use.

Another option is to encourage the use of more water-efficient crops, such as wheat, instead of rice. China banned rice production in the Beijing region. Moving down the food chain also saves water.

Although urban water use is relatively small compared with that used for irrigation, cities too can save water. Some cities now are beginning to recycle much if not most of the water they use. Singapore, whose freshwater supplies are severely restricted by geography, relies on a graduated water tax—the more water you use, the more you pay per gallon—and an extensive water recycling program to meet the needs of its 5 million residents.

The key to raising water use efficiency is price policy. Because water is routinely underpriced, especially that used for irrigation, it is used wastefully. Pricing water to encourage conservation could lead to huge gains in water use efficiency, in effect expanding the supply that could in turn be used to expand the irrigated area.

The third big supply-side challenge after stabilizing climate and raising water productivity is controlling soil erosion. With topsoil blowing away at a record rate and two huge dust bowls forming in Asia and Africa, stabilizing soils will take a heavy investment in conservation measures. Perhaps the best example of a large-scale effort to reduce soil erosion came in the 1930s, after a combination of overplowing and land mismanagement created a dust bowl that threatened to turn the U.S. Great Plains into a vast desert.

In response to this traumatic experience, the United States introduced revolutionary changes in agricultural practices, including returning highly erodible land to grass, terracing, and planting tree shelterbelts.

Another valuable tool in the soil conservation tool kit is no-till farming. Instead of the traditional practice of plowing land and discing or harrowing it to prepare the seedbed, and then using a mechanical cultivator to control weeds in row crops, farmers simply drill seeds directly through crop residues into undisturbed soil, controlling weeds with herbicides when necessary. In addition to reducing erosion, this practice retains water, raises soil organic matter content, and greatly reduces energy use for tillage.

In the United States, the no-till area went from 7 million hectares in 1990 to 26 million hectares (67 million acres) in 2007. Now widely used in the production of corn and soybeans, no-till agriculture has spread rapidly in the western hemisphere, covering 26 million hectares each in Brazil and Argentina and 13 million hectares in Canada. Australia, with 17 million hectares, rounds out the five leading no-till countries.

These initiatives do not constitute a menu from which to pick and choose. We need to take all these actions simultaneously. They reinforce each other. We will not likely be able to stabilize population unless we eradicate poverty. We will not likely be able to restore the earth's natural systems without stabilizing population and stabilizing climate. Nor can we eradicate poverty without reversing the decline of the earth's natural systems.

Achieving all these goals to reduce demand and increase supply requires that we redefine security. We have inherited a definition of security from the last century, a century dominated by two world wars and a cold war, that is almost exclusively military in focus. When the term national security comes up in Washington, people automatically think of expanded military budgets and more-advanced weapon systems. But armed aggression is no longer the principal threat to our future. The overriding threats in this century are climate change, population growth, spreading water shortages, rising food prices, and politically failing states.

It is no longer possible to separate food security and security more broadly defined. It is time to redefine security not just in an intellectual sense but also in a fiscal sense. We have the resources we need to fill the family planning gap, to eradicate poverty, and to raise water productivity, but these measures require a reallocation of our fiscal resources to respond to the new security threats.

Beyond this, diverting a big chunk of the largely obsolete military budget into incentives to invest in rooftop solar panels, wind farms, geothermal power plants, and more energy-efficient lighting and household appliances would accelerate the energy transition. The incentives needed to jump-start this massive energy restructuring are large, but not beyond our reach. We can justify this expense simply by considering the potentially unbearable costs of continuing with business as usual.

We have to mobilize quickly. Time is our scarcest resource. Success depends on moving at wartime speed. It means, for example, transforming the world energy economy at a pace reminiscent of the restructuring of the U.S. industrial economy in 1942 following the Japanese surprise attack on Pearl Harbor on December 7, 1941.

On January 6, 1942, a month after the attack, Franklin D. Roosevelt outlined arms production goals in his State of the Union address to the U.S. Congress and the American people.

He said the United States was going to produce 45,000 tanks, 60,000 planes, and thousands of ships. Given that the country was still in a depression-mode economy, people wondered how this could be done. It required a fundamental reordering of priorities and some bold moves. The key to the 1942 industrial restructuring was the government's ban on the sale of cars that forced the auto industry into arms manufacturing. The ban lasted from early 1942 until the end of 1944. Every one of President Roosevelt's arms production goals was exceeded.

If the United States could totally transform its industrial economy in a matter of months in 1942, then certainly it can lead the world in restructuring the energy economy, stabilizing population, and rebuilding world grain stocks. The stakes now are even higher than they were in 1942. The challenge then was to save the democratic way of life, which was threatened by the fast-expanding empires of Nazi Germany and Imperial Japan. Today the challenge is to save civilization itself.

Scientists and many other concerned individuals have long sensed that the world economy had moved onto an environmentally unsustainable path. This has been evident to anyone who tracks trends such as deforestation, soil erosion, aquifer depletion, collapsing fisheries, and the increase in carbon dioxide in the atmosphere. What was not so clear was exactly where this unsustainable path would lead. It now seems that the most imminent effect will be tightening supplies of food. Food is the weak link in our modern civilization—just as it was for the Sumerians, Mayans, and many other civilizations that have come and gone. They could not separate their fate from that of their food supply. Nor can we.

The challenge now is to move our early twenty-first-century civilization onto a sustainable path. Every one of us needs to be involved. This is not just a matter of adjusting lifestyles by changing light bulbs or recycling newspapers, important though those actions are. Environmentalists have talked for decades about saving the planet, but now the challenge is to save civilization itself. This is about restructuring the world energy economy and doing it before climate change spirals out of control and before food shortages overwhelm our political system. And this means becoming politically active, working to reach the goals outlined above.

We all need to select an issue and go to work on it. Find some friends who share your concern and get to work. The overriding priority is redefining security and reallocating fiscal resources accordingly. If your major concern is population growth, join one of the internationally oriented groups and lobby to fill the family planning gap. If your overriding concern is climate change, join the effort to close coal-fired power plants. We can prevent a breakdown of the food system, but it will require a huge political effort undertaken on many fronts and with a fierce sense of urgency.

We all have a stake in the future of civilization. Many of us have children. Some of us have grandchildren. We know what we have to do. It is up to you and me to do it. Saving civilization is not a spectator sport.

Critical Thinking

1. Why will there not be another green revolution to take care of the growing world food problem?

2. What trends have slowed down or reversed and worsened the food problem as a result?

3. Discuss the environmental aspects (land, soil loss, water scarcity, weather extremes, yield limits, etc.) of the food problem.

Internet References

Sociosite
    www.topsite.com/goto/sociosite.net
Socioweb
    www.topsite.com/goto/socioweb.com
Sociology—Study Sociology Online
    http://edu.learnsoc.org
Sociology Web Resources
    www.mhhe.com/socscience/sociology/resources/index.htm

The Washington Post has called **LESTER R. BROWN** "one of the world's most influential thinkers." He started his career as a farmer, growing tomatoes in New Jersey with his brother. After earning a degree in Agricultural Science from Rutgers University, he spent six months in rural India, an experience that changed his life and career. Brown founded the WorldWatch Institute and then the Earth Policy Institute, where he now serves as President. The purpose of the Earth Policy Institute is to provide a vision of an environmentally sustainable economy, a roadmap of how to get from here to there—as well as an ongoing assessment of progress. Brown has authored many books. His most recent is *Full Planet, Empty Plates: The New Geopolitics of Food Scarcity*. It is available online at www.earth-policy.org/books/fpep and at booksellers. Supporting data, endnotes, and additional resources are available for free on the website.

Article   Prepared by: Kurt Finsterbusch, *University of Maryland, College Park*

Synthesis of Papers by Blue Planet Laureates

Environment and Development Challenges: The Imperative to Act.

GRO HARLEM BRUNDTLAND, PAUL EHRLICH, JOSE GOLDEMBERG, JAMES HANSEN, AMORY LOVINS, GENE LIKENS, JAMES LOVELOCK, SUKI MANABE, BOB MAY, HAL MOONEY, KARL-HENRIK ROBERT, EMIL SALIM, GORDON SATO, SUSAN SOLOMON, NICHOLAS STERN, MS SWAMINATHAN, BOB WATSON, BAREFOOT COLLEGE, CONSERVATION INTERNATIONAL, INTERNATIONAL INSTITUTE OF ENVIRONMENT AND DEVELOPMENT, AND INTERNATIONAL UNION FOR THE CONSERVATION OF NATURE

Learning Outcomes

After reading this article, you will be able to:

- Describe the environmental situation today.
- Discuss the loss of biodiversity and its consequences.
- Explain what are the underlying drivers of the changes discussed in this article.

This paper is a synthesis of the key messages from the individual papers written by the BluePlanet Laureates (Annex I describes the Blue Planet Prize), and discusses the current and projected state of the global and regional environment, and the implications for environmental, social, and economic sustainability. It addresses the drivers for change, the implications for inaction, and what is needed to achieve economic development and growth among the poor, coupled with environmental and social sustainability, and the imperative of action now. The paper does not claim to comprehensively address all environment and development issues, but a subset that are deemed to be of particular importance.

Key Messages

- We have a dream—a world without poverty—a world that is equitable—a world that respects human rights—a world with increased and improved ethical behavior regarding poverty and natural resources—a world that is environmentally, socially, and economically sustainable, where the challenges such as climate change, loss of biodiversity, and social inequity have been successfully addressed. This is an achievable dream, but the current system is deeply flawed and our current pathway will not realize it.

- Population size and growth and related consumption patterns are critical elements in the many environmental degradation and social problems we currently face. The population issue should be urgently addressed by education and empowerment of women, including in the workforce and in rights, ownership and inheritance; health care of children and the elderly; and making modern contraception accessible to all.

- There is an urgent need to break the link between production and consumption on the one hand and environmental destruction on the other. This can allow risking material living standards for a period that would allow us to overcome world poverty. Indefinite material growth on a planet with finite and often fragile natural resources will, however, eventually be unsustainable. Unsustainable growth is promoted by environmentally damaging subsidies in areas such as energy, transportation, and agriculture and should be eliminated; external environmental and social costs should be internalized; and the market and nonmarket values of ecosystem goods and services should be taken into account in decision-making.

- The immense environmental, social, and economic risks we face as a world from our current path will be much harder to manage if we are unable to measure key aspects of the problem. For example, governments should recognize the serious limitations of GDP as a measure of economic activity and complement it with measures of the five forms of capital, built, financial, natural, human, and social capital, that is, a measure of wealth that integrates economic, environmental, and social dimensions. Green taxes and the elimination of subsidies should ensure that the natural resources needed to directly protect poor people are available rather than via subsidies that often only benefit the better off.

- The present energy system, which is heavily dependent on fossil fuels, underlies many of the problems we face today: exhaustion of easily accessible physical resources, security of access to fuels, and degradation of health and environmental conditions. Universal access to clean energy services is vital for the poor, and a transition to a low carbon economy will require rapid technological evolution in the efficiency of energy use, environmentally sound low carbon renewable energy sources and carbon capture and storage. The longer we wait to transition to a low carbon economy, the more we are locked into a high carbon energy system with consequent environmental damage to ecological and socioeconomic systems, including infrastructure.

- Emissions of GHG emissions are one of the greatest threats to our future prosperity. World emissions (flows) are currently around 50 billion tonnes of carbon dioxide-equivalent (CO_2e) per annum and are growing rapidly. As the terrestrial and oceanic ecosystems are unable to absorb all of the world's annual emissions, concentrations (stocks) of GHG emissions in the atmosphere have increased, to around 445 ppm of CO_2e today and increasing at a rate of around 2.5 ppm per year. Thus, we have a flow-stock problem. Without strong action to reduce emissions, over the course

of this century we would likely add at least 300 ppm CO_2e, taking concentrations to around 750 ppm CO_2e or higher at the end of the century or early in the next. The world's current commitments to reduce emissions are consistent with at least a 3°C rise (50–50 chance) in temperature: a temperature not seen on the planet for around 3 million years, with serious risks of 5°C rise: a temperature not seen on the planet for around 30 million years. Given there are some uncertainties present in all steps of the scientific chain (flows to stocks to temperatures to climate change and impacts), this is a problem of risk management and public action on a great scale.

- Biodiversity has essential social, economic, cultural, spiritual, and scientific values, and its protection is hugely important for human survival. The rapid loss of biodiversity, unprecedented in the last 65 million years, is jeopardizing the provision of ecosystem services that underpin human well-being. The Millennium Ecosystem Assessment concluded that 15 of the 24 ecosystem services evaluated were in decline, 4 were improving, and 5 were improving in some regions of the world and in decline in other regions. Measures to conserve biodiversity and make a sustainable society possible need to be greatly enhanced and integrated with social, political, and economic concerns. There is a need to value biodiversity and ecosystem services and create markets that can appropriate the value for these services as a basis for a "green" economy.

- There are serious short-comings in the decision-making systems at local, national, and global levels on which we rely in government, business, and society. The rules and institutions for decision-making are influenced by vested interests, with each interest having very different access over how decisions are made. Effective change in governance demands action at many levels to establish transparent means for holding those in power to account. At the local level, public hearings and social audits can bring the voices of marginalized groups into the forefront. At national level, parliamentary and press oversight are key. Globally, we must find better means to agree and implement measures to achieve collective goals. Governance failures also occur because decisions are being made in sectoral compartments, with environmental, social, and economic dimensions addressed by separate, competing structures.

- Decision makers should learn from ongoing grassroot actions and knowledge in areas such as energy, food, water, natural resources, finance, and governance. This is key, not the least in rural communities with a view to their management, control, and ownership of these resources. There is a need to scale up the grassroots actions by bringing together a complementary top-down and bottom-up approach to addressing these issues. Global cooperation can be improved by building on ongoing regional cooperation to deal with common sustainable development issues.

- Effective training programs should be implemented to multiply the number of competent decision makers in business and government. They must learn how to integrate programs and policies within sustainability constraints, to understand the business case thereof, and to acquire the skills to strategically move toward such sustainability goals.

- All of the problems mentioned above demand we increase investments in education, research, and assessments of knowledge.

- If we are to achieve our dream, the time to act is now, given the inertia in the socioeconomic system, and that the adverse effects of climate change and loss of biodiversity cannot be reversed for centuries or are irreversible (e.g., species loss). We know enough to act, but the current scientific uncertainties means that we are facing a problem of risk management on an immense scale. Failure to act will impoverish current and future generations.

The Problem Introduction

We have a dream—a world without poverty—a world that is equitable—a world that respects human rights—a world with increased and improved ethical behavior regarding poverty and natural resources—a world that is environmentally, socially, and economically sustainable, and where economic growth is accomplished within the constraints of realizing social objectives of poverty eradication and social equity and within the constraints of life support nature's carrying capacity, and a world where the challenges such as climate change, loss of biodiversity, and social inequity have been successfully addressed. This is an achievable dream, but the system is broken and our current pathway will not realize it.

Unfortunately, humanity's behavior remains utterly inappropriate for dealing with the potentially lethal fallout from a combination of increasingly rapid technological evolution matched with very slow ethical–social evolution. The human ability to do has vastly outstripped the ability to understand. As a result civilization is faced with a perfect storm of problems driven by overpopulation, overconsumption by the rich, the use of environmentally malign technologies, and gross inequalities. They include loss of the biodiversity that runs human life-support

systems, climate disruption, global toxification, alteration of critical biogeochemical cycles, increasing probability of vast epidemics, and the specter of a civilization-destroying nuclear war. These biophysical problems are interacting tightly with human governance systems, institutions, and civil societies that are now inadequate to deal with them.

The rapidly deteriorating biophysical situation is more than bad enough, but it is barely recognized by a global society infected by the irrational belief that physical economies can grow forever and disregarding the facts that the rich in developed and developing countries get richer and the poor are left behind. And the perpetual growth myth is enthusiastically embraced by politicians and economists as an excuse to avoid tough decisions facing humanity. This myth promotes the impossible idea that indiscriminate economic growth is the cure for all the world's problems, while it is actually (as currently practiced) the disease that is at the root cause of our unsustainable global practices.

In the face of an absolutely unprecedented emergency, society has no choice but to take dramatic action to avert a collapse of civilization. Either we will change our ways and build an entirely new kind of global society, or they will be changed for us.

In order to realize our dream of a more sustainable world, there is a need to understand the triple interdependence of economic, social, and environmental factors and integrate them into decision-making in governments and the private sector. One challenge facing many countries is how to manage natural resources in order to contribute to poverty alleviation while maintaining the ecological life support system. In economics, the main issue deals with what, where, and how much of the natural resources are required to alleviate poverty, while social issues deal with for whom and how much are resources developed, and environmental issues address how natural resources can be managed with minimum negative impact on ecosystems. The interaction between economic, social, and environment [is] enhanced and its coordination made more effective if their respective goals are translated into quantitative terms within a defined time scale. What is needed is to realize economic growth within the constraints of social and environmental sustainability.

Underlying Drivers of Change

The major indirect drivers of change are primarily demographic, economic, sociopolitical, technological, and cultural and religious. These affect climate change and biodiversity loss somewhat differently, although the number of people and their ability to purchase and consume energy and natural resources are common to both issues. Human-induced climate change is primarily driven by the aggregate consumption and choice of technologies to produce and use energy, which is influenced by energy subsidies and unaccounted costs, hence the current overreliance on burning fossil fuels. The loss of biodiversity and the degradation of ecosystems and their services are primarily due to the conversion of natural habitats, overexploitation of resources, air, land, and water pollution, introduction of exotic species and human-induced climate change.

Demographic: The global population, which has now passed 7 billion people, and the average per capita energy consumption have both increased sevenfold over the past 150 years, for an overall 50-fold increase in the emissions of carbon dioxide into the atmosphere. And both are still increasing. As a global average, total fertility rates are decreasing, as a result of more females completing primary and secondary education, along with availability of fertility control. But this global average conceals many local difficulties. In some parts of the world fertility remains high—and decline in these countries is by no means certain. More than 200 million women in developing countries still have unmet needs for family planning, and increased investment in reproductive health care and family planning programs along with education programs will be critical. Although the desire and the need are increasing, it is estimated that funding decreased by 30 percent between 1995 and 2008, not least as a result of legislative pressure from the religious right in the United States and elsewhere.

The aging of populations in many countries around the world is also a relevant sustainable development issue. The economic, social, and environmental implications are as yet unclear—but this trend will undoubtedly have an impact. Whether it is positive or negative depends to a large extent on how countries prepare, for example, in evaluating what an aging population will mean for economic productivity, consumption of goods and services, and in terms of urban planning, financial, health and social care systems, and so on.

Both culturally and genetically, human beings have always been small-group animals, evolved to deal with at most a few hundred other individuals. Humanity is suddenly, in ecological time, faced with an emergency requiring that it quickly design and implement a governance and economic system that is both more equitable and suitable for a global population of billions of people, and sustainable on a finite planet.

Economics: Uncontrolled economic growth is unsustainable on a finite planet. Governments should recognize the serious limitations of GDP as a measure of economic growth and complement it with measures of the five forms of capital, built (produced), natural, human, social, and institutional/financial capital, that is, a measure of wealth that integrates economic, social, and environmental dimensions and is a better method for determining a country's productive potential.

The failure of the economic system to internalize externalities leads to the continuation of environmentally damaging activities. If externalities are uncorrected then markets fail: they generate prices that do not reflect the true cost to society of our economic activities. Emissions of greenhouse gases represent a market failure as the damages caused by emissions from the burning of fossil fuels are not reflected in prices. The price of fossil fuels should reflect the true cost to society, resulting in a more level playing field for environmentally sound renewable energy technologies and a stimulus to conserve energy. There are a range of economic instruments for correcting the emissions market failure from taxes and emissions trading schemes, to standards and other regulations. All are likely to be needed.

There are a number of other relevant market failures that must also be corrected if we are to manage the risks of climate change: correcting the emissions externality on its own will not be sufficient. For example, there are market failures around research and development (innovation), there are imperfections in capital markets that prevent financing for low carbon infrastructure, there are network externalities, for example, around electricity grids and public transport, there are failures in the provision of information, and there are failures in valuing ecosystems and biodiversity. In addition, environmentally damaging subsidies in areas such as energy, transportation, and agriculture, which total about $1 trillion per year, cause further market distortion and are in general leading to environmental degradation and should be eliminated. We must act strongly across all these dimensions. Correcting the biodiversity and ecosystem market failure is particularly urgent and important. The benefits that we derive from the natural world (biodiversity and ecosystem services) and its constituent ecosystems are critically important to human well-being and economic prosperity, but are consistently undervalued in economic analysis and decision-making. Contemporary economic and participatory techniques allow us to take into account the monetary and nonmonetary values of a wide range of ecosystem services. These techniques need to be adopted in every day decision-making practice. Failure to include the valuation of nonmarket values in decision-making results in a less efficient resource allocation, with negative consequences for social well-being. Recognizing the value of ecosystem services would allow the world to move toward a more sustainable future, in which the benefits of ecosystem services are better realized and more equitably distributed.

Correcting these market failures is also important if developing countries are to continue to advance and improve their living standards. The economic emergence of the BRICS (Brazil, Russia, India, China, and South Africa) over recent decades has been a major success story. Their combined share of world GDP has increased from 23 percent to 32 percent over the last six decades. In contrast, over the same period the OECD share of world GDP has declined from 57 percent to 41 percent. This rapid economic growth has seen great improvements in health, literacy, and income. However, this rapid growth and development was achieved mostly through the increased use of fossil fuels (which in 2008 represented 90 percent of their energy consumption) and through the unsustainable exploitation of natural resources including oceans and forests. As a consequence of this energy intensive development, the emergence of the BRICS is associated with a significant increase in their GHG emissions (particularly CO_2), which have increased from 15 percent to 35 percent of global emissions over the last 60 years. This energy intensive development path is clearly unsustainable, and impacts are already being felt, for example, rapid increases in desertification in China and collapsing biodiversity in their oceans. Failure to shift to a low carbon development path, which will, among other actions, require correcting market failures and removing harmful energy subsidies, may result in damaging climate change and environmental damage. This would jeopardize future growth and put at risk these great advances in development over the past several decades. There are encouraging signs from BRIC countries. For example, in Brazil, deforestation in the Amazon has been cut by around 80 percent in the last 7 years and in China their 12th 5-year plan (2011–2015) indicates a change in strategy to a more sustainable low carbon economy. But much greater action is urgently needed.

Technology: The overreliance on fossil fuel energy (coal, oil, and gas) and inefficient end-use technologies has significantly increased the atmospheric concentrations of carbon dioxide and other greenhouse gases. We are currently putting one million years' worth of sequestered carbon into the atmosphere each year. Recent efforts to reduce the carbon intensity (CO_2/GDP) were made in a large number of countries particularly in China and Russia where the carbon content has declined significantly in the last 30 years albeit from very high levels. However, the carbon intensities of India, South Africa, and Brazil (including deforestation) have not declined significantly in that period. It is therefore clear that all countries have to take serious measures to reduce their CO_2 emissions in the next few decades. OECD countries alone, despite their efforts to reduce their carbon intensity (and carbon emissions), will not be able to avoid the world's growth of carbon emissions.

Sociopolitical: There are serious shortcomings in the decision-making systems on which we rely on government, business, and society. This is true at local, national, and global levels. The rules and institutions for decision-making are influenced by vested interests, yet each interest has very different access to how decisions are made. Effective change in governance demands action at many levels to establish transparent means for holding those in power to account. Governance failures also occur because decisions are being made in sectoral compartments, with environmental, social, and economic dimensions addressed by separate, competing structures.

The shift of many countries, and in particular the United States, toward corporate plutocracies, with wealth (and thus power) transferred in large quantities from the poor and middle classes to the very rich, is clearly doing enormous environmental damage. The successful campaign of many of the fossil fuel companies to downplay the threat of climate disruption in order to maintain the profits of their industry is a prominent example.

Cultural: The importance to reducing inequity in order to increase the chances of solving the human predicament is obvious just in the differences in access to food and other resources caused by the giant power gap between the rich and the poor. The lack of funding for issues such as the provision of family planning services and badly needed agricultural research contrasts sharply with the expenditures by the United States and some other rich nations to try to assure that oil flows to themselves and the rest of the industrialized world are uninterrupted. The central geopolitical role of oil continues unabated despite the dangerous conflicts oil-seeking already has generated and the probable catastrophic consequences its continued burning portends for the climate.

Current and Projected State of the Global and Regional Environment: Implications of climate change and loss of biodiversity and ecosystem services for Environmental, Economic, and Social Sustainability.

The Earth's environment is changing on all scales from local to global, in large measure due to human activities. The stratospheric ozone layer has been depleted, the climate is warming at a rate faster than at any time during the last 10,000 years, biodiversity is being lost at an unprecedented rate, fisheries are in decline in most of the world's oceans, air pollution is an increasing problem in and around many major cities, large numbers of people live in water stressed or water scarce areas, and large areas of land are being degraded. Much of this environmental degradation is due to the unsustainable production and use of energy, water, food, and other biological resources, and is already undermining efforts to alleviate poverty and stimulate sustainable development, and worse, the future projected changes in the environment are likely to have even more severe consequences.

Climate Change

There is no doubt that the composition of the atmosphere and the Earth's climate have changed since the industrial revolution predominantly due to human activities, and it is inevitable that if those activities do not shift markedly, these changes will continue regionally and globally. The atmospheric concentration of carbon dioxide has increased by over 30 percent since the preindustrial era primarily due to the combustion of fossil fuels and deforestation. Global mean surface temperature, which had been relatively stable for over 1,000 years, has already increased by about 0.75°C since the preindustrial era, and an additional 0.5–1.0°C is inevitable due to past emissions. It is projected to increase by an additional 1.2–6.4°C between 2000 and 2100, with land areas warming significantly more than the oceans and Arctic warming more than the tropic.

Critical Thinking

1. Why does the world face immense environmental, social, and economic risks today?

2. Explain why greenhouse gases are one of the greatest threats to our future prosperity?

3. Do you agree with the authors that a major problem is the "serious short-comings in the decision-making systems at local, national, and global levels on which we rely?"

Internet References

Sociology—Study Sociology Online
http://edu.learnsoc.org/

Sociology Web Resources
http://www.mhhe.com/socscience/sociology/resources/index.htm

Sociosite
http://www.topsite.com/goto/sociosite.net

Socioweb
http://www.topsite.com/goto/socioweb.com

Article   Prepared by: Kurt Finsterbusch, *University of Maryland, College Park*

How to Maintain America's Edge

Increase funding for basic science.

L. RAFAEL REIF

Learning Outcomes

After reading this article, you will be able to:

- Understand the importance of science for the progress of society.

- Describe how America can maintain its lead in science.

- Universities are key to the progress of science in America.

In February 2016, scientists from the Massachusetts Institute of Technology (MIT) and the California Institute of Technology, or Caltech, joined with the National Science Foundation (NSF) to share some remarkable news: two black holes 1.3 billion light-years away had collided, and the resulting gravitational waves had been "heard" by the twin detectors of the Laser Interferometer Gravitational-Wave Observatory (LIGO). This was the first time such waves—ripples in the space–time continuum caused by the violent acceleration of massive objects—had ever been directly observed. Albert Einstein had predicted such waves a century ago, but it was long doubted that instrumentation sensitive enough to confirm their existence could ever be created. It took more than four decades of work by a vast team of scientists to make the impossible possible.

LIGO has revealed thrilling new insights into the cosmos—but it has given the world some gifts of immediate practical value as well, which help illustrate the benefits of such investments in basic science. Over the years, the LIGO project has provided a crucial training ground for thousands of top young scientists and engineers, developing talent that has energized not only American universities but also American businesses. Because LIGO researchers had to measure displacements of mirrors one-10,000th the size of a proton, they were required

to invent an array of breathtakingly precise new tools, including ultrastable high-powered lasers, ultrasmooth mirrors mounted on ultraquiet vibration–isolation platforms, the world's largest ultrahigh-vacuum system, and software algorithms for extracting tiny signals from noisy data. Some of these technologies are already beginning to be used in commercial manufacturing. And if history is any guide, LIGO will lead to important innovations far down the road—just as 1940s, experiments with nuclear magnetic resonance led to the MRI scanner, a 1950s effort to create clocks to measure how gravity warps time made possible GPS, and research in the 1960s and 1970s gave the world the Internet.

LIGO, in short, is extraordinary. But it is also typical because it highlights the system the United States relies on to achieve great scientific discoveries: public support for university-based research, with large investments of time, cash, and patience. This support flows through federal agencies such as the NSF, the National Institutes of Health, and the Defense and Energy Departments. In the case of LIGO, its observatories were funded by the NSF and designed, constructed, and run by its university partners, with more than $1.1 billion spent over 40 years.

It often takes decades for fundamental research to yield practical applications.

Since World War II, the U.S. government has been the world's biggest supporter of potentially transformative science—which is a key reason why the country continues to have the highest share of knowledge- and technology-intensive industries in the world, amounting to nearly 40 percent of the economy. It often takes decades for fundamental research to yield practical applications, and those applications can be unpredictable (such as the cyclotrons devised for experiments in particle physics in the 1930s being put to use in cancer treatments now). Yet it is out of such attempts to expand human knowledge that powerful new businesses grow, with technology titans such as Apple and Google building world-class companies on the backs of technologies emerging from federal investments in research.

By now, one successful way to cultivate economic growth in the United States is clear: Government provides the resources for basic science, and universities supply the talent, the training, and the commitment. The results inspire innovation, private investment, and further research and development, generating new products, new industries, new jobs, and better lives on a large scale.

Indeed, a short walk from my office, I can see the physical embodiment of this process in Cambridge's Kendall Square, which has been transformed in recent decades from an aging industrial landscape. First, it became an informal gathering place for young scientists from MIT, Harvard, and Boston's great medical centers excited by molecular medicine and gene engineering, then the site of academic research centers focused on cancer, genomics, neuroscience, and biomedicine and a hotbed for start-ups in the biosciences. Now it is a home for large companies as well, in biotechnology, pharmaceuticals, information technology, and energy. Once dominated by shuttered candy factories and empty pavement, Kendall Square has been reborn as the biotech capital of the world, one of the most innovative square miles on the planet. Much of the work on the government-funded Human Genome Project took place in the area, and according to the Battelle Memorial Institute, a non-profit research-and-development organization, the $14.5 billion spent on that effort between 1988 and 2012 has helped generate an estimated $1 trillion in economic impact and more than four million job-years of employment.

Yet despite the remarkable success of the U.S. innovation economy, many players in both government and industry have been pulling back from the types of bold long-term investments in fundamental science that could seed the great companies of the future. The entire innovation ecosystem is becoming more shortsighted and cautious. And by failing to invest sufficiently in basic research today, Washington risks creating an innovation deficit that may hobble the U.S. economy for decades to come. This concern has become acute since the White House released its budget blueprint, which proposes crippling cuts to science funding. Now more than ever, the fate of this crucial national investment depends on Congress.

That Used to Be Us

While other nations are vigorously investing in scientific discovery, in recent years, total research-and-development spending in the United States, both private and public, has stagnated. Between 2008 and 2014, the entire U.S. research-and-development enterprise grew by just over 1 percent annually in inflation-adjusted dollars.

Most concerning, however, is the decline in federally supported research. Between 2009 and 2015, federal spending on research and development of all kinds decreased by nearly 20 percent in constant dollars. Universities suffered the longest downturn in federal support since the NSF began keeping track in 1972, and that has caused a great deal of promising work to stall—just when groundbreaking new tools, such as the LIGO detectors and CRISPR-Cas9 genome editing, have opened up enormous opportunities for new discoveries.

Such underinvestment in research and development is not merely a temporary effect of the Great Recession. The federal government now spends a significantly lower percentage of GDP on research than it did in the 1960s and 1970s and has particularly stinted research in essential fields such as the physical sciences, mathematics, computer science, and the environmental sciences. The result has been a shift over time in the source of the majority of research-and-development investment from the federal government to industry.

Industrial research and development is necessary and valuable, of course. But with some exceptions, it tends to focus on relatively narrow questions directed at specific commercial outcomes. Only about 6 percent of industry funding goes to basic research—to projects designed to expand humanity's store of knowledge rather than pass tests of immediate usefulness. This is understandable. Basic research is curiosity-driven, and the short-term returns from it are often not obvious. Yet we cannot do without it, because it is from such fundamental explorations that the world gets the startling breakthroughs that create entirely new industries.

Unfortunately, the United States' great corporate laboratories, such as Bell Labs and DuPont Central Research and Development, once hubs of both fundamental and applied science, are largely a thing of the past. As global competition intensified and firms lost their market dominance, funding such labs came to be seen as an extravagance. Since 1971, moreover, U.S. corporations have been required to report their earnings quarterly, a change that has made it more difficult for managers to focus on long-term results.

There is, however, a true bright spot in the innovation economy. A new generation of digital industry leaders is now funding applied research into various blue-sky technologies, such as low-cost space rockets, autonomous vehicles, holographic computing, Internet-beaming drones, and flying cars. Some are even taking on long-term biomedical challenges, such as devising interventions for aging. But however impressive such efforts are, one must not mistake the fruit for the tree it grew from. Even Astro Teller, the head of so adventurous a corporate laboratory as Alphabet's X, home of the fabled "moonshots," notes that basic research is outside his purview. "The word 'basic' implies 'unguided,'" Teller told The New York Times in 2014, "and 'unguided' is probably best put in government-funded universities rather than industry." Yet many of X's futuristic projects, Teller explained, "rely on the academic work of the last 30 or 40 years."

Universities have struggled to do their part. Over the past 40 years, they have doubled the share of academic research-and-development spending they provide themselves, to its highest level ever. They have found the money to invest steadily in new facilities, they continue to train the nation's young technical talent, and they continue to drive economic development, gaining ever more patents, licensing new technologies, and incubating start-ups. But budgets are tight, and university resources are too limited to sponsor basic research anywhere near the scale of LIGO.

Less Money, More Problems

Why is U.S. government funding for fundamental scientific research drying up? In part because sluggish economic growth since the end of the last economic downturn has made it difficult to justify funding projects with no projected returns for decades to come. There is also a sense that other countries will reap the profits of U.S. investment in basic research without helping cover the costs. And there is a concern that, in combination with globalization, innovation is contributing to the erosion of jobs.

But the process of scientific progress and technological change will not stop because Washington refuses to participate. Moreover, the growth of innovation clusters such as those around Silicon Valley and Kendall Square suggests that there is indeed a home-court advantage to those places where discoveries are made and that businesses like to stay physically close to the source of important ideas. In such places, start-ups linked to university-based research stay in the neighborhood to absorb talent and knowledge and are often joined by larger, more established firms.

And although an increasing percentage of Americans worry that science is forcing too much change on them too quickly, the route to rising incomes ultimately runs through new technologies. In 1987, the MIT professor Robert Solow was awarded the Nobel Prize in Economics for an economic growth model that proposed that rising real incomes are largely dependent on technological progress. Throttling back on investment in basic research is a way to increase economic insecurity, not reduce it, and threatens to shrink the country's horizons in several ways.

To start with, the United States' lead in technological innovation could fall to global competition, just as the country's domestic manufacturing base did, with major geopolitical and economic consequences. Cutting-edge science is equally vital to national security and the economy. Tellingly, other nations are already starting to catch up. As the United States' research-and-development spending stagnated between 2008 and 2013,

China's grew by 17 percent annually, and South Korea's, by 9 percent. Chinese nationals now publish almost as many peer-reviewed scientific journal articles as Americans do, and the quality of Chinese research is rising rapidly. (For as long as the U.S. Patent and Trademark Office has been monitoring how many patents have been granted to universities, MIT has ranked as the single institution with the greatest number, followed by other distinguished U.S. universities, such as Stanford and Caltech. In 2013, Beijing's Tsinghua University suddenly leapt ahead of Stanford.)

Further cuts in research budgets will discourage the cultivation of desperately needed young scientific and engineering talent. This is not merely an academic issue, because a high proportion of U.S. science and engineering PhD's go into industry. As a result, universities have a significant role in training the most sophisticated talent for U.S. businesses, and a crucial feature of U.S. graduate education in science and engineering is the involvement of students in cutting-edge academic research. Projects such as LIGO show graduate students that they can pursue the boldest of ideas, leading to further innovation down the road.

The benefits of public investment in science and technology must be broadly shared by citizens.

Continuing to starve basic research will also hamper the country's ability to attract top global talent, adding to the discouraging effect of recent restrictions on immigration. U.S. universities have long been a magnet for the world's most brilliant people, as both students and faculty. All six of the 2016 American Nobel laureates in science and economics were immigrants, for example, as have been 40 percent of the American Nobel laureates in chemistry, medicine, and physics in this century. At MIT, more than 40 percent of both the graduate students and the faculty were born outside the United States—including the Venezuelan-born author of this article. As research funding dries up, so, too, will the influx of foreign talent.

Fewer federal dollars will also reduce the diversity of the entire U.S. research enterprise. While philanthropic support is important and can focus resources and attention on particular areas of research at particular institutions in ways that may yield rapid results, it cannot substitute for the broad base of federal investment. The National Institutes of Health alone spends over $30 billion on medical research every year; imagine how many relentlessly generous billionaires it would take to match that. Furthermore, although some philanthropic funding goes to university research, the majority of it is directed to nonprofit research institutes, which, unlike universities, are not refreshed by a steady stream of new students and junior faculty. Because universities are forever young, they are uniquely creative.

Declining public investment in science is linked to another emerging threat: a less patient system of private investment to carry discoveries through to commercialization. From the

1960s through the early 1990s, federal investments in education and research produced well-trained young scientists and engineers who generated brilliant ideas. Big companies with big internal research-and-development operations would then hire many of those people, develop their ideas, and deliver them to the marketplace. When I joined MIT's electrical engineering faculty in 1980, that model was working well, translating discoveries from university labs across the country into market-ready innovations.

By the 1990s, however, as American corporations curtailed their own internal research operations, scientists and engineers were left with only one avenue to bring their innovations to market: seek risk capital and launch a start-up. Venture capital investment is typically not patient, however, and it has gravitated disproportionately to digital and biotechnology start-ups that offer a quick path to profitability or to the potentially outsize rewards of blockbuster therapeutics. Venture capital investment has not worked as well for many tangible products based on new science and technology, including sorely needed new energy technologies, which may require capital-intensive infrastructure and involve novel manufacturing processes that will take time to develop.

Danger, Will Robinson!

The future of U.S. scientific, technological, and economic innovation depends on increased federal funding for basic research and increased effort by the private sector to move new technologies into the marketplace. In 1964, at the height of the Cold War and the space race, federal spending on research and development came to 1.9 percent of GDP. Today it is less than half that—even in the face of threats such as terrorism, cyber-attacks, climate change, and potential pandemics. Given these challenges and the ratcheting up of international competition, a recommitment to U.S. leadership in science and innovation is critical.

Something more has to be done, also, to ensure a steady progression from ideas to investment to impact. Many universities have created incubators and accelerators to support start-ups emerging from their laboratories. At MIT, we are particularly concerned about the fate of "tough technologies" in fields such as clean energy, manufacturing, robotics, biotechnology, and medical devices—promising ideas that could potentially yield game-changing answers to enormous challenges but whose commercialization is too time- and capital-intensive to attract risk capital or strategic investment from a large corporation. To help such technologies reach the marketplace, we recently launched an enterprise we call The Engine. It will support up to 60 start-ups at a time by offering them affordable space near the MIT campus, access to specialized equipment and technical expertise, and patient capital through a venture capital investment arm relying on private funds. If this and similar projects elsewhere succeed, they could unleash waves of innovation that could benefit everyone.

The benefits of public investment in science and technology, finally, must be broadly shared by the citizens who shoulder the cost, and the economic and social disruptions triggered by the resulting advances must be addressed with systems that offer continuous training and retraining to American workers throughout their professional lives. Increasingly smart and nimble machines will eventually radically alter the workplace. Stopping such technological progress is impossible—so rather than wish the problem away, the public and private sectors should focus on helping people adapt successfully.

As soon as the world heard the first chirp signaling a gravitational wave emanating from black holes 1.3 billion light-years away, it was clear that the LIGO project was a triumph and would usher in a new kind of astronomy that would reveal new truths about the universe. LIGO shows that the United States still knows how to do truly bold science and do it well. But the breakthroughs today were built on the hard work and generous funding of past generations. If today's Americans want to leave similar legacies to their descendants, they need to refill the research pipelines and invest more in the nation's scientific infrastructure. If they don't, Americans should not be surprised when other countries take the lead.

Critical Thinking

1. What will be the likely result of the slowing of academic research in science and the slowing of government investment in science?

2. Do you agree with Solow that rising real incomes are largely dependent on technological progress?

3. What steps should be taken to minimize the negative impacts of new technologies?

Internet References

Sociology—Study Sociology Online
  http://edu.learnsoc.org/

Sociology Web Resources
  http://www.mhhe.com/socscience/sociology/resources/index.htm

Sociosite
  http://www.topsite.com/goto/sociosite.net

Socioweb
  http://www.topsite.com/goto/socioweb.com

Article   Prepared by: Kurt Finsterbusch, *University of Maryland, College Park*

The Axis of Climate Evil

PAUL KRUGMAN

Learning Outcomes

After reading this article, you will be able to:

- Describe Krugman's argument against the climate change deniers.

- Understand that the climate change deniers want more research to increase the confidence in the climate change theory before expensive policies are instituted.

- Speculate on the fate of the world.

"It's Not Your Imagination: Summers Are Getting Hotter." So read a recent headline in The Times, highlighting a decade-by-decade statistical analysis by climate expert James Hansen. "Most summers," the analysis concluded, "are now either hot or extremely hot compared with the mid-20th century."

So what else is new? At this point the evidence for human-caused global warming just keeps getting more overwhelming, and the plausible scenarios for the future—extreme weather events, rising sea levels, drought, and more—just keep getting scarier.

In a rational world urgent action to limit climate change would be the overwhelming policy priority for governments everywhere.

But the U.S. government is, of course, now controlled by a party within which climate denial—rejecting not just scientific evidence but also obvious lived experience, and fiercely opposing any effort to slow the trend—has become a defining marker of tribal identity.

Put it this way: Republicans can't seem to repeal Obamacare, and recriminations between Senate leaders and the tweeter in chief are making headlines. But the G.O.P. is completely united behind its project of destroying civilization, and it's making good progress toward that goal.

So where does climate denial come from?

Just to be clear, experts aren't always right; even an overwhelming scientific consensus sometimes turns out to have been wrong. And if someone offers a good-faith critique of conventional views, a serious effort to get at the truth, he or she deserves a hearing.

What becomes clear to anyone following the climate debate, however, is that hardly any climate skeptics are in fact trying to get at the truth. I'm not a climate scientist, but I do know what bogus arguments look like—and I can't think of a single prominent climate skeptic who isn't obviously arguing in bad faith.

Take, for example, all the people who seized on the fact that 1998 was an unusually warm year to claim that global warming stopped 20 years ago—as if one unseasonably hot day in May proves that summer is a myth. Or all the people who cited out-of-context quotes from climate researchers as evidence of a vast scientific conspiracy.

Or for that matter, think of anyone who cites "uncertainty" as a reason to do nothing—when it should be obvious that the risks of faster-than-expected climate change if we do too little dwarf the risks of doing too much if change is slower than expected.

But what's driving this epidemic of bad faith? The answer, I'd argue, is that there are actually three groups involved—a sort of axis of climate evil.

First, and most obvious, there's the fossil fuel industry—think of the Koch brothers—which has an obvious financial stake in continuing to sell dirty energy. And the industry—following the same well-worn path industry groups used to create doubt about the dangers of tobacco, acid rain, the ozone hole, and more—has systematically showered money on think tanks and scientists willing to express skepticism about climate change. Many—perhaps even most—authors purporting to cast doubt on global warming turn out, on investigation, to have received financial support from the fossil fuel sector.

Still, the mercenary interests of fossil fuel companies aren't the whole story here. There's also ideology.

An influential part of the U.S. political spectrum—think the Wall Street Journal editorial page—is opposed to any and all forms of government economic regulation; it's committed to Reagan's doctrine that government is always the problem, never the solution.

Such people have always had a problem with pollution: When unregulated individual actions impose costs on others, it's hard to see how you avoid supporting some form of government intervention. And climate change is the mother of all pollution issues.

Some conservatives are willing to face this reality and support market-friendly intervention to limit greenhouse gas emissions. But all too many prefer simply to deny the existence of the issue—if facts conflict with their ideology, they deny the facts.

Finally, there are a few public intellectuals—less important than the plutocrats and ideologues, but if you ask me even more shameful—who adopt a pose of climate skepticism out of sheer ego. In effect, they say: "Look at me! I'm smart! I'm contrarian! I'll show you how clever I am by denying the scientific consensus!" And for the sake of this posturing, they're willing to nudge us further down the road to catastrophe.

Which brings me back to the current political situation. Right now progressives are feeling better than they expected to a few months ago: Donald Trump and his frenemies in Congress are accomplishing a lot less than they hoped, and their opponents feared. But that doesn't change the reality that the axis of climate evil is now firmly in control of U.S. policy, and the world may never recover.

Critical Thinking

1. Do you agree with Krugman "that at this point the evidence for human-caused global warming just keeps getting more overwhelming, and the plausible scenarios for the future—extreme weather events, rising sea levels, drought, and more—just keep getting scarier"?

2. Is Krugman right to castigate the Republican Party for the climate change denial of most of its congressmen?

3. Do you agree with Krugman's explanation of the climate change deniers' behavior?

Internet References

Sociology—Study Sociology Online
   http://edu.learnsoc.org/
Sociology Web Resources
   http://www.mhhe.com/socscience/sociology/resources/index.htm
Sociosite
   http://www.topsite.com/goto/sociosite.net
Socioweb
   http://www.topsite.com/goto/socioweb.com

Article   Prepared by: Kurt Finsterbusch, *University of Maryland, College Park*

Can a Collapse of Global Civilization Be Avoided?

PAUL R. EHRLICH AND ANNE H. EHRLICH

Learning Outcomes

After reading this article, you will be able to:

- Evaluate the Ehrlichs' thesis about addressing environmental problems immediately or face the possibility of the collapse of global civilization.

- Give your assessment of how to deal with the problem of Americans overusing the environment.

- Lay out the steps that should be taken to make America sustainable.

1. Introduction

Virtually every past civilization has eventually undergone collapse, a loss of socio-political-economic complexity usually accompanied by a dramatic decline in population size. Some, such as those of Egypt and China, have recovered from collapses at various stages; others, such as that of Easter Island or the Classic Maya, were apparently permanent. All those previous collapses were local or regional; elsewhere, other societies and civilizations persisted unaffected. Sometimes, as in the Tigris and Euphrates valleys, new civilizations rose in succession. In many, if not most, cases, overexploitation of the environment was one proximate or an ultimate cause.

But today, for the first time, humanity's global civilization—the worldwide, increasingly interconnected, highly technological society in which we all are to one degree or another, embedded—is threatened with collapse by an array of environmental problems. Humankind finds itself engaged in what Prince Charles described as 'an act of suicide on a grand scale', facing what the UK's Chief Scientific Advisor John

Beddington called a 'perfect storm' of environmental problems. The most serious of these problems show signs of rapidly escalating severity, especially climate disruption. But other elements could potentially also contribute to a collapse: an accelerating extinction of animal and plant populations and species, which could lead to a loss of ecosystem services essential for human survival; land degradation and land-use change; a pole-to-pole spread of toxic compounds; ocean acidification and eutrophication (dead zones); worsening of some aspects of the epidemiological environment (factors that make human populations susceptible to infectious diseases); depletion of increasingly scarce resources, including especially groundwater, which is being overexploited in many key agricultural areas; and resource wars. These are not separate problems; rather they interact in two gigantic complex adaptive systems: the biosphere system and the human socio-economic system. The negative manifestations of these interactions are often referred to as 'the human predicament', and determining how to prevent it from generating a global collapse is perhaps the foremost challenge confronting humanity.

The human predicament is driven by overpopulation, over-consumption of natural resources and the use of unnecessarily environmentally damaging technologies and socio-economic-political arrangements to service Homo sapiens' aggregate consumption. How far the human population size now is above the planet's long-term carrying capacity is suggested (conservatively) by ecological footprint analysis. It shows that to support today's population of seven billion sustainably (i.e. with business as usual, including current technologies and standards of living) would require roughly half an additional planet; to do so, if all citizens of Earth consumed resources at the US level would take four to five more Earths. Adding the projected 2.5 billion more people by 2050 would make the human assault on civilization's life-support systems disproportionately worse, because almost everywhere people face systems with nonlinear responses, in which environmental damage increases at a rate that becomes faster with each additional person. Of course, the claim is often made that humanity will expand Earth's carrying capacity dramatically with technological innovation, but it is widely recognized that technologies can both add and subtract from carrying capacity. The plough evidently first expanded it and now appears to be reducing it. Overall, careful analysis of the prospects does not provide much confidence that technology will save us or that gross domestic product can be disengaged from resource use.

2. Do Current trends Portend a Collapse?

What is the likelihood of this set of interconnected predicaments leading to a global collapse in this century? There have been many definitions and much discussion of past 'collapses', but a future global collapse does not require a careful definition. It could be triggered by anything from a 'small' nuclear war, whose ecological effects could quickly end civilization, to a more gradual breakdown because famines, epidemics and resource shortages cause a disintegration of central control within nations, in concert with disruptions of trade and conflicts over increasingly scarce necessities. In either case, regardless of survivors or replacement societies, the world familiar to anyone reading this study and the well-being of the vast majority of people would disappear.

How likely is such a collapse to occur? No civilization can avoid collapse if it fails to feed its population. The world's success so far, and the prospective ability to feed future generations at least as well, has been under relatively intensive discussion for half a century. Agriculture made civilization possible, and over the last 80 years or so, an industrial agricultural revolution has created a technology-dependent global food system. That system, humanity's single biggest industry, has generated miracles of food production. But it has also created serious long-run vulnerabilities, especially in its dependence on stable climates, crop monocultures, industrially produced fertilizers and pesticides, petroleum, antibiotic feed supplements and rapid, efficient transportation.

Despite those food production miracles, today at least two billion people are hungry or poorly nourished. The Food and Agriculture Organization estimates that increasing food production by some 70 per cent would be required to feed a 35 per cent bigger and still growing human population adequately by 2050. What are the prospects that H. sapiens can produce and distribute sufficient food? To do so, it probably will be necessary to

accomplish many or all of the following tasks: severely limit climate disruption; restrict expansion of land area for agriculture (to preserve ecosystem services); raise yields where possible; put much more effort into soil conservation; increase efficiency in the use of fertilizers, water and energy; become more vegetarian; grow more food for people (not fuel for vehicles); reduce food wastage; stop degradation of the oceans and better regulate aquaculture; significantly increase investment in sustainable agricultural and aquacultural research; and move increasing equity and feeding everyone to the very top of the policy agenda.

Most of these long-recommended tasks require changes in human behaviour thus far elusive. The problem of food wastage and the need for more and better agricultural research have been discussed for decades. So have 'technology will save us' schemes such as building 'nuclear agro-industrial complexes', where energy would be so cheap that it could support a new kind of desert agriculture in 'food factories', where crops would be grown on desalinated water and precisely machine fertilized. Unhappily, sufficiently cheap energy has never been produced by nuclear power to enable large-scale agriculture to move in that direction. Nor has agriculture moved towards feeding people protein extracted from leaves or bacteria grown on petroleum. None of these schemes has even resulted in a coordinated development effort. Meanwhile, growing numbers of newly well-off people have increased demand for meat, thereby raising global demand for feed grains.

Perhaps even more critical, climate disruption may pose insurmountable biophysical barriers to increasing crop yields. Indeed, if humanity is very unlucky with the climate, there may be reductions in yields of major crops, although near-term this may be unlikely to affect harvests globally. Nonetheless, rising temperatures already seem to be slowing previous trends of increasing yields of basic grains, and unless greenhouse gas emissions are dramatically reduced, dangerous anthropogenic climate change could ravage agriculture. Also, in addition to falling yields from many oceanic fish stocks because of widespread overfishing, warming and acidification of the oceans threaten the protein supply of some of the most nutritionally vulnerable people, especially those who cannot afford to purchase farmed fish.

Unfortunately, the agricultural system has complex connections with all the chief drivers of environmental deterioration. Agriculture itself is a major emitter of greenhouse gases and thus is an important cause of climate disruption as well as being exceptionally vulnerable to its consequences. More than a millennium of change in temperature and precipitation patterns is apparently now entrained, with the prospect of increasingly severe storms, droughts, heat waves and floods, all of which seem already evident and all of which threaten agricultural production.

Land is an essential resource for farming, and one facing multiple threats. In addition to the serious and widespread problems of soil degradation, sea-level rise (the most certain consequence of global warming) will take important areas out of production either by inundating them (a 1 m rise would flood 17.5% of Bangladesh), exposing them to more frequent storm surges, or salinizing coastal aquifers essential for irrigation water. Another important problem for the food system is the loss of prime farmland to urbanization, a trend that seems certain to accelerate as population growth steadily erodes the per capita supply of farmland.

The critical importance of substantially boosting the inadequate current action on the demographic problem can be seen in the time required to change the trajectory of population growth humanely and sensibly. We know from such things as the World War II mobilizations that many consumption patterns can be altered dramatically within a year, given appropriate incentives. If food shortages became acute, then a rapid reaction would ensue as hunger became much more widespread. Food prices would rise, and diets would temporarily change (e.g. the number of meals consumed per day or amount of meat consumed) to compensate the shortage.

Over the long term, however, expanding the global food supply and distributing it more equitably would be a slow and difficult process. Even though a major famine might well provoke investment in long-needed improvements in food production and distribution, they would take time to plan, test and implement.

Furthermore, agriculture is a leading cause of losses of biodiversity and thus of the critical ecosystem services supplied to agriculture itself (e.g. pollination, pest control, soil fertility, climate stability) and other human enterprises. Farming is also a principal source of global toxification, as has been clear since the days of Carson, exposing the human population to myriad subtle poisons. These pose further potential risks to food production.

3. What Needs to be done to Avoid a Collapse?

The threat from climate disruption to food production alone means that humanity's entire system for mobilizing energy needs to be rapidly transformed. Warming must be held well below a potential 58C rise in global average temperature, a level that could well bring down civilization. The best estimate today may be that, failing rapid concerted action, the world is already committed to a 2.48C increase in global average temperature. This is significantly above the 28C estimated a decade ago by climate scientists to be a 'safe' limit, but now considered by some analysts to be too dangerous, a credible assessment,

given the effects seen already before reaching a one degree rise. There is evidence, moreover, that present models underestimate future temperature increase by overestimating the extent that growth of vegetation can serve as a carbon sink and underestimating positive feedbacks.

Many complexities plague the estimation of the precise threats of anthropogenic climate disruption, ranging from heat deaths and spread of tropical diseases to sea-level rise, crop failures and violent storms. One key to avoiding a global collapse, and thus an area requiring great effort and caution is avoiding climate-related mass famines. Our agricultural system evolved in a geological period of relatively constant and benign climate and was well attuned to twentieth-century conditions. That alone is cause for substantial concern as the planet's climates rapidly shift to new, less predictable regimes. It is essential to slow that process. That means dramatically transforming much of the existing energy mobilization infrastructure and changing human behaviour to make the energy system much more efficient. This is possible; indeed, sensible plans for doing it have been put forward, and some progress has been made. The central challenge, of course, is to phase out more than half of the global use of fossil fuels by 2050 in order to forestall the worst impacts of climate disruption, a challenge the latest International Energy Agency edition of World Energy Outlook makes look more severe. This highlights another dilemma. Fossil fuels are now essential to agriculture for fertilizer and pesticide manufacture, operation of farm machinery, irrigation (often wasteful), livestock husbandry, crop drying, food storage, transportation and distribution. Thus, the phase-out will need to include at least partial substitution of non-fossil fuels in these functions, and do so without greatly increasing food prices.

Unfortunately, essential steps such as curbing global emissions to peak by 2020 and reducing them to half of present levels by 2050 are extremely problematic economically and politically. Fossil fuel companies would have to leave most of their proven reserves in the ground, thus destroying much of the industry's economic value. Because the ethics of some businesses include knowingly continuing lethal but profitable activities, it is hardly surprising that interests with large financial stakes in fossil fuel burning have launched a gigantic and largely successful disinformation campaign in the USA to confuse people about climate disruption and block attempts to deal with it.

One recurrent theme in analyses of the food problem is the need for closing 'yield gaps'. That means raising yields in less productive systems to those typical of industrial agriculture. But climatic conditions may change sufficiently that those industrial high yields can themselves no longer be sustained. Thus, reducing the chances of a collapse calls for placing much more effort into genetic and ecological research related to agriculture and adopting already known environmental-friendly techniques, even though that may require trading off immediate corporate profits for social benefits or long-term sustainability.

Rationalizing energy mobilization alone may not be enough to be enough to maintain agricultural production, let alone allow its great expansion. Human water-handling infrastructure will have to be re-engineered for flexibility to bring water to crops in an environment of constantly changing precipitation patterns. This is critical, for although today only about 15 per cent of agricultural land is irrigated, it provides some 40 per cent of the grain crop yield. It seems likely that farming areas now rain-fed may someday need to be irrigated, whereas irrigation could become superfluous elsewhere, and both could change more or less continually. For this and many other reasons, the global food system will need to quickly evolve an unprecedented flexibility, never before even contemplated.

One factor making the challenges more severe is the major participation in the global system of giant nations whose populations have not previously enjoyed the fossil energy abundance that brought Western countries and Japan to positions of affluence. Now they are poised to repeat the West's energy 'success', and on an even greater scale. India alone, which recently suffered a gigantic blackout affecting 300 million people, is planning to bring 455 new coal plants on line. Worldwide more than 1200 plants with a total installed capacity of 1.4 million megawatts are planned, much of that in China, where electricity demand is expected to skyrocket. The resultant surge in greenhouse gases will interact with the increasing diversion of grain to livestock, stimulated by the desire for more meat in the diets of Indians, Chinese and others in a growing global middle class.

4. Dealing with Problems Beyond Food Supply

Another possible threat to the continuation of civilization is global toxification. Adverse symptoms of exposure to synthetic chemicals are making some scientists increasingly nervous about effects on the human population. Should a global threat materialize, however, no planned mitigating responses (analogous to the ecologically and politically risky 'geoengineering' projects often proposed to ameliorate climate disruption) are waiting in the wings ready for deployment.

Much the same can be said about aspects of the epidemiological environment and the prospect of epidemics being enhanced by rapid population growth in immune-weakened societies, increased contact with animal reservoirs, high speed transport and the misuse of antibiotics. Nobel laureate Joshua Lederberg had great concern for the epidemic problem, famously stating, 'The survival of the human species is not a preordained evolutionary program'. Some precautionary steps that should be considered include forbidding the use of antibiotics as growth

stimulators for livestock, building emergency stocks of key vaccines and drugs (such as Tamiflu), improving disease surveillance, expanding mothballed emergency medical facilities, preparing institutions for imposing quarantines and, of course, moving as rapidly as possible to humanely reduce the human population size. It has become increasingly clear that security has many dimensions beyond military security and that breaches of environmental security could risk the end of global civilization.

But much uncertainty about the human ability to avoid a collapse still hinges on military security, especially whether some elements of the human predicament might trigger a nuclear war. Recent research indicates that even a regional scale nuclear conflict, as is quite possible between India and Pakistan, could lead to a global collapse through widespread climatic consequences. Triggers to conflict beyond political and religious strife easily could include cross-border epidemics, a need to gain access to food supplies and farmland, and competition over other resources, especially agricultural water and (if the world does not come to its energy senses) oil. Finding ways to eliminate nuclear weapons and other instruments of mass destruction must move even higher on civilization's agenda, because nuclear war would be the quickest and surest route to a collapse.

In thinking about the probability of collapse, one must obviously consider the social disruptions associated with elements of the predicament. Perhaps at the top of the list should be that of environmental refugees. Recent predictions are that environmental refugees could number 50 million by 2020. Severe droughts, floods, famines and epidemics could greatly swell that number. If current 'official' predictions of sea-level rise are low (as many believe they are), coastal inundations alone could generate massive human movements; a 1 m rise would directly affect some 100 million people, whereas a 6 m rise would displace more than 400 million. Developing a more comprehensive system of international governance with institutions planning to ameliorate the impacts of such catastrophes would be a major way to reduce the odds of collapse.

5. The Role of Science

The scientific community has repeatedly warned humanity in the past of its peril, and the earlier warnings about the risks of population expansion and the 'limits to growth' have increasingly been shown to be on the right track. The warnings continue. Yet many scientists still tend to treat population growth as an exogenous variable, when it should be considered an endogenous one—indeed, a central factor. Too many studies asking 'how can we possibly feed 9.6 billion people by 2050?' should also be asking 'how can we humanely lower birth rates far enough to reduce that number to 8.6?' To our minds, the fundamental cure, reducing the scale of the human enterprise (including the size of the population) to keep its aggregate consumption within the carrying capacity of Earth, is obvious but too much neglected or denied. There are great social and psychological barriers in growth manic cultures to even considering it. This is especially true because of the 'endarkenment'—a rapidly growing movement towards religious orthodoxies that reject enlightenment values such as freedom of thought, democracy, separation of church and state, and basing beliefs and actions on empirical evidence. They are manifest in dangerous trends such as climate denial, failure to act on the loss of biodiversity and opposition to condoms (for AIDS control) as well as other forms of contraception. If ever there was a time for evidence-based (as opposed to faith-based) risk reduction strategies, it is now.

How can scientists do more to reduce the odds of a collapse? Both natural and social scientists should put more effort into finding the best ways of accomplishing the necessary re-modelling of energy and water infrastructure. They should develop better ways of evaluating and regulating the use of synthetic chemicals, a problem that might abate somewhat as availability of their fossil fuel sources fades (even though only about 5% of oil production flows into petrochemical production). The protection of Earth's remaining biodiversity (especially the crucial diversity of populations) must take centre stage for both scientific specialists and, through appropriate education, the public. Scientists must continually call attention to the need to improve the human epidemiological environment, and for control and eventual elimination of nuclear, chemical and biological weapons. Above all, they should expand efforts to understand the mechanisms through which cooperation evolves, because avoiding collapse will require unusual levels of international cooperation.

Is it too late for the global scientific community to collect itself and start to deal with the nexus of the two complex adaptive systems and then help generate the necessary actions to move towards sustainability? There are certainly many small scale science-based efforts, often local, that can provide hope if scaled up. For example, environmental non-govenmental organizations and others are continually struggling to halt the destruction of elements of biodiversity (and thus, in some cases, of vital ecosystem services), often with success. In the face of the building extinction crisis, they may be preserving nuclei from which Earth's biota and humanity's ecosystem services, might eventually be regenerated. And some positive efforts are scaling up. China now has some 25 per cent of its land in ecosystem function conservation areas designed to protect both natural capital and human well-being. The Natural Capital Project is helping improve the management of these areas. This is good news, but in our view, many too few scientists are involved in the efforts needed, especially in re-orienting at least part of their research towards mitigating the predicament and then bringing their results to the policy front.

6. The Need for Rapid Social/ Political Change

Until very recently, our ancestors had no reason to respond genetically or culturally to long-term issues. If the global climate were changing rapidly for Australopithecus or even ancient Romans, then they were not causing it and could do nothing about it. The forces of genetic and cultural selection were not creating brains or institutions capable of looking generations ahead; there would have been no selection pressures in that direction. Indeed, quite the opposite, selection probably favoured mechanisms to keep perception of the environmental background steady so that rapid changes (e.g. leopard approaching) would be obvious. But now slow changes in that background are the most lethal threats. Societies have a long history of mobilizing efforts, making sacrifices and changes, to defeat an enemy at the gates, or even just to compete more successfully with a rival. But there is not much evidence of societies mobilizing and making sacrifices to meet gradually worsening conditions that threaten real disaster for future generations. Yet that is exactly the sort of mobilization that we believe is required to avoid a collapse.

Perhaps the biggest challenge in avoiding collapse is convincing people, especially politicians and economists, to break this ancient mould and alter their behaviour relative to the basic population-consumption drivers of environmental deterioration. We know that simply informing people of the scientific consensus on a serious problem does not ordinarily produce rapid changes in institutional or individual behaviour. That was amply demonstrated in the case of cigarettes, air pollution and other environmental problems and is now being demonstrated in the obesity epidemic as well as climate disruption.

Obvious parallels exist regarding reproduction and overconsumption, which are especially visible in what amounts to a cultural addiction to continued economic growth among the already well-off. One might think that the mathematics of compound interest would have convinced everyone long ago that growth of an industrialized economy at 3.5 per cent annually cannot long continue. Unfortunately, most 'educated' people are immersed in a culture that does not recognize that, in the real world, a short history (a few centuries) of exponential growth does not imply a long future of such growth.

Besides focusing their research on ways to avoid collapse, there is a need for natural scientists to collaborate with social scientists, especially those who study the dynamics of social movements. Such collaborations could develop ways to stimulate a significant increase in popular support for decisive and immediate action on the predicament. Unfortunately, awareness among scientists that humanity is in deep trouble has not been accompanied by popular awareness and pressure to counter the political and economic influences implicated in the current crisis. Without significant pressure from the public demanding action, we fear there is little chance of changing course fast enough to forestall disaster.

The needed pressure, however, might be generated by a popular movement based in academia and civil society to help guide humanity towards developing a new multiple intelligence, 'foresight intelligence' to provide the long-term analysis and planning that markets cannot supply. Foresight intelligence could not only systematically look ahead but also guide cultural changes towards desirable outcomes such as increased socio-economic resilience. Helping develop such a movement and foresight intelligence are major challenges facing scientists today, a cutting edge for research that must slice fast if the chances of averting a collapse are to be improved.

If foresight intelligence became established, many more scientists and policy planners (and society) might, for example, understand the demographic contributions to the predicament, stop treating population growth as a 'given' and consider the nutritional, health and social benefits of humanely ending growth well below nine billion and starting a slow decline. This would be a monumental task, considering the momentum of population growth. Monumental, but not impossible if the political will could be generated globally to give full rights, education and opportunities to women, and provide all sexually active human beings with modern contraception and backup abortion. The degree to which those steps would reduce fertility rates is controversial, but they are a likely win-win for societies.

Obviously, especially with the growing endarkenment, there are huge cultural and institutional barriers to establishing such policies in some parts of the world. After all, there is not a single nation where women are truly treated as equal to men. Despite that, the population driver should not be ignored simply because limiting overconsumption can, at least in theory, be achieved more rapidly. The difficulties of changing demographic trajectories mean that the problem should have been addressed sooner, rather than later. That halting population growth inevitably leads to changes in age structure is no excuse for bemoaning drops in fertility rates, as is common in European government circles. Reduction of population size in those over-consuming nations is a very positive trend, and sensible planning can deal with the problems of population aging.

While rapid policy change to head off collapse is essential, fundamental institutional change to keep things on track is necessary as well. This is especially true of educational systems, which today fail to inform most people of how the world works

and thus perpetuate a vast culture gap. The academic challenge is especially great for economists, who could help set the background for avoiding collapse by designing steady-state economic systems, and along the way destroying fables such as 'growth can continue forever if it's in service industries', or 'technological innovation will save us'. Issues such as the importance of comparative advantage under current global circumstances, the development of new models that better reflect the irrational behaviour of individuals and groups, reduction of the worship of 'free' markets that infests the discipline, and tasks such as making information more symmetrical, moving towards sustainability and enhancing equity (including redistribution) all require re-examination. In that re-examination, they would be following the lead of distinguished economists in dealing with the real world of biophysical constraints and human well-being.

At the global level, the loose network of agreements that now tie countries together, developed in a relatively recent stage of cultural evolution since modern nation states appeared, is utterly inadequate to grapple with the human predicament. Strengthening global environmental governance and addressing the related problem of avoiding failed statehood are tasks humanity has so far refused to tackle comprehensively even as cultural evolution in technology has rendered the present international system (as it has educational systems) obsolete. Serious global environmental problems can only be solved and a collapse avoided with an unprecedented level of international cooperation. Regardless of one's estimate of civilization's potential longevity, the time to start restructuring the international system is right now. If people do not do that, nature will restructure civilization for us.

Similarly, widely based cultural change is required to reduce humanely both population size and overconsumption by the rich. Both go against cultural norms, and, as long feared, the overconsumption norm has understandably been adopted by the increasingly rich subpopulations of developing nations, notably India and China. One can be thrilled by the numbers of people raised from poverty while being apprehensive about the enormous and possibly lethal environmental and social costs that may eventually result. The industrial revolution set civilization on the road to collapse, spurring population growth, which contributed slightly more than overconsumption to environmental degradation. Now population combined with affluence growth may finish the job.

Needless to say, dealing with economic and racial inequities will be critically important in getting large numbers of people from culturally diverse groups to focus their minds on solving the human predicament, something globalization should help. These tasks will be pursued, along with an emphasis on developing 'foresight intelligence', by the nascent Millennium Alliance for Humanity and the Biosphere (the MAHB; http://mahb. stanford.edu). One of its central goals is to try to accelerate change towards sustainability. Since simply giving the scientific facts to the public will not do it, among other things, this means finding frames and narratives to convince the public of the need to make changes.

We know that societies can evolve fundamentally and unexpectedly, as was dramatically demonstrated by the collapse of communist regimes in Europe in 1989. Rather than tinkering around the edges and making feeble or empty gestures towards one or another of the interdependent problems we face, we need a powerful and comprehensive approach. In addressing climate change, for instance, developing nations need to be convinced that they (along with the rest of the world) cannot afford (and do not need) to delay action while they 'catch up' in development. Indeed, development on the old model is counterproductive; they have a great opportunity to pioneer new approaches and technologies. All nations need to stop waiting for others to act and be willing to do everything they can to mitigate emissions and hasten the energy transition, regardless of what others are doing.

With climate and many other global environmental problems, polycentric solutions may be more readily found than global ones. Complex, multi-level systems may be better able to cope with complex, multi-level problems, and institutional change is required at many levels in many polities. What scientists understand about cultural evolution suggests that, while improbable, it may be possible to move cultures in such directions. Whether solutions will be global or polycentric, international negotiations will be needed, existing international agencies that deal with them will need strengthening, and new institutions will need to be formed.

7. Conclusions

Do we think global society can avoid a collapse in this century? The answer is yes, because modern society has shown some capacity to deal with long-term threats, at least if they are obvious or continuously brought to attention (think of the risks of nuclear conflict). Humanity has the assets to get the job done, but the odds of avoiding collapse seem small because the risks are clearly not obvious to most people and the classic signs of impending collapse, especially diminishing returns to complexity, are everywhere. One central psychological barrier to taking dramatic action is the distribution of costs and benefits through time: the costs up front, the benefits accruing largely to unknown people in the future. But whether we or more optimistic observers are correct, our own ethical values compel us to think the benefits to those future generations are worth struggling for, to increase at least slightly the chances of avoiding a dissolution of today's global civilization as we know it.

We are especially grateful to Joan Diamond, Executive Director of the MAHB, for her ideas on foresight intelligence, and to the Beijer Institute of Ecological Economics for two decades of provocative discussions on topics related to this paper. This paper has benefited from comments from Ken Arrow, Scott Barrett, Andy Beattie, Dan Blumstein, Corey Bradshaw, Greg Bratman, Paul Brest, Jim Brown, Bob Brulle, Gretchen Daily, Lisa Daniel, Timothy Daniel, Partha Dasgupta, Nadia Diamond-Smith, Tom Dietz, Anantha Duraiappah, Riley Dunlap, Walter Falcon, Marc Feldman, Rachelle Gould, Larry Goulder, John Harte, Mel Harte, Ursula Heise, Tad Homer-Dixon, Bob Horn, Danny Karp, Don Kennedy, Michael Klare, Simon Levin, Jack Liu, David Lobell, Doug McAdam, Chase Mendenhall, Hal Mooney, Fathali Moghaddam, Dennis Pirages, Graham Pyke, Gene Rosa, Lee Ross, Jose Sarukhan, Kirk Smith, Sarah Soule, Chris Turnbull and Wren Wirth. Two of the best and most thorough anonymous reviewers we have ever encountered helped us improve the manuscript. The work was supported by Peter and Helen Bing and the Mertz Gilmore Foundation.

Critical Thinking

1. What is your assessment of the state of the planet?
2. What specifically are the most worrisome environmental problems?
3. The Ehrlichs wonder whether the collapse of global civilization can be avoided. Do they have convincing data supporting this conclusion?

Internet References

Sociosite
www.topsite.com/goto/sociosite.net

Socioweb
www.topsite.com/goto/socioweb.com

Sociology—Study Sociology Online
http://edu.learnsoc.org

Sociology Web Resources
www.mhhe.com/socscience/sociology/resources/index.htm

PAUL EHRLICH is a Professor of Biology and President of the Center for Conservation Biology at Stanford University, and Adjunct Professor at the University of Technology, Sydney. His research interests are in the ecology and evolution of natural populations of butterflies, reef fishes, birds and human beings. **ANNE EHRLICH** is a Senior Research Scientist in Biology at Stanford and focuses her research on policy issues related to the environment

Article   Prepared by: Kurt Finsterbusch, *University of Maryland, College Park*

How Innovation Could Save the Planet

Ideas may be our greatest natural resource, says a computer scientist and futurist. He argues that the world's most critical challenges—including population growth, peak oil, climate change, and limits to growth—could be met by encouraging innovation.

Ramez Naam

Learning Outcomes

After reading this article, you will be able to:

- Understand both the benefits and the costs of long-term economic progress.

- Evaluate Ramez Naam's thesis that "Innovation Could Save the Planet."

- Notice the many specific ideas and innovations that could address the major problems.

The Best of Times: Unprecedented Prosperity

There are many ways in which we are living in the most wonderful age ever. We can imagine we are heading toward a sort of science-fiction Utopia, where we are incredibly rich and incredibly prosperous, and the planet is healthy. But there are other reasons to fear that we're headed toward a dystopia of sorts.

On the positive side, life expectancy has been rising for the last 150 years, and faster since the early part of the twentieth century in the developing world than it has in the rich world. Along with that has come a massive reduction in poverty. The most fundamental empowerer of humans—education—has also soared, not just in the rich world, but throughout the world.

Another great empowerer of humanity is connectivity: Access to information and access to communication both have soared. The number of mobile phones on the planet was effectively zero in the early 1990s, and now it's in excess of 4 billion. More than three-quarters of humanity, in the span of one generation, have gotten access to connectivity that, as my

friend Peter Diamand is likes to say, is greater than any president before 1995 had. A reasonably well-off person in India or in Nigeria has better access to information than Ronald Reagan did during most of his career.

With increased connectivity has come an increase in democracy. As people have gotten richer, more educated, more able to access information, and more able to communicate, they have demanded more control over the places where they live. The fraction of nations that are functional democracies is at an all-time high in this world—more than double what it was in the 1970s, with the collapse of the Soviet Union.

Economically, the world is a more equal place than it has been in decades. In the West, and especially in the United States, we hear a lot about growing inequality, but on a global scale, the opposite is true. As billions are rising out of poverty around the world, the global middle classes are catching up with the global rich.

In many ways, this is the age of the greatest human prosperity, freedom, and potential that has ever been on the face of this planet. But in other ways, we are facing some of the largest risks ever.

The Worst of Times: The Greatest Risks

At its peak, the ancient Mayan city of Tikal was a metropolis, a city of 200,000 people inside of a civilization of about 20 million people. Now, if you walk around any Mayan city, you see mounds of dirt. That's because these structures were all abandoned by about the mid-900s AD. We know now what happened: The Mayan civilization grew too large. It overpopulated. To feed themselves, they had to convert forest into farmland. They chopped down all of the forest. That, in turn, led to soil erosion. It also worsened drought, because trees, among other things, trap moisture and create a precipitation cycle.

When that happened, and was met by some normal (not human-caused) climate change, the Mayans found they didn't have enough food. They exhausted their primary energy supply, which is food. That in turn led to more violence in their society and ultimately to a complete collapse.

The greatest energy source for human civilization today is fossil fuels. Among those, none is more important than oil. In 1956, M. King Hubbert looked at production in individual oil fields and predicted that the United States would see the peak of its oil production in 1970 or so, and then drop. His prediction largely came true: Oil production went up but did peak in the 1970s, then plummeted.

Oil production has recently gone up in the United States a little bit, but it's still just barely more than half of what it was in its peak in the 1970s.

Hubbert also predicted that the global oil market would peak in about 2000, and for a long time he looked very foolish. But it now has basically plateaued. Since 2004, oil production has increased by about 4%, whereas in the 1950s it rose by about 4% every three months.

We haven't hit a peak; oil production around the world is still rising a little bit. It's certainly not declining, but we do appear to be near a plateau; supply is definitely rising more slowly than demand. Though there's plenty of oil in the ground, the oil that remains is in smaller fields, further from shore, under lower pressure, and harder to pump out.

Water is another resource that is incredibly precious to us. The predominant way in which we use water is through the food that we eat: 70% of the freshwater that humanity uses goes into agriculture.

The Ogallala Aquifer, the giant body of freshwater under the surface of the Earth in the Great Plains of the United States, is fossil water left from the melting and the retreat of glaciers in the end of the last Ice Age, 12,000-14,000 years ago. Its refill time is somewhere between 5,000 and 10,000 years from normal rainfall. Since 1960, we've drained between a third and a half of the water in this body, depending on what estimate you look at. In some areas, the water table is dropping about three feet per year.

If this was a surface lake in the United States or Canada, and people saw that happening, they'd stop it. But because it's out of sight, it's just considered a resource that we can tap. And indeed, in the north Texas area, wells are starting to fail already, and farms are being abandoned in some cases, because they can't get to the water that they once did.

Perhaps the largest risk of all is climate change. We've increased the temperature of the planet by about 2°F in the last 130 years, and that rate is accelerating. This is primarily because of the carbon dioxide we've put into the atmosphere, along with methane and nitrous oxide. CO_2 levels, now at over 390 parts per million, are the highest they've been in about 15 million years. Ice cores go back at least a million years, and we know that they're the highest they've been in that time. Historically, when CO_2 levels are high, temperature is also high. But also, historically, in the lifetime of our species, we've actually never existed as human beings while CO_2 levels have been this high.

For example, glaciers such as the Bear and Pedersen in Alaska have disappeared just since 1920. As these glaciers melt, they produce water that goes into the seas and helps to raise sea levels. Over the next century, the seas are expected to rise about 3 to 6 feet. Most of that actually will not be melting glaciers; it's thermal expansion: As the ocean gets warmer, it gets a little bit bigger.

But 3 to 6 feet over a century doesn't sound like that big a deal to us, so we think of that as a distant problem. The reality is that there's a more severe problem with climate change: its impact on the weather and on agriculture.

In 2003, Europe went through its worst heat wave since 1540. Ukraine lost 75% of its wheat crop. In 2009, China had a once-in-a-century level drought; in 2010 they had another once-in-a-century level drought. That's twice. Wells that had given water continuously since the fifteenth century ran dry. When those rains returned, when the water that was soaked up by the atmosphere came back down, it came down on Pakistan, and half of Pakistan was under water in the floods of 2010. An area larger than Germany was under water.

Warmer air carries more water. Every degree Celsius that you increase the temperature value of air, it carries 7% more water. But it doesn't carry that water uniformly. It can suck water away from one place and then deliver it in a deluge in another place. So both the droughts are up and flooding is up simultaneously, as precipitation becomes more lumpy and more concentrated.

In Russia's 2010 heat wave, 55,000 people died, 11,000 of them in Moscow alone. In 2011, the United States had the driest 10-month period ever in the American South, and Texas saw its worst wildfires ever. And 2012 was the worst drought in the United States since the Dust Bowl—the corn crop shrank by 20%.

So that's the big risk the world faces: that radical weather will change how we grow food, which is still our most important energy source—even more important than fossil fuels.

A number of people in the environmentalist movement are saying that we have to just stop growing. For instance, in his book Peak Everything: Waking Up to the Century of Declines, Richard Heinberg of the Post-Carbon Institute says that the Earth is full. Get used to it, and get ready for a world where you live with less wealth, and where your children live with less wealth, than any before.

I don't think this idea of stopping growth is realistic, because there are a top billion people who live pretty well and there are another 6 billion who don't and are hungry for it. We see demand rising for everything—water, food, energy—and that demand is rising not in the United States or Europe or Canada or Australia. It's rising in the developing world. This is the area that will create all of the increased demand for physical resources.

Even if we could, by some chance, say That's enough, sorry, we're not going to let you use these resources, which is doubtful, it wouldn't be just, because the West got rich by using those natural resources. So we need to find a different way.

Ideas as a Resource Expander, Resource Preserver, and Waste Reducer

The best-selling environmental book of all time, Limits to Growth, was based on computer modeling. It was a simple model with only about eight variables of what would happen in the world. It showed that economic growth, more wealth, would inevitably lead to more pollution and more consumption of finite resources, which would in turn take us beyond the limits and lead ultimately to collapse.

While it's been widely reported recently that its predictions are coming true, that's actually not the case. If you look at the vast majority of the numbers that the researchers predict in this model, they're not coming true.

Why did they get these things wrong? The most important thing that the forecasters did was underestimate the power of new ideas to expand resources, or to expand wealth while using fewer resources. Ideas have done tremendous things for us. Let's start with food.

In *The Population Bomb* (1968), Paul Ehrlich predicted that food supply could not support the population, just as Malthus did. But what's happened is that we've doubled population since 1960, and we've nearly tripled the food supply in total. We've increased by 30%–40% the food supply per person since the 1960s.

Let's look at this on a very long time scale. How many people can you feed with an acre of land? Before the advent of agriculture, an acre of land could feed less than a thousandth of a person. Today it's about three people, on average, who can be fed by one acre of land. Pre-agriculture, it took 3,000 acres for one person to stay alive through hunting and gathering. With agriculture, that footprint has shrunk from 3,000 acres to one-third of one acre. That's not because there's any more sunlight, which is ultimately what food is; it's because we've changed the productivity of the resource by innovation in farming—and then thousands of innovations on top of that to increase it even more.

In fact, the reason we have the forests that we have on the planet is because we were able to handle a doubling of the population since 1960 without increasing farmland by more than about 10%. If we had to have doubled our farmland, we would have chopped down all the remaining forests on the planet.

Ideas can reduce resource use. I can give you many other examples. In the United States, the amount of energy used on farms per calorie grown has actually dropped by about half since the 1970s. That's in part because we now only use about a tenth of the energy to create synthetic nitrogen fertilizer, which is an important input.

The amount of food that you can grow per drop of water has roughly doubled since the 1980s. In wheat, it's actually more than tripled since 1960. The amount of water that we use in the United States per person has dropped by about a third since the 1970s, after rising for decades. As agriculture has gotten more efficient, we're using less water per person. So, again, ideas can reduce resource use.

Ideas can also find substitutes for scarce resources. We're at risk of running out of many things, right? Well, let's think about some things that have happened in the past.

The sperm whale was almost hunted into extinction. Sperm whales were, in the mid-1800s, the best source of illumination. Sperm whale oil—spermaceti—was the premier source of lighting. It burned without smoke, giving a clear, steady light, and the demand for it led to huge hunting of the sperm whales. In a period of about 30 years, we killed off about a third of the sperm whales on the planet.

That led to a phenomenon of "peak sperm-whale oil": The number of sperm whales that the fleet could bring in dropped over time as the sperm whales became more scarce and more afraid of human hunters. Demand rose as supply dropped, and the prices skyrocketed. So it looked a little bit like the situation with oil now.

That was solved not by the discovery of more sperm whales, nor by giving up on this thing of lighting. Rather, Abraham Gesner, a Canadian, discovered this thing called kerosene. He found that, if he took coal, heated it up, captured the fumes, and distilled them, he could create this fluid that burned very clear. And he could create it in quantities thousands of times greater than the sperm whales ever could have given up.

We have no information suggesting that Gesner was an environmentalist or that he cared about sperm whales at all. He was motivated by scientific curiosity and by the huge business opportunity of going after this lighting market. What he did was dramatically lower the cost of lighting while saving the sperm whales from extinction.

One more thing that ideas can do is transform waste into value. In places like Germany and Japan, people are mining landfills. Japan estimates that its landfills alone contain 10-year supplies of gold and rare-earth minerals for the world market.

Alcoa estimates that the world's landfills contain a 15-year supply of aluminum. So there's tremendous value.

When we throw things away, they're not destroyed. If we "consume" things like aluminum, we're not really consuming it, we're rearranging it. We're changing where it's located. And in some cases, the concentration of these resources in our landfills is actually higher than it was in our mines. What it takes is energy and technology to get that resource back out and put it back into circulation.

Ideas for Stretching the Limits

So ideas can reduce resource use, can find substitutes for scarce resources, and can transform waste into value. In that context, what are the limits to growth?

Is there a population limit? Yes, there certainly is, but it doesn't look like we're going to hit that. Projections right now are that, by the middle of this century, world population will peak between 9 billion and 10 billion, and then start to decline. In fact, we'll be talking much more about the graying of civilization, and perhaps underpopulation—too-low birthrates on a current trend.

What about physical resources? Are there limits to physical resource use on this planet? Absolutely. It really is a finite planet. But where are those limits?

To illustrate, let's start with energy. This is the most important resource that we use, in many ways. But when we consider all the fossil fuels that humanity uses today—all the oil, coal, natural gas, and so on—it pales in comparison to a much larger resource, all around us, which is the amount of energy coming in from our Sun every day.

The amount of energy from sunlight that strikes the top of the atmosphere is about 10,000 times as much as the energy that we use from fossil fuels on a daily basis. Ten seconds of sunlight hitting the Earth is as much energy as humanity uses in an entire day; one hour of sunlight hitting the Earth provides as much energy to the planet as a whole as humanity uses from all sources combined in one year.

This is an incredibly abundant resource. It manifests in many ways. It heats the atmosphere differentially, creating winds that we can capture for wind power. It evaporates water, which leads to precipitation elsewhere, which turns into things like rivers and waterfalls, which we can capture as hydropower.

But by far the largest fraction of it—more than half—is photons hitting the surface of the Earth. Those are so abundant that, with one-third of 1% of the Earth's land area, using current technology of about 14%-efficient solar cells, we could capture enough electricity to power all of current human needs.

The problem is not the abundance of the energy; the problem is cost. Our technology is primitive. Our technology for building solar cells is similar to our technology for manufacturing computer chips. They're built on silicon wafers in clean rooms at high temperatures, and so they're very, very expensive.

But innovation has been dropping that cost tremendously. Over the last 30 years, we've gone from a watt of solar power costing $20 to about $1. That's a factor of 20. We roughly drop the cost of solar by one-half every decade, more or less. That means that, in the sunniest parts of the world today, solar is now basically at parity in cost, without subsidies, with coal and natural gas. Over the next 12-15 years, that will spread to most of the planet. That's incredibly good news for us.

Of course, we don't just use energy while the Sun is shining. We use energy at night to power our cities; we use energy in things like vehicles that have to move and that have high energy densities. Both of these need storage, and today's storage is actually a bigger challenge than capturing energy. But there's reason to believe that we can tackle the storage problem, as well.

For example, consider lithium ion batteries—the batteries that are in your laptop, your cell phone, and so on. The demand to have longer-lasting devices drove tremendous innovations in these batteries in the 1990s and the early part of the 2000s. Between 1991 and 2005, the cost of storage in lithium ion batteries dropped by about a factor of nine, and the density of storage—how much energy you can store in an ounce of battery—increased by a little over double in that time. If we do that again, we would be at the point where grid-scale storage is affordable and we can store that energy overnight. Our electric vehicles have ranges similar to the range you can get in a gasoline-powered vehicle.

This is a tall order. This represents perhaps tens of billions of dollars in R&D, but it is something that is possible and for which there is precedent.

Another approach being taken is turning energy into fuel. When you use a fuel such as gasoline, it's not really an energy source. It's an energy carrier, an energy storage system, if you will. You can store a lot of energy in a very small amount.

Today, two pioneers in genome sequencing—Craig Venter and George Church—both have founded companies to create next-generation biofuels. What they're both leveraging is that gene-sequencing cost is the fastest quantitative area of progress on the planet.

What they're trying to do is engineer microorganisms that consume CO_2, sunlight, and sugar and actually excrete fuel as a byproduct. If we could do this, maybe just 1% of the Earth's surface—or a thirtieth of what we use for agriculture—could provide all the liquid fuels that we need. We would conveniently grow algae on saltwater and waste water, so biofuel production wouldn't compete for freshwater. And the possible yields are vast if we can get there.

If we can crack energy, we can crack everything else:

- Water. Water is life. We live in a water world, but only about a tenth of a percent of the water in the world is freshwater that's accessible to us in some way. Ninety-seven percent of the world's water is in the oceans and is salty. It used to be that desalination meant boiling water and then catching the steam and letting it condense.

Between the times of the ancient Greeks and 1960, desalination technology didn't really change. But then, it did. People started to create membranes modeled on what cells do, which is allow some things through but not others. They used plastics to force water through and get only the fresh and not the salty. As a result, the amount of energy it takes to desalinate a liter of water has dropped by about a factor of nine in that time. Now, in the world's largest desalination plants, the price of desalinated water is about a tenth of a cent per gallon. The technology has gotten to the point where it is starting to become a realistic option as an alternative to using up scarce freshwater resources.

- Food. Can we grow enough food? Between now and 2050, we have to increase food yield by about 70%. Is that possible? I think it is. In industrialized nations, food yields are already twice what they are in the world as a whole. That's because we have irrigation, tractors, better pesticides, and so on. Given such energy and wealth, we already know that we can grow enough food to feed the planet.

Another option that's probably cheaper would be to leverage some things that nature's already produced. What most people don't know is that the yield of corn per acre and in calories is about 70% higher than the yield of wheat. Corn is a C 4 photosynthesis crop: It uses a different way of turning sunlight and CO_2 into sugars that evolved only 30 million years ago. Now, scientists around the world are working on taking these C 4 genes from crops like corn and transplanting them into wheat and rice, which could right away increase the yield of those staple grains by more than 50%.

Physical limits do exist, but they are extremely distant. We cannot grow exponentially in our physical resource use forever, but that point is still at least centuries in the future. It's something we have to address eventually, but it's not a problem that's pressing right now.

- Wealth. One thing that people don't appreciate very much is that wealth has been decoupling from physical resource use on this planet. Energy use per capita is going up, CO_2 emissions per capita have been going up a little bit, but they are both widely outstripped by the amount of wealth that we're creating. That's

because we can be more efficient in everything—using less energy per unit of food grown, and so on.

This again might sound extremely counterintuitive, but let me give you one concrete example of how that happens. Compare the ENIAC—which in the 1940s was the first digital computer ever created—to an iPhone. An iPhone is billions of times smaller, uses billions of times less energy, and has billions of times more computing power than ENIAC. If you tried to create an iPhone using ENIAC technology, it would be a cube a mile on the side, and it would use more electricity than the state of California. And it wouldn't have access to the Internet, because you'd have to invent that, as well.

This is what I mean when I say ideas are the ultimate resource. The difference between an ENIAC and an iPhone is that the iPhone is embodied knowledge that allows you to do more with less resources. That phenomenon is not limited to high tech. It's everywhere around us.

So ideas are the ultimate resource. They're the only resource that accumulates over time. Our store of knowledge is actually larger than in the past, as opposed to all physical resources.

Challenges Ahead for Innovation

Today we are seeing a race between our rate of consumption and our rate of innovation, and there are multiple challenges. One challenge is the Darwinian process, survival of the fittest. In areas like green tech, there will be hundreds and even thousands of companies founded, and 99% of them will go under. That is how innovation happens.

The other problem is scale. Just as an example, one of the world's largest solar arrays is at Nellis Air Force Base in California, and we would need about 10 million of these in order to meet the world's electricity needs. We have the land, we have the solar energy coming in, but there's a lot of industrial production that has to happen before we get to that point.

Innovation is incredibly powerful, but the pace of innovation compared to the pace of consumption is very important. One thing we can do to increase the pace of innovation is to address the biggest challenge, which is market failure.

In 1967, you could stick your hand into the Cuyahoga River, in Ohio, and come up covered in muck and oil. At that time, the river was lined with businesses and factories, and for them the river was a free resource. It was cheaper to pump their waste into the river than it was to pay for disposal at some other sort of facility. The river was a commons that anybody could use or abuse, and the waste they were producing was an externality. To that business or factory, there was no cost to pumping waste into this river. But to the people who depended upon the river, there was a high cost overall.

That's what I mean by a market externality and a market failure, because this was an important resource to all of us. But no one owned it, no one bought or sold it, and so it was treated badly in a way that things with a price are not.

That ultimately culminated when, in June 1969, a railway car passing on a bridge threw a spark; the spark hit a slick of oil a mile long on the river, and the river burst into flames. The story made the cover of Time magazine. In many ways, the environmental movement was born of this event as much as it was of Rachel Carson's Silent Spring. In the following three years, the United States created the Environmental Protection Agency and passed the Clean Water and Clean Air acts.

Almost every environmental problem on the planet is an issue of the commons, whether it's chopping down forests that no one owns, draining lakes that no one owns, using up fish in the ocean that no one owns, or polluting the atmosphere because no one owns it, or heating up the planet. They're all issues of the commons. They're all issues where there is no cost to an individual entity to deplete something and no cost to overconsume something, but there is a greater cost that's externalized and pushed on everybody else who shares this.

Now let's come back again to what Limits to Growth said, which was that economic growth always led to more pollution and more consumption, put us beyond limits, and ends with collapse. So if that's the case, all those things we just talked about should be getting worse. But as the condition of the Cuyahoga River today illustrates, that is not the case.

GDP in the United States is three times what it was when the Cuyahoga River caught on fire, so shouldn't it be more polluted? It's not. Instead, it's the cleanest it's been in decades. That's not because we stopped growth. It's because we made intelligent choices about managing that commons.

Another example: In the 1970s, we discovered that the ozone layer was thinning to such an extent that it literally could drive the extinction of all land species on Earth. But it's actually getting better. It's turned a corner, it's improving ahead of schedule, and it's on track to being the healthiest it's been in a century. That's because we've reduced the emissions of CFCs, which destroy ozone; we've dropped the amount of them that we emit into the atmosphere basically to zero. And yet industry has not ground to a halt because of this, either. Economic growth has not faltered.

And one last example: Acid rain—which is primarily produced by sulfur dioxide emitted by coal-burning power plants—is mostly gone as an issue. Emissions of sulfur dioxide are down by about a factor of two. That's in part because we created a strategy called cap and trade: It capped the amount of SO_2 that you could emit, then allowed you to swap and buy emission credits from others to find the optimal way to do that.

The cost, interestingly enough, has always been lower than projected. In each of these cases, industry has said, This will

end things. Ronald Reagan's chief of staff said the economy would grind to a halt, and the EPA would come in with lower cost estimates. But the EPA has always been wrong: The EPA cost estimate has always been too high.

Analysis of all of these efforts in the past shows that reducing emissions is always cheaper than you expect, but cleaning up the mess afterwards is always more expensive than you'd guess.

Today, the biggest commons issue is that of climate change, with the CO_2 and other greenhouse gases that we're pumping into the atmosphere. A logical thing to do would be to put a price on these. If you pollute, if you're pumping CO_2 into the atmosphere and it's warming the planet, so you're causing harm to other people in a very diffuse way. Therefore, you should be paying in proportion to that harm you're doing to offset it.

But if we do that, won't that have a massive impact on the economy? This all relates to energy, which drives a huge fraction of the economy. Manufacturing depends on it. Transport depends on it. So wouldn't it be a huge problem if we were to actually put a price on these carbon emissions?

Well, there has been innovative thinking about that, as well. One thing that economists have always told us is that, if you're going to tax, tax the bad, not the good. Whatever it is that you tax, you will get less of it. So tax the bad, not the good.

The model that would be the ideal for putting a price on pollution is what we call a revenue-neutral model. Revenue-neutral carbon tax, revenue-neutral cap and trade. Let's model it as a tax: Today, a country makes a certain amount of revenue for its government in income tax, let's say. If you want to tax pollution, the way to do this without impacting the economy is to increase your pollution tax in the same manner that you decrease the income tax. The government then is capturing the same amount of money from the economy as a whole, so there's no economic slowdown as a result of this.

This has a positive effect on the environment because it tips the scales of price. Now, if you're shopping for energy, and you're looking at solar versus coal or natural gas, the carbon price has increased the price of coal and natural gas to you, but not the cost of solar. It shifts customer behavior from one to the other while having no net impact on the economy, and probably a net benefit on the economy in the long run as more investment in green energy drives the price down.

Toward a Wealthier, Cleaner Future

The number-one thing I want you to take away is that pollution and overconsumption are not inevitable outcomes of growth. While tripling the wealth of North America, for instance, we've gone from an ozone layer that was rapidly deteriorating to one that is bouncing back.

The fundamental issue is not one of limits to growth; it's one of the policy we choose, and it's one of how we structure our economy to value all the things we depend upon and not just those things that are owned privately.

What can we do, each of us? Four things:

First is to communicate. These issues are divisive, but we know that beliefs and attitudes on issues like this spread word of mouth. They spread person to person, from person you trust to person you trust. So talk about it. Many of us have friends or colleagues or family on the other side of these issues, but talk about it. You're better able to persuade them than anyone else is.

Second is to participate. By that I mean politically. Local governments, state and province governments, and national governments are responsive when they hear from their constituents about these issues. It changes their attitudes. Because so few constituents actually make a call to the office of their legislator, or write a letter, a few can make a very large impact.

Third is to innovate. These problems aren't solved yet. We don't have the technologies for these problems today. The trend lines look very good, but the next 10 years of those trend lines demand lots of bright people, lots of bright ideas, and lots of R&D. So if you're thinking about a career change, or if you know any young people trying to figure out what their career is now, these are careers that (A) will be very important to us in the future and (B) will probably be quite lucrative for them.

Last is to keep hope, because we have faced problems like this before and we have conquered them every time. The future isn't written in stone—it could go good or bad—but I'm very optimistic. I know we have the ability to do it, and I think we will. Ultimately, ideas are our most important natural resource.

Critical Thinking

1. Do the facts seem to support an optimistic future or a pessimistic future?

2. What is the potential of new ideas and new technologies?

3. Technologies have brought great benefits and considerable problems. Can technologies and new ideas now solve those problems?

Internet References

Sociosite
www.topsite.com/goto/sociosite.net

Socioweb
www.topsite.com/goto/socioweb.com

Sociology—Study Sociology Online
http://edu.learnsoc.org/

Sociology Web Resources
www.mhhe.com/socscience/sociology/resources/index.htm

RAMEZ NAAM is a computer scientist and author. He is a former Microsoft executive and current fellow of the Institute for Ethics and Emerging Technologies.

Article   Prepared by: Kurt Finsterbusch, *University of Maryland, College Park*

Is America Still Safe for Democracy? Why the United States Is in Danger of Backsliding

ROBERT MICKEY, STEVEN LEVITSKY, AND LUCAN AHMAD WAY

Learning Outcomes

After reading this article, you will be able to:

- Explain how the Civil Rights Act and its results contributed to the current political conflict and inaction.

- Understand that many organisms of government and society would be politicized and used by leaders to try to monopolize government power.

- Notice the actions of elected leaders in other countries as they become more authoritarian and imagine that the United States could follow the same path.

The election of Donald Trump as president of the United States—a man who has praised dictators, encouraged violence among supporters, threatened to jail his rival, and labeled the mainstream media as "the enemy"—has raised fears that the United States may be heading toward authoritarianism. While predictions of a descent into fascism are overblown, the Trump presidency could push the United States into a mild form of what we call "competitive authoritarianism"—a system in which meaningful democratic institutions exist yet the government abuses state power to disadvantage its opponents.

But the challenges facing American democracy have been emerging for decades, long before Trump arrived on the scene. Since the 1980s, deepening polarization and the radicalization of the Republican Party have weakened the institutional foundations that have long safeguarded U.S. democracy—making a Trump presidency considerably more dangerous today than it would have been in previous decades.

There is little reason to expect Americans' commitment to democracy to serve as a safeguard against democratic erosion.

Paradoxically, the polarizing dynamics that now threaten democracy are rooted in the United States' belated democratization. It was only in the early 1970s—once the civil rights movement and the federal government managed to stamp out authoritarianism in southern states—that the country truly became democratic. Yet this process also helped divide Congress, realigning voters along racial lines and pushing the Republican Party further to the right. The resulting polarization both facilitated Trump's rise and left democratic institutions more vulnerable to his autocratic behavior.

The safeguards of democracy may not come from the quarters one might expect. American society's purported commitment to democracy is no guarantee against backsliding; nor are constitutional checks and balances, the bureaucracy, or the free press. Ultimately, it may be Trump's ability to mobilize public support—limited if his administration performs poorly, but far greater in the event of a war or a major terrorist attack—that will determine American democracy's fate.

What Backsliding Looks Like

If democratic backsliding were to occur in the United States, it would not take the form of a coup d'état; there would be no declaration of martial law or imposition of single-party rule. Rather, the experience of most contemporary autocracies suggests that it would take place through a series of little-noticed, incremental steps, most of which are legal and many of which appear innocuous. Taken together, however, they would tilt the playing field in favor of the ruling party.

The ease and degree to which governments can accomplish this vary. Where democratic institutions and the rule of law are well entrenched and civic and opposition forces are robust, as in the United States, abuse both is more difficult to pull off and less consequential than it is in such countries as Russia, Turkey, and Venezuela. Nevertheless, such abuse has occurred in the United States in the recent past, and so it cannot be ruled out.

The first type of abuse entails politicizing state institutions and deploying them against the opposition. Modern states possess a variety of bodies that can investigate and punish wrongdoing by public officials or private citizens—the courts; public prosecutors; legislative oversight committees; and law enforcement, intelligence, tax, and regulatory agencies. Because these organs are designed to serve as neutral arbiters, they present both a challenge and an opportunity for would-be authoritarians. To the extent that investigative agencies remain independent, they may expose and even punish government abuse. If controlled by loyalists, however, they can cover up official malfeasance and serve as potent weapons against the government's opponents.

Elected autocrats thus have a powerful incentive to purge career civil servants and other independent-minded officials and replace them with partisans. Agencies that cannot be easily purged, such as the judiciary, may be politicized in other ways. Judges, for instance, may be bribed, bullied, or blackmailed into compliance, or be publicly vilified as incompetent, corrupt, or unpatriotic. In extreme cases, they may be targeted for impeachment.

Packing state agencies is like buying off the referees in a sporting match: not only can the home team avoid penalties but it can also subject its opponent to more of them. For one thing, the government can shield itself from investigations, lawsuits, and criminal charges, and it can rest assured that unconstitutional behavior will go unchecked. For another, it can selectively enforce the law, targeting rival politicians, businesses, and media outlets while leaving allies (or those who remain quiet) alone. Vladimir Putin, for example, eliminated most of his opponents after becoming president of Russia by prosecuting them for corruption while ignoring similar behavior by his allies.

A politicized police force, meanwhile, can be relied on to crack down on opposition protesters while tolerating violence by pro-government thugs—a tactic that has proved effective in Venezuela. Politicized intelligence agencies, for their part, can be used to spy on critics and dig up blackmail material. Malaysia's top opposition leader, Anwar Ibrahim, was sidelined in this way: after a dubious police investigation, he was convicted of sodomy in 1999 and imprisoned. To be sure, even bureaucracies in democratic countries are susceptible to politicization, but it is usually limited and punished when egregious.

In competitive authoritarian regimes, by contrast, it is systematic and consequential.

The second way elected autocrats may tilt the playing field by neutralizing key parts of civil society. Few contemporary autocracies seek to eliminate opposition outright. Rather, they attempt to co-opt, silence, or hobble groups that can mobilize it: media outlets, business leaders, labor unions, religious associations, and so on. The easiest route is co-optation. Thus, most authoritarian governments offer perks or outright bribes to major media, business, and religious figures. Friendly press outlets get privileged access; favored business leaders receive profitable resource concessions or government contracts. To handle those who resist, autocrats turn to the politicized authorities. Newspapers, television networks, and websites that denounce government wrongdoing face libel or defamation suits or are prosecuted for publishing material that supposedly promotes violence or threatens national security. Business leaders critical of the government are investigated for tax fraud or other infractions, and opposition politicians get mired in scandals dug up or simply invented by intelligence agencies.

Sustained harassment of this type can seriously weaken the opposition. The press may remain nominally independent but quietly censor itself, as in Turkey and Venezuela. Businesspeople may withdraw from politics rather than risk running afoul of tax or regulatory agencies, as in Russia. Over time, critical media coverage diminishes, and with leading businesses and labor unions cowed into political inactivity, opposition parties find it harder to fundraise, leaving them at a significant disadvantage.

Finally, elected autocrats often rewrite the rules of the political game—reforming the constitution, the electoral system, or other institutions—to make it harder for their rivals to compete. Such reforms are often justified on the grounds of combating corruption, cleaning up elections, or strengthening democracy, but their true aim is more sinister. In Ecuador, for example, an electoral reform pushed through by the government of President Rafael Correa in 2012 heavily restricted private campaign contributions, ostensibly to reduce the corrupting influence of money in politics. But in reality, the reform benefited Correa's governing party, whose unregulated access to government resources gave it a massive advantage.

In both Malaysia and Zimbabwe, the government has invoked the goal of decentralization to justify reforms that increased the electoral weight of sparsely populated rural areas at the expense of urban centers, where the opposition was strongest. Such institutional reforms are particularly dangerous because they maintain a veneer of legitimacy. Nevertheless, they systematically bias electoral outcomes and, in many cases, allow incumbents to lock in advantages created by their initial abuse of power.

A Young Democracy

It may be tempting to assume that the United States' centuries-old democracy is impervious to democratic erosion, but such confidence is misplaced. In fact, liberal democracy—with full adult suffrage and broad protection of civil and political liberties—is a relatively recent development in the United States. By contemporary standards, the country became fully democratic only in the 1970s.

Beginning in the 1890s, after the Civil War and the failure of Reconstruction, Democratic politicians in each of the 11 states of the old Confederacy built single-party, authoritarian enclaves. Having wrested some room to maneuver from the Supreme Court, the executive branch, and their national party, conservative Democrats disenfranchised Blacks and many poorer White voters, repressed opposition parties, and imposed racially separate—and significantly unfree—civic spheres. Their goal was to ensure cheap agricultural labor and White supremacy, and they used state-sponsored violence to achieve it.

For half a century, southern states capitalized on their influence in Congress and the national Democratic Party to shield themselves from outside reform efforts. In 1944, however, the U.S. Supreme Court struck down the region's White-only Democratic primaries. Beginning with that decision, Black activists compelled and capitalized on federal judicial rulings, congressional legislation, and national-party reforms to dismantle disenfranchisement, segregation, and state repression. By the early 1970s, the southern authoritarians had been defeated; today, some 6,000 Black elected officials serve southern constituencies.

But American authoritarianism has not been just a southern phenomenon. From the time the FBI, the CIA, and the National Security Agency were created, presidents used them to monitor White House staff, journalists, political opponents, and activists. Between 1956 and 1971, the FBI launched more than 2,000 operations to discredit and disrupt Black protest organizations, antiwar groups, and other perceived threats. It even provided Dwight Eisenhower with derogatory information about Adlai Stevenson, his Democratic rival in the 1952 election. Likewise, the Nixon administration deployed the U.S. Attorney General's Office and other agencies against its "enemies" in the Democratic Party and the media. And congressional investigations into alleged subversion further threatened civil rights and liberties. Like southern authoritarianism, the abuse of federal intelligence and law enforcement agencies largely ended in the 1970s, in this case after the post-Watergate reforms.

American democracy remains far from ideal. Ex-felons, who are disproportionately Black, are often prohibited from voting; many states are experimenting with an array of new voting restrictions; and the concentration of campaign donations among the wealthy raises serious concerns about how representative U.S. democracy truly is. Still, the United States has been a bona fide multiracial democracy for almost half a century.

Yet just as the United States fulfilled its democratic promise, the foundations of the system began to weaken. Ironically, the very process of democratization in the South generated the intense polarization that now threatens American democracy.

The Great Divide

Scholars have long identified political polarization as a central factor behind democratic breakdown. Extreme polarization leads politicians and their supporters to view their rivals as illegitimate and, in some cases, as an existential threat. Often, democratic norms weaken as politicians become willing to break the rules, cooperate with antidemocratic extremists, and even tolerate or encourage violence in order to keep their rivals out of power. Few democracies can survive for long under such conditions.

Until recently, the United States seemed immune from such threats. Indeed, traditions of restraint and cooperation helped the United States avoid the kinds of partisan fights to the death that destroyed democracies in Germany and Spain in the 1930s and Chile in the 1970s. In the United States, leading Democrats opposed President Franklin Roosevelt's efforts to pack the Supreme Court, and Republicans backed the investigation and impeachment of President Richard Nixon. The party controlling the White House never used the full extent of governmental powers against the other side. In fact, the systematic underutilization of power by presidents and congressional majorities has long served as a vital source of democratic stability in the United States.

But with the passage of the Civil Rights Act and the Voting Rights Act in the 1960s, the Democratic Party (long the guarantor of White supremacy) and the Republican Party ("the party of Lincoln") realigned national politics along racial lines. Southern Blacks entered the electorate as Democrats, and southern Whites became increasingly Republican. Many White southerners voted Republican for class reasons: the region's incomes were rising, thus enhancing the appeal of the GOP's economic policies. But many chose the Republicans for their conservative stances on racial issues and their appeals to "law and order."

This realignment helped change the composition of Congress. In the ensuing decades, the South transformed from a one-party, Democratic region into a Republican-dominated one. Whereas it once sent moderate Democrats to Congress, today it elects either Black or Hispanic liberal Democrats or, much more commonly, very conservative White Republicans. The ideological polarization of Congress has other sources, to be sure, but the democratization of the South represents a critical one. The result has been two much more ideologically homogeneous—and disciplined—parties. Gone are crosscutting issues that temper partisan conflict, along with moderate members within each party critical for crafting legislative deals.

The triumph of democracy in the South not only polarized Congress ideologically; it also polarized voters along party lines. Starting in the late 1960s, Democratic and Republican candidates began staking out increasingly distinctive views on public policy, first on racial matters (such as affirmative action) and then on a wider range of issues. As the political scientist Michael Tesler has argued, racially coded campaign appeals encourage voters to evaluate government programs in terms of the social groups they imagine as benefiting from them. Over time, white voters' racial attitudes have increasingly shaped their views about public policy, even on issues that seem unrelated to race, such as health care, Social Security, and taxes.

Elected autocrats have a powerful incentive to purge career civil servants and replace them with partisans.

Taking their cues from party leaders, voters are increasingly sorted into the ideologically "correct" party: few center-left Republican or center-right Democratic voters remain. And a greater share of Black voters back Democratic candidates than ever before, while a greater share of White voters support Republicans. Although just a small percentage of the American electorate is highly ideological (unlike their representatives in Congress), voters now exhibit heightened animosity toward politicians and voters of the other party—what the political scientists Alan Abramowitz and Steven Webster have termed "negative partisanship."

Partisan polarization has been reinforced by the weakening of the establishment news media, a critical component of democratic accountability. Until the 1990s, most Americans got their news from a handful of trusted television networks. Politicians themselves relied heavily on the press to get the public's attention, and so they could ill afford to alienate journalists. But over the last 20 years, the media have become increasingly polarized. The rise of Fox News kicked off the era of partisan news channels. The Internet, meanwhile, has made it easier for people to seek out news that confirms their existing beliefs and has played a role in the widespread closure of local and regional newspapers.

Today, Democrats and Republicans consume news from starkly different sources, and the traditional media's influence has declined precipitously. As a result, voters have grown more receptive to fake news and more trusting of party spokespeople. When events are filtered through fragmented and polarized media, Americans view nearly all political events through purely partisan lenses. Consider what happened after Trump, breaking with traditional Republican policy, embraced Putin:

one poll found that Putin's favorability rating among Republicans increased, from 10 percent in July 2014 to 37 percent in December 2016.

The growing gap between the richest Americans and the rest of the country has also accentuated polarization. U.S. income inequality has reached its highest level since the onset of the Great Depression. The explosive growth of incomes at the top has increased support among wealthy voters and campaign contributors for conservative economic policies, especially on taxes, and has moved Republican legislators to the right. The stagnation of working-class wages over the past three decades, moreover, has triggered a right-wing populist reaction with racial overtones, especially among rural Whites, who have directed their anger at liberal spending programs that they view as benefiting urban minorities.

The growing political differences over identity extend beyond the traditional Black–White binary. Since the 1970s, increased immigration has added more Hispanic and Asian Americans to the electorate, largely as Democrats, further solidifying the partisan gap between Whites and non-Whites. These trends have exacerbated anxieties among many White voters about losing their numerical, cultural, and political preeminence—just as White southerners feared before democratization. In many respects, then, the South's racial politics have gone national.

The Perils of Polarization

Partisan polarization poses several threats to U.S. democracy. First, it leads to gridlock, especially when different parties control the legislative and executive branches. As polarization increases, Congress passes fewer and fewer laws and leaves important issues unresolved. Such dysfunction has eroded public trust in political institutions, and along partisan lines. Voters backing the party that does not currently occupy the White House have astonishingly little trust in the government: in a 2010 poll conducted by the political scientists Marc Hetherington and Thomas Rudolph, a majority of Republican voters surveyed said they "never" trust the federal government.

Gridlock, in turn, encourages presidents to pursue unilateral action on the edges of constitutional limits. When there is divided government, with the party out of power determined to block the president's legislative agenda, frustrated presidents work around Congress. They expand their power through executive orders and other unilateral measures, and they centralize their control of the federal bureaucracy. At the same time, polarization makes it harder for Congress to exercise oversight of the White House, since members have a hard time forging a collective, bipartisan response to executive overreach.

When the same party controls both Congress and the White House, legislators have little incentive to exercise tough oversight of the president. Today, then, polarization reduces the chance that congressional Republicans will constrain Trump. Although many party elites would prefer a more predictable Republican in the White House, Trump's strong support among the party's voters means that any serious opposition would probably split the party and encourage primary challenges, as well as endanger the party's ambitious conservative agenda. Congressional Republicans are thus unlikely to follow in the footsteps of their predecessors who reined in Nixon. Indeed, so far, they have refused to seriously investigate Trump's conflicts of interest or accusations of collusion between his campaign and the Russian government.

Even more dangerous, the Republican Party has radicalized to the point of becoming, in the words of the scholars Thomas Mann and Norman Ornstein, "dismissive of the legitimacy of its political opposition." Over the last two decades, many Republican elected officials, activists, and media personalities have begun to treat their Democratic rivals as an existential threat—to national security or their way of life—and have ceased to recognize them as legitimate. Trump himself rose to political prominence by questioning President Barack Obama's citizenship. During the 2016 campaign, he repeatedly referred to his opponent, Hillary Clinton, as a criminal, and Republican leaders led chants of "lock her up" at their party's national convention.

It was only in the early 1970s that the United States truly became democratic.

Parties that view their rivals as illegitimate are more likely to resort to extreme measures to weaken them. Indeed, the Republican Party has increasingly abandoned established norms of restraint and cooperation—key pillars of U.S. political stability—in favor of tactics that, while legal, violate democratic traditions and raise the stakes of political conflict. House Republicans' impeachment of President Bill Clinton in 1998 represented an early instance. Senate Republicans' refusal to hold confirmation hearings for Obama's Supreme Court nominee in 2016 marked another.

At the state level, Republicans have gone even further, passing laws aimed at disadvantaging their rivals. The most blatant example comes from North Carolina, where in late 2016, the lame-duck Republican legislature passed a series of last-minute laws stripping powers from the newly elected Democratic governor. Meanwhile, Republicans in more than a dozen states have introduced legislation to criminalize certain kinds of protests. Even more disturbing are new restrictions on voting rights, which have been justified as efforts to combat massive voter fraud, a problem that simply does not exist. These laws have been concentrated in states where Republicans have recently taken control of the legislature but hold only a slim majority, suggesting that their true purpose is to lower the turnout of voters likely to back Democratic candidates, such as non-Whites. Trump, for his part, has given such initiatives a boost. Not only has he falsely claimed that the 2016 election was marred by massive illegal voting, undermining public trust in the electoral process, but his Department of Justice also looks poised to begin defending states facing lawsuits over their suffrage restrictions.

Trump has thus ascended to the presidency at an especially perilous time for American democracy. His party, which controls both houses of Congress and 33 governorships, has increasingly turned to hardball tactics aimed at weakening the opposition. As president, Trump himself has continued to violate democratic norms—attacking judges, the media, and the legitimacy of the electoral process. Were his administration to engage in outright authoritarian behavior, polarization has reduced the prospects that Congress would mobilize a bipartisan resistance or that the public would turn against him en masse.

The Fate of Democracy

What could halt the United States' democratic erosion? There is little reason to expect Americans' commitment to democracy to serve as a safeguard. Until the 1960s, most Americans tolerated serious restrictions on democracy in the South. Nor should one expect the Constitution on its own to impede backsliding. As the constitutional scholars Tom Ginsburg and Aziz Huq have argued, the ambiguities of the U.S. Constitution leave considerable room for executive abuse on various fronts—including the ability to pack government agencies with loyalists and appoint or dismiss U.S. attorneys for political reasons. In the absence of informal norms of restraint and cooperation, even the best-designed constitution cannot fully shield democracy.

The press is also unlikely to prevent backsliding. The mainstream media will continue to investigate and denounce wrongdoing in the Trump administration. But in the current media environment, even revelations of serious abuse will likely be eagerly consumed by Democrats and dismissed as partisan attacks by Trump supporters.

Those pinning their hopes on pushback from the bureaucracy are also likely to be disappointed. The United States lacks the kind of powerful career civil service found in European democracies, and Republicans' control of both the White House and Congress limits GOP legislators' incentive to monitor the president's treatment of federal agencies. Those staffing the agencies, meanwhile, may prove too intimidated to resist abuse by the White House. Moreover, Congress controls the agencies' budgets, and in January, House Republicans revived the

Holman Rule, an arcane 1876 provision that allows Congress to reduce any bureaucrat's salary to $1.

The United States' federal system of government and independent judiciary should provide more robust defenses against backsliding. Although the extreme decentralization of U.S. elections makes them uneven in quality, it also hampers any effort at coordinated electoral manipulation. And although U.S. courts have often failed to defend individual rights in the past (as when they permitted the internment of Japanese Americans during World War II), federal judges since the 1960s have generally strengthened civil rights and civil liberties. Still, even U.S. courts are not immune to political pressures from other branches of government.

It may be tempting to assume that the United States' centuries-old democracy is impervious to democratic erosion, but such confidence is misplaced.

Ultimately, the fate of American democracy under Trump may hinge on contingent events. The greatest brake on backsliding today is presidential unpopularity. Republican politicians troubled by Trump's behavior but worried about winning their party's nomination will have an easier time opposing the president if his support among Republican voters weakens. Declining support may also embolden federal judges to push back against executive aggrandizements more aggressively. Thus, factors that undermine Trump's popularity, such as an economic crisis or a "Katrina moment"—a high-profile disaster for which the government is widely viewed as responsible—may check his power.

But events could also have the opposite effect. If a war or a terrorist attack occurs, the commitment to civil liberties on the part of both politicians and the public will likely weaken. Already, Trump has framed the independent judiciary and the independent press as security threats, accusing the judge who struck down his initial travel ban of putting the country in "peril" and describing the mainstream media as "enemies." In the event of an attack comparable in scale to those of 9/11, any efforts to crack down on the media, dissent, or ethnic and religious minorities would face far fewer obstacles.

The Trump presidency has punctured many Americans' beliefs about their country's exceptionalism. U.S. democracy is not immune to backsliding. In fact, it now faces a challenge that extends well beyond Trump: sustaining the multiracial democracy that was born half a century ago. Few democracies have survived transitions in which historically dominant ethnic groups lose their majority status. If American democracy manages to do that, it will prove exceptional indeed.

Critical Thinking

1. Do you think that the move to authoritarianism will be incremental or be a sudden change?

2. Evaluate the conclusions of many scholars that identify political polarization as a central factor behind democratic breakdowns.

3. Why are so many states overwhelmingly red or blue?

Internet References

Sociology—Study Sociology Online
http://edu.learnsoc.org/

Sociology Web Resources
http://www.mhhe.com/socscience/sociology/resources/index.htm

Sociosite
http://www.topsite.com/goto/sociosite.net

Socioweb
http://www.topsite.com/goto/socioweb.com

Article

Prepared by: Kurt Finsterbusch, *University of Maryland, College Park*

The New Era of Monopoly Is Here

Today's markets are characterized by the persistence of high monopoly profits.

JOSEPH STIGLITZ

Learning Outcomes

After reading this article, you will be able to:

- Describe the two schools of thought on the causes of inequality.
- Discuss why monopoly is increasing.
- Discuss the role of technology in changing the distribution of income.

American banks persuaded US Congress to amend or repeal legislation separating commercial banking from other areas of finance, a naked example of market power. For 200 years, there have been two schools of thought about what determines the distribution of income—and how the economy functions. One, emanating from Adam Smith and 19th-century liberal economists, focuses on competitive markets. The other, cognizant of how Smith's brand of liberalism leads to rapid concentration of wealth and income, takes as its starting point unfettered markets' tendency toward monopoly. It is important to understand both, because our views about government policies and existing inequalities are shaped by which of the two schools of thought one believes provides a better description of reality.

For the 19th-century liberals and their latter-day acolytes, because markets are competitive, individuals' returns are related to their social contributions—their "marginal product," in the language of economists. Capitalists are rewarded for saving rather than consuming—for their *abstinence*, in the words of Nassau Senior, one of my predecessors in the Drummond Professorship of Political Economy at Oxford. Differences

in income were then related to their ownership of "assets"—human and financial capital. Scholars of inequality thus focused on the determinants of the distribution of assets, including how they are passed on across generations.

The second school of thought takes as its starting point "power," including the ability to exercise monopoly control or, in labor markets, to assert authority over workers. Scholars in this area have focused on what gives rise to power, how it is maintained and strengthened, and other features that may prevent markets from being competitive. Work on exploitation arising from asymmetries of information is an important example.

In the west in the post-second world war era, the liberal school of thought has dominated. Yet, as inequality has widened and concerns about it have grown, the competitive school, viewing individual returns in terms of marginal product, has become increasingly unable to explain how the economy works. So, today, the second school of thought is ascendant.

After all, the large bonuses paid to banks' CEOs as they led their firms to ruin and the economy to the brink of collapse are hard to reconcile with the belief that individuals' pay has *anything* to do with their social contributions. Of course, historically, the oppression of large groups—slaves, women, and minorities of various types—are obvious instances where inequalities are the result of power relationships, not marginal returns.

In today's economy, many sectors—telecoms, cable TV, digital branches from social media to Internet search, health insurance, pharmaceuticals, agro-business, and many more—cannot be understood through the lens of competition. In these sectors, what competition exists is oligopolistic, not the "pure" competition depicted in textbooks. A few sectors can be defined as "price taking"; firms are so small that they have no effect on market price. Agriculture is the clearest example, but government intervention in the sector is massive, and prices are not set primarily by market forces.

Barack Obama's council of economic advisers (CEA), led by Jason Furman, has attempted to tally the extent of the increase in market concentration and some of its implications. In most industries, according to the CEA, standard metrics show large—and in some cases, dramatic—increases in market concentration. The top 10 banks' share of the deposit market, for example, increased from about 20 percent to 50 percent in just 30 years, from 1980 to 2010.

Some of the increase in market power is the result of changes in technology and economic structure: consider network economies and the growth of locally provided service-sector industries. Some is because firms—Microsoft and drug companies are good examples—have learned better how to erect and maintain entry barriers, often assisted by conservative political forces that justify lax antitrust enforcement and the failure to limit market power on the grounds that markets are "naturally" competitive. And some of it reflects the naked abuse and leveraging of market power through the political process: Large banks, for example, lobbied the US Congress to amend or repeal legislation separating commercial banking from other areas of finance.

The consequences are evident in the data, with inequality rising at every level, not only across individuals but also across firms. The CEA report noted that the "90th percentile firm sees returns on investments in capital that are more than five times the median. This ratio was closer to two just a quarter of a century ago."

Joseph Schumpeter, one of the great economists of the 20th century, argued that one shouldn't be worried by monopoly power: monopolies would only be temporary. There would be fierce competition *for* the market and this would replace competition in the market and ensure that prices remained competitive. My own theoretical work long ago showed the flaws

in Schumpeter's analysis, and now empirical results provide strong confirmation. Today's markets are characterized by the persistence of high monopoly profits.

The implications of this are profound. Many of the assumptions about market economies are based on acceptance of the competitive model, with marginal returns commensurate with social contributions. This view has led to hesitancy about official intervention: If markets are fundamentally efficient and fair, there is little that even the best of governments could do to improve matters. But if markets are based on exploitation, the rationale for laissez-faire disappears. Indeed, in that case, the battle against entrenched power is not only a battle for democracy; it is also a battle for efficiency and shared prosperity.

Critical Thinking

1. Does the functioning of capitalism inevitably increase inequality?
2. What is the role of power in increasing inequality?
3. How can inequality be reduced in ways that have some chance passing?

Internet References

Sociology—Study Sociology Online
http://edu.learnsoc.org/
Sociology Web Resources
http://www.mhhe.com/socscience/sociology/resources/index.htm
Sociosite
http://www.topsite.com/goto/sociosite.net
Socioweb
http://www.topsite.com/goto/socioweb.com

JOSEPH STIGLITZ is a Nobel-prizewinning economist, professor at Columbia University, former senior chief economist of the World Bank and chair of the council of economic advisers under Bill Clinton.

Article   Prepared by: Kurt Finsterbusch, *University of Maryland, College Park*

The Greatest Story Too Rarely Told: America Is an Oligarchy

We live in a nation controlled by corporate power and the individually wealthy. And the major press, of course, is in on the con.

JOHN ATCHESON

Learning Outcomes

After reading this article, you will be able to:

- Explain Atcheson's thesis that the Republican Party has adopted lies over facts in many fields of knowledge.

- Explain the basis of Atcheson's attack on the news media.

- Understand the funding sources for theories and policies that support elite interests.

OK. Enough. It's time to quit being "balanced" or "nonpartisan" or whatever other euphemism the elite establishment media uses to justify ignoring the two biggest elephants in our national living room.

After Trump was elected there was a lot of concern about allowing his idiocy to become the "new normal." But in truth, we've been accepting an unacceptable level of insanity in our national body politic for decades now.

Elephant number one—and it's a huge honking beast squatting squarely on our ottoman—is the fact that the Republican Party has come unhinged and it's dragging us back to the Dark Ages. Literally. To be a Republican today you have to have complete disdain for facts, reality, empiricism, the scientific method, or any of the other underpinnings of the Enlightenment. This isn't merely a difference between two legitimate philosophies as the press insists on portraying it—rather, it is a self-limiting time bomb which is destroying any hope of a prosperous economy or a functioning society, not to mention

our country's standing in the world and the habitability of our planet.

The evidence is overwhelming. For starters, there's the insane denial of climate change when records are dropping like stones.

For example, February 2016 was an astounding 1.35 C (2.43 F) warmer than the average temperature for February based on the period from 1951 to 1980. That smashed the previous record for a monthly temperature increase by 0.21 C, another record. Oh, and that previous monthly record? It was set in January. February's 1.35 C increase was dangerously close to the 1.5 C increase that most scientists agree is as high as we can go without incurring serious and irreversible consequences.

Meanwhile, 16 of the hottest 17 years on record have occurred since 2000. The last three decades have also set records for the warmest decade on record, and this decade is on track to exceed them.

Or consider that the National Snow and Ice Data center announced that in 2016 and 2015 the Arctic sea ice maximum set a record for the lowest it's been since records have been kept, both breaking the previous record which was set—you guessed it, in 2014.

To deny the existence of climate change in the face of this kind of data is . . . well. . . irrational. Saying so is not partisan or biased, it's simply an accurate description of their behavior. The same is true of their position on health care, national budgets, state budgets, and tax policy. In all cases, their policies are counterfactual and counterproductive.

Doubt that? Consider the collapse of the economy in Kansas after they adopted supply-side and trickle-down-economics. Or the fact that the three biggest economic collapses in US history followed periods when the Republicans were in control and they'd implemented their destructive laisez-faire economic policies. Or watch as they fumble with health care, literally threatening death to hundreds of thousands in the process, and leaving 22 million more Americans uninsured.

But the press still covers all this in a way that is "balanced," rather than accurate. Oh, yes, they will often point out that the Republican "perspective" is opposed by most scientists, or that economists and health-care specialists take issue with their proposals, but they don't point out just how at odds their rhetoric is with reality. And that's the real story here. It's not that there are two different perspectives on climate, or the economy, or the consequences of taxation and fiscal policies or health care. It's that this Party is behaving as if it were literally insane. And that should be newsworthy. Throw in Trump's irrational, self-destructive, and contradictory tweets, and the press should be running above the fold headlines, and lead stories sounding the alarm.

Which begs a question: Why aren't they?

Well, they're wholly owned subsidiaries of corporate America, that's why. And that's who this four-decade long scam benefits, at least in the short term. They get to liquidate the earth and the environment for fun and profit with nothing but he-said/she-said stories from the elite establishment media.

Which brings us to Elephant number Two—the Democrat's embrace of the raw deal over the New Deal. The idea that there is a Party representing the left (or the people, for that matter) in the United States is ludicrous. We have a right-wing Party representing the Oligarchy—the Democrats— and an insanely right-wing Party—the Republicans—who represent an extremist fringe of the rich, including folks like the Koch Brothers, Betsy DeVos, and so on. More about this in a moment, but back to the Democrats for now.

Back before Bill Clinton brought "triangulation," centrism, and corporatism to the Democratic Party, about half of all eligible voters claimed to be Democrats, while only about 25 percent identified as Republican. Today, only about 29 percent identify as Democrat, and too many of them don't bother to vote because the choices are so abysmal.

In a race between those appealing to the passionately ignorant with contentious wedge issues and those paying lip service to progressivism while governing for plutocrats, the passionately ignorant will always win.

Now back to those rich folks who have created the right-wing revolution. In what has been the least reported, but most important issue of our times, a group of wealthy individuals essentially purchased the press and both parties. The bones of the takeover can be found in a memo drafted by Lewis Powell, dated August 23, 1971. In it, he outlined a systematic approach to turning the country to the right and making it more business friendly. He focused on the long term, on institution building, and on

influencing education at all levels, including what kind of textbooks should be allowed. He noted that most media outlets were owned by corporations, and thus, could be made to represent the perspective of corporate America. Powell's manifesto repeatedly used the terms "fair" and "balanced." Ring a bell?

Of course, any good coup needs resources, and that's where the right-wing fat cats come in. A cadre of uber-wealthy ultra-conservatives including Richard Scaiffe, Adolph Coors, the Koch brothers (as well as their father, who helped fund the John Birch Society), Alice and Jim Walton, John Olin, Lynde and Harry Bradley, and Betsy DeVos helped fund think tanks, foundations, and endowed university chairs designed to carry forward their assault on government, a mindless celebration of the free market, and a system that rewards the rich at the expense of the poor and middle class. They also fostered measures designed to initially roll back laws designed to assure the media functioned in an impartial manner and ultimately, once those laws were rolled back, to purchase it outright.

Today, there is a virtual army of think tanks who are paid to make the crazy sound sane; to lend legitimacy to the illegitimate; and to tamp down any signs of reason among the citizenry with a mixture of fear, hate, greed, blame, and xenophobia.

But the coup remains the greatest story never told, and the pretense of a left/right political dialectic goes on, with useful idiots like Democratic "strategist" Mark Penn suggesting we take the middle ground between the extreme right wing, and the merely right wing, compromising ourselves into the Dark Ages.

Critical Thinking

1. Do you agree with Atcheson that the Republican Party position on health care, national budgets, state budgets, and tax policy are counterfactual and counterproductive?

2. Is there a Party that represents the people?

3. Does Atcheson provide any hope that the situation will be corrected?

Internet References

Sociology—Study Sociology Online
   http://edu.learnsoc.org/
Sociology Web Resources
   http://www.mhhe.com/socscience/sociology/resources/index.htm
Sociosite
   http://www.topsite.com/goto/sociosite.net
Socioweb
   http://www.topsite.com/goto/socioweb.com

JOHN ATCHESON is an author of the novel, ***A Being Darkly Wise***.

Article Prepared by: Kurt Finsterbusch, *University of Maryland, College Park*

Understanding Populist Challenges to the Liberal Order

Pranab Bardhan

Learning Outcomes

After reading this article, you will be able to:

- Understand the populist challenge to the liberal order.

- Describe the many problems that many people have and blame the government for.

- Discuss the role of powerlessness in the political actions of many Americans today.

L ate on election night, November 8, 2016, Paul Krugman wrote in the *New York Times*: ". . . people like me, and probably like most readers of *The New York Times*, truly didn't understand the country we live in. We thought that our fellow citizens would not, in the end, vote for a candidate . . . so scary yet ludicrous." About two and half years before that night, many liberals in India felt something similar at Narendra Modi's massive victory—though one should say, Modi is scary but not ludicrous.

The right-wing populist challenge to the liberal order is by no means limited to Donald Trump's America or Modi's India. The popular appeal of Britain's Brexit, France's Marine Le Pen, Russia's Vladimir Putin, Hungary's Viktor Orbán, Poland's Jarosław Kaczyński, Turkey's Recep Tayyip Erdoğan, and the Philippines's Rodrigo Duterte has baffled social thinkers over the last few years. Meanwhile after a decades-long triumphal march of authoritarian and rapid economic growth, China's increasingly repressive regime seems to be winning all the marbles in the global power game.

In deciphering a pattern in the looming illiberal challenge, an explanation has often been sought in the inexorable and unconscionable rise of economic inequality. The standard measures of income and wealth inequality show a significant rise in recent years, not just in rich but also in middle- and low-income countries (with the possible exception of some Latin American countries, although the levels of inequality there remain quite high). Liberalism, by encouraging the free play of market forces and relentless global competition and integration—particularly with the lifting of restrictions on international trade and capital flows—has accentuated inequalities and eroded the foundations of job security and social protection. The resultant dislocation, anxiety, and despair have supposedly driven workers into the arms of populist demagogues.

The idea that the rise of populism was caused by market-driven inequalities fails to address why populism is so cozy with crony capitalists.

But this explanation, while plausible, has some major gaps.

On the contentious issue of globalization, the line to the rise of right-wing populist anger is not clear. A **2016 survey** in the *Economist* across 19 countries suggests that countries as diverse as Vietnam, the Philippines, India, Thailand, Malaysia, Indonesia, Germany, Sweden, Denmark, and Hong Kong view globalization quite favorably. If China had been included in the survey, it would likely have made the list as well. Yet right-wing populism is no less rampant in India and the Philippines, and to a lesser extent in Indonesia, Germany, and Denmark. Of course skepticism about globalization is often greater in wealthy countries whose historically dominant positions in the international economy are slowly eroding. But even in France, where only 37 percent of all respondents agree that globalization is positive, *77 percent* of those under the age of 24 concur. An earlier, 2014 Pew Research Center Survey of 44 countries yielded similar findings: 81 percent of respondents saw international trade and global business ties as good for their countries.

On the issue of jobs, as Thomas Piketty has shown in *Capital in the Twenty-first Century* (2013), market-driven losses for unskilled workers play only a small part in the large rise in inequality. The takeoff in the income and wealth of the top 1 percent may have more to do with the excessive financialization and the entrenchment of a financial oligarchy, as well as the astronomical salaries of super-managers. All these factors are more prominent in the United States than they are elsewhere.

Certainly in the manufacturing sector, the loss of jobs—or sluggish growth in the availability of good jobs—is starkly evident, not just in rich countries but also in many developing countries. The loss of manufacturing jobs in the United States due to competition from Chinese imports has now been widely documented. But this phenomenon is less documented in poor countries such as India, where job growth has been relatively stagnant while a surge in the youth population and an exodus from the agricultural sector continue unabated. In many cases, the impact of labor-replacing technological change is perhaps no less severe than that of cheap Chinese imports, though the latter often garners more attention. Even in traditional labor-intensive industries (such as footwear, electronic assembly, and textiles), manufacturing job expansion is stalled because of automation, chronic deficiencies in infrastructural facilities, and business and labor regulations, while China moves up the global value chain. In many cases, the anger and despair are felt not just by the unemployed or the worst-off, but also by workers who are worried about the sustainability of their jobs and about their children's futures. More than chronic job loss, the job churning brought about by domestic and foreign competition creates a climate of insecurity.

Finally, the idea that the phenomenal rise of China represents the greatest success in the global illiberal challenge over the last three decades is not entirely accurate. Many, both inside and outside China, now believe in the so-called Beijing Consensus on economic development. In practice, this consensus foregrounds an authoritarian, meritocratic state leadership in guiding a market economy toward long-term goals of massive infrastructural investment, as well as aggressive adoption of cutting-edge technology, all in a single-minded pursuit of nationalist glory. And all the while trampling upon minor encumbrances such as human rights and democratic processes. There is even a new though ill-defined term frequently used in Chinese strategic papers: the "China Solution" or *zhongguo fang'an*, touted as the cure for many of the world's major problems.

This, however, is not a solution if one values individual autonomy, participation, and deliberation as an intrinsic part of development, as Amartya Sen does in his book *Development as Freedom* (1999). Even if one does not, such a "solution" chokes the flow of independent information from below, thus delaying the correction of policy mistakes; suppresses institutions of open public scrutiny that can check official corruption or collusion with business in matters of land grabbing, work safety, or toxic pollution; and encourages debt-fueled overinvestment and excess capacity in state-controlled or politically connected firms. It is also worth keeping in mind that some of the beneficial aspects of Chinese governance follow less from illiberal practices and more from historically unique features of Chinese governmental organization, such as the meritocratic selection of bureaucrats, the systematic use of performance incentives in career promotion, and the remarkable combination of political centralization with a large degree of economic and administrative decentralization, quite unusual for an authoritarian system.

Is the culprit *Homo economicus*, with his hyperrational pursuit of greed and self-interest?

Perhaps above all, what the common explanation fails to explain is why, if global workers are angry with market-driven inequalities, they are gravitating toward leaders who are either plutocrats—such as Trump, Farage, Le Pen, Orbán, Erdoğan, and Putin—or are cozy with crony capitalists, such as Modi. Why, for example, are poor Louisianans more resentful, as Arlie Hochschild reports in *Strangers in Their Own Land* (2016), of ethnic minorities and immigrants than of the petrochemical companies that have ravaged their communities for decades?

Several new books try to answer these questions. Beyond these economic and governance-related challenges to liberalism, there is a general critique of liberal modernity, popular with postmodernists and cultural theorists that resonates ideologically with the turn toward populism. This critique usually associates modernity with cutthroat capitalism, and the ravages of imperialism with a presiding technocratic nation-state. It traces the poison all the way to the Enlightenment, even though Karl Marx and Mao Zedong are as much the children of this modernity as are Adam Smith and Milton Friedman. This critique of modernity is now quite familiar from the reading lists of any self-respecting cultural studies department. Here I shall confine myself to its exposition in a new book by Pankaj Mishra, *The Age of Anger* (2017), in which it is directly related to the populist anger that concerns us here. Going back to the eighteenth century, Mishra recalls Jean-Jacques Rousseau's romanticist reaction to the Enlightenment's rationalist narrative of unyielding progress, finding a reflection of that reaction in today's illiberal challenge, from the angry worker in the U.S. Rust Belt to the Islamist suicide bomber. Ressentiment, born out of "an intense mix of envy and sense of humiliation and powerlessness," is undermining civic society. *Homo economicus* in its hyperrational pursuit of greed and self-interest is the culprit, we are made to believe.

For all the faults of capitalism (and economics, for that matter), this is too sweeping a judgment. In trying to explain too much, it actually explains very little. Contrary to the image of an angry East reacting to the destabilizing effects of Western capitalism, this rage appears to be less intense in those parts of the East (such as East, Southeast, and South Asia), where capitalist growth has been relatively successful, than in West Asia and North Africa, where capitalist growth has been stunted and economic misery has been accentuated by corrupt political tyranny. The highly popular Arab Spring, now snuffed out, was a rebellion not against Western liberalism but against domestic tyranny and youth unemployment. The traditional Islamists seem disturbed less by the rational pursuit of money (Islam has nothing against profit-seeking) than by the collusion between domestic and foreign oligarchies. In fighting the "crusaders," the Islamists try to build an apparatus with all its modernist techno-military paraphernalia.

The working class seems angrier about *cultural* elites than about the *financial* elites who are the target of the left.

Contrary to Mishra's view, there is an intellectual tradition that suggests that economic interests can in fact tame human passions. In *The General Theory of Employment, Interest and Money* (1936), John Maynard Keynes writes, "Dangerous human proclivities can be canalized into comparatively harmless channels by the existence of opportunity for money-making and private wealth, which, if they cannot be satisfied in this way, may find their outlet in cruelty, the reckless pursuit of personal power and authority, and other forms of self-aggrandizement." Albert O. Hirschman's *The Passions and the Interests* (1977) has a more nuanced discussion of the relationship between interests and passions. However, both Keynes and Hirschman were talking about earlier times in Europe. Today, when the opportunities for money-making have opened up in countries such as China and India, passions are channeled by the ruling party in both countries into the service of a national aggrandizement that capitalist growth has at last made possible.

But Rousseau's romantic search for community may be relevant to the present crisis. A common element of reactions across rich and poor countries is that the working class seems angrier about the *cultural* elite than about the *financial* elites who are the target of the left (incidentally, coming from Geneva, Rousseau himself felt like an outsider in the Parisian salons of high culture). For many populist supporters, the liberal elite's lofty preaching of multiculturalism and cosmopolitanism offends their sense of cultural rootedness in family, community, and nation, making them easy prey for the militant ethnic nationalism that is often the first refuge of demagogues. Likewise, liberal criticism of demagogues is often easily dismissed as elitist and anti-national. Meanwhile, minorities and immigrants are demonized by populist leaders as obstacles to national unity; historical facts about the role those minorities and immigrants played in nation-building are not allowed to interfere with nationalist myths. As nineteenth-century French philosopher and historian Ernest Renan famously quipped, "Getting its history wrong is part of being a nation."

This is how immigration as part of a globally fluid economy becomes a sensitive issue. It is also why economists' usual arguments about the value of immigrants to the economy do not cut much ice. In the *Economist* survey cited above, only a minority of respondents in 17 of the 19 countries considered the effect of immigrants on their countries to be positive.

This anti-immigrant sentiment is part of a larger majoritarian perception of siege and victimhood, exacerbated by the majority community's perception that it is now less secure or privileged than it was in the past. In widely noted research by Anne Case and Angus Deaton about the "deaths of despair" from suicide, drug overdose, or alcohol abuse among middle-aged Whites in the United States, the authors document how the rising mortality rates of people with a high school degree or less for Whites are now converging with those of similar less-educated Blacks.

In India, Muslims are on average socially and economically much worse off than Hindus, and yet Hindu resentments provide fuel for the right-wing resurgence. Hindus constitute about 80 percent of the population, while Muslims constitute a mere 13 percent, and yet the supposed higher fertility rates of Muslims is cited to stoke fears among Hindus about becoming outnumbered. Fearmongering about the threat of terrorism only adds to this. The traumatic history of Partition and the proximity of Muslim-majority Pakistan make Muslims an easy suspect. In the United States, Europe, and India, crime and violence are routinely attributed to minorities (Muslims, Gypsies, Hispanics, and Blacks), and the blatant discrimination and ghettoization of these minority groups can often make such perceptions self-fulfilling.

In the United States, Europe, India, Turkey, and elsewhere, the perceived *appeasement* of minorities—which is assumed to be implicit in the liberal *support* for minority rights—fosters resentment among the majority, which find the liberal rhetoric of diversity and political correctness condescending if not outright threatening. Conversely a Trump or a Modi's thinly veiled rantings, taken as anti-establishment raw spontaneity, energize this base. In Hochschild's book, her White working-class respondents in Louisiana sense that all demographic groups other than theirs receive sympathy from liberals. Hochschild quotes a gospel singer and avid Rush Limbaugh fan saying, "Oh, liberals think that Bible-believing Southerners are ignorant, backward, rednecks, and losers. They think we're racist, sexist, homophobic, and maybe fat." A Tea Party enthusiast claims, "People think we're not good people if we don't feel sorry for Blacks and immigrants and Syrian refugees. . . . But I am a good person and I don't feel sorry for them."

There is an intellectual tradition that suggests that economic interests can in fact tame human passions.

In recent years, the gulf between the working class and the liberal elite has widened. Elites have become isolated by effectively segregating themselves in large gentrified cities, marrying within their class, and adopting mostly professional occupations. The consequences of this disjuncture are particularly important in the context of the shrinking influence of worker organizations. With wage stagnation and job losses, blue-collar trade unions cannot deliver on their economic promises, and membership continues to decline. With this decline of trade unions all over the world, the traditional institutions that used to tame and transcend nativist passions and intolerance of working-class families are now sorely missing.

In different parts of the world, political leaders who are adept in machine politics are cognizant of the electoral payoff of stoking feelings of siege and victimhood in majority communities. The current ruling parties in the two largest democracies, India and the United States, have mastered this. As a result, there is now considerable tension between the politics of electoral mobilization and the procedural aspects of democracy. Mobilized followers do not care much about the procedural niceties of a liberal order. They often show impatience with the encumbrances of due process and affirmative action. They hanker for strong leaders who can embody the "will of the people," surpass those encumbrances, and provide seductively simple solutions to problems. The organizational norms of traditional political parties that once disciplined mass fanaticism are being cast aside—voters are choosing political outsiders, or, within established political parties, leaders who defy traditionalists.

The hard-to-define word *populism* is used in political discourse in many senses. Economists use it to mean pandering to short-term interests at the expense of the long-term. They often point to left-wing populism (familiar in Latin American history) that is prone to encouraging fiscal extravagance. Here I use it to mean when a leader claims to organically embody the popular will, thereby rendering standard institutions of representative democracy (along with minority rights and procedures) less relevant. From the procedural point of view, they enjoy a culture of impunity in violating liberal norms and dismissing critical media as purveyors of "fake news." In Hungary, Orban openly advocates an "illiberal democracy." Of course, institutions of checks and balances are still much stronger in the United States than they are in India, Turkey, or Hungary.

Such populism is right wing in the sense of being both business-friendly and congenial to ethnic hubris and muscular nationalism. But it is not right wing in the sense of insisting on a minimalist state. It calls for an active role of the state in both boardrooms and bedrooms. Paradoxically, China may also fall under this category of right-wing populism. The ruling party (represented by its "core" leader) is supposed to embody the popular will by being business-friendly, ultra-nationalist, and a vigorous proponent of state policy. But China is not populist in the economist's sense of short-termist.

Political leaders adept at machine politics are cognizant of the payoff of stoking feelings of siege and victimhood in majority communities.

Going back to Rousseau's idea of the community, many people today believe that their basic values, as well as their nostalgia for a (false) golden past, are disrespected by a cosmopolitan elite whose liberalism prioritizes individual freedom over community bonding and traditional loyalties. In this sense, liberty and fraternity are clearly not always in harmony.

A deeper conflict in the conception of the individual may also be at stake here. In his recent book, *On Human Nature* (2017), the conservative philosopher Roger Scruton distinguishes between the liberal individual, self-possessed in her autonomous decisions, consent, contract, and trade, and the conservative individual who endows meaning to her life mainly through her identity in relation to a community with established traditions. If there is anything to this, then the traditional role of trade unions and other worker associations in linking up with neighborhoods and communities in local cultural and social activities becomes all the more important, beyond mere wage bargaining. Their role in sustaining politically the network of social insurance and protection is also crucial in keeping despondent workers away from demagogues.

The trend of rising White mortality rates in the United States, highlighted by the Case-Deaton study, does not apply to Whites in Western Europe or Canada. One possible reason for this is that structures of social insurance (along with worker retraining programs) are much stronger there. Perhaps there is a shred of hope in the fact that Trump is finding it difficult to decimate U.S. health-care provisions for the poor, or that Modi has decided to keep India's minimal welfare measures intact, which he had earlier dismissively described as "dole." Focusing on measures to alleviate the financial insecurity of workers—including those from the majority community and religious conservatives—with active involvement of worker associations in those communities may help relieve some of their perceived cultural insecurities. Worker and religious organizations may in fact find some common cause on matters of social and environmental protection.

If sluggish wage and job growth continue, fueling mass disaffection with liberal politics, and the pace of automation becomes inexorable, worker organizations should give serious consideration to demanding more public investment in job-creating renewable energy and public health-care services; more participation in the internal governance of firms, particularly in decisions to outsource and relocate; and the institution of a basic income.

The labor movement is weak today. In rich countries, many blue-collar workers have dropped out of unions, and other workers, such as professionals and those in the so-called gig economy, never belonged to one. In poor countries, most workers are in the informal sector outside unions. The demand for a basic income as part of a citizen's rights may provide a common bridge for the currently divided labor force. In general, the labor movement has been dissipated by the constant threat of capital moving abroad, facilitated by the part of globalization not emphasized enough in the standard attitude surveys (like those cited above), that of opening up the capital account. In demanding some restrictions on capital movement and other universal pro-labor measures such as basic income, the strengthening of the structure of unions toward a more coordinated and confederate mode may become necessary. For now, outside Nordic countries and Central Europe, labor unions are much too fragmented to achieve such countrywide goals.

Critical Thinking

1. Why are so many poor more resentful of ethnic minorities and immigrants than of the capitalist companies that have adversely affected them?

2. Explain the decline of many of the organizations that worked for the interests of the poor and the manual workers.

3. Explain populism.

Internet References

Sociology—Study Sociology Online
http://edu.learnsoc.org/

Sociology Web Resources
http://www.mhhe.com/socscience/sociology/resources/index.htm

Sociosite
http://www.topsite.com/goto/sociosite.net

Socioweb
http://www.topsite.com/goto/socioweb.com

Bardhan, Pranab. "Understanding Populist Challenges to the Liberal Order," *Boston Review*, May 2017. Copyright ©2017 by Pranab Bardhan. Used with permission.